W9-ANT-785   16.2

HUMBER COLLEGE L. R C. (LAKESHORE)

DATE DUE

AUG 0 3 2004		
MAR 1 4 2016		APR 08 2016

CARR McLEAN, TORONTO FORM #38-297

MANAGING REPUTATIONAL RISK

Current and Forthcoming Titles in the IIA Series

Series Editor: Andrew Chambers

MANAGING REPUTATIONAL RISK

curbing threats, leveraging opportunities

JENNY RAYNER

160201

WILEY

The Institute of Internal Auditors
UK and Ireland

Published in 2003 by John Wiley & Sons Ltd,
The Atrium, Southern Gate, Chichester,
West Sussex PO19 8SQ, England

Telephone   (+44) 1243 779777

Email (for orders and customer service enquiries): cs-books@wiley.co.uk
Visit our Home Page on www.wileyeurope.com or www.wiley.com

Other Wiley Editorial Offices

John Wiley & Sons Inc., 111 River Street, Hoboken, NJ 07030, USA

Jossey-Bass, 989 Market Street, San Francisco, CA 94103-1741, USA

Wiley-VCH Verlag GmbH, Boschstr. 12, D-69469 Weinheim, Germany

John Wiley & Sons Australia Ltd, 33 Park Road, Milton, Queensland 4064, Australia

John Wiley & Sons (Asia) Pte Ltd, 2 Clementi Loop #02-01, Jin Xing Distripark, Singapore 129809

John Wiley & Sons Canada Ltd, 22 Worcester Road, Etobicoke, Ontario, Canada M9W 1L1

Wiley also publishes its books in a variety of electronic formats. Some content that appears
in print may not be available in electronic books.

Library of Congress Cataloging-in-Publication Data

Rayner, Jenny.
Managing reputational risk : curbing threats, leveraging opportunities / Jenny Rayner.
    p.   cm.
Includes bibliographical references (p.) and index.
ISBN 0-471-49951-X (cloth : alk. paper)
1. Corporate image. 2. Business ethics. 3. Risk management. I. Title.
HD59.2.R39 2003
659.2—dc21   2003009971

British Library Cataloguing in Publication Data

A catalogue record for this book is available from the British Library

ISBN 0-471-49951-X

Typeset in 10/12pt Times by TechBooks, New Delhi, India
Printed and bound in Great Britain by Antony Rowe Ltd, Chippenham, Wiltshire
This book is printed on acid-free paper responsibly manufactured from sustainable forestry
in which at least two trees are planted for each one used for paper production.

contents

CONTENTS

figures

tables

preface

Warning signs that suggest a patient may not be suitable for cosmetic surgery include: expectations of an appearance enhanced beyond possibility; unrealistic expectations of lifestyle/career/relationship effects; an unwillingness to change the behaviour that led to the problem.

(Plastic Surgery Information Service)

Many books have been written on reputation management, which position it as the prime focus of the public relations department and its spin-doctors. This book is different. It places reputation and its associated risks – both threats and opportunities – squarely in the domain of the boardroom, at the heart of prudent business management, good corporate governance, leading-edge strategy development, effective risk management, corporate responsibility, comprehensive assurance and transparent communications.

In this book I have tried to make sense of the seemingly specialist subjects of reputation management and risk management in a way that is accessible to all. I have endeavoured to unravel reputation management for the board of directors, demystify risk management for the public relations professional, clarify corporate governance for the financial manager, explain the essence of corporate social responsibility to the risk or audit manager and argue the case for transparent communication, backed up by solid assurance, for all those involved in preparing and validating data for internal and external reporting. It is only when all these disparate interested parties work together – contributing their individual insights and exercising their influence – that a truly excellent reputation can be achieved and sustained.

Experience has shown that a sustainable reputation cannot purely be built 'outside in' by responding to external expectations and moulding one's image accordingly. Reputation must

xiii

primarily be built 'inside out' and should be based on a solid foundation of corporate vision and consistently upheld values, underpinned by robust management policies and ways of working, if it is to endure and enable a business to thrive. The analogy with cosmetic surgery in the opening quotation is therefore most apt. Putting a positive PR gloss on an inherently sick business will not result in a good reputation that endures in the longer term; investing in a carefully thought-through set of actions to nurture reputation, by curbing threats and leveraging opportunities to it, is much more likely to deliver.

In this book I have attempted to draw together the key lessons from a number of sectors and disciplines and from the practical experience of leading organisations that have learned to build and capitalise on their reputations to underpin their success.

It is my intention that this book should be of value to a wide range of readers: from executive and non-executive directors to risk managers and internal auditors, from company secretaries to corporate affairs and investor relations professionals, from fund managers to communications consultants. The lessons to be learned from the many examples of good – and bad – practice discussed are relevant to all types and sizes of organisation whether they are in the private, public or not-for-profit sectors.

The book will take the reader on a journey from rising interest in reputation as a key intangible asset, through increasingly rigorous corporate governance, risk management and investor requirements, to the growing clamour for socially responsible behaviour. It will offer some simple tools to help to identify and manage the risks to your business's reputation. It will explore the key drivers of reputation and the practical ways in which pace-setting organisations are not only managing threats to safeguard their reputations, but are also actively exploiting opportunities to bolster their standing, as a key enabler in building a successful and sustainable future. That is not to say that the book has to be read from cover to cover. If you are an experienced risk manager you may wish to skip Chapter 3, 'Risk management: an overview'. Communications professionals may decide to skim Chapter 9, 'Bolstering reputation through transparent reporting'.

However you choose to use this book, I trust that you will enjoy the journey and will discover new ideas, insights, tools and techniques along the route that will enable you to play a more positive and active role in protecting and enhancing the reputation of your own organisation.

Jenny Rayner
June 2003

acknowledgements

I would like to thank the countless individuals and organisations that have knowingly or unwittingly inspired me in the writing of the book. My gratitude goes in particular to those businesses which have kindly allowed their insights and best practice models to be reproduced so that others might benefit from them. I am indebted to the UK's Institute of Business Ethics for giving me the opportunity to conduct earlier research into the management of reputation risk among their members – work that formed the foundations of my thinking in this book.

I am also most grateful to the Institute of Internal Auditors – UK and Ireland for sponsoring this series on risk management topics, and to the series editor, Professor Andrew Chambers, for his original suggestion that I undertake this project. Thanks are also due to my friend and colleague Walter Raven, whose encouragement and flow of cuttings have helped to keep me sane. And last, but not least, my heartfelt thanks go to my husband Keith and daughters Jo and Dani for their understanding, forbearance and refreshments service as deadlines approached.

one

reputation unravelled

WHAT IS REPUTATION?

The beliefs or opinions that are generally held about someone or something.

(Compact Oxford English Dictionary)

The standard dictionary definition given above hints at the complexity of the reputation concept. Reputation is fundamentally about perception and beliefs; it is not necessarily an accurate reflection of reality. But in the eyes of the beholder perception *is* reality – perception is what counts. This is one of the features that differentiate the management of reputation, and its associated risks, from the management of other, more tangible assets.

Reputation is as relevant to individuals as it is to organisations. Although organisations are the prime focus of this book, the personal reputation of individual directors and other prominent employees can, and often does, influence corporate reputation as many of the examples cited will show.

- *Reputation is a collection of perceptions and beliefs, both past and present, which reside in the consciousness of an organisation's stakeholders* – its customers, suppliers, business partners, employees, investors, analysts, communities, regulators, governments, pressure groups, non-governmental organisations and the public at large.

These perceptions and beliefs are often built over a period of many years: every contact, every media mention, every rumour, every leak, every piece of gossip will play its part in forming an overall impression of an organisation's standing.

1

> If image is the immediate external perception of an organisation, it could be argued that reputation is the historic and cultural dimension of that image – a stakeholder community's 'social memory' of the sum total of a company and its activities.
>
> (Michael L Sherman, AIG[1])

Reputation often can't be quantified, compared against hard benchmarks or analysed in the same way as financial or other numerical data. Its management requires softer skills such as sound judgement, an ability to anticipate future trends and requirements, understand stakeholder concerns, listen carefully, consider dispassionately and respond constructively.

Another key distinguishing feature of reputation is its potential transience. Although a 'good' corporate reputation can take many long years to build, it can be destroyed in an instant through an ill-considered 'off the record' remark, a lapse in personal behaviour, an ethical blunder in the supply chain or an inadequate response to a crisis.

> It takes twenty years to build a reputation and five minutes to destroy it.
>
> (Warren Buffett, CEO, Berkshire Hathaway)

In this era of instant, real-time communications there is no hiding place. Like fish in a goldfish bowl, today's businesses are subject to constant, often unforgiving scrutiny.

Thirdly, reputation can be impacted by virtually anyone in the organisation or anyone in its supply chain, such as outsourced service providers, raw material suppliers, distributors – or even external auditors, as the Enron/Andersen débâcle has demonstrated. Everyone directly involved with an organisation plays a part in moulding and upholding its reputation.

The perception-based, potentially transient and all-embracing nature of reputation poses particular challenges for directors, managers, auditors and corporate affairs specialists. How can you:

- recognise and prioritise the issues that are most likely to impact corporate reputation?
- assure yourselves that your major risks to reputation are identified and well managed?
- ensure that everyone representing your organisation will act in a way that protects and enhances corporate reputation?
- track the changing requirements and expectations of key stakeholder groups?
- demonstrate to your major stakeholders that you are living up to the claims your organisation makes of itself – as well as meeting their expectations?

Possible solutions to these challenges will be suggested in the chapters that follow.

WHY DOES REPUTATION MATTER?

Why is so much emphasis now put on the management of reputation? The management of reputation has, in the past ten years, shifted from being the preserve of public relations specialists and corporate spin-doctors to become a mainstream boardroom issue. It is increasingly recognised that a good corporate reputation is a highly prized intangible asset – one which, if nurtured and protected, can continue to grow in value over time. Reputation management is therefore a topic that now merits board airtime and may warrant the specific deployment of other resources. So what has brought this about?

The broader environment in which business operates has radically altered. Four key developments have influenced this:

- the stakeholder imperative
- globalisation
- the technological and media revolution
- the rise of intangible assets.

the stakeholder imperative

Since the advent of the industrial revolution and the birth of the limited liability public company some 150 years ago, the primary goal of company directors has been to create wealth for their shareholders – initially large institutions or wealthy private investors. In this relatively uncomplicated world, industrialists wielded unprecedented power and influence. The ends – increased production and rising profits – justified the means, which often resulted in unsafe working conditions and poverty line wages. Such industrialists were rarely challenged; the media were generally in awe of them and their achievements. They were trusted and revered members of society. There was no environmental lobbying and little concern about the scant regard paid to worker welfare. This was, after all, progress.

There were, of course, a handful of prominent philanthropists whose religious and moral convictions – combined with the recognition that a local supply of skilled, healthy and committed labour was necessary to fulfil their business ambitions – inspired them to build houses, schools, roads and indeed whole communities to accommodate their burgeoning workforces. Leading exponents of this blend of moral values and self-interest include Hershey in the USA, Cadbury and Rowntree in the UK and Krupps in Germany. Although both individual and corporate reputations were no doubt enhanced by such visible acts of corporate philanthropy, the primary focus was on wealth generation. A company's continued 'licence to operate' was virtually automatic if its financial and output targets were met.

How different is the business environment today. Now, before applying for planning permission for a building extension or launching a technologically innovative product, businesses generally feel the need to consult widely with their stakeholders[2] – environmental lobby groups, employees, suppliers, local communities and governments – in an attempt to reach consensus or, at least, to agree a *modus vivendi*. Over the past 20 years there has been an exponential rise in the demands, expectations and influence of these stakeholder groups, without whose implied 'permission' a business's licence to operate can be jeopardised and its legitimacy threatened.

> 'The global nature of our business also drives . . . the need to be involved in the societies of which we are a part. . . . Not out of altruism, but out of enlightened self-interest, because we believe that if big companies are not seen to be making constructive social investments their licence to operate will in the end be limited. And if your ability to operate is limited, then your performance is limited.'
> (Sir John Browne, chief executive, BP[3])

Business leaders are often simply not trusted. In the wake of the Enron, WorldCom and Tyco scandals, Lawrence Weinbach, chairman and chief executive of Unisys, the US information technology, commented at a meeting of the G100 club of top chief executives:

> None of us feel good right now. If you are a CEO it's almost like you have to prove that you're not doing something wrong, whereas before it was taken for granted that you were doing something right.[4]

Campaigning organisations now often enjoy more public trust than company leaders. Research by the global public relations company Edelman in 2002 showed that over 50% of European leaders trust campaigning organisations compared to 41% who trust companies[5] – and this was before the WorldCom and Xerox scandals broke.

In the public sector, too, politicians are little trusted; their every word is scrutinised by pressure groups and a voracious media for signs of inconsistency, lack of integrity or a hint of policy change. The proportion of British adults distrusting politicians stood at a massive 73% in February 2002, with only 19% trusting them (Figure 1-1). This fell further to 18% a year later, putting politicians on a par with journalists.

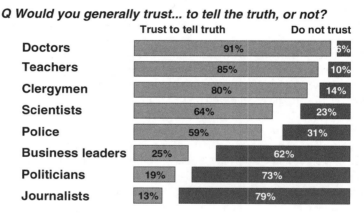

Figure 1-1   Trust in integrity. (Reprinted by permission of MORI (Market & Opinion Research International))

In February 2002, in the wake of the US scandals, the proportion of respondents who trust business leaders stood at only 25%, with those distrusting at 62%. A year later, this figure had risen by three percentage points to 28%, with a hefty 60% (compared with 62% in 2002) still distrusting business leaders.

The age-old respect for leaders in business or public life is long gone. It has been replaced by scepticism, aggressive challenging and demands for incontrovertible evidence – preferably from an external independent third party (Figure 1-2).

This insatiable thirst for information and quest for 'the truth' has been fuelled by the technological revolution, discussed later in this chapter.

Trust me   Show me   ...and prove it!

Figure 1-2   Shifting stakeholder expectations.

The rise in stakeholder power is often seen as a threat, but in fact presents a huge opportunity, if harnessed properly, for businesses to gain a competitive edge and enhance their standing. Reputation can play a crucial role in determining how an organisation's major stakeholders are likely to behave towards it. The actions they decide to take will, in turn, play their part in shaping the organisation's future reputation. A business's reputation can influence:

- investors' decisions to hold its shares
- consumers' willingness to buy from it
- suppliers' willingness to partner with it
- competitors' determination to enter its market
- media coverage and pressure group activity
- regulators' attitude towards it
- its cost of capital
- potential recruits' eagerness to join it and existing employees' motivation to stay
- stakeholders' willingness to give it the benefit of the doubt when a problem or crisis occurs.

This final point can be a significant benefit. There are many examples of how accumulating 'reputational capital' with stakeholders can help a business to weather the occasional storm. The occasional lapse of a reputationally strong company is likely to be regarded as a one-off aberration, because it has a solid track record and its values and business ethos are clearly understood. The reaction will most probably be a shrug and a 'that's not like them' rather than a 'there they go again'.

A study in the late 1990s of the performance of US companies during the 1987 stock market crash found that the shares of the ten most admired companies dropped less and recovered faster, while the shares of the ten least admired companies plunged three times as far[6] – a very strong indication that having a good reputation can pay real dividends. The total return of the top ten firms in *Fortune* magazine's 2003 America's Most Admired Companies survey was −8.63%, more than 13% higher than the total return of the S&P 500.[7] Good reputations, however, can only be built by understanding and responding to the requirements and expectations of your major stakeholders so that their confidence and trust in your business is fostered and maintained. It is therefore perfectly logical that discussion of shifting stakeholder demands and perceptions should find its way onto today's boardroom agendas.

globalisation

The past 15 to 20 years have witnessed a dramatic shift in the respective roles of government, business and society. Governments have encouraged businesses to offer services previously provided by the State through public–private partnerships. Large multinational corporations have spread their tentacles into many parts of the developing as well as the developed world. The ubiquitous McDonald's golden arches can now be seen from Manhattan to Manila, from Boston to Bombay. Whether you believe that multinationals are a force for good by creating jobs in communities where unemployment and hunger are rife, or a force for evil by eroding local culture and paying subsistence wages, the fact remains that globalisation is a major influence in the world today.

The annual turnover of some major multinationals dwarfs the GDP of many national economies. Twenty-nine of the world's 100 biggest economic entities are multinational companies, according to the United Nations Conference on Trade and Development (UNCTAD). According to UNCTAD,[8] the activities of the 100 biggest companies, measured on the basis of value-added – the yardstick used to calculate a country's gross domestic product – accounted for 4.3% of world GDP in 2000, up from 3.5% in 1990. The US energy group Exxon is larger than all but 44 national economies.

> Exxon, with estimated value-added of $63 billion, was about the same size as the economy of Pakistan and larger than Peru's, while Ford, DaimlerChrysler, General Electric and Toyota were all comparable in size to the economy of Nigeria. Philip Morris, the tobacco group, was on a par with Tunisia, Slovakia and Guatemala, while BP, Wal-Mart, IBM and Volkswagen all ranked in size between Libya and Cuba. GlaxoSmithKline and BT, the smallest of the top 100 multinationals, were equal in size to Syria.[9]

As a result, public and political expectations of business have steadily increased. In many cases corporations are now expected to plug the gap left by governments through provision of the economic support, infrastructure and even the moral guidance needed to boost the local economy. The potential power of transnational corporations to bring about change was amply demonstrated at the August 2002 World Summit on Sustainable Development in Johannesburg. Speaking prior to the summit, president of the World Bank, James Wolfensohn, said: 'Companies have more of a role than ever to play in reducing the poverty and social exclusion that widens the gap between the haves and have nots.'[10] The traditional boundaries between the roles of government, business and society have blurred and are now sometimes transposed.

As a consequence of these heightened and, at times, unreasonable expectations, companies are under intense scrutiny from pressure groups and the media. Are they acting consistently across the globe? Is there a local lapse in their ethical standards which indicates that they are ruthlessly exploiting cheap local labour and are not enforcing their head office generated 'codes of conduct'? Are they abusing their corporate power?

The reality of globalisation is that the corporate reputation of multinational companies can be jeopardised by the words or action of any employee or supply chain partner in any country of operation in the world.

The reality of globalisation is also the globalisation of competition. Products and services jockey for position in a cost-sensitive worldwide market in which differentiation is ever more difficult. Reputation may, in the final analysis, be the only factor that distinguishes your offering from that of your competitors.

the technological and media revolution

Another crucial change has been the technological and media revolution – the advent of real-time communications and the rise of the Internet – which has resulted in businesses and public organisations responding to crises as they unfold under the harsh spotlight of the global media gaze. If an environmental incident, code of conduct violation or even flippant remark attracts the attention of the media it can be splattered across the headlines not just in Chittagong, where the transgression originally occurred, but almost instantaneously in Chicago, most probably catching Head Office on the defensive. A report may appear in Internet on-line newsgroups, with comment from a relevant 'expert', before the organisation itself has had a chance to respond.

The voracious media, ever quick to detect a chink in the corporate armour, will bay for blood if they spot a story that has potential appeal and could fill column inches over a period of weeks or months; emotionally laden issues such as human rights abuses prove particularly popular. These days the media have scant respect for rank or authority. Whether the prominent figure or business in question is a government body or a major multinational, anyone or anything is fair game – provided it sells copy or airtime. A virulent or even personal attack can almost always be justified as being 'in the public interest' or 'for the sake of transparency and openness'.

As a result, organisations have to be constantly vigilant and available for comment. As well as trying to maintain cordial relations with the media in their major countries of operation, businesses are now exposed wherever they – or indeed their major suppliers – operate in the world. Nor is it only newspapers and magazines that have to be scanned to keep pace with shifting stakeholder moods: chat rooms, on-line newsgroups, spoof defamatory websites also need to be monitored regularly to ensure that emerging issues are understood and managed actively where possible. In addition to this, organisations' own websites are frequently the first port of call for journalists, pressure groups, investors and rating agencies seeking information. Woe betide an organisation whose website provides inadequate or opaque information on key aspects of its activities or fails to acknowledge a breaking crisis. The media abhors an information vacuum and will seek comment from an unauthorised source in its relentless quest for news.

The unprecedented availability and accessibility of data via the Internet and global telecommunications networks have had the knock-on effect of providing ammunition for stakeholders to be more challenging and sceptical than ever before. This has, in turn, fuelled stakeholder demands for yet more information and more transparency. The ability of businesses to provide the right information, in the right form at the right time – the ability to communicate effectively – has itself become a key business competence and a driver of reputation.

the rise of intangible assets

The need to satisfy shareholders has historically been catered for by a narrow range of financial indicators, with the primary focus on earnings. However the wave of accounting scandals in the USA in 2001–2 has shown that easily manipulable earnings are often not a reliable indicator of a company's true worth – and are certainly no guarantee of its future performance. Popular shareholder value benchmarks such as EBITDA (Earnings before interest, tax, depreciation and amortisation) have become discredited. Post the WorldCom scandal, EBITDA was playfully referred to as Earnings Before I Tricked the Dumb Auditor!

It is now apparent that blinkered focus on financial parameters can be a recipe for disaster: excessive interest in achieving short-term financial goals – and the director share options and bonuses linked to them – may not be in the best long-term interests of shareholders, let alone employees, suppliers and other stakeholders. A survey of 200 US companies conducted by PricewaterhouseCoopers tested the belief that the market had become too short-term oriented. Fifty-eight per cent of respondents strongly agreed that the financial community tended to focus on short-term earnings; another 35% agreed, with only 6% disagreeing.[11]

There's much more to running a successful, sustainable business than meeting short-term financial targets. Traditional annual reports alone provide insufficient information on the true health and future prospects of a business: their primary focus is on past financial performance. In today's knowledge economy, a business's intangible assets – such as corporate reputation, vision and leadership, the quality, skills and motivation of employees, the ability to leverage knowledge and innovate, intellectual property, products in the development pipeline, brands and the quality of business relationships with key stakeholders – can account for 70% to well over 90% of a business's market worth.

Much of this is 'off balance sheet' and does not form part of the business's quoted net assets, its 'capital'. Current global accounting methods do not normally allow for inclusion of internally generated intangible assets, only those attained via acquisition.[12] Even acquired assets are usually lumped together in an overall 'goodwill' figure (the premium paid for a business in excess of its net assets).

For the most part, therefore, the true value of a business's intangible assets can only be estimated by deducting its net book assets shown on the balance sheet from its total market capitalisation (share price multiplied by number of shares). The gap between the two figures represents the business's intangible assets.

The 'market to book' ratio (market capitalisation divided by net assets) can be as high as 10–15 for 'high tech' companies. More traditionally based companies are also affected by the increasing reliance on intangibles. A US study in 1994 showed that tangible assets accounted for just a third of the stock market value of more than 2000 US manufacturing firms. Just a decade earlier, these book assets had accounted for almost two-thirds of their value.[13]

The knowledge-driven economy is not just about new high-tech industries built on a science base like software and biotechnology. Nor is it confined to new technology. For it is about new sources of competitive advantage: the ability to innovate and create new products and exploit new markets. It applies to all industries, high-tech and low-tech, manufacturing and services, retailing and agriculture. The key to competitiveness increasingly turns on the way people combine, marshal and commercialise their knowledge.

(Charles Leadbetter[14])

Professor Baruch Lev, from the Stern School of Business at New York University, estimated that in 1998 US industrial companies invested as much in intangible assets such as R&D and training as they did in physical plant and equipment.[15] However, although investment in tangible assets is capitalised on the balance sheet, investment in intangibles is treated as an expense against revenue, even though a number of academic studies have shown a clear correlation between the level of investment in intangibles and future profits.

Intangible assets such as reputation are particularly valuable as they are difficult to imitate and can therefore act as powerful barriers to entry for potential new competitors, thereby helping to maintain a business's competitive edge.

Having so much of a business's true value 'off balance sheet' does not augur well for correct valuation by the market or, indeed, in the wake of Enron's off-balance sheet shenanigans, for investor confidence. When the market lacks information it regards as important, it tends to err on the side of caution and is likely to value a company at a level below its management's expectations. It is therefore not surprising that 30% of high-tech company managers believe that their companies' shares are substantially undervalued, 45% believe that they are somewhat undervalued and only 18% regard their valuation as correct.[16]

Some governments, such as in the UK, are encouraging businesses to include much more information in their annual reports on the non-financial aspects of their activities to enable investors and other stakeholders to have better information on which to base their decisions.[17] The US corporate scandals have strengthened governments' resolve and have accelerated moves to introduce both voluntary and mandatory reporting requirements to underpin accountability and transparency. In the USA the Financial Accounting Standards Board (FASB) is working on rules that will require US companies to disclose information regarding intangible assets such as customer lists, brands and technology. Professor Baruch Lev wants the FASB to ask companies to disclose detailed information about everything from staff training and turnover to investment in information technology. He would like to see disclosure of both inputs – the amount of money spent on training, for example – and outputs, such as staff turnover.[18]

Although the FASB is unlikely to go as far at Professor Lev would like, the tide has undoubtedly turned: there is an irreversible interest in intangible assets as a key indicator of future prospects – and reputation is a key component of this.

REPUTATION AND BRAND

Before progressing too far in the analysis of reputation drivers and their associated risks, it may be helpful to define terms. Is corporate reputation the same as brand reputation? If not, what is the relationship between them?

For some organisations the concept of product or service brand does not enter the equation: corporate reputation is synonymous with the corporate brand. This is likely to be the case for a local government organisation, pressure group or a business manufacturing a single product.

However, a large and diverse conglomerate such as Procter & Gamble will have an overall 'corporate reputation' to which its many individual brands contribute. Those diverse brands, such as Crest, Pampers, Olay, Pringles, Sunny Delight and Tampax, will each enjoy their own brand reputation. A problem with one discrete product can often be contained and may not affect the reputation of other unrelated brands, even though they share a corporate umbrella. A product brand-related crisis may therefore have only a minimal effect on share price, dependent on the importance of the affected product or service in the overall business portfolio.

Conversely 'corporate reputation' issues, such as questionable boardroom ethics or director integrity, can rock the entire corporate edifice, and send the share price spiralling downwards – as the Tyco and WorldCom débâcles have demonstrated. It may also affect customer confidence in individual product brands, although this may not necessarily occur.

The extent of any reaction will depend in part on whether the organisation leverages its corporate brand in promoting individual product and service brands or whether its individual brands predominate. The name of Diageo, the global drinks company, may mean little to the average consumer as the group's strategy is to strongly promote its individual product brands including Johnnie Walker, Guinness, Smirnoff, J&B, Baileys, Captain Morgan, Cuervo and Tanqueray and to subordinate the corporate brand. Such a strategy can limit cross-contamination of other brands or corporate reputation when a single brand is tarnished.

At the other end of the spectrum, the corporate reputations of businesses such as British Airways, Delta and Singapore Airlines are almost indistinguishable from their brands. A hit to either overall corporate reputation or one of the service brands is therefore more likely to lose the confidence of both investors and consumers.

Even an apparently homogeneous business like the UK-based Virgin Group, which trades on its corporate image and the colourful personality and high profile of its founder and chairman, Sir Richard Branson, enjoys different reputations in relation to its many branded businesses. These are all brands spawned by capitalising on Virgin's corporate image: Virgin the airline operator, Virgin the train operator, Virgin financial services, Virgin records. However, due to the ubiquity of the Virgin name, these individual business brands are afforded little protection when one of them is attacked. When Virgin Rail was under siege in 2000–2001 for its poor performance and fare increases (demonstrated by headlines such as 'Virgin Trains face fresh attack over poor performance figures'[19] and a cartoon depicting a frustrated would-be commuter with the caption: 'Virgin Trains: Train cancelled – Branson's reputation on the line'[20]), the media lost no time in highlighting problem areas elsewhere in the Virgin empire.

However, an academic debate on the whys and wherefors of corporate reputation versus brand reputation is not additive in a publication that focuses on the management of *risks* to reputation. The basic techniques for assessing and acting on risks to reputation are the same, whether the reputation in question is of the 'corporate' or 'brand' variety. The term 'reputation' or 'corporate reputation' will be used throughout this book and is relevant to all types and sizes of organisation. Readers will need to determine for themselves the extent to which it is helpful to separate out the risks to individual 'brands' when evaluating risks for their own business.

MEASURING AND VALUING REPUTATION

Owing to the importance of corporate reputation as a driver of business performance and stakeholder behaviours, a number of methodologies have been developed which attempt to measure and value corporate reputation. These are designed to help business leaders to focus on the right levers as they endeavour to manage their businesses' reputations. Such models are helpful in identifying and managing risks to reputation as they provide a good indication of the key sources of reputational threats and opportunities.

One of the best-known reputation surveys is *Fortune* magazine's annual listing of the most admired companies in America, which began in 1983.[21] A similar *Fortune* annual survey is conducted for the world's most admired companies.[22] For the global survey 10,000 directors, executives and managers at 345 companies around the world are asked to rate eligible[23] companies against nine attributes:

- Quality of management
- Quality of products and services
- Innovation
- Long-term investment value
- Financial soundness
- Employee talent
- Social responsibility
- Use of corporate assets
- Globalness.

Top-league players in the 50–strong All-Star global listing for 2003 included Wal-Mart at number one (up from second place), nudging General Electric into the number two spot after heading the league table for four years, and Microsoft retaining third position.

A similar survey is conducted by the UK's *Management Today* magazine (Britain's Most Admired Companies). The *Management Today* criteria are virtually identical to *Fortune*'s apart from a 'Quality of marketing' category in place of 'Globalness'.[24] Similar regional reputation surveys are carried out in Asia by *Asian Business* and the *Far Eastern Economic Review*.

A global survey conducted by the UK newspaper the *Financial Times* (World's Most Respected Companies for 2002[25]), conducted annually since 1998, involves 1,000 CEOs in 20 countries. It seeks to identify those companies and business leaders most respected by their peers and to establish the reasons for this. As well as being asked to nominate the three companies they respect most in the world and in their industry sector, and their top three business leaders, participants were asked for the first time in 2001 to name companies that delivered value in three separate areas:

- Value creation for customers
- Value creation for shareholders
- Best management of environmental resources.

For each of the three 'value' questions a relevant stakeholder group was also surveyed to provide a contrast to CEO opinion (members of the general public for customers, fund managers world wide for shareholders and media commentators and NGOs for environmental resources). This new twist to the survey highlights recognition of the growing importance of public opinion, pressure groups and the media in shaping corporate reputation.

> Reputation, rather like beauty, is something that largely exists in the eye of the beholder. For corporations that beholder is the myriad stakeholders whose perceptions combine across interests and geographies to create a corporate reputation.
> (Andrew Pharoah, managing director, Public and Corporate Affairs, Hill & Knowlton[26])

The 2002 *Financial Times* survey also asked CEOs to nominate the companies they felt displayed the greatest integrity and those that would make the most impact over the next five to ten years on economic and social issues in emerging economies.

Table 1-1. Reputation Quotient attributes[29] (Reproduced by permission of Harris Interactive)

Category	Specific attributes
Emotional appeal	• Have a good feeling about the company • Admire and respect the company • Trust the company a great deal
Products and services	• Stands behind its products and services • Develops innovative products and services • Offers high-quality products and services • Offers products and services that are good value for money
Financial performance	• Has a strong record of profitability • Looks like a low-risk investment • Looks like a company with strong prospects for future growth • Tends to outperform its competitors
Vision and leadership	• Has excellent leadership • Has a clear vision for its future • Recognises and takes advantage of market opportunities
Workplace environment	• Reward employees fairly • Looks like a good company to work for • Looks like a company that would have good employees
Social responsibility	• Supports good causes • Is an environmentally responsible company • Behaves responsibly towards the people in the communities where it operates

Another widely used methodology, the Harris–Fombrun Reputation Quotient[SM] (RQ), was developed by research company Harris Interactive in conjunction with Dr. Charles J. Fombrun[27] of the Stern School of Business of New York University and Executive Director of the Reputation Institute. To ensure that perceptions of companies could be measured across companies and many stakeholder groups, the RQ methodology, was based on the output from focus groups in the USA where people were asked to name companies they did and didn't like or respect and explain why.[28] The series of pilot tests that followed determined the optimal 20 attributes that were grouped into six categories that became the Reputation Quotient[SM] (Table 1-1).

The criteria used to assess reputation are not only relevant to large corporations: even if your business has only a single product and a handful of employees or operates in the public or not-for-profit sector, many of the attributes in Table 1-1 will be considered by your stakeholders in evaluating you as a potential employer, supplier or partner.

The criteria used by the various organisations offering reputation rating services are therefore a useful guide to the generic drivers of reputation and the threats and opportunities that surround them. But understanding what drives the reputation of a specific organisation requires deeper analysis and an exploration of the reputational threats and opportunities relevant to its unique circumstances.

WHAT DRIVES REPUTATION?

If reputation is a product of the way in which many different people and groups perceive an organisation, what makes the difference between a good and a bad reputation? The answer to this is straightforward.

A good reputation will be enjoyed by an organisation that consistently meets or exceeds the requirements and expectations of its major stakeholder groups so that stakeholder experience matches expectation.

A bad reputation results when the words or deeds of an organisation fall short of stakeholder demands and expectations. A lack of alignment will start to erode confidence in the organisation and, if not corrected, may ultimately destroy it.

This concept is simply expressed in the reputation equation in Figure 1-3.

Reputation = experience – expectations

Beliefs about what a business is for and how it does it

Beliefs inform our

expectations about how a business would behave in a

particular situation

Against which we measure our

experience of what a business actually did

© Oonagh Mary Harpur

Figure 1-3   The reputation equation.[30] **(Reproduced by permission of Oonagh Mary Harper)**

It follows that keeping in tune with the requirements and changing expectations of major stakeholder groups, ensuring that their beliefs are soundly based and that their expectations match the reality of their day-to-day experience will yield a good and sustainable reputation. Finding innovative ways of exceeding expectations can actually enhance reputation by building trust and increasing stakeholder confidence. In theory it really is as simple as that. However, putting this into practice is both challenging and demanding as it requires both an 'inside out' and an 'outside in' approach: 'inside out' by ensuring that reputation is built on a solid foundation of core purpose, values and ways of working; 'outside in' by responding to the changing demands of the broader environment in which the business operates.

A practice deemed acceptable today in areas such as boardroom remuneration, environmental impacts, use of youth labour or territories of operation, may no longer be permissible in 12 months' or two years' time. And it is not necessarily a change in law or regulations that will bring this about: a shift in opinion of key stakeholder groups fuelled by the media may suffice. As stakeholders become better informed, their expectations will continue to rise and their tolerance of 'bad' practice will diminish – particularly if that practice could adversely impact reputation, stock price, earnings or their confidence.

This publication explores the risks to reputation – both threats and opportunities – arising from seven drivers of reputation (Figure 1-4):

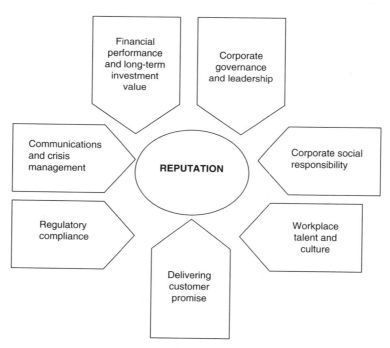

Figure 1-4   Drivers of reputation.

- *Financial performance and long-term investment value* Does the business have a solid financial track record? What are its future prospects? Will it prove a good investment in the longer term?
- *Corporate governance and leadership* Does the top team set an appropriate tone for the organisation? Do its leaders have integrity? Does the business have a compelling but realistic vision for the future? Does it display good corporate governance?
- *Regulatory compliance* Does the business comply with relevant laws and regulations? Does it anticipate and keep pace with regulatory developments? Does it become embroiled in litigation?
- *Delivering customer promise* Does the business provide consistently good-quality products and services? How good is its customer service? Does it innovate and successfully launch new products and services? How responsible is its marketing? How does it handle complaints?
- *Workplace talent and culture* How well does the business treat its employees? Is it able to recruit, develop and retain high quality staff? What does it feel like to work there?
- *Corporate social responsibility (CSR)* Does the business understand its social, ethical and environmental impacts? Is it receptive to the requirements and expectations of its key stakeholders? How does it respond?
- *Communications and crisis management* Does the business provide meaningful and transparent information which allows stakeholders to understand its values, goals, performance and future prospects? How would it handle a crisis?

These criteria are an amalgam of the reputation attributes described above, but have been adapted to reflect heightened interest in fundamental issues such as corporate governance, compliance with laws and regulations, the personal integrity of directors and the transparency of reporting and communications, following the scandals at Enron, Andersen, Tyco, WorldCom and others.

In discussing these seven criteria, this book will consider the relevance of each to major stakeholder groups and the implications for an organisation's core purpose, values, policies and practice. 'Inside out' and 'outside in' will work simultaneously to provide an integrated and workable approach to

Managing reputation is not just about avoiding media attention. It's also about the upside — the opportunities for reputation enhancement, performance improvement and competitive advantage that will add real value to the bottom line.

There are many benefits to be derived from managing down the threats and leveraging the opportunities associated with reputation. Creating and maintaining a positive reputation can lead to a variety of positive outcomes, including:

- attracting investors and securing capital at a lower cost
- attracting customers and creating consumer loyalty
- commanding a price premium for goods and services
- recruiting and retaining high-quality employees
- creating a barrier to entry for potential competitors

- providing an edge in competitive markets
- underpinning long-term supplier partnerships
- fostering a positive relationship with regulators and the media and
- providing protection against the occasional crisis.

A positive and sustainable reputation is now a major determinant of a business's future ability to generate wealth and succeed in the longer term. Corporate reputation is not only a measure of past performance – it is an indicator of future promise.

The next chapter will explore how, by systematically identifying risks to reputation, organisations can achieve the twin goals of safeguarding, while at the same time enhancing, their reputation.

NOTES AND REFERENCES

1. Sherman, Michael L., chief operating officer, AIG Europe (UK) Ltd quoted in Institute of Directors (1999) *Reputation Management: Strategies for protecting companies, their brands and their directors.* London, Director Publications, p. 11.
2. The stakeholder concept is defined and further examined in Chapter 4.
3. Sir John Browne (now Lord Browne) from a speech about what it means to be 'admired' at a dinner organised by *Management Today*, 30 November 2000.
4. Quoted in the *Financial Times*, 1 July 2002.
5. Quoted in the *Financial Times*, 5 June 2002.
6. The Brouillard study, based on the companies featured in *Fortune* magazine's 15th annual survey of America's Most Admired Companies as reported in *Reputation Management* (1999).
7. As reported in the 2003 America's Most Admired Companies survey, *Fortune* magazine, 3 March 2003.
8. www.unctad.org.
9. Reported in *The Guardian*, 13 August 2002.
10. *Financial Times*, 23 August 2003.
11. Eccles, R.G., Herz, R.H., Keegan, E.M. and Phillips, D.M.H. (2001) *The ValueReporting Revolution: Moving beyond the Earnings Game*. John Wiley & Sons, Inc, Chapter 5.
12. National accounting conventions differ, but the general rule is that intangible assets generated in-house can only be capitalised and regarded as assets if they have a readily ascertainable market value. Similarly only those elements of acquired 'goodwill' which have a clear market value should be separated out. This is the approach currently taken by accounting standards FRS 10 in the UK and FASB 141 and 142 in the USA. These standards do not assume that goodwill will automatically depreciate. In the USA there is now an annual 'impairment' test whereby only if the goodwill is deemed to have diminished it should be written down and depreciated (amortised) through the profit and loss account (revenue account). Otherwise it can be held at cost. The value of acquired product brands (arrived at by using a variety of valuation techniques such as Interbrand's methodology, Y&R's Brand Asset Valuator®, and WPP's Brandz) and other acquired intangibles for which a value can be calculated, such as the value of products in the development pipeline for a pharmaceutical company, is sometimes visible as an asset in balance sheet. However, strict accounting standards combined with a reticence to display commercially sensitive data mean that, in practice, this is still the exception

rather than the rule. Even in Australia, where current accounting policy allows internally created brands to appear on the balance sheet at fair value based on directors' or experts' estimates, many Australian companies still choose not to separate out their brand values. National differences in accounting rules also make it difficult for investors and analysts to make cross-border comparisons between companies. This may change with the advent of International Accounting Standards (IAS), to be known as International Financial Reporting Standards (IFRS) in 2005.

13. Leadbeater, C. (2000) *New Measures for the New Economy*. London: ICAEW Centre for Business Performance, p. 9.
14. Leadbeater, C. (2000) *New Measures for the New Economy*. London: ICAEW Centre for Business Performance, p. 5.
15. Institute of Chartered Accountants of England and Wales (ICAEW), P.D. Leake lectures, Oxford, April 1998.
16. Eccles, R.G., Herz, R.H., Keegan, E.M. and Phillips, D.M.H. (2001) *The ValueReporting Revolution: Moving beyond the Earnings Game*. John Wiley & Sons, Inc., Chapter 7.
17. See Chapter 2 for background to this in the section on governmental and regulatory drivers relating to the UK's plans to reform company law.
18. Reported in the *Financial Times*, 5 March 2002.
19. *The Guardian*, 12 April 2001.
20. *The Guardian*, 13 January 2001.
21. Results of the 2003 America's Most Admired Companies survey were published in *Fortune* magazine on 3 March 2003. Also available from www.fortune.com/fortune/mostadmired.
22. Results of the 2003 World's Most Admired Companies survey were published in *Fortune* magazine, 3 March 2003. Also available from www.fortune.com/fortune/globaladmired.
23. To be eligible, companies had to have revenues of at least $8 billion in 2001.
24. The assessment criteria and results of 2002 *Management Today*'s Britain's Most Admired Companies survey can be viewed on their website at www.clickmt.com.
25. The assessment criteria and results of the 2002 World's Most Respected Companies survey can be found in the *Financial Times*, 20 January 2003. The fieldwork for the 2002 survey was conducted between October and November 2002. See www.ft.com/wmr2002. for details of the 2002 survey and for results going back to 1998.
26. Quoted in the *Financial Times*, 16 September 2002.
27. Dr. Charles J. Fombrun is professor of management at the Stern School of Business of New York University and Executive Director of the Reputation Institute. He is co-founder and editor-in-chief of the quarterly journal *Corporate Reputation Review*. See the Reputation Institute website at www.reputationinstitute.com.
28. From article entitled 'The value to be found in corporate reputation' by Dr. Charles J. Fombrun, in the *Financial Times*, 4 December 2000.
29. Reproduced by permission of Harris Interactive www.harrisinteractive.com.
30. Harpur, Oonagh Mary, in *Corporate Social Responsibility Monitor* (2002). London: Gee Publishing, Chapter B4.

two

the business case for reputation risk management

WHAT IS REPUTATION RISK?

The term 'reputation risk' or 'reputational risk' is frequently bandied about as if it were a discrete risk category alongside 'financial risk' and 'operational risk'. But what is meant by it? What precisely is reputation risk?

First it is necessary to dispel a myth. There is no such thing as 'reputation risk' – only risks *to* reputation. The term 'reputation risk' is a convenient catchall for all those risks, from whichever source, that can *impact* reputation, as shown in Figure 2-1.

In 1990 the benzene contamination of natural spring water, produced and bottled by the French company Perrier, caused severe reputational damage, decimated market share and ultimately led to the takeover by Nestlé of this icon of French business in 1992. The source of the risk was a product quality problem which impacted both brand and corporate reputation.

Similarly, in 1999 the reputation of British Nuclear Fuels was in tatters and customers and the general public had lost confidence in the company. The origin of this risk to reputation was an organisational culture of sloppiness, non-compliance and lack of accountability that had been allowed to take root – not something that one would reasonably hope or expect in the hazardous and high-profile nuclear industry.

Although in the strict sense of the term 'reputation risk' does not exist, its use can sometimes be helpful. There are occasions when specific use of the term can help to grab management's attention and persuade them to focus on this often neglected area of risk, for example when establishing risk categories for a structured brainstorm or when presenting risk workshop output data to top management.

Figure 2-1   Reputation risk.

In fact, it is such a useful term that this book will continue to employ it as convenient shorthand for 'risks to reputation'. For the sake of clarity, the following working definition of reputation risk may be helpful:

> *Reputation risk is any action, event or circumstance that could adversely or beneficially impact an organisation's reputation.*

WHY DEVOTE A BOOK TO REPUTATION RISK MANAGEMENT?

So, if 'reputation risk' is really 'risks to reputation' in disguise, isn't the subject already adequately covered by the numerous learned tomes on general risk management theory? Why dedicate a whole book to the topic? There are two answers to this question. First, reputation is now a key corporate asset – often the single most significant asset a business possesses. Second, although concepts of formal risk management have been around for a number of years, businesses still often find it easier to focus on risks that have a clear and quantifiable financial impact. As a result, risks to reputation which may have 'soft' root causes and hard-to-quantify impacts, are frequently ignored, underplayed or, at best, sidelined. They are too often shunted into the 'too difficult' pile as they may require lateral thinking, innovative solutions and, in some cases, a fundamental rethink of strategy. This is paradoxical, as significant risks to reputation are often those 'killer risks' that can jeopardise a business's very existence.

To illustrate this, try this simple 'cornflake' test. Imagine you are coming downstairs for breakfast, ready to attack your morning bowl of cornflakes. The newspaper has just arrived. What is the headline you would least like to see about your organisation? Is it the revelation that your supposedly environmentally friendly products are not quite as 'green' as your publicity implies? Is it an exposé on the bullying and domineering style of your chief executive and the powerlessness of your lightweight, overcommitted non-executive directors? Is it a quote from a major institutional investor that they have lost confidence in your management's strategic vision, are impatient with the failure to deliver and want a change of leadership? Is it the latest in a string of racial discrimination cases, an award for stress or for unequal pay? Or is it the death of a contractor on one of your manufacturing sites?

Whatever your 'killer headline', what is the underlying risk? Does this risk appear on your corporate risk profile (if you have one)? Is it discussed in the boardroom? What is being done

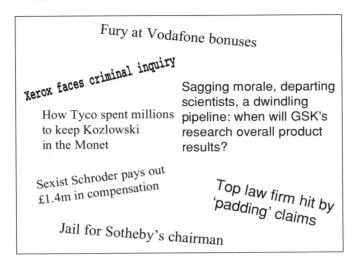

Fury at Vodafone bonuses

Xerox faces criminal inquiry

How Tyco spent millions to keep Kozlowski in the Monet

Sagging morale, departing scientists, a dwindling pipeline: when will GSK's research overall product results?

Sexist Schroder pays out £1.4m in compensation

Top law firm hit by 'padding' claims

Jail for Sotheby's chairman

Figure 2-2   News headlines.

to reduce the likelihood of it happening? And if, heaven forbid, it should occur, what would its impact be and how would you manage the ensuing crisis?

On a daily basis, newspaper readers are exposed to headlines which impact, either positively or negatively, their view of the targeted individuals, organisations and market sectors – and their reputations (Figure 2-2). Yet so often, the issues and circumstances that could spark these potential 'killer headlines' don't feature in the risk profile. Assumptions such as 'that'll never happen', 'we can handle it if it does', 'what's the point of worrying – there's nothing we can do about it' or even 'we've got more important things to do – like running this darn business!', are rife. But the corporate graveyard is littered with businesses that didn't anticipate and positively manage risks that were fundamental to their reputation and their continued success.

In almost all cases, there were warning signs that either management chose to ignore or others in the organisation chose not to communicate. That is why risk management can be such a powerful enabler. Basic risk management tools can be harnessed to involve *all* employees in the active management of risks to reputation so that the significance of those 'killer risks' is understood and they receive attention at the right level. Appropriate action can then be taken before it is too late.

A survey conducted in 2001 by the insurance company Aon, which polled the UK's top 2000 private and public organisations, showed that 'loss of reputation' was seen as the greatest risk, followed by 'failure to change'. This was a significant shift from the previous study in 1999 when reputation was ranked in fourth position.[1] A survey by Corporate Reputation Watch of 600 US-based senior executives in February 2002 found that 49% were concerned about negative press in the print and broadcast media as a major threat to reputation, and 42% of respondents saw unethical behaviour as most likely to imperil a company's reputation.[2] This survey was carried out around the same time that a *BusinessWeek*/Harris poll found that 79% of adults believed that the executives of many large companies were, as at Enron, putting their own personal interests ahead of those of workers and shareholders.[3] Corporate behaviour, business ethics and the integrity of individual directors have become inextricably entwined as drivers of reputation. As Ron Hartwig, executive vice president of Hill & Knowlton, commented: 'Senior executives now understand that an ethical lapse can devastate a company's reputation, and that behavior is a critical component to how a company is perceived.'[4]

In spite of the importance attached to reputation and the risks to it, a US survey by consultancy firm McKinsey showed that directors would like to understand more about the risks their companies face and have a particularly poor understanding of non-financial risks. The survey found that CEOs and directors are more knowledgeable about financial risk and therefore tend to focus on it. As a result, non-financial risk receives only 'anecdotal treatment' and 'boards absolutely do not understand the risks their companies face'. While 43% of directors could not effectively identify, safeguard against and plan for key risks, 36% did not understand the major risks facing the company.[5]

So why devote a book to reputation risk management? Perhaps such a book will persuade organisations to give mission-critical risks to reputation the attention they deserve by providing a route-map for identifying and dealing with them.

WHY BOTHER TO MANAGE REPUTATION RISKS?

Chapter 1 explored why reputation is such a crucial intangible asset and examined some of the environmental factors that have led to its change in status (the stakeholder imperative, globalisation, the technological and media revolution, the rise of intangible assets). This backcloth has resulted in raised stakeholder expectations of the businesses they invest in, buy from and work for. There are calls for greater transparency and accountability and for consistently responsible and ethical behaviour. If expectations are not met, stakeholders are increasingly willing to 'vote with their feet' by selling those shares, boycotting that product or choosing not to work for that company. These factors may, in themselves, provide a compelling business case for the proactive management of reputational risks. However, if you're still not convinced that seeking out risks to reputation is a worthwhile activity, here are some other key developments around the globe that may change your mind. These are all factors specific to individual stakeholder groups; some, or perhaps all of them, will be relevant to your own organisation.

governmental and regulatory drivers

Spurred on by the loss of market confidence caused by the US corporate scandals, governments and regulators around the globe have been seeking to ensure that the businesses in their jurisdiction fully understand the risks they are running, and, to avoid unwelcome surprises, loss of value and damage to reputation, are controlling them well and providing adequate information to shareholders and other stakeholders.

❏   UK

In the UK, market confidence issues have been on the agenda since a spate of corporate scandals in the late 1980s, including the plundering of pension funds by Robert Maxwell's publishing empire and high-profile corporate collapses at Polly Peck and BCCI. The response was a series of corporate governance codes introduced during the 1990s. These codes sought to moderate boardroom behaviour, executive remuneration and improve control of the business by, for example, recommending that the roles of chairman and chief executive be split so that an autocratic CEO could no longer dominate the company's directors.

The most recent of these codes, the Combined Code, published in June 1998, amalgamated all that had gone before into a single cohesive document. A separate committee chaired by Sir Nigel Turnbull, then executive director of Rank Group plc, was established to provide further guidance on the aspects of the Combined Code related to controlling a business. The guidance produced by the committee, known as the Turnbull report (issued September 1999), has had far-reaching consequences. It makes an explicit link between a company's business goals, the risks to delivering them and the internal controls established to manage those risks; its guidance is based on companies taking a risk-based approach to internal control. For the first time it urges companies to consider not just financial risks but *all* significant risks, including those related to 'legal, health and safety and environmental, reputation and business probity issues'.[6]

The Turnbull guidance stresses that risk-taking is necessary to generate profit, but that risks should be managed and controlled appropriately. To comply with Turnbull, companies have to state in their annual reports that they have established ongoing processes to identify, evaluate and manage significant risks to the business and that the board has reviewed the effectiveness of these processes. UK stock exchange listing rules have required all companies listed in the UK to comply fully with the Combined Code and Turnbull guidance since the end of 2000, or state where they have not complied and explain why. The 'comply or explain' approach is a basic tenet of UK corporate governance policy.

The Turnbull guidance has been widely adopted as best practice by much of the public sector and parts of the private and not-for-profit sectors. This means that a wide range of UK businesses and organisations now have to systematically identify, assess and actively manage their risks – specifically including those risks related to reputation.

The UK government has also undertaken a major review of company law which culminated in a white paper (draft bill) in July 2002. This will, if accepted, ultimately become a new Companies Act, possibly by 2004. The importance of corporate reputation is underlined by the white paper which recognises that companies are 'increasingly reliant on intangible assets such as the skills and knowledge of their employees, their business relationships and their reputation'.[7] It proposes that directors should aim to run a company successfully in the best interests of its shareholders while taking into account the relationships on which the company depends and both the long- and short-term consequences of their actions. To discharge this responsibility, directors should recognise, as circumstances require:

...the company's need to foster relationships with its employees, customers and suppliers, its need to maintain its business reputation, and its need to consider the company's impact, on the community and the working environment.[8]

The white paper demands proof of action – not just words. It wants a company to demonstrate what it is actually doing by reporting more fully on its critical intangible assets and risks to allow an 'informed assessment' of its operations, its financial position and its future business strategies and prospects. It proposes that directors include in a mandatory Operating and Financial Review (OFR), as part of their annual report, any material factors which they, in good faith, deem relevant to that 'informed assessment'. This may include the company's policies and performance on employment, environmental social and community issues and any other matters 'which affect, or may affect, the company's reputation'.[9] The proposals are designed to significantly improve both the quantity and quality of information available on a company, inform decision-making and enable investors to hold directors to account.

As the new act will apply not only to public companies (with a turnover in excess of £50 million) but also to large privately owned companies (with a turnover above £500 million), it will have a broader impact than the Turnbull guidance – and will position reputation and its associated risks centre stage.

The proposed changes in company law were supplemented in January 2003 by new guidance on the role of non-executive directors (the Higgs report), the role of audit committees (the Smith report) and on auditing and accounting matters.[10] The recommendations from these reports are to be incorporated into the Combined Code with the usual requirement for companies to 'comply or explain'. Overall, these changes represent a significant strengthening of UK corporate governance arrangements – moves that should help to safeguard business reputations.

☐ USA

The Enron, WorldCom and other corporate scandals have led to hard-hitting and swift action from government and regulators in the USA in response to outraged public opinion. Global confidence in Wall Street and in the reputation of US business had to be restored. The cancer of what Harvey Pitt, the then chairman of the US Securities and Exchange Commission, described as 'breathtaking failures of corporate governance' and 'revolting misfeasance by corporate leaders'[11] needed to be tackled, and quickly.

The new 'get tough on business' hard-line attitude was encapsulated by the images of disgraced WorldCom executives Scott Sullivan and David Meyers appearing handcuffed in a New York courtroom in August 2002, flanked by burly FBI agents.

The government's response, the Sarbanes–Oxley Act, was signed into US law by Congress on 30 July 2002 and took immediate effect. The act was described by US President George Bush as 'the most far-reaching reforms of American business practice since the time of Franklin Delano Roosevelt'.

This new law sends very clear messages that all concerned must heed. This law says to every dishonest corporate leader: you will be exposed and punished; the era of low standards and false profits is over; no boardroom in America is above or beyond the law. . . .

This law says to corporate accountants: the high standards of your profession will be enforced without exception; the auditors will be audited; the accountants will be held to account. This law says to shareholders that the financial information you receive from a company will be true and reliable, for those who deliberately sign their names to deception will be punished. . . . Today, we are taking practical steps to encourage honest enterprise in our nation. Under this law, CEOs and chief financial officers must personally vouch for the truth and fairness of their companies' disclosures. Those financial disclosures will be broader and better for the sake of shareholders and investors.

(George Bush, US President, July 2002)

The new act, known as SOx, indeed represents the most significant change to US corporate governance since the enactment of the Securities Exchange Act of 1934. It sets new standards for company executives, accountants and auditors. Companies listed in the USA must now comply with a number of new measures including:

- chief executive and chief financial officer to attest to the accuracy and completeness of the accounts
- disclosure of off-balance sheet transactions
- evidence that the necessary processes have been put in place to prove that their accounts are not misleading
- an internal control report, within the annual report, affirming the responsibility of management for the adequacy of the internal control structure and financial reporting procedures and providing an assessment of them[12]
- adoption of a code of ethics for senior financial officers with confirmation disclosed in annual reports
- mandatory internal audit function
- audit committees to be mandatory and to have greater control over the company's relationships with its external auditor including hiring, firing, spending authority, pre-approval of audit or non-audit work and oversight
- company audit committees to be composed exclusively of independent directors
- audit committees to contain at least one member who is a 'financial expert'
- a ban on company loans to directors and executives
- disclosure of share dealings of directors and officers within two days to the SEC and NYSE
- forfeiting of bonuses by company executives if accounts have to be restated
- prohibition on audit firms performing audit services for a client whose CEO, CFO, controller or chief accounting officer was previously employed by the auditor and participated in the client's audit during the previous 12-month period
- restrictions on consulting and other non-auditing services that accounting firms can provide to their clients with periodic disclosure of any non-audit services provided
- protection for corporate whistleblowers.

And those are just the edited highlights! Failure to comply could result in harsh civil and criminal penalties. The Act will be reinforced by implementation rules to be introduced by the Securities and Exchange Commission (SEC). New listing standards have also been brought in by the New York Stock Exchange (NYSE)[13] and Nasdaq, requiring listed companies to: gain shareholder approval for all stock-option plans; have a majority of independent directors on their board; have exclusively independent directors on the audit committee and committees that select executives (nomination committee) and determine executive pay (compensation committee); adopt a code of business conduct and ethics and adopt corporate governance guidelines and charters for audit, compensation and nomination committees.

In common with the UK's company law proposals, SOx seeks to encourage improved and more complete disclosure, greater transparency and heightened accountability to enable stakeholders to have a better understanding of a business's performance and the threats and opportunities facing it.

The interesting point about these legislative and regulatory actions – or over-reactions as some would argue – is that they were introduced because US business was patently incapable of a standard of self-regulation that would satisfy key stakeholders and maintain the reputation of US business in the global economy. 'Self-regulate effectively or you'll be regulated against' is a recurrent theme in many jurisdictions. But therein lies the potential competitive advantage: being an early adopter can bolster reputation and stakeholder trust. What SOx and the accompanying regulations provide is an excellent checklist of current corporate governance 'hot topics'. Whether or not you are a company listed in the USA or indeed a company, you could do worse than use these criteria as a benchmark to critically assess corporate governance standards in your own organisation – before the media or a disenchanted institutional investor does it for you! The growing importance of good corporate governance as a driver of reputation will be returned to in Chapter 6.

◻   ELSEWHERE

In other countries moves are also afoot to tighten corporate governance in order to safeguard the reputation of business and shore up financial markets. In May 2003 the European Commission unveiled an action plan to enhance corporate governance in Europe. The proposals target areas including directors' pay, broader financial and non-financial disclosure, the role of independent directors and shareholder rights.[14]

The Organisation of Economic Cooperation and Development (OECD) has also announced plans to revise and expand its 1999 principles of corporate governance[15] to help to rebuild investor confidence. The preamble to the current OECD Corporate Governance principles states:

> factors such as business ethics and corporate awareness of the environmental and societal interests of the communities in which it operates can also have an impact on the reputation and the long-term success of a company.[16]

In South Africa an updated version of the 1994 King report on Corporate Governance was published in 2002. 'King 2' is widely regarded as the most comprehensive publication on the subject as it adopts best practice from around the world. It embraces the 'inclusive' or 'stake-holder' approach to corporate governance which puts responsibilities to stakeholders at the heart of the business. Like the Turnbull report, it takes a risk-based approach to internal control and requires businesses to consider the gamut of business risks, including risks to reputation.[17]

Some governments are pressing for more disclosure on environmental and social issues, primarily to establish the extent to which businesses are contributing to the delivery of po-litical objectives in these areas. There has, however, been little appetite for legislation, with the notable exception of the French government which, in February 2002, announced a new law, the 'Nouvelles Régulations Economiques' (NRE – New Economic Regulations), which makes social and environmental reporting mandatory for the top 200 publicly listed compa-nies. Data on performance in areas such as labour standards, workforce diversity, community involvement, stakeholder engagement and emissions are to be included.[18] Other governments have favoured a more 'softly softly' approach, some choosing to 'name and shame' compa-nies for failing to report on environmental and social issues. The UK's Environment Agency has, for example, on its website a 'hall of shame', listing the most fined and prosecuted UK polluters.[19]

☐ SECTORAL REGULATION

Another recent development is the growing number of codes and guidelines from regulators on issues that could tarnish the reputations of the sectors they serve. One example of this is the UK's financial watchdog, the Financial Services Authority (FSA), one of whose key aims is to maintain market confidence. In October 2002 the FSA launched its new 'Ethical Framework for Financial Services' which states:

> Reputation, reputation, reputation! – behaviour perceived as unethical can carry a significant bottom line cost – and not only for one year. The 'ripple effect' of being linked, or being seen to be linked, to an unethical firm or situation can be very damaging for other parties too. And the stench can be difficult to get away from. Reputational issues rarely respect national boundaries![20]

It then outlines the opportunity this presents for both maintaining and increasing market con-fidence: 'Distinguishing the UK financial services sector as being renowned for good ethical practice could help it to absorb some "shocks".'[21] The document concludes the section on 'why ethics matter' by stating:

> In summary, reputation is the key to the business case for ethics, and reputation and of the sector and the firms within it is important to all of us. We threaten no stick as such but we would emphasise a significant carrot; good, ethical behaviour can also be a competitive advantage, and, in time, a way to lighter regulation.[22]

The document presents a cogent, opportunity-based business case for reputation risk manage-ment which applies equally to private, public and not-for-profit sectors. What a refreshingly upbeat stance for a regulator! If you exemplify responsible and ethical behaviour you will not only maintain and potentially enhance the reputation of your organisation, but that of the entire sector, thereby creating competitive advantage for your organisation while guarding against sectoral collateral damage. As an added bonus, your good behaviour and unimpeachable reputation may convince regulators that a lighter regulatory touch is warranted.

Not all regulators, however, take such an upbeat view. The European Agency for the Evaluation of Medicines (EMEA – the European medicines regulator), is planning to force pharmaceutical companies to provide more information about their new drugs, including products that fail to gain regulatory approval. This move is in response to concerns among investors about the way in which the industry communicates key information about the status of products in the development–approval–launch pipeline. Selective or late disclosure by AstraZeneca, the Anglo-Swiss group, the Dutch firm Akzo Nobel, UK-based PowderJect and others has not only dented the reputations of the individual companies but has also threatened to undermine investor confidence in the industry.[23]

Even the UK's FSA, in the very same month that it launched its ethical framework, threatened to start 'naming and shaming' financial institutions it found in breach of its tightened money-laundering rules[24] – an effective way of impacting the reputation of targeted companies!

Wherever one looks, there is growing recognition of the importance of reputation as a key intangible asset. Governments and regulators are now cognisant of the need to guard against threats to reputation and to exploit opportunities to enhance it so as to maintain and increase stakeholder confidence in individual businesses, sectors and markets. It is generally accepted that that the broader aspects of governance, not just the conduct of directors themselves, but also the maintenance of those key relationships with stakeholders and the environment on which the business's future success depends, are inextricably linked with an organisation's reputation and its future prospects. If businesses are not able to keep their own houses in order through proactive self-regulation, the hostile, post-Enron mood may lead to further legislation and regulation.

investor engagement and activism

☐   THE NEW ACTIVISM

Another key development that has focused boardroom attention on reputation is the emphasis major investors are now putting on a 'good' reputation and the factors that contribute to it. But aren't investors only interested in profitability and performance? Why would they get excited about reputation? The explanation for this is simple:

> A hit to reputation is a hit to long-term shareholder value.
>
> (Dr Craig Mackenzie[25])

Investors will often pay a premium for equity in companies with a good corporate reputation and robust governance because the risk is lower. McKinsey's 2002 global investor study[26] found that, around the world, 73–78% of investors are prepared to pay a premium for companies exhibiting high governance standards. The premium differs widely, however, from territory to territory – from 12–14% in North America and Western Europe to 20–25% in Asia and Latin America and over 30% in Eastern Europe and Africa.

Investors are now recognising both the upside and downside nature of reputation: strong corporate reputations can enhance future prospects and earnings potential whereas a damaged reputation often results in a lower share price and a diminished shareholder value. Once reputation is recognised as key business asset, the need to actively track threats and opportunities to it, in order to safeguard one's investment, becomes axiomatic. The fact that investors are probing into sources of reputation risk such as boardroom behaviour and social, environmental and ethical impacts (SEE) should therefore come as no surprise.

In some countries, this broader investor focus on softer risks has been fuelled by changes in legislation. The UK was the first country to introduce legislation that forced investors to consider SEE risks. A new Pensions Act Regulation, which took effect from 3 July 2000, required trustees of occupational pension funds to disclose in their Statement of Investment Principles (SIP) *'the extent (if at all) to which social, environmental and ethical considerations are taken into account in the selection, retention and realisation of investments'*.[27] As this regulation related to over £800 billion of funds and over 20 million people who were members or beneficiaries of an occupational pension fund, its effect has been significant. It has put under the spotlight the ethical and socially responsible basis of pension fund investment and has required institutional investors to devise means of screening the companies in their portfolio as, in many cases, pension fund trustees have delegated responsibility to their fund managers.

One response has been from the Association of British Insurers (ABI), whose members control around 25% of the UK stock market. The ABI has asked UK listed companies to disclose in their annual reports what they are doing on SEE issues. The preface to the Association of British Insurers' 2001 report on investing in social responsibility, which contains the ABI's disclosure guidelines, articulates the case well:

> [The report] reflects growing concern in the business and investor communities that companies' exposure to social, ethical and environmental risk has been increasing over the past few years, and that these increased risks may not have been recognised, especially by companies which are not obviously exposed to potential controversies.[28]

> . . . Companies of all sizes, across the whole range of business sectors, face heightened risks from failing to meet society's expectations. At the same time, a full understanding and effective management of a company's impact on society can help to build shareholder value, especially in the 21st century economy where intangible assets and relationships are critical to business success.[29]

The aim is to persuade companies to integrate SEE risks into their risk management frameworks and corporate governance structures. And the UK is not alone. Similar pensions legislation is now under consideration in other European countries such as Germany, Austria and Switzerland, and in Australia.

Since the start of the new millennium, there has been a marked change in the approach of institutional investors to underperforming companies in their portfolios. There was a time when index tracking – a passive investment strategy – was the rule, with activist funds such as the TIAA-Cref and CalPERS[30] pension funds in the USA the exception. CalPERS, for example, publish annually a list of the best and worst US boards. These pockets of activity have not, however, protected US fund managers from accusations of dereliction of duty in the wake of high-profile accounting scandals!

Disenchantment with company performance following the burst of the dot.com bubble and the US accounting scandals has led to a sea change in investor activism. Institutional investors have always had a duty to secure value for the ultimate beneficiaries of the investment – pension scheme members, insurance policyholders and individual savers – by continuously monitoring the performance of the companies in their portfolio. But there is now an expectation from governments, regulators and the general public that the true owners of publicly listed companies – their investors – should also act more like owners and should *actively engage* with poorly performing investees to try to improve their performance. The new activism means that direct and active engagement should be employed by institutional investors where companies are underperforming, and that they should be held to account if they fail in this basic duty. Anne Mulcahy, chief executive of Xerox, has described shareholder pressure on companies as being 'at an all time high.'[31]

Bob Monks, one of the USA's best-known corporate activists, is to join with William Lerach, a leading US corporate lawyer, to push a radical shareholder rights agenda through the US judicial system. They plan to mount a series of legal actions against companies that have failed to listen to shareholder concerns and whose share price has plummeted. Their aim is to extract from companies not only damages, but also a commitment to improve corporate governance. This new and more aggressive approach to shareholder activism had been labelled 'corporate governance at gunpoint'.[32]

In the UK, a statement of principles on shareholder activism issued in October 2002 by the Institutional Shareholders' Committee[33] (ISC – whose members control the vast majority of UK institutional funds), suggests that it may be appropriate for institutional investors to intervene when they have concerns about:

- the company's strategy
- the company's operational performance
- the company's acquisition/disposal strategy
- independent directors failing to hold executive management properly to account
- internal controls failing
- inadequate succession planning
- an unjustifiable failure to comply with the Combined Code (the UK corporate governance code)
- inappropriate remuneration levels/incentive packages/severance packages and
- the company's approach to corporate social responsibility.

If companies persistently fail to respond to investors' concerns, investors are urged to register an abstention or vote against the board at general meetings. Investor policies on activism will be published and written into client contracts. The ISC statement was a bid to demonstrate effective self-regulation in attempt to ward off threatened legislation which would compel investors to intervene in underperforming companies.

This is a useful checklist for the key issues that excite institutional investors – and can, and already have, caused damage to the both the reputation and share price of many prominent companies!

In some areas fund managers are coordinating their activities and acting in concert to bring about change on general corporate governance improvements or other specific issues. Alongside the UK's ISC principles, collective institutional investor initiatives include:

- The International Corporate Governance Network (whose members control $10 000 billion of assets)[34] pressing for radical changes on the way companies are run on issues such as improved board independence, better board oversight and executive remuneration.
- In May 2002, 35 institutional investors with combined assets in excess of $4500 billion (£2884 billion) wrote to the world's 500 largest companies urging them to disclose the projected financial impacts of climate change on their company and to reveal what measures, if any, they proposed to minimise them. The Carbon Disclosure project involves big names such as Allianz Dresdner, Munich Re, Swiss Re, Credit Suisse and the UK's University Superannuation Scheme.
- The UK's Association of British Insurers' (ABI) disclosure guidelines on social responsibility[35] require investees to disclose in their annual report whether the board has identified, assessed and put in place systems to manage significant risks to the company's long- and short-term value arising from social, environmental and ethical (SEE) matters as well as opportunities to enhance value that could arise from an appropriate response, and to include information on such risks.
- The UK's National Association of Pension Funds (NAPF) *Independent Directors – what investors expect* (2002)[36] provides guidance on the role and accountabilities of independent directors. These include prompting the board to consider threats and opportunities arising from its ethical behaviour, its interactions with stakeholders and communities and its impact on the environment.

Individual fund managers have also launched their own initiatives:

- The TIAA-Cref and CalPERS campaign targeting excessive executive pay and their campaign for legislative changes which would boost the influence of shareholders in the boardroom.
- Hermes has launched the Hermes Principles – a document setting out what shareholders expect of public companies and what companies should expect of their investors.[37] Hermes states that 'a company's primary consideration should be the generation of long-term shareholder value, and this should be based on appropriate financial disciplines, competitive advantage and within a framework which is economically, ethically and socially responsible and sustainable'.
- Insight Investment's[38] Global Business Principles project, launched on November 2002, calls for companies to comply with internationally recognised business principles with regard to governance and corporate responsibility, particularly in developing countries.

- Morley Fund Management, the London-based asset management business with over £100 billion under management, has since 2001 had a policy of voting against the annual accounts of the top 100 UK companies unless they include an environmental report and to abstain for FTSE 250 high-risk companies. In May 2002 Morley launched their 'sustainabililty matrix' – a league table ranking the top 100 UK listed companies on their commitment to social and environmental issues. Lower ranked companies are excluded from Morley's sustainability funds. Morley argued that it is not a blacklist but rather a tool to encourage management to change their practices.
- ISIS Asset Management,[39] the UK fund manager's September 2002 launch of a 'green' league table of ten European banks with a combined market capitalisation of 389 billion euros. The focus is on the banks' lending policies to environmentally damaging projects. ISIS's stance is that banks associated with 'dirty' companies run the risk of damaging their reputation which can, in turn, 'harm brand value, employee morale, ability to recruit and in some cases write business especially in the retail market'.[40] ISIS plan to extend the initiative to cover other banks and insurance companies.

These initiatives demonstrate the ever-broadening concerns of investors, and their growing requirement for information on both financial and non-financial risks. Some investors cite political pressures from governments, increased scrutiny from non-governmental organisations and the rising number of ethical benchmarks and indices as drivers of their heightened interest. But many of these initiatives have at their core the drive for improved governance and a growing concern that some of the threats and opportunities associated with intangible assets – such as brands, knowledge, intellectual property and relationships with employees, local communities and the environment – are not being effectively managed. As the ABI puts it, 'these major investors want assurance that companies they invest in are fully aware of the risks and have effective management systems to deal with them'.[41] If things go wrong an investee's reputation can be in tatters and its share price can spiral downwards. Investors therefore have a responsibility to ensure that these areas are managed well; not just paid lip service to, but supported by robust management, monitoring and reporting processes. Businesses ignore these new demands at their peril.

And how are investors voicing their new activism? Why can this group's actions be so damaging to reputation? Although much investor engagement is still played out in private, in closed meetings, video links and written communications with corporate executives, the climate has changed. As well as abstaining or voting against resolutions at company annual general meetings and voting against the re-election of directors, disgruntled investors are now often prepared to voice their concerns to the media though the publication of league tables, sharing of previously confidential research, and through overtly critical comments on individual companies and their directors. Fearing punitive legislation if they fail to act, the major investors cannot risk being accused of being asleep on the watch, or of dilatoriness in safeguarding the investments entrusted to them.

The UK's Institutional Shareholders' Committee statement of principles on shareholder activism provides some useful pointers on how investors might progressively escalate action when boards fail to 'respond constructively' to their concerns:

- holding additional meetings with management specifically to discuss concerns
- expressing concern through the company's advisers
- meeting with the chairman, senior independent director, or with all independent directors
- intervening jointly with other institutions on particular issues
- making a public statement in advance of an AGM or EGM
- submitting resolutions at shareholders' meetings, and
- requisitioning an EGM, possibly to change the board.[42]

The US Investor Responsibility Centre, which monitors proxy voting, revealed that, in the run up to the 2003 annual general meeting season, more than 850 resolutions had been added to the meeting agendas of the 2000 listed companies they monitor, compared with 802 in the whole of 2002. It seems that, on both sides of the Atlantic, shareholder activism is on the increase.

The thirst for more information about the strength of corporate governance and attention to social, environmental and ethical issues, has also spawned a wave of new initiatives from analysts and rating agencies to help investors and their advisers to evaluate corporate performance. The US credit rating agency, Standard & Poors, has launched a new unit to rate US companies' governance standards; US-based Moody's Investors Services is to integrate corporate governance into its fundamental credit analysis; and organisations such as Innovest and CoreRatings offer analyses of corporate performance. As new national and international good practice benchmarks emerge, boards find themselves under increasing pressure to ensure that their company doesn't lie at the bottom of a league table. Research organisations are also jumping on the bandwagon by providing additional ammunition to investors to aid proactive engagement. In November 2002, the Corporate Library,[43] a US-based corporate governance research website, launched a database that enables subscribers to track interlocking director-ships and to spot board 'back scratching' and potential conflicts of interest. At least 20 US executives or chairmen currently sit on each other's boards. The problem is greater still in Europe.[44] Therefore, if one or more of your major investors charges you of failing to respond to their concerns, it may be prudent to take corrective action before they are provoked into a more public display of disgruntlement and take their grievances to take the media.

☐ SOCIALLY RESPONSIBLE INVESTMENT (SRI)

This general interest from investors in governance, social, ethical and environmental issues which could impact reputation has also been fuelled by the rapid growth in specifically screened responsible and ethical funds – socially responsible investment (or SRI).

SRI has been defined by the UK Social Investment Forum as:

> Investment that combines investors' financial objectives with their commitment to social concerns, such as social justices, human rights, economic development, peace or a healthy environment

The investment decision-making process takes into account not only financial risk/return parameters, but also social, ethical and environmental impacts and performance. SRI is most usually deemed to include funds that have been specifically 'ethically screened' . This is done either:

- negatively – by excluding companies in certain industries (such as arms, nuclear power/fuel, tobacco, gambling, pornography, alcohol, animal experimentation, etc.); or
- positively – by including companies whose products or services are seen to be sustainable and to provide long-term environmental or social benefit – for example, firms championing energy conservation or manufacturing recycling equipment.

SRI funds have continued to attract new money and in some territories have expanded faster than general funds. EIRIS,[45] a research consultancy, has estimated that there is £3.5 billion ($5.5 billion) of retail money in UK by based SRI funds and £10 billion for Europe as a whole. Pension fund money invested in SRI funds is over and above this figure and is set to rise as SEE-related pension fund legislation starts to bite. An October 2001 Europe-wide survey of 300 financial analysts and fund managers found that 33% currently offer SRI products and 15% have plans to introduce them.[46] In the USA, one dollar in eight under professional management is already believed to be invested in socially responsible portfolios.

In addition to specific funds marketed by individual fund managers (such as Henderson Ethical and Jupiter Ecology), there are a number of ethical indices which rank quoted companies by their SEE credentials. Two of the best known are the Dow Jones Sustainability Index (launched in 1999) and FTSE4Good[47] (launched 2001). FTSE4 Good is a series of benchmark and tradable indices for the UK, Europe, the USA and global, which include only companies that meet defined standards for corporate social responsibility.

FTSE4Good screens companies on the basis of:

- working towards environmental sustainability
- developing positive relations with stakeholders
- upholding and supporting human rights.

FTSE4Good made it clear at the outset that inclusion criteria would be progressively made more stringent as better indicators became available. In May 2002, the FTSE announced that the environmental screening criteria were to be tightened. From March 2003 all companies listed in the index must have a publicly available environmental policy. Companies designated 'medium impact' by the FTSE will also have to provide evidence of an environmental management system (EMS) by September 2003 or they could be dropped from the index. The human rights criteria have also been strengthened.

Inclusion in such responsible indices can only enhance a company's reputation; failure to be included or, worse still, subsequently being publicly dropped, could cause acute embarrassment and dent a company's reputation. The message from institutional investors, rating agencies and the index providers is clear: the bar will continue to be raised (Figure 2-3). Companies cannot afford to be complacent; those that fail to meet the ever more exacting requirements may see their reputations suffer.

In a sense, ethically conscious investors are investing in a 'good reputation': they trust the companies they self-select or those included in ethical indices or funds not to let them down.

Doing nothing – or standing still – are no longer options.

The bar is constantly being raised

Figure 2-3   The impact of investor engagement and SRI

Although socially responsible investment (SRI) is a fast-growing area in many countries, it is still a relatively small proportion of the total market. The jury is still out regarding whether SRI funds will outperform general stock indices in the longer term. However, it is already clear that investors in such funds are less volatile and less swayed by short-term market movements; they tend to commit for the longer term. Whatever the final judgement, specialist ethical indices and SRI funds will continue to induce companies to act more responsibly and be reputable.

the rise and rise of pressure groups

Today's business and political agenda is increasingly set by the pronouncements and actions of an ever more powerful group of pressure groups and NGOs. These organisations have learned how to mobilise public opinion by skilful and timely use of the media, and how to work, when necessary, with other stakeholder groups to maximise impact. With trust in business at an all time low, such pressure groups currently enjoy almost automatic legitimacy, with their own credentials and reputations rarely questioned. Once the butt of disparaging jokes, NGOs can now be found commenting on the robustness of stakeholder dialogue in a company annual report, verifying the authenticity of environmental impact data, sitting on an 'ethics and environmental' subcommittee of the board or assisting with the development of new standards and guidelines. Indeed, they now often form part of the political and regulatory process itself, and are invited to consult with governments, regulators and professional bodies to bring challenge and external perspective to the formulation of new laws, regulations and codes. The agenda of activist campaigns includes not just the targeted issue but also raising the profile of the organisation itself. As Glen Peters astutely observes: 'Being the first to humble some lumbering corporation would bring recognition, more members, more subscriptions and inevitably more resources.'[48]

The growing influence of NGOs is recognised by businesses and major investor groups alike. The UK's National Association of Pension Funds has stated:

NGOs . . . will increasingly be scrutinising company CSR [corporate social responsibility] statements and performance to expose inconsistencies. As these assessments are published at a time to cause maximum commercial impact there are inevitable risks to company value when these instances arise.[49]

This new-found legitimacy is well articulated by Tony Juniper, then Policy and Campaigns Director of environmental pressure group, Friends of the Earth:

> Ten years ago, companies would have seen the environment as utterly irrelevant and regard it as something that the government cared about. Now, though, non-government organisations like ourselves are getting a seat at the big table and we are listened to and asked for advice from a whole range of leading companies from all sectors as they increasingly rely on a good reputation to run a good business. We can help them get a good reputation if they do the right thing, but we can certainly harm them if they don't.[50]

In early 2003 Friends of the Earth announced that it had bought a token shareholding in 18 publicly listed companies which it claims are putting profits before people and the environment, to give it a legitimate voice on specfic issues of concern. Herein lies both a perilous threat and a fertile opportunity: inciting the wrath of pressure groups can cause irreparable reputational damage. In contrast, working in collaboration with an NGO could convert your most vociferous critic into your most ardent fan and goodwill ambassador. Of course, real life is not always as straightforward. The ethos and approach of some pressure groups may preclude any form of discussion or collaboration with the 'enemy'. However, that in itself can sometimes be turned to advantage by slipping into a public statement the fact that pressure group x declined an invitation to discuss issue y. Whichever approach an organisation decides to take, doing nothing is rarely a sensible option when a pressure group has you in its sights.

employee expectations

Employees, too, have ever more demanding expectations of the organisations they work for. Research has shown that a good reputation for responsible behaviour is a significant factor in recruitment, particularly of graduates. A report by the Industrial Society found that 82% of UK professionals would not work for an organisation whose values they did not believe in, and 59% had chosen an employer because they believe in what it does and what it stands for.[51]

No one, by choice, would want to admit during a cocktail party that they work for a discredited company or in a disreputable industry. In a highly mobile labour market, where 30-year long-service awards are a rarity and a CV showing changes of employment is more likely to get you that next job, employees enjoy more real choice than ever before. If your business's reputation is poor, you are likely to have difficulty both recruiting and retaining high-quality staff. If it is good, you enter into a virtuous circle where you attract high-quality recruits who, by their very presence, further enhance your reputation and entice the next wave of potential high-flyers.

consumer power and the voice of the people

Consumers, fired by a new-found ethical awareness and an abundance of supporting data (provided by the media, pressure groups and the Internet) are faced with a bewildering choice of products and services. They are in an ideal position to switch brands or boycott products if they have concerns about the reputation of the supplier.

The boycott of ExxonMobil-owned service stations world wide, masterminded by environmental pressure groups (including Greenpeace's StopEsso campaign[52] and Friends of the

Earth), has rallied consumer opposition to the company's stance on global warming, its rejection of the Kyoto protocol on reducing greenhouse gas emissions and refusal to invest in renewable energy. The Greenpeace website offers free downloads of campaigning material such as stickers, placards and factsheets to help consumers to mobilise effectively. Although the campaign is not yet believed to have had a material impact on Exxon's revenues, the negative headlines it has generated in many territories have damaged the company's image in the eyes of the public and have resulted in the company being shunned by ethical investment funds. Demonised by campaigners as environmental enemy number one, Exxon stands in stark contrast to its rivals BP and Shell which both back Kyoto and are investing in renewables.

The US-based CampaignExxonMobil[53] (which has the memorable by-line 'Can we save the tiger from ExxonMobil?') – a coalition of religious shareholders and national environmental organisations – also urges consumers to take direct action and endeavours to make the business case for a change in ExxonMobil's position. In conjunction with US shareholder activist Bob Monks and the NGO CERES,[54] it sponsored the paper *Risking Shareholder Value? ExxonMobil and Climate Change. An investigation of unnecessary risks and missed opportunities*. The paper estimates that ExxonMobil's strategy on global warming could have a negative impact of $2–3 billion on brand value and that the broader consequences of a damaged reputation, in areas such as staff motivation and political access, could amount to $10–50 billion of market value. It argues that the impact would be particularly damaging as ExxonMobil's activities on climate change are 'deliberate, aggressively pursued and identified with senior management'.[55] It seems unlikely that ExxonMobil's donation of $100 million to a Stanford University Project to tackle global warming (dismissed by Greenpeace as 'a delaying tactic'[56]) will succeed in silencing its critics.

However, it would be unwise to assume that consumers always do as they say. When approached by a market research company the majority of consumers do not always have the gall to say what they really think if it may be construed as politically incorrect. Perhaps, in truth, they don't really care whether a product is sourced from a factory using child labour as long as the price is kept low. It is, therefore, not surprising that many polls depict consumers as far more 'ethical' in their purchasing habits than is borne out in practice. This is at the root of what researchers have called 'the 30 : 3 syndrome' – the fact that around a third of consumers claim to care about business policies and performance on social responsibility, but that products marketed as 'ethical' struggle to exceed 3% of the market share.[57]

Nevertheless, repeat research indicates a rising underlying trend. A survey in the UK conducted by MORI[58] in 2001 showed that the proportion of people who regard an organisation's social responsibility as 'very important' when selecting a product has risen from 28% in 1998 to 46% in 2001. Businesses would be foolish to dismiss the fact that consumers are often now prepared – when given a well-aimed nudge – to vote with their feet.

stakeholder convergence

The various stakeholders discussed in this chapter are often not discrete, mutually exclusive groups; they frequently have overlapping interests. An individual may wear a number of stakeholder 'hats' in relation to a single organisation, particularly in this era of unprecedented shareholdings by private citizens. An individual may be an employee, customer, supplier or shareholder of a specific business as well as a member of the local community in which the business operates. Since the advent of the Internet and mass telecommunications, each group's voice resonates not only within its peer group but can also be heard by, and can influence, other stakeholder groups. This has allowed cross-pollination of ideas and convergence of interests. It has led, in some cases, to the emergence of powerful new cross-stakeholder alliances which have the ability to make, or break, the reputations of the biggest transnational businesses and public sector organisations.

CampaignExxonMobil, discussed above, is a good example of this growing phenomenon. Here shareholders and environmental groups have joined together in an attempt to persuade a major corporation to change its policy. Although the rationale for action may differ between the interested parties – ranging from religious conviction to concern for the environment to preservation of shareholder value – these disparate groups have united to wage a powerful and focused campaign. Such alliances can also result in NGO-sponsored shareholder resolutions at company annual general meetings and well-orchestrated media campaigns.

Another example of stakeholder convergence is the campaign waged early in 2001 by the British-based charity Oxfam, to communicate the message that global pharmaceutical companies were in part responsible for limiting access to medicines in developing countries through high prices and restrictive patents. Oxfam's campaign focused on the 39 pharmaceutical companies that were bringing a lawsuit against the South African government for infringement of intellectual property rights on drugs. Big Pharma wanted the South African government to abolish a law which allowed the government to 'buy patented drugs from suppliers other than the manufacturers, or generics from factories in India or Brazil, when patented medicines were "unaffordable" or there was a "health emergency" such as Aids.'[59] Damaging headlines began to appear such as 'At the mercy of drug giants; millions struggle with disease as pharmaceutical firms go to court to protect profits'.[60]

Oxfam made effective use of the media in getting the message across and allied itself with other non-governmental organisations such as Médecins sans Frontières and the South African Treatment Action Campaign. But the campaign also had some new distinguishing characteristics. Not only did Oxfam engage in direct talks with many pharmaceutical companies that contributed to price reductions, but also worked in concert with influential institutional investors who could put direct pressure on companies to act:

> It also led to new alliances, this time with the increasingly active socially responsible investment community. Oxfam understood that to be successful it would need to make a strong business case for change. It was possible to build on the understanding of a growing number of investors that failure to consider the human impact of policies that benefited the companies was posing serious risks to the regulatory environment in which the industry operated.
>
> (Sophia Tickell, Senior Policy Adviser, Oxfam[61])

Oxfam enlisted the support of Friends Ivory & Sime and Hendersons, investors in the newly merged drugs giant GlaxoSmithKline, which suddenly found itself in the spotlight. GlaxoSmithKline was the first to break rank by pledging more cut price anti-Aids and HIV drugs for terminally ill patients in Africa ('Glaxo relents on Aids drugs'[62]).

Oxfam's campaign caught the imagination of the media and the general public and also won additional support from an unexpected source – bestselling author John le Carré who had just published a new novel, *The Constant Gardener,* on the power wielded by pharmaceutical giants. Le Carré penned several well-aimed articles exposing the alleged abuses perpetrated by Big Pharma.

The campaign was highly effective. One by one the major pharmaceutical companies made concessions on the price of Aids, malaria and other drugs in an attempt to restore their battered reputations ('Embarrassed firms slash Aids drugs prices'[63]) and weeks later Big Pharma abandoned the damaging South African lawsuit. The decision to mount the court case was widely regarded as a public relations disaster for the pharmaceutical industry. Its business practices came under intense scrutiny and it was criticised around the globe for being greedy and unethical. This example illustrates an important 'don't' in reputation risk management: don't go to court unless you are certain that moral, as well as legal, right is on your side!

the rise of corporate social responsibility

Many of the issues discussed in this chapter relate to what is often termed 'corporate social responsibility' (CSR), which has been defined by the World Business Council for Sustainable Development as:

> . . . the commitment of business to contribute to sustainable economic development, working with employees, their families, the local community and society at large to improve their quality of life.[64]

In the UK, the National Association of Pension Funds' explanation of what CSR comprises provides further, and helpful, clarification:

> CSR covers a wide spectrum of interdependent areas. Broadly, they are the environmental impacts of a company's operations and products, its community interactions, its interactions with staff, customers, suppliers and other key stakeholder groups, and its ethical behaviour. It encompasses the principle of sustainability and, at is most general, sets the challenge of improving the environment and society, or at least leaving them in an equivalent state as a result of company operations and products.[65]

Often these are the very issues that delight the media as they relate to human stories of abuse, unjust treatment and unethical behaviour – particularly flavoursome if perpetrated by overweight, overpaid and overhyped executives! Such tales appeal not just to investors and business people on the business pages of the broadsheets, but to consumers and the general public on the front pages of the tabloids. These are the some of the risks that can result in catastrophic reputational damage.

As previously discussed, the investment community has now recognised the importance of identifying and actively managing exposure to social, ethical and environmental risks and the value of strong stakeholder relationships. Embracing CSR principles and being socially responsible is seen as a vital prerequisite for a good reputation, hence the growing number of codes, guidelines and disclosure requirements developed in an attempt to keep businesses in check. There is also mounting evidence that companies that integrate and embed CSR principles throughout their operations tend to be better run and therefore present a less risky investment.

An April 2002 Deloitte & Touche survey on trends in socially responsible investment found that over 90% of respondents saw corporate social responsibility as key to a company's reputation and brand value. A majority of fund managers believed that CSR would become an important feature in their investment decision-making in the next three years. The 20 largest also believed that the financial performance of companies exhibiting good environmental, social and ethical management was likely to outstrip that of their peers.[66]

The investor angle is crystallised in the Hermes Principles, a statement by UK fund manager Hermes on what shareholders expect of public companies and what companies should expect of their investors.[67]

> Hermes' overriding requirement is that companies be run in the long term interest of shareholders. Companies adhering to this principle will not only benefit their shareholders, but also we would argue, the wider economy in which the company and its shareholders participate. We believe a company run in the long term interest of shareholders will need to manage effectively relationships with its employees, suppliers and customers, to behave ethically and to have regard for the environment and society as a whole.

A survey of European business leaders conducted in 2002 by Business in the Community[68] asked leaders to rate the top issues affecting performance in the next five years. The top three were:

- Attracting and retaining staff
- Ability to innovate
- Corporate reputation.

The same study also found that:

- 78% agree that companies that integrate responsible practices will be more competitive;
- 73% agree that sustained social and environmental engagement can significantly improve profitability; and
- 66% agree that innovation and creativity are helped by responsible business practices

although a much smaller proportion were actually doing anything about it!

The mood of the general public has also shifted. According to MORI survey data, in the late seventies, the public agreed by 2:1 that the profits of large companies benefited their customers; but the public now disagrees by 2:1 (Figure 2-4). CSR is often seen as means of building a *new* basis of trust with consumers and the general public.

The Millennium poll, a May 1999 survey of 25 000 adults in 23 countries conducted by MORI/Environics, showed that more people were influenced by corporate responsibility (to employees, communities, the environment and ethics) than were swayed by either product brand/quality/value or by business/financial performance in forming an opinion of a particular business (Figure 2-5).

The new-found emphasis on corporate social responsibility is an entirely natural development. CSR is no longer the preserve of wild and woolly tree-hugging green activists or of

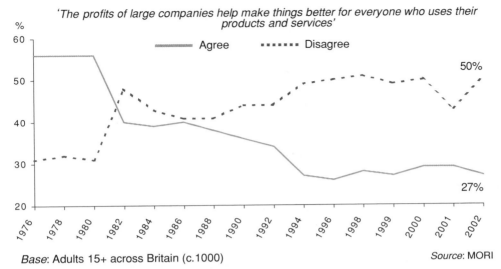

Figure 2-4   The effect of large companies' profits. (Reproduced by permission of MORI (Market & Opinion Research International))

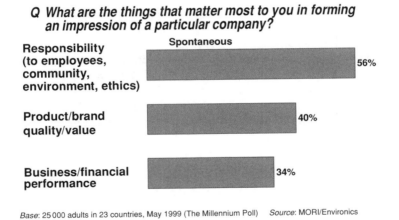

Figure 2-5   Criteria for judging companies world wide. (Reproduced by permission of MORI (Market & Opinion Research International))

ageing hippies investing in squeaky clean ethical funds with all traces of dirty tobacco and armaments expunged. Thanks to a nudge from legislators, burgeoning interest from investors and rising public expectations, CSR has entered the business mainstream.

Embracing CSR in some form is no longer an optional extra: it's a necessity and a prerequisite to a business to having high self-esteem and enjoying a good reputation with its key

towards successful and sustainable businesses that enjoy the trust and confidence of their stakeholders

Figure 2-6   Convergence of agendas.

stakeholders. The essence of CSR is ensuring that social, ethical and environmental impacts and risks are identified and actively managed so that organisations focus not just on the generation of profits and on meeting targets but also on *how* those results are achieved. It's also about operating in harmony with the expectations of the business's key stakeholders. CSR therefore introduces a number of qualitative considerations, such as ethics, integrity, accountability, transparency, responsiveness, flexibility and stakeholder dialogue. What better way of managing these threats and opportunities – many of which have a direct impact on reputation – than by incorporating them into your overall risk management framework and treating them as an integral part of good corporate governance?

The previously disparate disciplines of corporate governance, risk management, reputation management and CSR are increasingly converging (Figure 2-6), making it difficult to segregate the distinct strands and to establish who is responsible for them. That is why a holistic risk-based approach can be a highly effective way of managing the various elements in a fully integrated manner. Such an approach can also give the most critical threats and opportunities an adequate airing where they belong – in the boardroom.

IN SUMMARY

In the wake of the US corporate scandals there is a groundswell of rising expectations for business behaviour. Yet this goes hand-in-hand with a deep mistrust of business and business leaders. This gap presents a fertile opportunity to enhance corporate reputation by being reliable, trustworthy, accountable and transparent, and demonstrating this not just by fine words, but through positive action. Organisations that actively rise to the challenges presented by these new demands and expectations have a unique opportunity to enhance their reputations. Those that choose to ignore the new imperatives may see their reputations – and their performance and prospects – dwindle.

Are you now convinced that risks to reputation are worth considering and warrant management attention? If so, the next chapter will look at what risk management is, what it does and how to go about implementing a formal risk management system that can help you to identify and manage those elusive reputational threats and opportunities.

NOTES AND REFERENCES

1. Aon Biennial Risk Management and Risk Financing Survey 2001. The 2001 survey was the seventh in a series which commenced in 1989. See www.aon.co.uk for details.
2. From February 2002 Corporate Reputation Watch survey, as reported in a press release on the Hill & Knowlton website www.hillandknowlton.com. The global public relations firm Hill & Knowlton jointly sponsored the survey in conjunction with *Chief Executive* magazine.
3. *Business Week*/Harris Poll conducted 16–21 January 2002, as reported in *Business Week*, 4 February 2002.
4. From the press release for the February 2002 Corporate Reputation Watch survey on www.hillandknowlton.com.
5. From the McKinsey study *Inside the Boardroom*, a survey of 200 directors sitting on some 500 boards and interviews with 50 directors, governance experts and investors which explored what directors think about the demand for corporate governance reform in corporate America. The survey was conducted during April/May 2002.
6. Turnbull report (1999) *Internal Control for Directors on the Combined Code*. London: ICAEW, Appendix, paragraph 1. The Appendix to the Turnbull report is reproduced in full as Appendix B. See also www.icaew.co.uk/internalcontrol.
7. Company Law White Paper: Department of Trade and Industry, *Modernising Company Law*, July 2002. London: The Stationery Office, Volume 1, Part 2, Paragraph 4.30.
8. Company Law White Paper: Department of Trade and Industry, Modernising Company Law, July 2002. London: The Stationery Office, Volume 1, Part 2, para. 3.3.
9. Company Law White Paper: Department of Trade and Industry, *Modernising Company Law*, July 2002. London: The Stationery Office, Volume 2, draft clauses 73–75.
10. All four reviews are available from the Department of Trade and Industry website at www.dti.gov.uk. Some of the best practice implications are considered in the corporate governance section of Chapter 6.
11. As reported in the *Financial Times*, 11 October 2002.
12. This supplements the existing US Securities and Exchange Commission requirement for companies to detail 'risk factors' in their Form 20-F submission and will require directors to attest to the adequacy of their internal control framework in managing business risks. SOx goes beyond the UK's Turnbull guidelines, which require directors only to conduct an annual review of the effectiveness of internal controls and reports that they have done so, not to provide an opinion on what they have found.
13. The NYSE's 42-page document Corporate Governance Role Proposals. Reflecting recommendations from the NYSE Corporate Accountability and Listing Standards Committee as approved by the NYSE Board of Directors was published on 1 August 2002. It can be downloaded from the NYSE website www.nyse.com.
14. Modernising Company Law and Enhancing Corporate Governance in the European Union – A Plan to Move Forward, published by the EC Commission, 21 May 2003.

15. Reported in the *Financial Times*, 15 November 2002. The 1999 OECD Principles of Corporate Governance are available from www.oecd.org.

16. OECD (1999) *Principles of Corporate Governance*. p. 2. Available from www.oecd.org.

17. See www.iodsa.co.za.

18. See www.bsr.org for a summary of the new reporting requirements.

19. See Environment Agency website at www.environment-agency.gov.uk.

20. *An Ethical Framework for Financial Services* (October 2002). London: FSA, p. 6.

21. *An Ethical Framework for Financial services* (October 2002). London: FSA, p. 7.

22. *An Ethical Framework for Financial services* (October 2002). London: FSA, p. 7.

23. As reported in the *Financial Times*, 14 and 16 August 2002.

24. Reported in the *Financial Times*, 16 October 2002.

25. Statement by Dr Craig Mackenzie when he was Director, Governance and Socially Responsible Investment, at UK fund manager Friends Ivory & Sime. Dr Mackenzie is now head of investor responsibility at Insight Investment Management Ltd, the asset management arm of HBOS plc and is Deputy Chair of the FTSE4Good ethical share index committee.

26. McKinsey and Company's Global Investor Opinion Survey was undertaken between April and May 2002 in cooperation with the Global Corporate Governance Forum. The survey was based on responses from over 200 institutional investors, collectively responsible for some USD 2 trillion of assets under management. See www.mckinsey.com/governance for further details.

27. *Occupational Pension Schemes (Investment) Regulations 1996* (Regulation 11A).

28. *Investing in Social Responsibility: Risks and Opportunities* (2001). London: Association of British Insurers, p. 2 (can be downloaded from www.abi.org.uk).

29. *Investing in Social Responsibility: Risks and Opportunities* (2001). London: Association of British Insurers, p. 4.

30. CalPERS the California Public Employees' Retirement System, the largest US pension fund, manages $150 billion of assets for California's public employees. TIAA-CREF is the US teachers' retirement fund.

31. Quoted in the *Financial Times*, 10 October 2002.

32. Reported in the *Financial Times*, 4 November 2002.

33. From *The Responsibilities of Institutional Shareholders and Agents* issued by the UK's Institutional Shareholders' Committee (ISC), October 2002. The ISC's membership includes the Association of British Insurers (ABI), the Association of Investment Trust Companies (AITC), the Investment Management Association (IMA) and the National Association of Pension Funds (NAPF). It speaks for a membership that controls the vast majority of institutional funds in the UK.

34. The International Corporate Governance Network was founded in 1995. Its members include some of the world's largest investors: the US-based CalPERS and TIAA-CREF; ABP Europe's largest pension fund; BT Pension fund, the UK's largest as well as several fund management houses. Its members control $10 000 billion of assets.

35. An appendix to *Investing in Social Responsibility: Risks and Opportunities* (2001). London: Association of British Insurers (can be downloaded from www.abi.org.uk).

36. *Independent Directors – What Investors Expect* (2002). London: National Association of Pension Funds.

37. See also Appendix A for details of the ten Hermes Principles. The document can be downloaded in full at www.hermes.co.uk.

38. Insight Investment Management Ltd is the asset management arm of UK financial services group HBOS plc. A report setting out the rationale and objectives of the Global Business Principles Project is available from www.insightinvestment.com/responsibilty.

39. ISIS Asset Management is the new investment company formed by the merger of Friends, Ivory & Sime and Royal SunAlliance investments.

40. See press release on ISIS website and accompanying report *Environmental Credit Risk Factors in the Pan-European Banking Sector* at www.isisam.com.

41. *Investing in Social Responsibility: Risks and Opportunities* (2001). London: Association of British Insurers, p. 4.

42. From *The Responsibilities of Institutional Shareholders and Agents* issued by the UK's Institutional Shareholders' Committee (ISC), October 2002.

43. See website at www.thecorporatelibrary.com.

44. Reported in the *Financial Times*, 25 November 2002.

45. The UK-based Ethical Investment Research Service (EIRIS) provides research into companies' social, environmental and ethical performance to allow ethical investors to make informed decisions. EIRIS provides data and screening services for the FTSE4Good indices.

46. Euronext/CSR Europe Survey, October 2001.

47. An explanation of the principles behind FTSE4Good and details of the screening criteria are available from www.ftse4goodcom.

48. Peters, G. (1999) *Waltzing with the Raptors: A practical roadmap to protecting your company's reputation*. New York: John Wiley & Sons Inc, p. 4.

49. *Independent Directors – What Investors Expect* (2002). London: National Association of Pension Funds, p. 17.

50. Quoted in quoted in *Internal Auditing and Business Risk*, February 2001, p. 25.

51. *Corporate Nirvana – Is The Future Socially Responsible?* (2000). London: Industrial Society.

52. Esso is the brand name under which Exxon sell petrol in Europe. The international Greenpeace campaign website can be found at www.stopesso.org or for details of the US campaign, see www.greenpeace.org/exxonmobil.

53. See www.campaignexxonmobil.org.

54. CERES (the Coalition for Environmentally Responsible Economies) is a coalition of 85 investor and public interest groups working with major companies to increase corporate responsibility world wide. Since its inception in 1989, CERES has persuaded dozens of companies to endorse the CERES principles and co-founded the Global Reporting Initiative (GRI). The CERES Sustainable Governance Project seeks to bring together the sustainability and corporate governance movements to improve policies on climate change and other social environmental and governance issues. See www.ceres.org.

55. Mansley, M. (May, 2002) *Risking Shareholder Value? ExxonMobil and Climate Change: An investigation of unnecessary risks and missed opportunities*. Claros Consulting Discussion Paper (available for download from www.campaignexxonmobil.org).

56. Rob Gueterbock, Greenpeace campaign organiser, quoted in *The Guardian*, 21 November 2002.

57. From Research by the Future Foundation for the UK-based Co-operative Group entitled: *Who are the Ethical Consumers?* (October 2000) by Roger Cowe and Simon Williams.

58. Results of 2001 MORI poll quoted in the UK Department of Trade and Industry's *Business and Society: Corporate Social Responsibility Report 2002*.

59. *The Guardian*, 5 March 2001.

60. *The Guardian*, 12 February 2001.

61. *Corporate Social Responsibility Monitor* (2002). London: Gee Publishing, Chapter B5:4.

62. *The Guardian*, 22 February 2001.

63. *The Guardian*, 14 March 2001.

64. *Corporate Social Responsibility: Making Good Business Sense* (January 2000). WBCSD, Geneva, p. 10.
65. *Independent Directors – What Investors Expect* (2002). London: National Association of Pension Funds, p. 17.
66. *Socially Responsible Investment Survey 2002, Envrionment and Sustainability Series* (April 2002), Deloitte & Touche. The survey covered 65 fund managers responsible for over £1400 billion of assets. See www.deloitte.co.uk/sri.pdf.
67. See Appendix A for details of the Hermes Principles. The document can be downloaded in full at www.hermes.co.uk.
68. Business in the Community Study of European business leaders. See www.bitc.org.uk.

three

risk management: an overview

WHAT'S IT ALL ABOUT?

So what is this mythical beast called 'risk management', which needs to be 'embedded' – presumably along with its voracious 'appetite'? It's mercifully nowhere as fearsome as it sounds, as this chapter will demonstrate. Also, the good news is that – once you've mastered it – risk management is the perfect tool for dealing with those threats and opportunities to reputation that can make such a difference to your business's performance and prospects.

The purpose of risk management is quite simple: to identify and manage issues and situations that could prevent a business from achieving its goals and being successful. In essence it's about being wise *before* the event. Traditionally the term 'risk' has had negative connotations. It's been about downsides, about fires, floods and other adverse events, many of which can be covered by insurance. But thinking about risks in a purely negative way is not helpful as risks can be opportunities as well as threats.[1] Risks may be situations in the marketplace which, if exploited, could enable your business to exceed its goals for market share, not just meet them. They could be ideas for new products or services which, if you act swiftly, could give you a real edge over your competitors. Risks can, of course, equally be more of the 'downside' variety such as changing regulatory requirements which, if not met in full, could lose your business's reputation and even its licence to operate.

It is useful to think about risk as the *uncertainties* surrounding your business. Risk management (Figure 3-1) is about deciding which of those uncertainties present threats, which present opportunities and taking appropriate action to achieve the best results for your specific business situation. It also involves deciding which threats could, with a little positive and lateral thinking, be converted into opportunities. As you will see in Chapter 6, many of the apparent threats to reputation are potential opportunities in disguise. That's why you should

47

Risk management is about
making sure...

- good things happen

- and bad things don't

Risks can be opportunities as
well as threats

Figure 3-1   Defining risk management.

think of risk as a healthy and positive aspect of business life, not as something to be feared and preferably eradicated. If you are too risk averse, you may miss fertile opportunities to advance and improve your business to generate returns for your shareholders and benefits for customers, suppliers and employees.

The UK's Turnbull Report sums this up neatly by stating that 'profits are, in part, the reward for successful risk-taking in business' and that organisations should therefore aim to 'manage and control risk appropriately rather than to eliminate it'.[2]

Risk management is also about putting systems in place to give the organisation confidence that it is on track for successful delivery and, if it starts to veer off course, to give the earliest possible warning to enable corrective action to be taken. Finally it's about being able to demonstrate to your stakeholders that you're fully in control and are likely to remain so.

'We're doing that already – that's management's role' you may well think. And of course you'd be right. Boards of directors should indeed be considering threats and opportunities in strategic planning and target-setting, managers should be thinking about risks as they embark on new projects and launch new products and services. But all too often this is done in a haphazard, ad hoc way with different assumptions being made about the level of risk exposure that is acceptable to the organisation and differing risk controls being put in place as a result. It's usually implicit, not explicit, so discrepancies between different parts of the organisation may not be picked up before it's too late (look at how major frauds were perpetrated at Barings Singapore[3] and at Allfirst – the US subsidiary of Allied Irish Banks[4]). All too frequently the focus is more on tangible risks than on the softer, intangible risks that can impact reputation.

Today's risk management requires a level of formality that has not previously existed. Identification of risks should be as *systematic* as possible and the risks, once identified, should be *documented*. Directors need to have an understanding of their business's *most significant risks* – whether they arise in small trading office in Singapore or in a major US subsidiary. Within an organisation, whether it is a small one-site business or a sprawling multinational, there should ideally be a *common language for describing risk* and *a consistent means of assessing risks* across the organisation. This will allow risk exposures arising in different areas of operations to be compared and contrasted. It will also enable priorities for action and resource allocation to be determined in a structured way. These key components of a formalised risk management system will be examined later in this chapter.

The risk management process should also be able to withstand scrutiny both internally (perhaps from internal audit or an audit or risk committee) and externally (from external auditors, investors and other key stakeholders with a legitimate interest in the business). Risk management is now seen as an integral part of good corporate governance and directors will therefore be held to account if risk management systems are not in place or are not operating properly. This in itself can be a source of risk to both corporate and personal reputation, as managers at AIB have found to their cost.

> Susan Keating, the US head of fraud-hit Allied Irish Banks, has finally fallen on her sword, becoming the ninth executive to leave the company. Ms Keating had faced criticism for staying on as chief executive of Allfirst, the US arm of AIB which this year uncovered a £450m fraud, when more junior staff were forced out.[5]

So what does risk management involve?

KEY STEPS IN RISK MANAGEMENT

Risk management can be made extremely complex and many organisations (aided and abetted by consultants) appear to do precisely that! But it really isn't rocket science. The basic principles behind risk management are very simple and should be easily explainable to anyone in your organisation.

Figure 3-2 condenses risk management into five essential steps, which are generally accepted as the key building blocks for effective risk management.[6] Many bells and whistles can be added to this foundation: there is no magic 'one size fits all' solution. You will need to decide whether some of the items described below are 'nice to haves' or essentials in the context of your own business.

The remainder of this chapter focuses on the critical initial step in Figure 3-2, which is about building the right foundation for successful risk management. Steps two, three and four are examined in Chapter 4 and the monitoring and reporting aspects are explored in Chapters 7, 8 and 9.

BOARD/EXECUTIVE COMMITMENT AND TONE-SETTING

The importance of this step cannot be overemphasised. Many organisations have embarked on a risk management programme only to find that it stalls or does not achieve the desired results. This is so often because the top team has merely paid lip service to the initiative and has delegated responsibility for implementation to some unsuspecting insurance or audit manager. If the senior team is visibly not committed to risk management, other employees are unlikely

Board/executive commitment
and tone-setting

Risk identification

Risk assessment

Risk response planning

Monitoring and reporting

Information for assurance, disclosure,
decision making and future improvement

Figure 3-2   The risk management process.

to be persuaded to embrace the concept with enthusiasm. It is also more likely to be seen as on an 'add-on' to business activities – one of those ephemeral management fads that is here today and gone tomorrow – rather than a mainstream activity which involves everyone and is fundamental to business success.

The top team in any organisation, whether it operates in the private, public or not-for-profit sector, has a crucial role to play in promoting the importance of risk management and in setting the tone for the organisation. This involves putting in place the core components of an enabling *risk management framework* and promoting an *organisational climate* that aims to support – not thwart – effective risk management.

For businesses at the forefront of good risk management this usually includes:

1. Establishing and communicating a clear vision, values and strategy for the business to provide the context and perspective for risk decisions to be made. Demonstrating personal commitment to the values and goals through both words and deeds.
2. Clarifying the business's tolerance of risk (or risk appetite) so that risk exposures are understood by everyone in the organisation and can be maintained within acceptable limits.
3. Putting in place supporting policies, processes, procedures and ways of working which guide the behaviours and actions of employees and key partners.
4. Ensuring that a consistent risk management framework is in operation which provides a common language and methodology for identifying and assessing risks across the business. It should also include common monitoring and reporting mechanisms that give the top team confidence that risks are under control – and early warning if they're not.

5. Promoting a climate of trust and openness in which employees are willing to express their concerns and bright ideas, and provide the relevant personnel with early warning of potential risks.

VISION, VALUES AND STRATEGY

It is essential that all employees understand what their business is there to do and how it does it. Business strategy, objectives and organisational values should be unambiguous and embodied by top management, both in their words and in their deeds.

> Credibility is mostly about consistency between words and deeds. People listen to the words and measure the deeds. Then they measure the congruence.[7]

The same can, of course, be said for reputation itself. But more of that later!

Vision and values are the glue which bind together a business's activities and should encourage congruence of approach and behaviour throughout all areas of operation. An explicit vision and unequivocal values provide a much-needed perspective for an organisation's employees – and its business partners. In the aftermath of the Enron, WorldCom and Xerox scandals, it is clear that this component of 'tone setting' should be a key role for the Chief Executive, directors and senior management team. Having established the business's vision and values, it is essential that they personally practise what they preach and act as role models for the entire organisation. They also need to reinforce the importance of their employees adhering at all times to the business ethos – or risks may be taken which generate unacceptable exposures and could tarnish corporate reputation.

A broad understanding of the organisation's goals and the context in which it operates is also vital in providing the backcloth for the everyday decisions, actions and responses of its staff to the risks surrounding it. As the UK's Turnbull report states, objectives should be communicated 'so as to provide effective direction to employees on risk assessment and control issues'.[8] This may all seem obvious, but so often there is a mismatch between the strategy being pursued by directors and the way in which it is received throughout the organisation. This may be because of failure to articulate a compelling yet achievable vision which inspires the workforce, patchy cascade of strategic goals or simply lack of time to devise consistent lower-tier goals that dovetail with the new corporate direction during a period of change. It can equally be caused by mixed messages.

Plant operators may see directors driving at breakneck speed through the manufacturing site, ignoring speed limits, and take away the message that safety is not as important as they previously thought. A procurement officer may have been told that ensuring full traceability of raw materials is vital, but may see this as less than essential when their boss selects the lowest cost supplier who hasn't yet put in place the necessary procedures. Any form of discrimination may be deemed to be counter-culture until the chief executive tells an offensive racist joke at the office Christmas party.

Everyone needs to understand that if safety is deemed to be paramount it is never knowingly compromised; that if integrity of raw material sourcing is a key selling point, it is never intentionally undermined; and that any form of discrimination is unacceptable and could lead to disciplinary action or dismissal. Trade-offs are inevitable in a business. If employees are not clear on the 'no-go' areas where compromise is unthinkable, risks may be taken that could damage the business – and its reputation. Policies and procedures are an excellent means of conveying this to all staff and external stakeholders.

One company that understands the importance of articulating clear values is the oil and gas conglomerate BP, which now comprises British Petroleum, Amoco, Arco, Burmah Castrol and Mobil Europe. BP has transformed itself from a lacklustre British oil company in the early 1990s into a successful and innovative global player in the oil and gas industry. BP has ranked in 'most admired company' surveys both in the UK and globally and has won awards for responsible capitalism. Its CEO, Lord John Browne, won the UK's coveted *Management Today* 'most admired business leader' award for the fourth successive year in 2002. BP was also voted the most admired company in the same year.

BP's values are stated as:

- A respect for the individual and for the diversity of mankind
- A responsibility to protect the natural environment
- A belief in honest exchange
- An awareness that a strong reputation is essential for business success.

These values are summed up in the BP corporate brand:

- Innovative
- Performance driven
- Environmental leadership
- Progressive – always alive to the things that can and should be improved.

BP believe that in all areas of operation:

> . . . our activities should generate economic benefits and opportunities for an enhanced quality of life for those whom our business impacts; that our conduct should be a positive influence; that our relationships should be honest and open; and that we should be held accountable for our actions.[9]

These values are reflected in BP's policies, which are discussed below.

RISK APPETITE

Tolerance of risk or risk appetite within a business should also be clearly set out by the top team. A business may regard itself as more or less 'risk averse' or 'risk-taking' but a complex organisation is unlikely to have a single risk appetite. The manufacturing plant of a pharmaceutical company will probably have a very low tolerance for deviations in product quality.

	Low competence	High competence
Risk-taker	Gambler	Winner
Risk averse	Loser	Also-ran

Figure 3-3   Risk appetite vs competence in controlling risk.

However, the marketing department of the same company may be prepared to take significant calculated risks in penetrating new markets. Such divergent risk appetites are perfectly permissible, provided they are understood and approved by the board, and are not just the preferred personal style of a rogue trader in a far-flung corner of the corporate empire!

The Turnbull report is again eloquent on this. The board should consider 'the extent and categories of risk which it regards as acceptable for the company to bear',[10] and should ensure that there is a 'clear understanding by management and others within the company of what risks are acceptable to the board'.[11]

In practice, organisations often consider their tolerance to risk exposure against individual risks or areas of risk. If the agreed exposure threshold is out of step with competence in controlling risk, the effect can be catastrophic. You need look no further than the speculative operations at Allfirst in the USA and Barings Singapore for examples. Conversely, unwillingness to take sufficient risk can be a risk in itself. A conservative company that sticks doggedly with its traditional product offerings – making no attempt to modify them in line with changing consumer tastes – is likely become a 'loser' in its market sector (Figure 3-3).

Defining and communicating risk appetite is a crucial component of any risk management system and a key enabler for a supportive organisational culture. If the board's attitude to risk exposures is not clear, how can managers and other employees be expected to know what risks they can take in their own areas? Staff need to understand which activities are 'no-go' and prohibited in all circumstances (such as anti-competitive activity, giving or taking bribes, insider trading), which activities are permissible within limits (such as purchases within agreed authority limits or capital expenditure if due process is followed) and in which activities they have full rein to act as they feel is appropriate. Policies and procedures can be useful tools in communicating acceptable exposure levels throughout the organisation.

SUPPORTING POLICIES AND PROCEDURES

Policies and procedures can underpin good governance as well as guiding behaviours and setting clear boundaries for action. A growing number of organisations have finally grasped that turgid tomes of policies gathering dust on managers' shelves are not only a waste of space but also an unfortunate waste of resource. Positioning policies as living documents which are updated in the light of experience and making them available to all employees (via the business intranet) and to investors, customers, suppliers and other stakeholders (via the website and annual reports) can be a highly effective use of resource. They are an excellent means of truly 'embedding' risk management thinking into day-to-day working practices.

Fund managers, analysts and even NGOs now acknowledge that well-designed and properly implemented policies are a major plank of good corporate governance. Rating agencies and fund-screening criteria increasingly check the existence of key policies (perhaps relating to the company's stance on ethics, the environment or indeed on risk management itself) and seek evidence of compliance with them as a way of assessing the robustness of management systems within a business.

BP make active and deliberate use of policies in providing a framework to guide actions and behaviours in their operations worldwide. BP's business policies focus on five areas:

- Ethical conduct
- Employees
- Relationships (with customers, contractors, suppliers, partners, communities, governments, NGOs and individuals)
- Health, safety and environmental performance
- Control and finance (including risk management).

The policy statement (or Policy Commitment as BP call it) is designed to ensure that performance targets are delivered in the way intended, and consistent with company values. 'Policy commitments are the foundation on which we build and conduct our business. We expect everyone who works for BP to live up to these commitments'. Each Policy Commitment is supported by further guidance (Policy Expectations) which describe the boundaries of what is and is not acceptable practice. The Policy Commitments also clarify what people can expect in their dealings with BP.

BP's commitment to ethical conduct and the supporting policy expectations can be found in Appendix C. They clearly delineate the 'thou shalt not' activities such as political donations from those activities that are acceptable provided key principles are adhered to – such as deciding to make a major investment in a new area. BP also seeks to extend the commitment to third parties acting directly on its behalf. Finally, BP promotes the 'when in doubt shout' principle and encourages staff to seek guidance when they are unsure about the correct course of action.

CONSISTENT RISK MANAGEMENT FRAMEWORK

If risk management is to help and not hinder a business, its top team needs to ensure that the structures put in place to manage risk fit the ethos of the business and are integrated as far as possible with existing ways of working. The core components of the risk framework include:

- *A common definition of risk* – which encourages the fullest possible capture of potential threats and opportunities to the business. (See Chapter 4 where risk identification will be examined in detail.)

- *A consistent methodology for assessing and responding to risks* – which allows risks to be compared and contrasted across the organisation, enables the most significant risks to be singled out for priority attention and suggests ways in which risks can be managed in keeping with the defined tolerances to exposure, or risk appetite. (See Chapter 4.)
- *Clarity on roles and responsibilities* – which outline the respective roles of executive and non-executive directors, management, other employees and key business partners for managing risk. (See Chapter 5 for an exploration of how to make risk management everyone's business – a key element in protecting and enhancing reputation.)
- *A common monitoring and reporting process* – which will provide confirmation that things are on track and early warning if they're not, so that corrective action can be taken (see Chapters 7 and 8). It can also give directors confidence to improve the transparency and relevance of external reporting, which, in turn, can boost stakeholder confidence and reputation (see Chapter 9).

Many organisations have found it useful to include these core components in a brief *risk management policy* which can be used to communicate to all concerned the importance of risk management, its objectives and how the system works. Such a policy can also help to demonstrate to investors, regulators and other stakeholders that the business takes risk management seriously and has introduced formal steps to positively identify and manage its risks.

But isn't this process and formality inhibiting? Doesn't it deter staff from using their initiative and from taking risks to benefit the business? Paradoxically it doesn't appear to. It's rather like a child–parent situation where, as the child internalises the house rules and becomes familiar with the boundaries, he or she grows more confident and street-wise. In a business situation, being crystal clear on 'freedom to act', and providing guidance and support on calculated risk taking, can liberate staff by giving them not only the skills to manage threats, but the confidence to spot and leverage opportunities. A much more fulfilling activity!

This, however, can only work if it is underpinned by a supportive organisational climate.

ORGANISATIONAL CULTURE

An old-style 'command and control culture' will most probably undermine efforts to embed risk management. An autocratic board, with a penchant for shooting the messenger, is unlikely to pick up the first rumblings of impending crisis. Those lower down the organisation, who spot the early signs, may be afraid to speak up or may have their concerns edited out by managers keen to serve up to the board their usual sanitised view of reality. Equally, this type of culture so often constrains initiative and innovation – when new ideas come from anywhere other than the board itself!

Marks & Spencer (M&S), the quintessentially British store – a magnet for overseas visitors and, in spring 1998, the second most profitable retailer in the world – suffered a spectacular fall from grace in 1998 when its profits suddenly plummeted by 23% at a time when the board was still confidently predicting a 10% growth in sales.[12] M&S had simply lost the plot and

Table 3-1. Organisational culture characteristics

Risk averse	Risk seeking
• 'Stick with what we know'	• 'Let's go for it' – Can do'
• New ideas rejected	• New and creative ideas welcomed
• Stability and experience highly valued	• Innovation and motivation highly valued
• Focus on problem solving	• Focus on exploiting opportunities
• 'Command and control'	• People empowered/use initiative
• Primary focus internal	• Primary focus external
• Difficult to change strategies and policies	• Strategies and policies modified to reflect changed circumstances
• Mistakes personalised	• Mistakes tolerated/learned from
• Blame culture	• Supportive culture

disappointed its loyal following largely because its autocratic 'top down' style, which had served it well in its early days, was no longer appropriate for an international business on the eve of the twenty-first century. Customers, and employees, were becoming increasingly disenchanted with what was on offer. The warning signs were there and were known to middle management, but they were neither acknowledged nor acted on by the top team.

> Thinking for yourself, taking initiative, unless it was to point out faulty products, were not encouraged. Head office decided what goods would be sent where, how they would be displayed and what price they would be. Store managers were expected to follow instructions to the letter. Total obedience combined with a zeal for quality products were what counted and so those who rose towards the top naturally displayed these qualities.[13]

Establishing a climate of trust and openness, in which employers feel able to express concerns, air their views on threats and opportunities, share new ideas, take calculated risks and ask for help when in doubt, should be a key part of the board's remit. The characteristics of a 'risk averse' versus a 'risk-seeking' organisation are suggested in Table 3-1.

An open and trusting climate is important to the success of any risk management initiative, but particularly vital for the management of risks to reputation. The early warning signs of a threat or opportunity to reputation can appear anywhere in a business and can involve anyone working for it. If mechanisms do not exist for identifying, channelling and acting on these early signs, a reputational crisis or missed business opportunity can ensue.

TOP TIPS FOR EMBEDDING RISK MANAGEMENT

Formalised risk management has been around for a number of years. There is therefore much to be learned from those pioneering organisations that have already blazed the trail.

The goal, as you will have gathered by now, is that risk management ultimately becomes 'embedded' in all areas of operations (as emphasised in Figure 3-4): when people throughout

```
┌─────────────────────────────────────┐
│        Risk management is            │
│        embedded when...              │
│                                      │
│   ...risk management thinking and    │
│ practices are seamlessly integrated  │
│    into the day-day-fabric of the    │
│     organisation at all levels       │
└─────────────────────────────────────┘
```

Figure 3-4   'Embedding' risk management.

the organisation understand and use the language of risk management, take responsibility for risks in their area of activity and talk naturally about risk in their daily work. It's also 'embedded' when risk management concepts are integrated into policies, procedures and ways of working, and when the tone set by the top team and the entire organisational culture supports active and positive risk management.

To maximise your chances of successfully implementing risk management:

- Position risk management as a mainstream activity, not as an 'add on'
- Ensure that top team commitment to risk management is visible and active
- Be clear on the benefits – accentuate the positive
- Keep the language and framework simple and non-bureaucratic
- Link to business and personal objectives
- Get people involved and make them accountable
- Win hearts and minds by going for quick wins
- Build where possible on what's already in place.

If your top team takes the time to establish a solid foundation by being visibly committed to risk management and by setting an appropriate tone, it will be much easier to successfully implement the remaining elements of your risk management framework.

NOTES AND REFERENCES

1. *ISO/IEC Guide 73 Risk management – Vocabulary – Guidelines for use in standards,* issued by the International Standards Organisation (ISO) and International Electrotechnical Committee (IEC), both Geneva based, in 2002, recognises that risk management is about both averting threats and realising opportunities. It therefore tackles risk from both the positive and negative perspectives. The guide aims to provide basic vocabulary to develop common understanding among organisations internationally. It provides standards writers with generic definitions of risk management terms that can be used in the preparation or revision of standards which have risk management aspects.
2. Turnbull report (1999) *Internal Control for Directors on the Combined Code*. London: ICAEW, para 13.

3. Nick Leeson, a futures trader in Barings' Singapore office, caused the long-established bank to collapse in 1995 after he ran up losses of £830 million through unauthorised trading in derivatives. Barings' liquidator attempted to sue Deloitte & Touche, which audited its operations in the early 1990s, for negligence. In June 2003 the High Court ruled that Deloitte and Touche was negligent in its auditing of the accounts of Barings Futures Singapore and that Barings' management was also guilty of a 'high level of fault'.

4. John Rusnak, a foreign exchange trader at Allfirst, Allied Irish Banks' US subsidiary, was indicted in June 2002 for bank fraud and false entry into bank records in a scandal that lost the bank $691 million. The sale of the Allfirst subsidiary to the US Bank, M&T, was agreed in September 2002.

5. *The Guardian*, 19 July 2002.

6. There is currently no recognised global standard for risk management. However, a standard issued in 1999 in Australia and New Zealand (AS/NZS 4360: 1999) is commonly referred to and provides some useful guidance and templates. AS/NZS 4360: 1999 Risk Management Standard was developed by the Joint Standards Australia/Standards New Zealand Committee OB/7 on Risk Management as a revision of AS/NZS 4360: 1995 Risk Management. It is available from www.riskmanagement.com.au.

   A new British standard was launched in October 2002 which was jointly developed by The Association of Insurance and Risk Managers (AIRMIC), the National Forum for Risk Management in the Public Sector (ALARM), and the Institute of Risk Management (IRM). A key feature of the Standard is its recognition that risk has an upside as well as a downside and can represent both threat and opportunity. The Standard can be downloaded from websites of the three sponsoring bodies at www.theIRM.org, www.airmic.co.uk or www.alarm-uk.com.

7. Kouzes, J.M. and Posner, B.Z. (1993) *Credibility*. Jossey Bass Inc.

8. Turnbull report (1999) *Internal Control for Directors on the Combined Code*. London: ICAEW, Appendix, section 1 'Risk assessment'. The Appendix to the Turnbull report provides a useful checklist for directors when assessing the effectiveness of the risk and control processes in place within the business. The Appendix to Turnbull is reproduced in full as Appendix B.

9. Extract from BP's website at www.bp.com as at June 2003. Reproduced by permission of BP plc.

10. Turnbull report (1999) *Internal Control for Directors on the Combined Code*. London: ICAEW, para. 17.

11. Turnbull report (1999) *Internal Control for Directors on the Combined Code*. London: ICAEW, Appendix. The useful appendix to the Turnbull report is reproduced in Appendix B.

12. Bevan, J. (2001) *The Rise and Fall of Marks and Spencer* Profile Books, London, pp. 5–8. Marks & Spencer figures for first half of 1998, announced on 3 November 1998, showed a 23% fall in profits.

13. Bevan, J. (2001) *The Rise and Fall of Marks and Spencer*. Profile Books, London, p. 38.

four

identifying, prioritising and responding to risks

NEXT STEPS

Chapter 3 examined the essence of risk management and outlined its constituent parts. After ensuring that the top team is visibly committed to risk management, has played its part in setting up the right framework and actively promotes a supportive organisational culture (although changes here clearly cannot be effected overnight), the stage is set for risk management proper: identifying, assessing and responding to risks.

This chapter explores these next steps in the context of managing risks to reputation.

COMPREHENSIVE RISK CAPTURE

The first and most critical stage is identifying risks. True to the 'garbage in/garbage out' principle, if initial capture of risks is not systematic and comprehensive, the end result is unlikely to be satisfactory. Indeed, a major risk might be missed which could jeopardise the business's very existence.

One cannot but speculate, for example, whether Tyco considered director ethics and integrity as a potential risk area. If directors and finance managers had seen this as an issue that could seriously impact Tyco's reputation, they might have seen fit to challenge the $135m of loans and 'expenses' paid to former chairman and chief executive Dennis Kozlowski. These monies, from Tyco's corporate coffers, allegedly helped to fund a $13m art collection (on which Kozlowski was subsequently charged with $1m tax evasion), a lavish lifestyle including several homes, three yachts, decorating bills and a $2m junket to Sardinia to celebrate his wife's fortieth birthday, in addition to multimillion dollar 'personal' charitable donations.[1] Kozlowski's greed and blatant disregard for basic standards of corporate governance spawned eye-catching headlines such as 'How Tyco spent millions to keep Kozlowski in the Monet'.[2] and 'Tale of our times: a case study in corporate greed. How Tyco boss used company as his personal piggy bank'[3] This catastrophic failure to curb Kozlowski's excesses led to a dramatic fall in share price as the scandal unfurled (from $60 in December 2001 to around $13 in early August 2002) and has cost other board members their jobs.[4]

definition of risk

When identifying risks, a good starting point is an all-embracing risk definition. It should encourage the capture of any threats that could materialise, any opportunities that you might fail to exploit, risks about compliance, risks about performance, internal and external risks – past, present and future (see Figure 4-1).

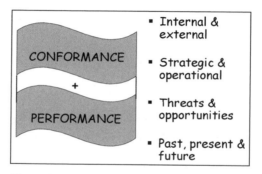

Figure 4-1   Which risks should be considered?

A risk definition such as 'Risk is the possibility that adverse circumstances will be experienced as the result of an event or circumstance' is unlikely to stimulate innovative thinking on new opportunities in the external environment which could enhance performance and reputation. An all-embracing definition, such as that suggested in Figure 4-2, is more likely to have the desired effect.

> Risk is...
>
> an event or situation which could adversely or beneficially affect the business's ability to achieve its objectives, maintain a good reputation and meet stakeholder expectations.

Figure 4-2   Definition of risk.

Your risk definition should be relevant to your business so that it makes sense to all personnel and can help to pinpoint the most significant risks to your business – that is, those with which the top team should be actively involved. The risk definition should be endorsed and signed off by the top team, ideally as part of your risk management policy, to give it full credibility.

options for risk capture

Now that you have a risk definition and your first piece of risk language, you can start capturing the risks to your business.

Risks can be identified using questionnaires, one-to-one interviews, brainstorming sessions, round table discussion or interactive workshops. Some form of interactive workshop can often work best, as participants are able to challenge and spark off one another, unearthing risks that were previously not recognised. This collaborative approach can be particularly helpful in identifying risks to reputation, the sources of which are not always immediately apparent and often need to be teased out through debate.

Many risk consultancies offer sophisticated software containing a 'universe of risks' on every conceivable topic – enabling managers literally to tick the risks that seem relevant to their circumstances. Although such tools can act as a useful cross-check that no major areas have been missed, they should not be regarded as a magic solution. There is no quick fix. Every business is unique in the circumstances and challenges it faces. There is no real substitute for well-briefed managers and staff engaging their brains in considering the risks to their own business. Those who work in the business and know it intimately are undoubtedly best placed to identify and assess the risks to its future success – even if they receive helpful prompts and challenges from internal audit, in-house risk managers, external risk consultants, risk management software and their stakeholders.

These group sessions, which can be organised by department, function or cutting across the business, should be structured to ensure optimal representation. And the top team itself should not be forgotten. In so many organisations the board or executive has never participated directly in a risk identification exercise, apparently believing itself to be somehow immune – a bewildering stance when it is usually directors and top managers who mastermind the big strategic throws of portfolio change, infrastructure investment, new product or service launches and radical internal restructuring! The use of an experienced facilitator – external to the group but not necessarily to the business – can help to keep the process on track.

To structure the risk identification workshop, it is helpful to ask participants to think in advance about the risks to the business: those that affect the organisation as a whole and those pertinent to their own department or area of operation. They could be asked to come to the workshop with pre-prepared 'Post-It' slips stating their top five or top ten risks. Participants should be encouraged to think laterally, to be negative as well as positive and to challenge historic assumptions. They should consider all the uncertainties surrounding the business: those with potentially negative impacts (threats) and those with positive impacts (opportunities); those that merely help the business to 'conform' to standards, regulations and the goals it has set itself and those that would enable it to 'perform' better and exceed expectations.

Focusing on risks to corporate objectives can provide an excellent starting point, provided business goals are clearly articulated and well communicated. However, it may not always be sufficient. Corporate objectives are sometimes too internally oriented and do not always take into account the changing requirements and expectations of major business stakeholders. If there is blinkered focus on strategic objectives without due consideration of relevant external developments, a major reputational risk could be missed. Furthermore, the corporate objectives may have been set by managers unaware of some of the new and exciting prospects offered by changing external circumstances. Using techniques that enable staff to cast aside their blinkers and look afresh at the environment in which the business operates can be hugely beneficial.

To encourage this, it can be helpful to suggest risk categories, instead of or in addition to corporate objectives to obtain the best possible capture of the risks surrounding a business. These categories should be relevant and meaningful to the organisation involved. It is most efficient to start from the outside in, from the high level to the low level, to ensure that topics are discussed in a logical sequence. Categories could include:

- *External environment/stakeholder relations*, such as:
  - political, market, regulatory and technological developments,
  - external stakeholder perceptions, requirements and expectations.
- *Strategic*, such as:
  - leadership/direction and tone setting
  - stakeholder relations and communications
  - strategic planning and policy development
  - target setting
  - performance monitoring.
- *People*, such as:
  - recruitment, retention, manpower/succession planning
  - competence, training, career development
  - remuneration package
  - role clarity, freedom to act
  - morale, motivation
  - workload, stress
  - health, safety, security.
- *Compliance and governance*, such as:
  - compliance with relevant local and international laws and regulations
  - compliance with internal policies, standards, guidelines and procedures
  - compliance with good governance practice.
- *Operational*, such as:
  - quality of decision-making
  - information/knowledge management
  - data and information security
  - internal/external communications
  - management of change
  - project management

- systems and processes
- infrastructure
- financial management and budgetary control
- business continuity and crisis management.

To tease out those softer issues that can damage, or boost, reputation, it can also be helpful to have a separate reputation category. This forces people to focus on those adverse, or positive, newspaper headlines and the issues that could give rise to them.

- *Reputation*, such as issues that could impact:
  - your legitimacy and 'licence to operate'
  - your competitive advantage
  - your local/international standing
  - stakeholder loyalty, trust and confidence
  - pressure group interest
  - media relations.

Workshop participants can place their pre-prepared 'Post-It' slips on the relevant flipchart (marked up with the strategic objective and/or category heading prior to the session). The facilitator can then run through the flipcharts in a logical sequence, pooling ideas and getting people to articulate the risk to enable a consensus view to be developed on the top risks to the business, the operating unit, department or project. The 'Post-It' approach has the advantage of enabling everyone to express a viewpoint – without feeling intimidated by an overbearing colleague or boss. However, if the 'Post-It' method doesn't appeal, the facilitator can orchestrate a plenary discussion using the agreed categories.

If this isn't high-tech enough for you, there are a number of sophisticated risk management electronic database and voting systems that may suit better. Whichever method you choose, and however you decide to support it, the key principles remain the same:

- Get the right people involved
- Brief them adequately
- Give them the right tools
- Encourage them to think 'out of the box'
- And keep it simple – or you'll lose them!

tools for risk capture

To flesh out the approach outlined above and to provide more structure if deemed necessary, there are some other specific tools that can help.

◻ SWOT ANALYSIS

This is a strategic planning and marketing tool that can be useful in risk identification. It requires an analysis of the strengths/opportunities facing a business as well as the weaknesses/threats.

Internal	STRENGTHS	WEAKNESSES
External	OPPORTUNITIES	THREATS

Figure 4-3   SWOT analysis.

A SWOT approach can help to avoid an undue focus on downsides, at the expense of the often less obvious upsides.

Structuring the discussion so that participants explore strengths prior to weaknesses and opportunities prior to threats can help to counter the natural tendency to focus on the negative. After all, bad news about your organisation, particularly if it is the responsibility of another department, is so much more satisfying to air in pubic than potential good news – which could land back on your desk to deliver!

❏   FORCE FIELD ANALYSIS

Force field analysis is an approach used in strategic planning to test the feasibility of implementation. It involves considering the forces that will impact, both positively and negatively, the achievement of your strategic objectives. Which actions, events and situations could smooth your path to success? Which factors could obstruct you in achieving your goals? Analysing the positive and negative forces in Figure 4-4 can provide a fertile source of both threats and opportunities.

❏   FIVE FORCES ANALYSIS

This approach, developed by management guru Michael Porter in the mid 1980s,[5] is useful in establishing a business's uniqueness and competitive advantage – factors that need to be considered in managing reputation risk. Porter's approach encourages evaluation of changing conditions in the business environment, the forces which have an impact on the organisation, the sector in which it operates and the overall market. It requires examination of five major forces:

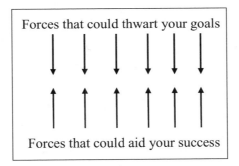

Figure 4-4   Force field analysis.

- Threat of new entrants (barriers to entry)
- Threat of substitute products or services
- Bargaining power of buyers
- Bargaining power of suppliers
- Rivalry among existing competitors.

A solid reputation can itself be a powerful barrier to entry; it can deter potential new competitors while maintaining a loyal clientele.

☐   PEST ANALYSIS

An in-depth evaluation of the political, economic, social and technological influences on a business. This is a useful means of tackling the External Environment risk category.

☐   SCENARIO PLANNING

Scenario planning is a tool that facilitates structured appraisal of possible future scenarios and their associated risks. It is not an attempt to predict the future but a well-tried approach to exploring uncertainty. It can help organisations to think 'out of the box' and create a series of 'what if' scenarios that may present different sets of threats and opportunities to the business.

Scenario planning was originally developed as a tool for use by the US services. After the Second World War it was modified by the Hudson Institute for commercial use. The global conglomerate Shell pioneered the use of scenario planning, both globally and locally, as an input to strategy development and has been an active practitioner for over 30 years. Some of the early scenarios developed by Shell in the early 1970s addressed the price of crude oil. One scenario explored a world of strong OPEC market power in which prices rose rapidly – in sharp contrast to prevailing wisdom at the time. Shell's preparedness for the consequent OPEC price hike helped them to secure a leading position in the industry.

Shell describes scenarios as:

Carefully crafted stories about the future embodying a wide variety of ideas and integrating them in a way that is communicable and useful. They help us link the uncertainties we hold about the future to the decisions we must make today. When we reflect on situations, we see the world through our own frames of reference. The purpose of scenario work is to uncover what these frames are, respecting differences rather than aiming for a consensus that puts them to one side.[6]

Shell find scenarios particularly useful in situations where there is a desire to put challenges on the agenda proactively (for example, where there are leadership changes and major impending decisions) and where changes in the global business environment are recognised but not well understood (such as major political changes and new emerging technologies).[7]

Scenario planning can be a useful tool in exploring uncertainty and teasing out those difficult-to-get-at risks that can impact corporate reputation. It can be particularly helpful in considering the sets of circumstances that could spark a reputational crisis. Scenario planning essentially involves:

- Diagnosis of the issues facing the organisation
- Investigation and development of strategic options
- Development of scenarios (to test the options)
- Evaluation of the options
- Implementation of the selected options via strategy
- Review.[8]

☐ STAKEHOLDER ANALYSIS AND ENGAGEMENT

This involves identifying the organisation's stakeholders and deciding which are the most influential in terms of the negative or positive impact they could have on your business and its reputation.

It may be helpful to pause for a moment to consider in a little more detail what is meant by the term 'stakeholder'. Traditionally stakeholders were seen as groups that had a financial 'stake' in a business. This included the business's investors, customers and suppliers. In recent years the term has been used more loosely to describe groups that have an impact on, or are impacted by, the organisation.

> An organisation's stakeholders are those groups who affect and/or are affected by the organisation and its activities

Source: AccountAbility[9]

Figure 4-5   Stakeholders: a definition.

For most organisations, the core relationships are with five major stakeholder groups:

- Employees who work for it
- Customers who buy or receive its goods and services
- Suppliers who provide it with goods and services
- The community/communities in which operates
- Shareholders and investors.

However, stakeholders can encompass a far wider circle of interested parties dependent on the nature of the business. Examples include other business partners, lenders, analysts, insurers, trustees, members (of cooperative, mutual or friendly societies), regulators, government, the electorate and other government departments (for public sector bodies), trade/industry associations, professional bodies, trades unions, the media, competitors, non-governmental organisations (NGOs), pressure groups, the natural environment and even future generations. Each group will have its own unique set of interests that will evolve over time, although these may well overlap with the interests of other stakeholder groups. For example, investors and suppliers will have a keen interest in a business's financial performance and viability. Customers may be less interested in this (unless they are also investors) and are more likely to value the quality, value and availability of the product or service. As discussed in Chapter 2, the convergence of stakeholder interests and the emergence of powerful cross-stakeholder coalitions is a growing feature in today's business environment.

A global study by the World Business Council for Sustainable Development (WBCSD), published in 2000,[10] identified nine categories of stakeholder:

- Company owners/shareholders/investors
- Employees
- Customers
- Business partners
- Suppliers
- Competitors
- Government/regulators
- NGOs, pressure groups/influencers
- Communities.

The WBCSD list includes those groups that have a clear, direct and legitimate financial or other 'stake' in the business (such as its employees and investors), as well as groups that have an indirect interest (such as NGOs, pressure groups and other influencers). These latter groups often see themselves as vociferous 'proxies', representing voiceless or disenfranchised communities, the general public, animals or the natural environment.

For effective reputation risk management, it will be prudent initially to consider the perceptions, requirements and expectations of *all* your stakeholders. Restricting the focus to only those with a clear direct stake in your business may well exclude the very groups, such as NGOs, that can radically impact your reputation.

Some stakeholders will clearly wield more real power and influence than others. Once you have developed a comprehensive list of stakeholders relevant to your business, the challenge

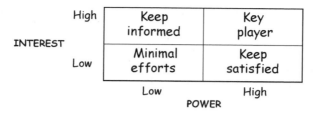

Figure 4-6   The power–interest matrix.

is to establish which are the most critical and to ensure that, as a minimum, their needs and expectations are met, both now and in the future.

Various methodologies have been developed for this. The World Business Council for Sustainable Development (WBCSD) advocates initial screening of stakeholders by asking:

- *Legitimacy*   Is a particular stakeholder group representative of issues that are relevant to your business and accountable to those with a legitimate interest in the way you do business?
- *Contribution/influence*   Does the stakeholder group have a contribution to make in helping you to run the business more responsibly or significant influence on your company's business and/or on other stakeholders?
- *Outcome*   Is the engagement likely to result in a productive outcome in the long run?[11]

The WBCSD suggests that those for whom the answers are 'Yes' should be considered key stakeholders and should be the priority focus for stakeholder dialogue.

An alternative way of prioritising stakeholders is suggested by Johnson and Scholes.[12] Their approach is to group stakeholders into four categories based on the power a stakeholder has in influencing a business's strategy and their level of interest in the business – i.e. their willingness to communicate their experiences with regard to the company's strategy (Figure 4-6). This allows an organisation to ensure it is investing time and effort in building and leveraging the relationships that really count for future strategy development and for protecting and enhancing reputation – and is not wasting resource on non-value-adding relationships. It also helps to ensure that the business is focusing on the right issues, in areas where there will be an ultimate pay-back.

After you have established who your major stakeholders are, the next step is to solicit their views and perceptions by engaging with them. This can take a number of forms including:

- One-to-one interviews, face-to-face and distance
- Group interviews
- Focus groups
- Workshops and seminars.
- Public meetings
- Questionnaires – face-to-face, by letter, telephone, internet, or other techniques.[13]

Looking with fresh eyes at the mass of information on stakeholders that already resides in your business can be a useful and low–cost starting point. A closer look at those tiresome questionnaires from analysts, institutional investors and rating agencies can, for example, provide vital early indications of how demands and expectations are shifting. A more detailed appraisal of those whingeing employee, customer and supplier surveys may yield equally valuable clues on opportunities to bolster those key relationships and build trust.

Whatever form it takes, the aim of the 'engagement' with stakeholders is to understand their perceptions, demands and expectations and to identify issues, threats and opportunities relating to the organisation's activities and performance. A key question is: What would make this stakeholder feel differently – either positively or negatively – about the organisation?

Engagement with stakeholders is fundamental to reputation risk management. As

$$Reputation = Experience - Expectations$$

it's vital that any business is fully tuned into its major stakeholders, is accountable to them and endeavours to meet their expectations. The benefits are many:

Meaningful engagement with stakeholders can help to:
(a) Anticipate and manage conflicts;
(b) Improve decision-making from management, employees, investors and other external stakeholders;
(c) Build consensus amongst diverse views;
(d) Create stakeholder identification with the outcomes of the organisation's activities;
(e) Build trust in the organisation.[14]

Engagement with stakeholders can also provide a rich seam of ideas for new products and services and information on embryonic market trends which can help a business to maintain its competitive edge – and its good reputation.

Stakeholder engagement should not be seen as a 'one-off' exercise. Stakeholders' concerns – and the alliances they choose to form – will change and evolve over time. To keep pace with developments, businesses need to put in place regular stakeholder monitoring, engagement and dialogue processes so that feedback is sufficiently frequent to ensure that no important new issue or emerging alliance is missed or misjudged.

In summary, analysing and engaging with your stakeholders is critical to successful reputation risk management. The key steps include:

- Identifying all stakeholders (with both a direct and indirect interest)
- Characterising the nature of the relationship with each (aims, requirements and expectations of both parties as you see it)
- Prioritising stakeholders so that key stakeholders are agreed
- Engaging with key stakeholders to identify perceptions, issues, concerns, requirements and expectations[15]
- Building the emerging threats and opportunities into your risk profile and, where appropriate, into your strategic planning process; recalibrating aims and values as required
- Repeating the process sufficiently frequently to ensure that no new issues or emerging alliances are overlooked.

DOCUMENTING, PRIORITISING AND RESPONDING TO RISKS

The final section of this chapter focuses on how to document the risks you have identified, how to assess and prioritise them and how to decide on an appropriate response. To complete the picture, it will also touch briefly on monitoring and assurance activities, although these aspects will be dealt with in detail in Chapters 7 and 8.

As part of your risk management framework you will need to record the risks identified and the risk response plans agreed to ensure that they are carried out and are effective. A simple template for expressing this is shown in Table 4-1. This type of simple 'risk register' can be used both for managing and for reporting risks. It can be made as sophisticated and detailed as is appropriate for the business[16] and can be usefully brought to life via spreadsheets and databases which allow information to be collated, sifted, compared and contrasted across the organisation. It covers the key steps for effectively managing risk discussed in Chapter 3: risk identification, risk assessment, risk response planning and monitoring and reporting.

The process in Table 4-1 may seem to be a trifle bureaucratic, but it's actually quite simple and logical. The good news is that this approach is valid for any type of risk, including risks to reputation. To demonstrate this, sample threats and opportunities to reputation will be run through the various stages of the process, which are:

- *Risk description*   What is the nature of risk and how will it impact the organisation expressed as: *Event/situation resulting in consequence/impact.* Give each risk a unique number so you can keep track of it (risk number in column 1)
- *Root cause(s)*   What could trigger the risk or make it more likely to occur?
- *Description of existing controls*   What are you already doing – if anything – to manage the risk? Is there a policy or procedure that is designed to keep it in check? Is it covered by working practices? Have you put in place specific actions or measures to manage it? Note the main ones.
- *Adequacy of existing controls*   How effective are the measures you have in place in actually controlling the risk? Are they adequate (A), inadequate (I) or are you uncertain (U)?
- *Assessment of risk*   Taking into account the controls that are already in place and their known effectiveness, how likely is it that the risk will actually occur? What would be its impact if it did? So how significant is it?
- *Owner*   Dependent on the significance of the risk, who should be responsible for managing it and ensuring actions are taken to bring or keep it under control?
- *Risk response and agreed actions*   How will you respond to the risk? Is the exposure acceptable given the appetite for risk that your business has? Will you tolerate, transfer, terminate or treat it? What specific additional actions, if any, are needed to control it? Who will develop and implement them? By when?
- *Assurance activities*   What is in place to give the business confidence (assurance) that the risks are and will remain under control? What level of monitoring and review occurs? Assurance activities could include reviews by management, surveys, self-assessment questionnaires, internal audits, reviews/audits by external bodies, benchmarking and a host of other performance indicators and reporting mechanisms.

Table 4-1. Risk register template

Risk no.	Risk description	Root cause(s)	Description of existing controls	Adequacy of existing controls (A/I/U)	Assessment of risk		Owner	Risk response and agreed actions (who, what, by when)	Assurance activities
					L	I			

Key: Adequacy of controls: A = Adequate;   I = Inadequate;   U = Uncertain

Risk assessment   L = Likelihood;   I = Impact;   H, M, L = High, Medium, Low

Figure 4-7   The risk management process.

The whole process (Figure 4-7), when working properly, should provide the top team with reliable information and assurance that risks have been properly identified and are well controlled, and that the business's position has been optimised by taking steps to increase the likelihood of success and reduce the possibility of failure. This will enable the top team to make appropriate disclosures to stakeholders on the business's risk and control arrangements, which should increase their confidence and enhance the business's reputation.

Here are some tips on how to make the risk management process work for you, rather than against you.

identifying risk descriptions and root causes

Once a risk has been identified, it should be framed in a way that makes it easy to understand and to manage subsequently. A useful format is:

Event/situation resulting in consequence/impact

For example:
Threats
1. Non-compliance with health and safety legislation results in litigation, censure and reputational damage.
2. Labour abuses at supplier factory lead to consumer boycott and adverse media coverage.

Opportunities
3. Being seen as good employer attracts high-quality staff, increases morale and enhances reputation.

4. Response to growing market demand for environmentally friendly goods results in launch of profitable new products, satisfied customers and a reputation for successful innovation.

The risk description should encapsulate the fundamental uncertainty, which can be either a threat or an opportunity to the business. Circumstances, actions or situations that could cause the risk to occur – its root causes or triggers – should be analysed and noted separately (Table 4-2). It is important to be clear about what precisely constitutes the risk, as distinct from its root cause. When you reach the stage of deciding how best to manage the risk, it is the root causes you will be seeking to control, so it will save time if you clarify what they are.

Table 4-2. Risk description and root cause(s)

Risk no.	Risk description	Root cause(s)
1	Non-compliance with health and safety legislation results in litigation, censure and reputational damage	• Difficult to track changes in legislation • Relevant policies and procedures not implemented • Relevant policies and procedures not implemented • Managers inadequately trained • Staff don't see as important • Inadequate internal review process to check compliance
2	Labour abuses at supplier factory lead to consumer boycott and adverse media coverage	• Required standards not clear • Suppliers not adhering to agreed standards • Lack of resource to check compliance in overseas factories • NGO and media interest
3	Being seen as good employer attracts high quality staff, increases morale and enhances reputation	• Good pay and conditions • Employees valued, trusted and respected • Excellent training and development processes • CV enhancing • Well promoted externally • Listed in 'best employer' survey
4	Response to growing market demand for environmentally friendly goods results in launch of profitable new products, satisfied customers and a reputation for successful innovation	• Entrepreneurial culture/innovation rewarded • Effective market research • Good customer feedback mechanisms • Research capability/track record on innovation • Effective marketing • External publicity • NGO support

It is important to try to make the risk as concrete as possible to enable it to be managed and controlled in practice. A risk register containing 'motherhood and apple pie' risks that are so generic that they are virtually meaningless and elicit a 'Well yes – but so what?' reaction will waste everyone's time and give risk management a bad name.

Table 4-3. Risk description and existing controls

Risk No.	Risk Description	Description of existing controls	Adequacy existing of controls (A/I/U)
1	Non-compliance with health and safety legislation results in litigation, censure and reputational damage	• Health and Safety department tracks pending legislative and regulatory changes • Health and Safety Policy • Management training on H&S on induction • H&S department compliance checks • Monthly board reporting of H&S incidents	U
2	Labour abuses at supplier factory lead to consumer boycott and adverse media coverage	• Group policy and code of conduct on labour standards in the supply chain • Rolling programme of supplier audits (Europe only); self-assessment at overseas sites as part of contract terms.	I
3	Being seen as good employer attracts high quality staff, increases morale and enhances reputation	• Flexible remuneration package • Career development and performance management processes	I
4	Response to growing market demand for environmentally friendly goods results in launch of profitable new products, satisfied customers and a reputation for successful innovation.	• Research and development programme • Three-yearly customer satisfaction surveys • Marketing and promotional activities	I

describing existing controls and establishing their adequacy

Having defined a risk, consider what actions, policies, standards, processes, procedures, and ways of working are in place to control it. Do you have any performance measures or other indicators to monitor its status? How adequate are those controls in managing the risk – are they adequate (A), inadequate (I) or are you uncertain (U)? In making this assessment, look back to the root causes. Is there a good match with the controls you currently have in place? If not, a gap may need to be filled. Or perhaps you realise that, although the controls are in place, they are not working as intended. There may have been a previous incident or near miss. There may be a recent audit report indicating that all is not well. If so, the controls are probably inadequate and need to be strengthened (Table 4-3). If in doubt, err on the side of caution. You can always validate the controls and modify your assessment at a later date.

assessing risks

This is an important step as it determines whether a risk is significant and worthy of attention – and, if so, at what level in the organisation. This is where you will need another simple piece of risk language and framework: a consistent means of ranking risks by impact and likelihood across the organisation.

This can be as straightforward or as complex as you wish. It can range from a simple three-by-three matrix, ranking each risk by High, Medium or Low for both the likelihood of its occurrence and its impact if it does, to more sophisticated models which rate impact and likelihood on a 10-or 12-point scale. Figure 4.8 shows the possible form of a simple three-by-matrix.

Likelihood		Impact	
Low	Unlikely	**Low**	Minor
Medium	Possible	**Medium**	Moderate
High	Probable	**High**	Major

Figure 4-8   Likelihood/impact matrix (three-by-three).

To give the likelihood scale perspective, it can be helpful to provide a time horizon relevant to your business. As many organisations work on a three-year planning cycle, 'within three years' can offer a relevant and meaningful timescale.

Remember that the same criteria are being use to evaluate both threats and opportunities. In the case of threats, the likelihood is of a negative outcome; in the case of opportunities, the likelihood relates to the prospects of a positive outcome.[17]

Another commonly used model is a five-point scale such as that in Table 4-4.[18]

Table 4-4. Likelihood/impact matrix (five-point scale)

Likelihood	Impact
A. Rare	1. Insignificant
B. Unlikely	2. Minor
C. Possible	3. Moderate
D. Likely	4. Major
E. Almost Certain	5. Massive

To bring these charts to life, the impacts can be expanded by using word-model descriptors against a set of pertinent and meaningful risk impact categories. As a minimum you should include both financial impacts and impacts on reputation. An example is given in Table 4-5 of a five-point scale impact guide chart for a major international business.

Table 4-5. Impact guide chart (five-point scale)

Impact	Financial	Reputation
1. Insignificant	< £0.1 million	Minor local reputation impact
2. Minor	£0.1 to < £1.0 million	Local media coverage
3. Moderate	£1.0 < to £10 million	National media coverage
4. Major	£10 to £10 million	International shortterm media coverage
5. Catastrophic	> £100 million	International adverse media coverage over more than one year

It's worth devoting some time to tailoring a guide chart that will enable people to make a quick assessment of the risks identified in a way that feels relevant to the organisation. It may be helpful to include other pertinent prompts that will assist you in understanding and prioritising the risks facing your business. For example, if your worst nightmare is your organisation being hauled up in front of a particular regulator, being prosecuted in court or causing fatalities, build this into your risk assessment criteria and use your own business vocabulary so that it instantly feels familiar. Equally, if your major challenge is increasing market share, developing new services or recruiting high-quality personnel, include some prompts in your guide chart that will reflect these potential areas of opportunity. You should also make sure that the assessment criteria are valid both for 'top down' and 'bottom up' use throughout the organisation to enable them to be employed in all areas of operation.

Table 4-6 shows an alternative guide chart for a public sector organisation, whose focus is primarily on reputation maintenance and service delivery within budget. It reflects both threats and opportunities to the organisation through judicious use of language and uses a simple high, medium and low ranking. In establishing the impact of a particular risk it makes sense to select the most relevant area impacted. If there is more than one, as is often the case since many risks may have both a financial and a reputational impact, you should again err on the side of caution to ensure that the risk receives appropriate attention at the right level.

To avoid any subjective bias in assessing impact and likelihood, relevant data should be used where possible. You have already done this in part by assessing the adequacy of existing controls. Now, taking these existing controls into account, you need to rank each risk by likelihood and impact. At this stage you should also consider:

- past experience: has this, or anything similar ever happened before?
- the experience of competitors/similar organisations
- the results of internal or external reviews, audits, benchmarking exercises, etc. (i.e. assurance activities)
- an assessment of the organisational culture (control environment)

Table 4-6. Sample guide chart

Area impacted	Low	Medium	High
Reputation	• Localised complaint /tribute • Minor change in stakeholder confidence • Impact less than one month	• Local press/TV coverage • Moderate change in stakeholder confidence • Criticism/ endorsement by regulatory authorities • Impact lasts one to three months	• National press/TV coverage • Censure by/accolade from regulatory authorities • Substantial change in stakeholder confidence • Impact lasts for three months or longer
Service provision	• Minor disruption or impact on operational performance	• Moderate disruption or impact on operational performance	• Substantial disruption or impact on operational performance
Regulatory/ Health and Safety	• Minor non-compliance with regulation • Minor injuries	• warning by regulatory bodies • Major injuries	• Fatality Censure/fine by regulatory bodies • Litigation
Financial	• Minor deviation from budget (below £10k)	• Moderate deviation from budget (>£10k and <£0.5m) • Adverse external audit management letter	• Substantial deviation from budget (>£0.5m) • External audit qualify accounts

- current or impending portfolio, organisational, personnel or systems changes that could trigger a risk
- trends and changes in the external environment, in stakeholder perceptions and expectations that could make a risk more or less likely to happen or increase/decrease its potential consequences.

It should never merely be assumed that controls are working as intended when there is no hard evidence for this. A previously unblemished record is no guarantee that catastrophe is not just around the corner![19]

Once risks have been assessed, the impact and likelihood ranking for each should be entered in the relevant column on the risk register. To portray their relative importance, the risks can then be charted on a risk profile according to the in-house assessment scale. You can give instant visibility to those risks requiring speedy attention and positive action by marking them red, those needing less urgent attention amber, and those risks where current management controls are deemed to be effective, green. The size and shape of your 'red, amber and green' zones will be determined by your business's definition of 'risk appetite' and the amount of exposure it is prepared to bear. Profiling allows risks to be quickly prioritised and resources allocated in accordance with risk exposures. An example of a risk profile is shown in Figure 4-9. All you are trying to do at this stage is to sort the risks by relative importance so that an appropriate response can be developed for each.

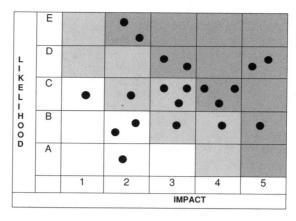

Key: ▨ Red;   ▨ Amber;   ☐ Green

Figure 4-9   Example of a risk profile.

By using a risk profile you can see at a glance which risks warrant active management attention, specific action and allocation of resource; which risks might be best handled by contingency plans; and which risks should be put on the back burner for now and be reviewed occasionally to check that their status hasn't changed as a result of market, regulatory or organisational developments (Figure 4-10).

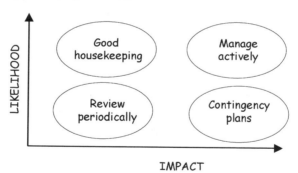

Figure 4-10   Risk assessment and response.

When it comes to planning actions for the risk response, you will need to consider whether the 'risk' is a threat or an opportunity (Figure 4-11). If a threat, your basic goal will be to reduce its impact and likelihood, thereby minimising negative effects (assuming the cost of action is warranted and the risk can actually be controlled). For opportunities, the name of the game is to enhance the conditions for its likelihood and impact to be maximised, so its benefits can be fully reaped. This means that, although, both threats and opportunities can be featured on the same risk profile, they will be pulling in opposite directions. You may wish to

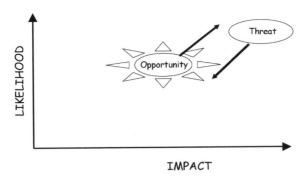

Figure 4-11   Response to threats and opportunities.

use a different shape or colour to denote your opportunities so that their status over time can be easily tracked.[20] Whether threats or opportunities, those risks appearing in the designated 'red' zone warrant senior management attention.

ownership, risk response and action planning

An owner should be designated for each risk. That person should have overall responsibility for ensuring that any actions agreed to mitigate the risk are carried out and have the desired effect – although the actions themselves can be delegated. The owner should also report back on progress to the relevant level in the organisation. The top 15–20 of risks deemed 'significant' to the business as a whole should be owned by a board member or senior executive and the status of risks should be regularly reviewed by the board (and/or audit or risk committee). If directors are not focusing on active management of significant threats and opportunities to the business, what other more worthwhile activities are they engaged in?

Consensus now needs to be reached on whether the residual exposure created by a risk (after current controls are taken into account) is acceptable to the business, i.e. whether it falls within the boundaries of the business's 'risk appetite' or risk tolerance. A decision can then be made on whether to tolerate, transfer, terminate or treat the risk, as depicted in Figure 4-12.

❒   TOLERATE

If the risk is deemed acceptable it can be managed passively and 'tolerated', i.e. taking no additional actions currently but reviewing the risk occasionally to check that its status is unchanged and that any controls are continuing to operate as intended. This can be applied to both threats and opportunities.

Acceptance of a risk should always be a conscious, considered and positive decision – not a default position because the business has not taken the trouble to analyse the risk and think about the best way of handling it. If the exposure is one requiring positive action, there are a number of active options available: transfer, terminate or treat.

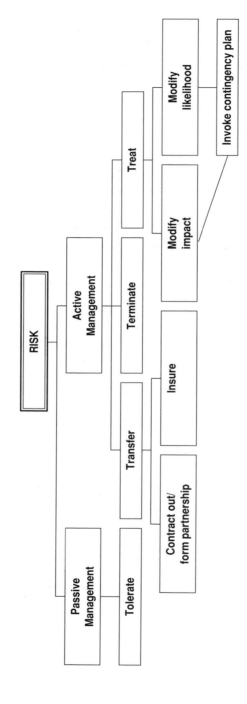

Figure 4-12   Risk response options.

☐ TRANSFER

This means sharing the risk in whole or in part with another party (perhaps with a subcontractor, joint venture partner or by outsourcing the activity) or by insuring all or part of the risk. But, of course, transferring the risk to another party does not necessarily exonerate you from blame when things go wrong – or give you all the kudos when things go right. The fact that Nike owns no factories itself to manufacture clothing has not protected it from damaging claims of tolerating sweatshop conditions and workplace abuses in its suppliers' manufacturing facilities. Headlines such as 'Sacking dispute hits Nike',[21] 'Indonesian Nike workers allege sexual harassment',[22] and 'Nike accused of tolerating sweatshops',[23] and a research report snappily entitled 'Still waiting for Nike to do it',[24] continued to dog the company, three years after it pledged to improve conditions for its 500 000 strong global workforce.

Similarly UK rail infrastructure operator Railtrack's decision to outsource its maintenance operations to third-party contractors did nothing to prevent its own image from being sullied when blame for a series of rail disasters was pinned partially on lax maintenance standards. Headlines such as 'Hatfield track the "worst ever seen"',[25] 'Hatfield: the warnings that Railtrack ignored',[26] and the public, investor and pressure group outcry they engendered, led to top-level management changes at Railtrack and contributed ultimately to the demise of the publicly quoted company.

The concept of risk transfer can apply both to threats and opportunities.

☐ TERMINATE

If a negative risk exposure could fundamentally jeopardise the business's performance and reputation, it may be wise to withdraw from the activity or avoid situations that could trigger it. The terminate option applies only to threats; it involves taking steps to ensure that the risk cannot possibly occur.

Leading software suppliers and construction contractors now routinely assess the risks of new projects on their own corporate reputation before embarking on them. If the client is known for weak management and has a track record of late project delivery, the risk to the supplier's reputation of the project failing, coming in late or over budget could be greater than any financial benefit of winning the contract. The contractor may decide to terminate or avoid the risk by not bidding. Even in situations where the risk was initially deemed acceptable, it may be prudent to terminate at a later stage if additional negative factors emerge.

The construction company Balfour Beatty decided to back out of a highly controversial deal to build the Ilisu dam on the Tigris river in south-east Turkey in an attempt to restore its battered reputation – even though it had already invested heavily in the project. The decision was taken after the company had faced a storm of protest from environmental, human rights campaigners and investors regarding the social and environmental impacts of the project and potential displacement of thousands of Kurds. Balfour Beatty announced in November 2001 that it was withdrawing as a result of outstanding commercial, environmental and social issues and believed it was 'not in the best interests of its stakeholders to pursue the project further'.[27] Chief executive, Mike Welton, commented that the company had 'clearly reached a point where 'no further action nor any further expenditure by Balfour Beatty on this project is likely to resolve the outstanding issues in a reasonable timescale.'[28] Balfour Beatty's climb-down was hailed as a major victory by environmental campaigners. Charles Secrett, then director of Friends of the Earth, called it a 'tremendous win against a disastrous project'.[29]

Announcing such a high-profile U-turn can only make sense in exceptional circumstances, when any other course of action could be yet more damaging. The fact that Balfour Beatty was one of the maintenance contractors caught up in the Railtrack débâcle over the Hatfield incident was no doubt also a factor. The Balfour Beatty experience illustrates that a careful and systematic appraisal of *all* the risks of a new project – including those to reputation – before you are committed, will always be resource well spent.

☐   TREAT

A risk is 'treated' when the exposure it creates is judged too great for the business to tolerate. In such cases, the business may need or choose to bear the risk, but its impact and/or likelihood needs to be actively modified to make the exposure acceptable. Profit is, after all, a reward for successful risk-taking; risk management is always a trade-off between risk and reward.

In the case of a threat, the name of the game is to lower the risk exposure by reducing the impact and/or likelihood of the threat occurring. So what does this mean in practice? The likelihood of the threat occurring could be reduced by improving training, by putting in place new policies and procedures, by tightening up contract terms or by checking that controls are working as intended though self-assessment or audit. The risk's impact could be reduced by contingency planning (such as disaster recovery and crisis plans) and by nurturing strong relationships with the relevant stakeholders. In deciding what needs to be controlled and how to control it, you need to look again at the root causes noted when the risks were first identified.

For an opportunity, the objective is to boost the prospects of it occurring and yielding benefits by increasing its likelihood and/or impact. Examples of increasing likelihood could include recruiting expertise crucial to the project, bolstering your sales effort in the potential market or raising advertising spend. Impact could be maximised by raising stock levels to ensure that additional demand can be catered for, by ensuring that staff are fully competent to exploit the new opportunity or by using public relations expertise to publicise your success and enhance your reputation.

For threats or opportunities the cost of any actions taken must be justifiable. Many internal threats can be virtually eliminated by implementing a battery of controls, checks and balances, but the cost of this may prove exorbitant both in terms of the sheer effort expended in operating the controls and in the negative impact it could have on employee morale. Part of the decision-making process is therefore to consider, as the Turnbull report puts it, 'the costs of operating particular controls relative to the benefit thereby obtained in managing the related risks'.[30]

Many apparent threats to reputation are also potential opportunities to enhance your standing – dependent on your mindset. In Chapter 6 a number of examples will be provided of businesses that have successfully combined threat reduction and opportunity maximisation on the same issue, to both safeguard and enhance their reputation.

A risk profile can also highlight those threats where, although the likelihood of occurrence is low, the impact could be catastrophic. This could include natural disasters such as fire or flood or terrorist attack or a completely unexpected virulent pressure group campaign. The risk may be impossible or very costly to control and is therefore probably best tackled via some form of contingency plan (a business continuity or crisis plan) which can be invoked if the event comes to pass; such a plan can be coupled with insurance where feasible. As you will see in Chapter 6, having an up-to-date crisis management plan is critical if reputation is to be safeguarded; and a swift and positive response to a crisis can actually enhance reputation.

An opportunity that has a very low likelihood but an exceptionally high positive impact will probably need to be disregarded as the cost of making it happen would be exorbitant. However, the situation should be kept under review in case a competitor feels able to seize the opportunity and leave you behind. It may be prudent to develop a contingency plan to counter any adverse impacts if this occurs.

Alternatively, if the opportunity is long-term one (perhaps stretching beyond the three-year time horizon of the strategic plan), the business may choose to make fundamental changes to its capability to exploit the opportunity, e.g. by acquiring a company with the requisite know-how or by actively building in-house skills and expertise over the medium term.

Table 4-7 shows the risk register, with risk rankings, risk responses and actions plans completed, and with designated owners, for the two threats and two opportunities discussed earlier. Using this method you have a simple time-phased action plan with measurable objectives, owned by named individuals to respond to each risk. Progress against individual risks can be tracked and monitored as an integral part of your management reporting system.

The standard or recommended responses of your organisation to various types of risk can be summarised in a 'risk management policy', reinforced by other corporate policies on issues such as business conduct to clearly delineate the 'thou shalt nots' and 'thou mays if due process is followed'.

Finally:

assurance activities

The last column on the risk register notes all the activities that are in place to give the business confidence (assurance) that the risks are and will remain under control. This could include embedded monitoring devices that are built into the reporting and management systems, performance measures and 'early warning indicators' to give advance warning of a risk materialising, and various forms of internal and external review and audit. The final column, once completed, will be similar to that shown in Table 4-8.

The risk response actions may recommend additional elements of assurance to make sure that management of the risk is rock solid and can be relied upon. Risks where potential impact is high but the likelihood is low because of 'adequate controls' are prime candidates for occasional review; if those critical controls cease to operate and the risk spirals out of control, the effect could be devastating. The risk register can therefore also be useful in focusing the activities of auditors (both internal and external) to ensure that the organisation gets maximum 'bang for its buck'. The role of monitoring and assurance will be examined in more detail in Chapters 7 and 8.

At least every six months, the risk response plans should be reviewed to ensure that implementation is on track and that any new controls are having the desired effect. Once the top team and/or audit or risk committee is confident that the controls are effective, the 'old' risks can be re-rated for likelihood and impact. Update your stakeholders in your annual report on the progress and successes of your risk management programme; this will give them confidence that their investment is in safe hands.

The process should be kept dynamic by ensuring that any emerging risks are captured and appropriate action plans developed in response to them. As it can prove quite a challenge to maintain management interest and ensure that the risk profile is regularly refreshed, some ideas on maintaining momentum are explored in Chapter 10.

So there you have it – the bare bones of a risk management system that will allow you to manage *all* the risks to your business, including threats and opportunities to your reputation. It will only be effective, however, if the right people are actively involved. For risks to reputation, where potential triggers can lurk in every nook and cranny of the organisation, this means making reputation risk management everyone's business – which just happens to be the title of the next chapter.

NOTES AND REFERENCES

1. *Sunday Times*, 11 August 2002 and *The Guardian*, 20 August 2002. The author's personal favourite is the $4m donation to Cambridge University in 2001 – to fund studies on corporate governance!
2. *The Guardian*, 8 August 2002.
3. *The Business*, 18/19 August 2002.
4. *Financial Times*, 20 August 2002. The previous day, shares in Tyco surged by 12% (up by $1.65 to $14.95) on the news that certain Tyco directors wanted all board members who had served under Kozlowski to resign to make a 'clean break with the conglomerate's troubled past'. It was proposed that all directors except the newly appointed chief executive Edward Breen and John Krol step down by the next annual meeting, early in 2003.
5. Porter, M. E. (1985) *Competitive Advantage*. New York: The Free Press.
6. Extract from the section on scenarios on Shell's website www.shell.com: *What are Scenarios?* Reproduced by permission of Shell International Ltd.
7. Extract from the section on scenarios on Shell's website www.shell.com: *Building and Using Scenarios*. Reproduced by permission of Shell International Ltd.
8. From 'Application of Scenario Planning to Corporate Social Responsibility', by Gill Ringland and Adrian H.T. Davies in the *Corporate Social Responsibility Monitor* (2002). London: Gee Publishing, Chapter C5, www.gee.co.uk.
9. AccountAbility 1000 (AA1000) framework: Exposure draft – November 1999, London: AccountAbility, p. 3.

10. Holme, R. and Watts, P. (2000) *Corporate Social Responsibility: Making Good Business Sense.* Geneva: World Business Council for Sustainable Development, p. 16.
11. Holme, R. and Watts, P. (2000) *Corporate Social Responsibility: Making Good Business Sense.* Geneva: World Business Council for Sustainable Development, p. 15.
12. Johnston, G. and Scholes, K. (1999) *Exploring Corporate Strategy.* Prentice Hall Europe.
13. AccountAbility 1000 (AA1000) framework: Exposure draft – November 1999, London: Account-Ability, p. 24.
14. AccountAbility 1000 (AA1000) framework: Exposure draft – November 1999, London: Account-Ability, p. 63.
15. Some argue that all stakeholders should be included in the process. AccountAbility 1000 (AA1000) a foundation standard for social and ethical accounting, auditing and reporting, developed by the UK-based Institute of Social and Ethical Accountability (ISEA) in 1999 is based on effective stakeholder engagement. One of its core principles is that of 'inclusivity' i.e. that *all* stakeholder groups should be involved, including 'voiceless', ones such as future generations and the environment. AA1000 provides helpful guidelines for stakeholder engagement. See www.accountabiliy.org.
16. The Australia and New Zealand risk management standard (AS/NZS 4360: 1999) contains some useful templates for risk capture and treatment.
17. *A Risk Management Standard* (2002), the UK standard developed by AIRMIC, ALARM and the IRM, advocates the use of different definitions for estimating the likelihood of threats and opportunities. It suggests that, for threats, High (probable) could mean 'likely to occur each year or more than a 25 per cent chance of occurrence'; Medium (possible) could mean 'likely to occur in a ten year time period or less than a 25 per cent chance of occurrence', Low (remote) could mean 'not likely to occur in a ten year period or less than 2 per cent chance of occurrence'. For opportunities, High could mean 'favourable outcome is likely to be achieved in a year or better than 75 per cent chance of occurrence'; Medium could mean 'Reasonable prospects of favourable results in one year or 25–75 per cent chance of occurrence'; High could mean 'Some chance of favourable outcome in the medium term or less than 25 per cent chance of occurrence'. The standard suggests that impact criteria, if neutrally framed (e.g. financial impact of £x) are valid for both threats and opportunities. The standard is available for download from www.airmic.co.uk, www.theirm.org and www.alarm.uk.com.
18. Adapted from *Australia and New Zealand Risk Management Standard* (AS/NZS 4360:1999) Appendix E.
19. Some organisations choose to rank their risks both before and after controls have been applied. Dual ranking of 'gross risk' (before controls are applied) and of 'net risk' or 'residual risk' (after controls have been implemented) can be helpful in showing the real effect of controls on impact and/or likelihood and thus on overall exposure. It can also help to focus attention on whether a control is really producing the desired effect and can provide useful data on whether the cost of the control is justified. Other organisations see it as artificial and non-value adding to think about a world in which no controls exist and believe it is sufficient to focus only on net risks. Both methods can work well, but caution should be exercised in the 'net risk' model to ensure that the true effectiveness of controls is not glossed over and unsubstantiated assumptions made that all is well.
20. An alternative means of tackling this is to use a double risk profile with threats on one side and opportunities on the other side of the vertical axis, with the horizontal axis for threats relating to negative impacts and the horizontal axis for opportunities relating to positive impacts. This approach is explained in a paper by Dr David Hillson of UK project management consultancy PMProfessional. Although the focus here is on projects, the same principles apply to risk management in the business as a whole The paper 'Extending the Risk Process to Manage Opportunities' was presented at the

Fourth European Project Management conference, PMI Europe in June 2001. It can be downloaded from www.risksig.com/articles/euro2001/hillson.pdf.

21. *Financial Times*, 19 January 2001.
22. *Financial Times*, 22 February 2001.
23. *The Observer*, 20 May 2001.
24. *Still waiting for Nike to do it*, published by the San Francisco based Global Exchange, May 2001.
25. *Financial Times*, 24 January 2001.
26. *The Guardian*, 16 January 2001.
27. Balfour Beatty press release, 13 November 2001. Text available in full from www. balfourbeatty.co.uk.
28. Balfour Beatty press release, 13 November 2001. Text available in full from www. balfourbeatty.co.uk.
29. As reported in *The Guardian*, 14 November 2001.
30. Turnbull report (1999) *Internal Control for Directors on the Combined Code*. London: ICAEW, para. 17.

Table 4-7. Risk responses, action plans and owners (as at 1 March 2003)

Risk no.	Risk description	Root cause(s)	Description of existing controls	Adequacy of existing controls A/I/U	Assessment of risk L	Assessment of risk I	Owner	Risk response and agreed actions (who, what, by when)
1	Non-compliance with health and safety legislation results in litigation, censure and reputational damage	• Difficult to track changes in legislation • Relevant policies and procedures not implemented • Managers inadequately trained • Staff don't see as important • Inadequate internal review process to check compliance	• Health and Safety department tracks pending legislative and regulatory changes • Health and Safety Policy • Management training on H&S on induction • H&S department compliance checks • Monthly board reporting of H&S incidents	U	M	H	SOS	**Treat threat** • Special one-off review by external consultancy to benchmark robustness of approach. (SLR by 31/5/03) • Review adequacy of resource for tracking regulatory changes. (SLR by 30/6/03) • Institute annual manager refresher training and incorporate new measure in monthly board reporting. (JMF by 30/9/03) • Internal audit to review compliance programme for completeness and frequency and report to audit committee (LJR by 30/9/03)

Table 4-7. continued

Risk no.	Risk description	Root cause(s)	Description of existing controls	Adequacy of existing controls A/I/U	Assessment of risk L	Assessment of risk I	Owner	Risk response and agreed actions (who, what, by when)
2	Labour abuses at supplier factory lead to consumer boycott and adverse media coverage	• Required standards not clear Suppliers not adhering to agreed standards • Lack of resource to check compliance in overseas factories • NGO and media interest	• Group policy and code of conduct on labour standards in the supply chain • Rolling programme of supplier audits (Europe only); self-assessment at overseas sites as part of contract terms	I	H	H	ANO	**Treat threat** • Paper to board on status of supplier factory audits world wide. (NGW by 2/4/03) • External consultancy to advise on third-party assessment at overseas sites. (ANO by 31/5/03) • Global assessment programme to be in place by 30/9/03. (NGW) • Results of supplier assessments summarised for board quarterly (NGW from 1/1/04); major non-conformances to be reported as part of monthly report. (NGW-immediate)

				I			RUF	Tolerate opportunity
3	Being seen as good employer attracts high-quality staff, increases morale and enhances reputation	• Good pay and conditions • Employees valued, trusted and respected • Excellent training and development processes • CV enhancing • Well promoted externally • Listed in 'best employer' survey	• Flexible remuneration package • Career development and performance management processes • Staff turnover/outstanding vacancies reported monthly to board	I	M	M	RUF	**Tolerate opportunity** No further action justified currently as recruitment/retention satisfactory. Keep under review
4	Response to growing market demand for environmentally friendly goods results in launch of profitable new products, satisfied customers and a reputation for successful innovation	• Entrepreneurial culture/innovation rewarded • Effective market research • Good customer feedback mechanisms • Research capability/track record on innovation • Effective marketing • External publicity • NGO support	• Research and development programme • Three-yearly customer satisfaction surveys • Marketing and promotional activities	I	L	H	ALF	**Treat opportunity – reposition over medium term to reap benefits.** **Initial actions:** • Establish customer focus groups to help define new product needs. (ALF by 30/9/03) • Review gaps in-house expertise to deliver new range of environmentally friendly products. (JSR to report with recommendations by 30/12/03) • Quarterly report to board of new launches of environmentally friendly products in sector. (ALF from 1/7/03)

Table 4-8. Risk assurance activities (as at 1 March 2003)

Risk no.	Risk response and agreed actions (who, what, by when)	Assurance activities
1	**Treat threat** • Special one-off review by external consultancy to benchmark robustness of approach. (SLR by 31/5/03) • Review adequacy of resource for tracking regulatory changes. (SLR by 30/6/03) • Institute annual manager refresher training and incorporate new measure in monthly board reporting. (JMF by 30/9/03) • Internal audit to review compliance check programme for completeness and frequency and report to audit committee. (LJR by 30/9/03)	• H&S compliance checks and monthly incident reporting • Manager training performance measure in monthly reporting (from 30/9/03) • External review of procedures. (SLR by 31/5/030) • Internal audit review of compliance programme (by 30/9/03). Annual thereafter
2	**Treat threat** • Paper to board on status of supplier factory audits world wide. (NGW by 2/4/03) • External consultancy to advise on third-party assessment at overseas sites. (ANO by 31/5/03) • Global assessment programme to be in place by 30/9/03. (NGW) • Results of supplier assessments summarised for board quarterly (NGW from 1/1/04); major non-conformances to be reported as part of monthly report. (NGW-immediate)	• Major supplier non-conformances to be included in monthly report. (NGW-immediate) • Quarterly summary of supplier assessments to board. (NGW from 1/1/04)
3	**Tolerate opportunity** • No further action justified currently as recruitment/retention satisfactory. Keep under review	• Staff turnover/outstanding vacancies reported monthly to board
4	**Treat opportunity: reposition over medium term to reap benefits. Initial actions:** • Establish customer focus groups to help define new product needs. (ALF by 30/9/03) • Review gaps in in-house expertise to deliver new range of environmentally friendly products. (JSR to report with recommendations by 30/12/03) • Quarterly report to board of new launches of environmentally friendly products in sector. (ALF from 1/7/03)	• To be agreed after initial review completed

five

making reputation risk management everyone's business

WHO SHOULD BE INVOLVED?

The importance of trying to involve everyone in an organisation in managing its risks has already been mentioned. In no area is this a more worthwhile goal than in managing risks to reputation. An organisation's reputation can be damaged as much by a tactless remark from a director or spokesperson as by a lackadaisical warehouse clerk who despatches the wrong goods, a customer service manager who fails to spot the significance of a spate of complaints or a procurement officer who doesn't adequately check the credentials of a new supplier.

If the behaviour of any individual working for the organisation or its supply chain is out of kilter with the beliefs and expectations of a stakeholder, that stakeholder's confidence and trust in the organisation can suffer. If the behaviour recurs, or is replicated by other employees so that it affects the perceptions of a number of stakeholders, it can begin to undermine corporate reputation. Consistently meeting and sometimes exceeding stakeholder expectations can, conversely, enhance reputation and build trust.

> Reputations reflect the behaviour you exhibit day in and day out through a hundred small things. The way you manage your reputation is by always thinking and trying to do the right thing every day.
>
> (Ralph S. Larsen, former chairman and CEO, Johnson & Johnson)

The goal should be for the management of risks – particularly of those that could impact reputation – to be a basic component of *everyone's* job. Risk management will be truly 'embedded' when everyone in the organisation considers risk as an integral part of 'the way we do things around here'. Risk thinking will be seamlessly integrated into everyday decision-making, into strategy development and into the organisation's policies, processes and procedures. People

91

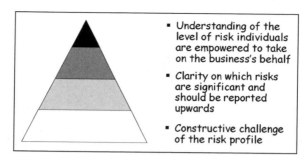

- Understanding of the level of risk individuals are empowered to take on the business's behalf
- Clarity on which risks are significant and should be reported upwards
- Constructive challenge of the risk profile

Figure 5-1   The 'freedom to act' risk management hierarchy.

will understand the implications of their actions and inactions, and see how this fits into the broader business perspective. Crucially, they will have a good understanding of the major sources of risk to reputation and the boundaries of risk tolerance in their specific business context; they will also know how to spot the early signs of a risk materialising and know what to do about it, and be prepared to act. The organisational climate will encourage people to be frank and speak up about areas of concern, and to critique the corporate risk profile. In this way, a risk management 'freedom to act' hierarchy will be established that creates a healthy tension and counterbalance to the occasional vagaries and excesses of executive directors! (Figure 5-1.)

Although everyone representing an organisation – including its suppliers and partners – bears some responsibility for upholding its reputation, the lead should, as ever, come from the top – from the organisation's board and senior executives, who bear the ultimate responsibility for ensuring that risks are understood and are properly controlled.

THE ROLE OF THE TOP TEAM

Apart from the board's vital role in establishing the organisation's vision, values and strategy, setting its cultural tone, establishing an appropriate framework for managing risks and setting risk tolerance boundaries (as discussed in Chapter 3), directors and senior executives should also play an active role in identifying and assessing the organisation's risks. They should act as the final arbiters on those risks considered to be the most significant to the business as a whole. The key corporate risks are, in the final analysis, those for which directors can be held accountable and those in which investors and other stakeholders have the greatest interest.

In the case of risks to reputation, an individual or single department or operating unit may lack the strategic overview needed to identify and assess potential impacts to the business overall. The active involvement of directors in managing reputation risk may therefore be crucial if potential killer risks are not to be overlooked or underestimated.

In spite of the seemingly unquestionable logic, however, not all boards *do* become actively involved in identifying and managing risks. Directors may acknowledge the theoretical need for their involvement but may be reluctant to roll up their sleeves and apply themselves. As the previously quoted US director survey conducted by McKinsey in spring 2002[1] showed, 36% of directors 'do not understand the major risks facing the company' and 43% cannot 'effectively identify, safeguard against and plan for key risks'. The same survey showed that CEOs and directors tend to focus on financial risk, of which they are more knowledgeable, to the detriment of non-financial risk, which 'only gets anecdotal treatment'. And this despite the fact that boards apparently want to understand more about the risks their companies face, with 73% of directors in favour of increasing the audit committee's responsibility for risk and 52% supporting establishment of a risk management committee. Could it be that directors are keen for risk management to take place – but don't see the need to dirty their own hands in the process?

If that is the case, they are abdicating their responsibility to their stakeholders. If a business's directors are not playing an active part in ensuring that significant risks to the business are identified and controlled so that exposures are acceptable and opportunities exploited, they are failing in their primary duty to safeguard shareholders' investment and the business's assets. If they cannot be certain that the right risks have found their way onto the corporate risk profile, or have doubts on whether they are being adequately controlled, how can they provide the requisite assurances to shareholders and other stakeholders through the annual reporting process? Company directors are, after all, responsible for the accuracy of public disclosures; developments such as the Sarbanes–Oxley Act in the USA have made this an unequivocal legal requirement.

Executive directors also play an important role in ensuring that fellow independent directors and employees have the proper information on which to make risk judgements. Independent directors and staff deprived of key risk information by reticent or self-serving executive directors are an under-utilised asset.

CONSCIENCE-PRICKERS: THE ROLE OF INDEPENDENT DIRECTORS

Boards generally contain a number of non-executive or independent[2] directors, increasingly even in public sector organisations. They can make a distinct contribution to managing reputation risk, which springs from their objectivity and helicopter view of the business from a position of detachment. If carefully selected for their knowledge of competitive activity in an industry sector, the dynamics of the investment community, environmental impacts, the forces and motivations that drive pressure groups or merely for the breadth of their experience, they can provide a valuable sanity check for an organisation's risk profile.

- Does it contain the issues directors really lose sleep about?
- Is anything significant missing?
- Is it sufficiently outward looking?
- Does it take into account the requirements and expectations of the business's major stakeholder groups?
- Is the business reporting to its stakeholders on the issues that count?
- Have risks been fairly assessed in terms of their potential impact – both on the bottom line and on reputation?

- Will the actions planned be adequate in bringing risk exposures down to an acceptable level?
- Have opportunities been spotted and leveraged that will create competitive advantage and bolster reputation?

The benefits of such a sanity check are obvious. But are independent directors capable of performing this task? Do they have the understanding of the business, time and inclination to provide that much-needed constructive challenge? Recent corporate débâcles in the USA, Europe and elsewhere would suggest that often they do not. Charismatic and domineering chief executives can still dominate a boardroom and run rings round their fellow directors. On both sides of the Atlantic there are calls for the net to be cast more widely to put an end to the old boys' network – the 'self-perpetuating oligarchy'[3] – and attract independent directors from more diverse backgrounds who are prepared to rock the boat if necessary and will 'relish the opportunity to prick the ego of cocky chief executives . . . far too may still collect directorships like golf club memberships'.[4]

The UK government-sponsored Higgs review into the role and effectiveness of non-executive directors reinforced the need to broaden the gene pool. It showed that UK company non-executive directors are overwhelmingly white, male and middle aged, with only 1% from ethnic minorities, 7% of non-British origin and 6% female. The average age of non-executives in the FTSE 100 is 59.[5] Ultimately, as the Higgs report states, people – their behaviours and relationships – hold the key to board effectiveness. Raising the quality of appointees is critical to improving the effectiveness of non-executive directors.[6]

Integrity, independence of thought, the ability to remain dispassionate under pressure and willingness to speak out are vital prerequisites for an effective independent director:

> Board tables are often like fish-bowls, ringed by panoplies of senior managers, consultants and investment bankers. In this consensual environment, directors may ask thoughtful, probing questions. But there is a big difference between polite inquiry and challenging the prevailing viewpoint.
>
> (Cynthia Montgomery and Rhonda Kaufman, Harvard Business School[7])

The willingness to stand up and be counted and be prepared to resign on principle if concerns are not satisfactorily addressed should, perhaps, feature in the selection criteria for independent directors – that is, of course, if they actually undergo a selection process! According to a UK survey, four out of five non-executive directors are appointed without a formal selection procedure. The majority were offered their positions by a company's existing director or professional advisers. Almost a third admitted they secured the position from an executive director 'whom I knew' or 'who was given my name by someone else'.[8]

The UK's National Association of Pension Funds' guide[9] for independent directors enumerates eight key qualities the investment community expects of independent directors:

- A willingness to contribute to strategy and to challenge executives on strategy and other matters, as necessary
- A readiness to challenge the company's mergers and acquisitions policy
- An ability to contribute to financial and capitalisation issues
- Relevant experience for the needs of the company's business

- Independence of mind
- Individuals with sufficient time to devote to the needs of the business
- Integrity and a preparedness to resign over matters of principle, should that be necessary
- A willingness to learn and continue to learn, not only about the business and its market sectors but about the role of the independent director.

Independent directors who embody these qualities and utilise their objectivity and breadth of vision to provide independent constructive challenge, can play a pivotal role in focusing the business on the real issues – however unpalatable they may be.

As Edmund Truell, chairman of the British Venture Capital Association, has said on the role of independent directors:

> They should ensure that the company takes a strong ethical position in the market and in the way it conducts its business. In a sense non-executives should be the ultimate guardians of a company's reputation.[10]

BOARD COMMITTEES

Many organisations in both the private and public sectors have established a series of board committees to assist directors in the task of running and controlling the business. These commonly include audit, remuneration and nomination committees which are composed, either exclusively or in part, of independent directors to provide the objectivity required in these sensitive areas. Burgeoning interest in risk management and external social, ethical and environmental issues in recent years has led to the broadening of the traditional role of the audit committee in many businesses. In some, the audit committee's title has been changed to 'risk and audit committee' while in others, a separate 'risk committee' has been established, additional to the audit committee. In some businesses new committees have been formed with a specific focus on softer or external risks (such as BP's Ethics and Environment Assurance Committee and Kingfisher's Social Responsibility Committee).

In the wake of the US accounting scandals and the introduction of the Sarbanes–Oxley Act in the USA, there has been much debate across the globe on the role and composition of audit committees. Should external auditors be appointed by and be answerable to the audit committee, rather than the executive directors (usually the finance director)? Should audit committees consist exclusively of independent directors? Should there be a requirement for independent directors to meet alone with the external auditors, away from the pervasive influence of overbearing executive directors?

The correct response will depend on the circumstances of your own business and the specific jurisdiction in which it operates. However, as the demands on business from a broad range of stakeholders continue to escalate, the role of these board committees will clearly grow in importance, as these are the committees that, if appropriately constituted, can provide objective assurance that the major issues of concern to stakeholders are under control. Concerns hitting the headlines in recent times have included director remuneration, board appointments, ethics and integrity, relationships with external auditors, succession planning, whistleblowing, and social and environmental risks – the very issues that form the mainstay of many board committees' work.

Such committees have the potential to go further, by creating the right sort of climate for good corporate governance and risk management to thrive. As the UK government-sponsored Smith report on the work of the audit committee suggests:

> [It] should go beyond catching inappropriate reporting or inadequate auditing. Rather its work should be more pervasive and seek to build into the organisation a culture of compliance and fair reporting, an environment in which issues are openly discussed and resolved before they become matters of real concern.[11]

If the composition, remit and activities of these committees are clear and well communicated (via the organisation's website and/or annual report) they can also help to build the stakeholder trust that is central to a sustainable reputation. Such committees can also provide a reputational safety net, by intercepting and dealing with issues that could dent the business's standing.

THE MANAGEMENT CHALLENGE

What, then, is the role of management – those senior and middle managers on the receiving end of board diktats who marshal the organisation's operational assets and are responsible for managing risks on a day-to-day basis? It is management's role to identify and manage risk, to implement the board's policies on risk and control and to design, operate and monitor the control systems, making sure that they work as intended. They also play a part in promoting risk awareness so that their staff understand risks in their own specific business context and area of operation.

Management are also tasked with identifying key strategic and operational risks that could have a significant impact on the organisation's reputation or finances and bringing them to the attention of the board of directors. The most fertile areas for risks to reputation often lie at the interface with major stakeholder groups: the customer service department, procurement, investor relations, regulatory affairs and in the functional areas such as legal, human resources, safety, health and environment and IT. Management's role opposite reputation risk is therefore vital, as they manage the teams that interact directly with those stakeholders. Management face the dual challenge of first identifying those killer risks, then devising systems to manage and control them – where possible building in early-warning indicators that will flag a potential problem so that it can be resolved before it becomes a crisis.

EMPLOYEES

Of course, not only managers and directors, but all other employees should play a part in upholding a business's reputation. Everyone in an organisation bears some responsibility for the management of risk as part of their accountability for achieving their objectives. As the UK's Turnbull report succinctly puts it:

> They [all employees] collectively, should have the necessary knowledge, skills, information and authority to establish, operate and monitor the system of internal control. This will require an understanding of the company, its objectives, the industries and markets in which it operates, and the risks it faces.[12]

The behaviours, remarks, decisions and actions of individual employees can affect the organisation's standing in the eyes of its stakeholders. Raising risk awareness through training, role-play and case studies can help to communicate the message that everyone's contribution counts in sustaining business's reputation.

RISK MANAGERS

If your organisation is practising some form of risk management it may, dependent on its size, have a dedicated risk management department, a single individual or a part-time risk champion who acts as an enabler in setting risk policies, building a risk aware culture, establishing an appropriate management and reporting framework and overseeing the risk management process.

Dedicated risk management personnel can ensure that the process runs smoothly and that key risks are not inadvertently filtered out (perhaps because their impact cannot be precisely quantified), thereby potentially excluding some major risks to reputation.

INTERNAL AUDIT

In some organisations it is the internal audit team that fulfils an enabling role on risk management. Where this is the case, the business needs to satisfy itself that the involvement of internal audit in risk management does not undermine its independence, as independence is crucial to its ability to discharge its primary function: the provision of assurance on the process of managing risk and the effectiveness of the responses put in place to control individual risks.

The theme of internal audit providing 'assurance' on the management of risks to reputation will be explored in more depth in Chapter 8.

PUBLIC RELATIONS

Whatever you choose to call it – corporate affairs, corporate communications or public relations – any sizeable organisation usually employs an individual or group to manage its image and communications. A very large company may even split its corporate communications team into those responsible for investor relations, employee relations and others. Visit the website of any major corporate entity and you will often find its home page divided into areas of interest to specific stakeholder groups.

Your communications team will no doubt regard maintaining and enhancing the organisation's image and reputation as its primary goal. Yet public relations are often called in at the eleventh hour to handle the latest crisis to erupt – when in the majority of cases the warning signs have been staring management in the face for weeks, but were neither spotted nor seen as significant.

Getting your communications team directly involved in risk management can provide a useful additional perspective and invaluable professional input. Some of the advantages of including specialist communications personnel include:

- Establishing relevant and meaningful wording for the reputation line of your impact guide chart (see Chapter 4). What would a 'high' impact on reputation feel like? Would it involve coverage on international, national or just local media? How quickly would you recover from it (one day, one week, one month, one year)?
- Ensuring that the reputational impact of all key risks is considered. Some organisations involve communications personnel directly in risk workshops to ensure that the reputation angle is adequately taken into account.

BUSINESS PARTNERS

Reputational damage is not just caused by the actions or inactions of employees; it can equally result from the behaviour of business partners in the supply chain who fall short of the requirements and expectations of major stakeholders. The discovery of labour abuses and the use of child labour in manufacturing facilities run by Nike and Gap led to harmful headlines in the tabloids and broadsheets and to investigative television documentaries that probed deep into the companies' operations in far-flung overseas territories. If abusive use of child labour is found in the supply chain, it is the corporate entity's name that will be splashed across the headlines: the fact that the affected employees are not on its payroll but that of an unknown local supplier will not diminish its culpability in the eyes of the public.

Businesses are therefore increasingly looking to their key suppliers for reputation maintenance by insisting that they adhere to codes of conduct or undertakings on environmental emissions if the business relationship is to prosper. With few exceptions the 'when in Rome, do as the Romans do' principle no longer applies: stakeholders expect a business to behave in Rome, Jakarta or Bombay just as it would in Melbourne, London or Washington. If it cannot, it should disclose this and explain how it plans to move towards a more acceptable position.

WINNING HEARTS AND MINDS

Reputation risk management can be rewarding and exciting. It can be easier to engage people on reputational risks that often have a clear upside of opportunity than on dull-as-ditchwater downside threats like fraud and business continuity.

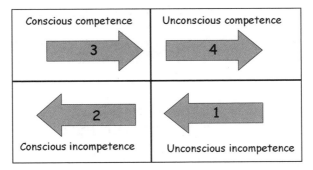

Figure 5-2   Reputation risk management: the unconscious competence.

The keys to success are enabling risk management through awareness raising, reinforcing risk management as a core value, making responsibility for reputation risk management integral to individuals' roles and recognising and rewarding good risk management practice. This could include:

- Supporting staff with tailored risk management training
- Including risk management in organisational value statements
- Integrating risk management accountabilities in individual role descriptions and objectives (ideally starting with the top team!)
- Linking good risk management to remuneration through the performance management system
- Recruiting risk-takers
- Management walking the talk.

Businesses are more likely to spot issues early and be able to take corrective action before a crisis erupts if everyone involved within or supplying the business:

- understands the business's values, strategic objectives and underpinning policies
- is alert to the major potential sources of risk in their specific business context
- knows where to turn for help and advice if in doubt on the course of action to take
- knows where to refer risks which are, or could escalate, outside their personal 'freedom to act' or departmental/business unit risk exposure limits
- contributes actively to a continuous flow of information on potential threats and opportunities to the business and its reputation.

A free flow of information is vital so that people throughout the organisation have the relevant information on which to make informed decisions and assessments of risk. Once everyone is playing their part, reputation risk management will become second nature, the unconscious competence (Figure 5-2).

Successful reputation risk management only occurs as a result of a total team effort, when executive and independent directors, managers, employees, risk, audit and PR professionals, and major business partners are pulling in the same direction under an over-arching set of values and policies that govern their every action.

When you have established your risk management framework and have recognised the importance of making reputation risk management everyone's business, the focus can shift to a more detailed examination of typical threats and opportunities to reputation and how to address them.

NOTES AND REFERENCES

1. Findings of McKinsey survey *Inside the Boardroom* based on discussions with 200 directors who collectively sit on some 500 US boards and 50 directors, governance experts and investors conducted during April–May 2002. Available from the McKinsey website www.mckinsey.com.
2. Independent directors should be entirely free of conflict of interest so they are able think and act objectively and impartially. Criteria for the 'independence' of directors are considered in the corporate governance section of Chapter 6.
3. The term used by Paul Myners, former head of Gartmore Investment Management and author of a UK government-sponsored report into institutional investment in the UK (*The Myners Report*) to describe non-executive directors.
4. Dan Roberts writing in the *Financial Times*, 19 August 2002.
5. Higgs, D. (January 2003) *Review of the Role and Effectiveness of Non-executive Directors*. London: The Stationery Office, p. 18. The report is available for download from the UK's Department of Trade and Industry website at www.dti.gov.uk/cld/non_exec_review.
6. Higgs, D. (January 2003) *Review of the Role and Effectiveness of Non-executive Directors*. London: The Stationery Office, p. 13. The report is available for download from the UK's Department of Trade and Industry website at www.dti.gov.uk/cld/non_exec_review.
7. Cynthia Montgomery and Rhonda Kaufman, Harvard Business School, writing in the *Financial Times*, 8 August 2002.
8. From a survey of 250 non-executive chairmen and directors serving on the boards of more than 800 quoted British companies carried out by headhunter Voices of Experience in 2002, reported in the *Sunday Times*, 8 September 2002.
9. From *Independent Directors – What Investors Expect: An NAPF guide for independent non-executive directors* (2002). London: NAPF, p. 3. The UK's National Association of Pension Funds (NAPF) represents circa 1000 pension schemes with collective assets of $600 billion. See the NAPF website at www.napf.co.uk. Reproduced by permission of NAPF Ltd.
10. Edmund Truell, chairman of the British Venture Capital Association writing in the *Financial Times*, 27 May 2002.
11. Smith, R. (January 2003) *Audit Committees Combined Code Guidance*. London: Financial Reporting Council, p. 23, para. 12. The full text of the Smith report is available for download from the Financial Reporting Council website at www.frc.org.uk/publications.
12. Turnbull report (1999) *Internal Control for Directors on the Combined Code*. London: ICAEW, para. 19.

six

managing threats and opportunities to reputation

INTRODUCTION

A number of potential sources of risks to reputation have been alluded to in the preceding chapters. Now it is time to take a more systematic look at reputation risk by examining in depth the seven drivers of reputation (Figure 6-1) identified in Chapter 1.

In discussing each of the seven drivers, external factors, such as the requirements and expectations of major stakeholder groups, will be explored as well as internal factors, such as the implications for an organisation's core purpose, values, policies, working practices and communications. First, however, it may be helpful to consider three generic points about managing risks to reputation which can permeate all seven areas: risks to your corporate legitimacy; risks to your uniqueness; and the impact of collateral damage.

safeguarding your legitimacy

The fall of Andersen is an excellent example of how risks that impact the very legitimacy of an organisation can have disastrous consequences. In May 2002, the Texas State Board of Public Accountancy filed a motion to revoke Andersen's licence to carry out audits in the state. The filing stated:

> Andersen's failure to comply with professional standards was not the result of the actions of one 'rogue' partner or 'out of control' office, but resulted from Andersen's organisational structure and corporate climate that created a lack of independence, integrity and objectivity[1]

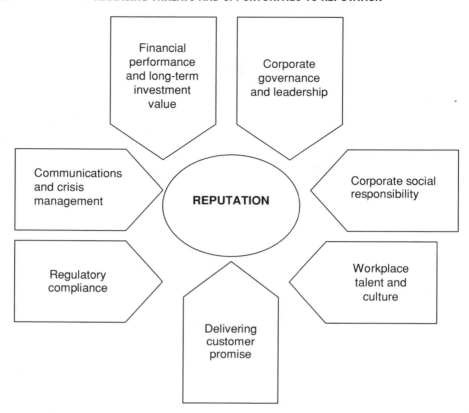

Figure 6-1   Drivers of reputation.

This damning indictment, whether founded on the whole truth or not, was the perception at the time. It was the basis for a series of swift actions which robbed Andersen almost overnight of their 'licence to operate'. The company founded by Arthur Andersen in 1913 had grown by 2001 to employ 85 000 people world-wide with annual revenues of $9.3 billion. By September 2002, less than a year after the initial rumblings at Enron, only 3000 staff remained: almost every country practice outside the USA had gone to a rival and the majority of the 26 000 US-based staff had exited piecemeal.[2] The discredited audit firm was found guilty of obstructing justice by shredding documents relating to audit client Enron as the investigators moved in. How could the downfall of one of the world's most respected companies be so precipitous? The answer is simple: its stakeholders simply lost confidence in its ability to perform its basic duties to the required standard. Andersen no longer had legitimacy. An auditor whose integrity is in question and who is seen to lack independence and objectivity simply cannot operate.

A key lesson from the sorry saga of Andersen is that when considering risks to reputation, you should begin by pinpointing the basis of your legitimacy. Identify those factors that (a) give you the right to do whatever you do as an organisation, and (b) underpin your licence to operate. Try to distil them into manageable chunks and encapsulate them in a single word or short phrase. Just a few key words will suffice.

For Andersen these might have been:

Independence – Integrity – Objectivity – Professionalism – Consistency

For a rail operator the key words might be:

Safety – Reliability – Efficiency

For a pharmaceutical company they could be:

Quality – Dependability – Safety – Integrity – Efficacy

These key words should sum up the very essence of what it takes to be an audit firm, a rail operator or a pharmaceutical manufacturer – leaving aside for a moment any special uniqueness or competitive edge. Once you have identified the key legitimacy elements for your business, consider including them in a corporate purpose statement or a set of corporate values so that all your employees, business partners and major stakeholders are clear that this is what you stand for, and that these things are sacrosanct and must be upheld. You may find that such terms already form part of your corporate mission and value statements. If so, you might like to sanity check them, with your new-found risk management mindset, to ensure that no critical component has been omitted.

These key pillars of your legitimacy should be at the back of your mind when you start to think about specific risks to reputation. Any risk that could undermine them could irreparably damage your reputation, erode stakeholder confidence and result in the loss of your licence to operate.

preserving your uniqueness

Moving beyond basic legitimacy issues, it is also illuminating to consider what makes your organisation unique. What are those attributes, unique to your business, that differentiate you from other providers of goods and services? A word of caution: this is not intended to be a wish list, but an accurate and objective statement of where you are currently, ideally substantiated by the results of customer research, employee surveys, vendor questionnaires and other forms of stakeholder feedback.

- What is your unique selling proposition (USP)? Why do consumers buy canned beans from you rather than AN Other? Why does a prospective client select your website development service when there are a hundred others to choose from?
- Why do young graduates choose to work for your business rather than the one based in a fancier part of town?

- What intellectual property, such as patents or licences, do you hold that your competitors would love to get their hands on?
- What knowledge do you have – market, technical or other – that gives you an edge in the market?
- Do you enjoy any special relationships with customers, suppliers, regulators or other stakeholders that makes it difficult to compete with you?

When the name Arthur Andersen changed to just Andersen in March 2001, the then chief executive, Joseph Berardino, said:

> There is extraordinary power in our name because it stands for time-tested values, a unique one-firm global operating approach and recognised superior performance.

Before Andersen's demise, their uniqueness attributes might have been considered to be:

Long-established name   –   Cohesive global approach   –   Solid track record
Extensive global client list   –   Superior performance   –   Clear values

A rail operator's might include:

Superior safety record   –   Superior punctuality   –   Excellent staff relations
Value for money

and for a pharmaceutical company:

Strong product brands   –   Trusted
Innovation excellence   –   Strong development pipeline
Speed of new products to market   –   Good relationship with regulators

Once you have listed those special attributes that make your organisation unique, keep them also at the back of your mind when thinking about specific risks to reputation. Threats that could adversely impact these unique attributes could knock you off the perch of market supremacy, shatter your reputation and turn your business into a has-been. Building on these unique attributes and introducing new ones could, on the other hand, help you to maintain or increase that competitive edge and sustain your reputation.

Indeed, if you are seeking new sources of competitive advantage, your pillars of legitimacy could be a good place to start. Opportunities to be the one who acts with the greatest integrity, the one with the best safety record, the one who can always be relied on, can be leveraged to differentiate you within your sector and enhance your reputation – while assuring your future licence to operate.

Note your pillars of legitimacy and uniqueness attributes in an aide-memoire (see Table 6-1) and refer to them, particularly when assessing the practical impact of threats and opportunities on your business. The impact could be greater than at first apparent if your pillars of legitimacy or uniqueness attributes are affected.

Finally there is a third consideration that may affect you through no direct fault of your own: collateral damage.

Table 6-1. Pillars of legitimacy and uniqueness attributes

	Pillars of legitimacy	Uniqueness attributes
The audit firm	• Independence • Integrity • Objectivity • Professionalism • Consistency	• Long-established name • Cohesive global approach • Solid track record • Global client list • Superior performance • Clear values
The rail operator	• Safety • Reliability • Efficiency	• Superior safety record • Superior punctuality • Excellent staff relations • Value for money
The pharmaceutical manufacturer	• Quality • Dependability • Safety • Integrity • Efficacy	• Strong product brands • Trusted • Innovation excellence • Strong development pipeline • Speed of new products to market • Good relationship with regulators

collateral damage

Fall out from the Andersen débâcle inflicted collateral reputational damage on the auditing profession globally. The remaining 'big four' players, PwC, KPMG, Deloitte and Ernst & Young, and some of their largest clients, found themselves under suspicion from a number of quarters.

> Tarnished by the collapse of international companies such as Enron, WorldCom, Global Crossing and Elan, the accounting profession is facing the kind of onslaught that it has never seen before. It stands accused of being in cahoots with management, of massaging audit figures in order to pick up lucrative consulting contracts and of operating in a four-partner cartel in auditing the books of the world's biggest companies.[3]

Aggressive questioning by investors and shareholder resolutions at company Annual General Meetings sought answers to why significantly higher amounts had been paid to the same firm for non-audit work than for audit work. Could auditors be truly independent if they were auditing areas where they had previously provided advice as consultants? Wasn't this a conflict of interest? Walt Disney was one of the companies affected:

> Stock owners submitted a shareholder resolution demanding that the company stop giving lucrative consulting contracts to its auditor, PricewaterhouseCoopers. With Enron Corp. still splashing regularly across the front pages, investors worried that the auditor was making five times as much consulting to the Magic Kingdom as it was from the audit. Could they skeptically review its books?[4]

Disney responded, long before its February 2002 annual meeting, by voluntarily separating auditing from consulting. Many other companies quickly followed suit. Anticipating a potential crisis, they decided not to wait for the deliberations of politicians and regulators, but moved swiftly to dispel any concerns by announcing that they would no longer use their external audit firm for non-audit related assignments. Companies including Disney, Bristol Myers Squibb, Apple Computer Inc. and Philips (the Dutch electronic firm) found that their rapid 'first mover' action had spin-off reputational benefits, with positive headlines appearing in the financial press. These announcements resulted in a frenzied 'shuffling of the pack' with the 'big four' losing non-audit work at some clients where there was potential for a conflict of interest, but gaining it at others. The cosmetic shuffling did not address the fundamental issue of there being only four global firms to choose from – but that highly-charged debate goes beyond the remit of this book.

What, then, are the lessons from this? Collateral damage clearly cannot always be avoided or its precise potential source anticipated. However, on the 'forewarned is forearmed' principle, you can safely assume that a collateral damage crisis will occur at some point and that it will be advisable to have a general contingency plan that can be tweaked to fit the specific circumstances. You may even wish to use scenario planning techniques to develop a series of more specific crisis response plans. The trick is to respond quickly and positively by bringing those uniqueness attributes to the fore, by reminding your stakeholders of what you stand for and what attributes differentiate you from the pack. There may even be the opportunity, if you move swiftly, to create a new reputation-enhancing differentiator, such as displaying decisiveness and integrity by voluntarily excluding your external auditor from non-audit work. The theme of boosting reputation through first mover advantage, by converting potential threats into opportunities, will be revisited later in the book.

Throughout this chapter, each of the seven major drivers of reputational risk will be linked to the major stakeholder groups most likely to be interested in it. As you read, you may wish to complete the reputation risk driver/stakeholder matrix (see Table 6-2) for your own organisation, to provide an initial indication of potential reputational 'hot spots'. You may wish to consider whether extending this basic list of stakeholders to include others with specific relevance to your business, such as analysts, insurers, lenders, trustees, trade unions, trade/industry associations, professional bodies or the media, might make the exercise even more valuable.

As each source of reputational risk is discussed, consider the stakeholders for whom this area is of interest. If they are key players, with both a high interest in the business and a strong influence on it (see Figure 4-6 in Chapter 4), hence a **strong** potential impact, mark the box with 'S' (or shade red); if they wield a considerable power but have little interest and could have a **moderate** impact, mark the box with 'M' (or shade amber); if they have high interest but little power, thus **limited** potential impact, mark with 'L' (or shade green). Leave the box blank if they have no discernible interest or power, and thus negligible potential impact on the business's reputation. Once completed, the chart will show at a glance your most critical stakeholders and those areas that could have the greatest impact on your reputation and on stakeholder confidence in your business.[5] These are the areas on which you should prioritise your quest for specific threats and opportunities, using the initial assessment you have made of stakeholder impact to help to gauge the potential consequences of the risk.

Table 6-2. Reputation risk driver/stakeholder matrix

	Financial performance and long-term investment value	Corporate governance and leadership	Regulatory compliance	Delivering customer promise	Workplace talent and culture	Corporate social responsibility	Communications and crisis management
Employees							
Customers							
Suppliers							
Communities							
Shareholders/ investors							
Regulators							
NGOs/ pressure groups							

Having set the scene, attention can now be turned to the first of the seven drivers of reputation: financial performance and long-term investment value.

FINANCIAL PERFORMANCE AND LONG-TERM INVESTMENT VALUE

Robust financial performance, profitability and being a safe investment, with the ability to create value going forward, is perhaps the most important driver of reputation in the private sector. In the public and not-for-profit sectors this translates to ability to balance the books, break even and utilise funds effectively.

Which stakeholder groups are most interested in financial performance?

- Institutional and private shareholders (including the growing number of employees involved in profit-sharing and share option schemes)
- Lenders and other backers
- Analysts and rating agencies
- Employees (both existing and prospective) who may need reassurance that their futures (and occupational pensions!) are safe
- Unions representing employees
- Suppliers
- Governments (for public sector bodies).

Some general requirements and expectations of stakeholders relating to a business's finances are shown in the Table 6.3.

Individual consumers, faced with considerable choice in the retail market, generally have little interest in the detail of a business's financial performance unless it goes under and fails to deliver an already paid-for item or there is some other direct impact on them personally. Businesses that are customers are likely to regard the accounts of their suppliers in a very different light. Financial problems resulting in failure to supply could disrupt production or provision of services resulting in loss of revenues and reputation for the customer. Accounts are likely to face particularly careful scrutiny if there is a single or dual source supply situation.

long-term shareholder value

In 2002, the UK-based fund manager Hermes – one of the largest fund managers in the UK with £40 billion of managed assets, including four of the top seven UK pension funds – published 'The Hermes Principles', a document setting out what shareholders expect of public companies and what companies should expect of their investors.[6]

Hermes states that 'a company's primary consideration should be the generation of long-term shareholder value, and this should be based on appropriate financial disciplines, competitive advantage and within a framework which is economically, ethically and socially responsible and sustainable'.

Table 6-3. Stakeholder requirements and expectations on financials

Stakeholder group	Requirements and expectations
Shareholders/Investors (Institutional and private)	• Solid financial track record • Clarity on value drivers and sources of future growth to generate long-term shareholder value
Analysts and rating agencies	• Transparency – policies and principles clear; no critical issues concealed
Lenders	• Reliable, relevant and timely information • Honest, accurate and consistent accounts – not 'earnings management' • Active management of major risks to an acceptable exposure level • Effective use of assets and minimisation of cost of capital • Investor expectations met • No frauds or other surprises!
Employees Unions	• Profitable going concern • Sustainable financial future so jobs safe • Security of pension fund
Suppliers	• Will stay in business and grow • Financial position allows continuing honouring of commitments
Community	• Will stay in business contributing to local economy and providing jobs
Governments (for pubic sector bodies)	• Strong budget management • No deficit • Effective use of funds
Customers	• Continue to trade and honour commitments (business clients and consumers) • Sustainable future (business clients)

Hermes' focus is on the generation of long-term shareholder value. Five of the ten Hermes Principles relate to financial issues (Table 6-4).

Companies that have fallen foul of their investors on financial issues bear the scars, both the impact on corporate reputation and on the management team, as executive heads can roll. Conversely, meeting stakeholder expectations and avoiding surprises can yield a number of benefits:

All other things being equal, a company where management has a reputation for 'no surprises' will enjoy the lowest sustainable cost of capital and the highest sustainable share price.[7]

Table 6-4. The Hermes Principles relating to financial issues (Reproduced by permission of Hermes Pensions Ltd)

Principle 2	Companies should have appropriate measures and systems in place to ensure that they know which activities and competencies contribute most to maximising shareholder value.
Principle 3	Companies should ensure all investment plans have been honestly and critically tested in terms of their ability to deliver long-term shareholder value.
Principle 4	Companies should allocate capital for investment by seeking fully and creatively to exploit opportunities for growth within their core businesses rather than seeking unrelated diversification. This is particularly true when considering acquisitive growth.
Principle 5	Companies should have performance evaluation and incentive systems designed cost-effectively to incentivise managers to deliver long- term shareholder value.
Principle 6	Companies should have an efficient capital structure which will minimise the long-term cost of capital.

honest and transparent accounts

Investors do not like to be misled by fraudulent or dishonest managers who are economical with the truth or bend it to their advantage. Investors were furious to learn that US telecommunications company WorldCom had boosted EBITDA and flouted accounting rules by booking $3.8 billion of operating expenses as capital expenditure. This allowed WorldCom to improve their results by spreading the bill over a number of years, rather than writing off ongoing costs as they occurred.[8] The massive fraud came to light during a routine internal audit only two months after Bernie Ebbers, WorldCom's chief executive, was forced to step down after awarding himself a $408 million personal loan from the company. The scandal prompted headlines such as 'The world after Worldcon'.[9] Further revelations of accounting irregularities increased the fraud at the company to a staggering £7.6 billion during a period of just over three years.[10] On 21 July 2002 WorldCom filed for bankruptcy in New York. This was the biggest ever Chapter 11 filing in US corporate history and marked 'an ignominious fall from grace for one of the tech boom's highest flying players'.[11]

Investors must have confidence in companies' financial statements. However, the proportion of companies restating their accounts has grown exponentially in recent years with about 10% of US public companies restating their accounts in the past six years. The percentage of US companies restating accounts was expected to have risen 170% by the end of 2002 compared to 1997.[12]

The fraud at WorldCom, the off-balance sheet shenanigans at Enron and accounting irregularities at Global Crossing, Adelphia Communications, Quest Communications, Dynergy and Xerox have caused investors and analysts to look much more closely at the books of other companies in the same sectors or with similar accounting structures. The accounts of firms involved in complex off-balance sheet special purpose entities or other forms of 'aggressive' or 'creative' accounting which could artificially inflate earnings, have been pored over by analysts, investors and audit firms. Collateral damage ensued in a number of cases: share prices and reputations fell when the companies were unable to pass muster.

UK-based tour operator MyTravel (previously known as Airtours) stunned investors and analysts in October 2002 by issuing a third profits warning in five months and scrapping its final dividend. Before the first profits warning in May, analysts were expecting pre-tax profits of around £150 million on a turnover of approaching £5 billion; by October the company stated that the outturn could be as low as £50 million. MyTravel's shares plunged over 62% on this latest announcement, bringing the total fall in share price to 90% since February 2002. The accounting 'irregularities' had come to light following the takeover of Andersen UK's activities by Deloitte & Touche and the abandonment of previous aggressive accounting policies. Concerns were raised about the way in which MyTravel dealt with insurance policies, discounts, promotional spending, valuation of its core assets (aircraft and cruise ships) and a host of other issues.

Outraged investors called for the scalps of David Crossland, the company's chairman and founder, and David Jardine, finance director (a former partner at Andersen, previously MyTravel's auditors). The head of chief executive, Tim Byrne, had already rolled by the time of the second profits warning.[13] As the adjusted figures related only to MyTravel's UK operations; there were fears that the worst could yet be to come when the outcome of the company's comprehensive review of its global commercial and financial activities was announced in November 2002. Investors and analysts were furious that they had been kept in the dark; at the time of the third profits warning not a single MyTravel executive was available for comment.

With investor confidence shaken to the core and the UK's Financial Services Authority regulator announcing an investigation into the way in which MyTravel had released information to the stock market, the group's future depended largely on the reaction of its customers. Financial performance is not automatically of concern to customers unless a company fails and they are directly affected. In MyTravel's case there were fears that travellers could be left stranded overseas or be prevented from travelling. Would MyTravel's customers desert the company in droves? Would they cancel existing bookings? Although MyTravel were at pains to reassure their customers that there was 'no cause for alarm whatsoever' and that all of the group's holidays were 'safe and secure',[14] the company's prospects were not helped by rival tour operators exploiting the adverse publicity by removing MyTravel holiday brochures from their shelves.

MyTravel's non-executives moved swiftly to try to limit the damage. They met privately in London in an attempt to block a compensation payment of £900 000 to ousted chief executive Tim Byrne[15] and to review the future position of founder and chairman David Crossland, whose remuneration had increased from over £0.6 to £1.04 million for the year to September 2001.[16] They also announced a five-week drive to produce proper accounts. Thanks to the prompt intervention of the non-executives and a number of board changes, by early 2003 it looked as if the company would survive – albeit with a tarnished reputation.

The warning signs of an impending crisis are often there, but are not acted upon. In February 2003, the revelation of significant accounting irregularities at Netherlands-based Ahold, the world's third largest food retailer, forced the resignation of the company's chief executive and finance director. The company announced that its earnings in 2001 and 2002 may have been overstated by more than 500 million euros, resulting from questionable accounting practices in its US and South American operations. The media were quick to point out that the alarm bells had been ringing for some time. The company had grown rapidly through some 50 acquisitions and had a double-digit target for earnings growth. Sales had doubled within three years, but long-term debt had almost tripled. In April 2002, a 36% rise in 2001 net earnings became an 85% drop in profits after generally accepted accounting principles were applied.[17] The US Securities and Exchange Commission launched an investigation into US Foodservice, Ahold's US subsidiary, where the bulk of the earnings had gone missing, and the Dutch securities regulator opened an inquiry into additional allegations of insider trading and failure to disclose market sensitive information. In the aftermath of the revelations, Ahold's shares crashed over 60% to just above 3 euros.[18]

In Europe and the USA there have been moves to require businesses to announce material changes in their outlook as early as possible and to tighten up on 'earnings management' and apparent adherence to basic accounting principles while deliberately misleading stakeholders. It is no longer sufficient merely to comply with accounting rules so that there is no technical breach; to restore confidence in the markets, investors also want companies to respect the spirit of the standards.

accountability and comparability

As a consequence of plummeting confidence in the accuracy and truthfulness of financial accounts, regulators have moved swiftly to make top executives directly accountable for the honesty and integrity of their financial statements. The Sarbanes–Oxley Act, effective on August 2002 in the USA, requires the chief executive and chief financial officer of US and overseas companies listed in the USA to make a sworn statement certifying the accuracy of their accounts.

The accounting scandals also gave fresh impetus to the drive for internationally recognised accounting and auditing standards. The quality of company accounts emerged as the most important factor influencing the decisions of institutional investors according to a mid-2002 global survey conducted by McKinsey[19] The same survey showed that 90% of respondents supported a single international accounting standard, although views differed on whether this should be GAAP (favoured by the USA and Latin America) or the new International Accounting Standard (favoured in Europe, Asia and Africa). Currently, the variety of accounting policies and principles used within and across national boundaries makes cross-company comparisons highly problematic.

the challenge ahead

So what can be done on financials to safeguard and even bolster reputation? Transparency, honesty, integrity and 'no surprises' are the bywords:

- Transparency of accounting policies and principles so that stakeholders, particularly investors and analysts, can have confidence in your historic and projected performance. Aim for consistent reporting that facilitates year-on-year comparisons. Opaque reporting and ever-changing accounting principles will arouse suspicion.

- Back this up by evidence of supporting internal standards, procedures and controls that are regularly reviewed and audited to ensure continuing compliance. Assure your stakeholders that you are complying fully, both in letter and in spirit. Tell them where you have gone beyond minimum compliance and are embracing best practice.

- Be honest and display integrity in your dealings with stakeholders so that bad news is communicated promptly; explain any problems and act quickly to correct them.

- Avoid surprising capital markets and stakeholders by managing risk well and by managing stakeholder expectations on volatility. Spell out your arrangements for managing and monitoring financial risk exposures and for avoiding fraud.

- Outline your value drivers and sources of future growth so that the markets have faith in your ability to provide investment value in the longer term.

Most organisations are likely to suffer some reputational damage if their financial prospects or track record is in question. However, if your organisation's pillars of legitimacy or uniqueness attributes are largely dependent on financial probity – perhaps because you are a bank or accountancy firm – the impact of a major financial crisis could be catastrophic for your reputation, and even terminal for your business.

To end this section on a more positive note, a consistent track record of solid financial performance, openness and transparency, observing both the spirit and the letter of accounting standards, can help to accumulate that critical store of reputational capital that can protect you from the occasional ill wind. Stakeholder belief that their 'investment'– whether in stock, loans, labour or supply/purchase agreements – in your business is safe and will continue to deliver, may make them less inclined to dissect performance in other areas of operation. However, once concerns about financial performance have been sparked, other aspects of your reputation are likely to be placed under scrutiny.

CORPORATE GOVERNANCE AND LEADERSHIP

Corporate Governance has been defined as: 'the system by which companies are directed and controlled'.[20] The Organisation for Economic Cooperation and Development expands on this by defining corporate governance as involving:

> ... a set of relationships between a company's management, its board, its shareholders and other stakeholders. Corporate governance also provides the structure through which the objectives of

the company are set, and the means of attaining those objectives and monitoring performance are determined. Good corporate governance should provide proper incentives for the board and management to pursue objectives that are in the interests of the company and shareholders and should facilitate effective monitoring, thereby encouraging firms to use resources more efficiently.[21]

It may be useful to think about the starting point for corporate governance as simply 'setting the tone from the top', for the principal duty of any board of directors is to lead and control their organisation. This is done by developing a clear vision, values, strategy and objectives, by articulating tolerance to risk, by building an appropriate organisational culture and by implementing policies, procedures and ways of working to set the business on track for success.

Given the importance of 'tone setting', the first step is naturally to ensure that the board itself is operating effectively and contains the right people, with the right balance of skills and experience. As Sir Robert Smith, chairman of the Weir Group and author of a UK government-sponsored report on the role of audit committees, has observed: 'My experience is that it doesn't matter how many rules you put in place. It is the people and the culture that matter.'[22]

The irony of the knee-jerk reactions to the 2001/2 corporate débâcles in the USA and elsewhere is that no amount of new rules and box-ticking will eliminate future disasters if directors do not act honestly and with integrity. If directors are hell-bent on inflating their own personal fortunes and images, just about any rule can be broken, manipulated or circumvented. Therefore, selecting the right executive and non-executive directors and putting in place suitable checks and balances to ensure that no one individual or clique can dominate board proceedings, is a vital prerequisite for good corporate governance – and a good reputation.

And once the top team is in place, their role in implementing a sound governance infrastructure and fostering the right climate – both at board level and throughout the business – is fundamental to effective risk management and the safeguarding of corporate reputation and stakeholder confidence.

Which stakeholders, therefore, are interested in governance issues? In the aftermath of recent corporate disasters, it is fair to say that no single stakeholder group has a monopoly interest in corporate governance. In fact, almost all have displayed heightened interest in governance and have acknowledged the importance of 'tone-setting' in ensuring that businesses are run not only to maximise shareholder value, but also to embrace the legitimate expectations of employees, customers and other stakeholders.

The previously cited McKinsey 2002 global investor study found that the vast majority of investors around the world are prepared to pay a premium for companies exhibiting high governance standards (Figure 6-2). Even more interesting was the revelation that investors believe corporate governance to be as important or more important than financial indicators when evaluating investment decisions (56–57% of respondents in North America and Western Europe and 82–85% in Asia, Latin America, Eastern Europe and Africa).[23]

Given the importance of good corporate governance to the overall standing of an organisation, no apologies will be made for devoting a hefty chunk of this chapter to the topic.

Corporate governance is at the heart of investment decisions

- Investors state that they still put corporate governance on a par with financial indicators when evaluating investment decisions.

- An overwhelming majority of investors are prepared to pay a premium for companies exhibiting high governance standards.

McKinsey Global Investor Opinion Survey 2002

Figure 6-2   The importance of corporate governance.

And what, then, do stakeholders require and expect of business under the corporate governance banner (Table 6-5)? There is an interesting convergence of interests here, with some specific additional expectations from individual groups.

Table 6-5. Stakeholder requirements and expectations on corporate governance

Stakeholder group	Requirements and expectations
Shareholders/Investors Analysts Rating agencies Lenders Regulators Government	• Compelling vision and strategy • Responsible, accountable and dynamic leadership • Balanced and effective board • Independent, challenging and proactive non-executive directors • Appropriate remuneration and incentives • Relevant and effective board committees • Comprehensive and cohesive risk management and internal control systems • Robust oversight and assurance • Full and transparent disclosure • Availability and responsiveness
Employees	• Compelling vision and strategy • Inspiring and responsible leadership • Concern for employee welfare as well as shareholder value
Suppliers	• Deliverable strategy that will keep the organisation in business
Communities	• Considers social and economic impact on local community
NGOs/Pressure groups	• Appropriate policies in place for social, ethical and environmental impacts: implemented and compliance monitored

So how can corporate governance impact reputation? What can go wrong? Can good corporate governance actually enhance reputation? What does best practice look like?

compelling vision and strategy

It is clear vision, strategy and objectives that provide the backcloth for an organisation's activities. If these are not well defined, are incoherent, opaque, poorly communicated, keep changing or simply fail to inspire confidence, the markets get nervous. It is no surprise to see 'the company's strategy' featuring top of the list of grounds for shareholder intervention in the ISC's statement of principles on shareholder activism.[24] Equally if a business's long-term strategy is not properly articulated, it should not be disappointed if it is judged only on short-term results.

In early 2001 UK telecommunications giant, BT, found itself under attack from investors as a result of frequently changing business strategy, falling profits and diminishing share price. Frustrated and furious investors demanded the scalps of Sir Iain Vallance and Sir Peter Bonfield, BT's chairman and chief executive, as a condition of supporting a £5.9 billion rights issue to shore up the company's finances. A leader in *The Guardian* encapsulated the dilemma faced by the beleaguered company:

not managing very well

The state of BT is sad and disturbing

Oh, how the mighty have fallen. British Telecom, once the global showpiece for privatisation, is now accused by its own investors of having lost its way. They want heads to roll, and roll they must if BT is to recover its self-confidence. Hardly anyone has a good word to say for the company these days. Its international strategy has failed: its balance sheet is reeling under the burden of £30 billion of debts . . . ; critics assail it for not rolling out high-speed 'broadband' access fast enough and customers for high charges. At the start of the new millennium, its shares were traded at over 1513p, yesterday they were 469p. . . . For all the excuses, this is a failure of management, and highly paid management too. BT is too important for the economy, let alone its shareholders, to be allowed to wither in power, esteem and sense of purpose. Unless they can change their spots overnight, it is time for those responsible for BT's demise to move over and let someone else have a go.[25]

And 'move over' they did. Within a month, Ian Vallance had stepped down as chairman. Sir Peter Bonfield announced his resignation six months later.

To satisfy employees, the vision and strategy must be not only coherent but also compelling and deliverable – setting out clear targets that are seen internally as realistic and achievable, albeit challenging. For a board's failure to motivate for success can result in a disenchanted and disillusioned workforce and damaging whispers, leaks and defections.

A vote of 'no confidence' in a business's strategy can lead to bitter battles played out not only within the confines of the boardroom, but increasingly in the public eye. These quarrels can become embarrassingly personal – focusing on the performance, track record, morals and lifestyle of top business executives.

responsible, accountable and dynamic leadership

Stakeholders want assurance that their stake in a business is in safe hands; they want to feel confident that the management is fully in control and can create value in a way that will not subsequently backfire and rebound on reputation; they want management to be held accountable if they fail or fall short of the mark. Enron and other corporate débâcles have severely dented confidence and eroded trust in business. Recent scandals have also illustrated the importance of the tone set by key individuals: the chief executive, chief financial officer and board members. As a result, the personal ethics and leadership style of top management have come under intense scrutiny.

US President George Bush stressed the importance of corporate executives setting the right tone in his speech in July 2002 in response to the spate of corporate scandals:

> Our leaders of business must set high and clear expectations of conduct, demonstrated by their own conduct. Responsible business leaders do not jump ship during hard times. Responsible leaders do not collect huge bonus packages when the value of their company dramatically declines. Responsible leaders do not take home tens of millions of dollars in compensation as their companies prepare to file for bankruptcy devastating the holdings of their investors. Everyone in a company should live up to high standards. But the burden of leadership rightly belongs to the chief executive officer. CEOs set the ethical direction for their companies. They set a moral tone by the decisions they make, the respect they show their employees, and the willingness to be held accountable for their actions. They set a moral tone by showing their disapproval to other executives who bring discredit to the business world.
>
> (President George W. Bush, 9 July 2002)

It is said that at WorldCom no one was prepared to question the tough talking and bullying chief executive, Bernie Ebbers, 'an intimidating figure' who 'liked to get in "one-on-one" confrontations with his staff, which often ended in humiliation for them'.[26] Those in his coveted inner circle, such as the now disgraced former chief financial officer Scott Sullivan, were apparently the only ones spared his vitriol.

Similarly oppressive and dictatorial regimes were presided over by Kenneth Lay at Enron and Dennis Kozlowski at Tyco. The vast majority of employees were unlikely to take a stand against such tyrannical overlords; these leaders dominated their boards, often preventing directors from playing the vital oversight role required for a healthy system of corporate governance:

> . . . it is no surprise that, as the background and detail unfolds, the biggest corporate collapses on the American scene have been characterised by bullying behaviour from chief executives.[27]

That is not to say that charismatic, decisive and powerful leaders are necessarily a source of evil. That would be grossly misleading. The ability to create a compelling vision that inspires and motivates employees and to drive it through to reality is a prime function of the chief executive. A colourful character who commands respect is much more likely to deliver this and to embody the entrepreneurial and risk-taking spirit required to succeed in business. After all, even benevolent dictatorships have *some* merits! However, a distinction must be made between autocratic and dynamic leadership. As John Argenti observes:

> An overbearing leader is frequently a prime trigger of corporate failure. Not because powerful personalities are anathema to success, but because strategic decisions become disproportionately risky when the decision maker's eyes or ears are closed. It is important to distinguish between an autocrat and a dynamic leader. The autocrat *is* the company. He does not listen to others and he does not share authority. Signs of this may be the merging of executive roles, the rise of passive directors and skewed skills at board level. As team input diminishes, the weaknesses of the individual at the top become the weaknesses of the entire company.[28]

Research has shown that the personal reputation of the CEO is a key contributor to corporate reputation. The 2002 Corporate Reputation Watch survey[29] found that 42% of US executives believed unethical behaviour most imperils corporate reputation and 80% that CEO reputation strongly influences it. A US poll in July 2002 found that an overwhelming 73% of respondents felt that CEOs of large corporates could not be trusted (the comparative figure for car dealers came worryingly close at 81%!) with 79% of those polled believing that the practice of top executives taking 'improper actions to help themselves at the expense of the corporation' was 'very or somewhat widespread'.[30] The unethical behaviour of a chief executive can be catastrophic for corporate reputation – as the recent US scandals have demonstrated.

The US Conference Board's Commission on Public Trust and Private Enterprise – established to address the abuses leading to corporate scandals, declining public trust in companies, their leaders and US capital markets – recommends that boards should be responsible for overseeing ethical behaviour in and by the corporation. It argues that 'ethical standards and the skills required to foster ethical practice throughout the organisation' should be among the selection criteria for the CEO and other senior positions.[31]

Stakeholders now attempt to get behind the rhetoric of the PR spin-doctors to spot the early signs of boardroom tyranny or dissent; they endeavour to detect symptoms of non-alignment elsewhere in an organisation. Is there a mismatch between avowed corporate values and the actual behaviour of individual board members? Are directors walking the talk? Do directors have any conflicts of interest? Have the strategy and targets disseminated by directors actually been communicated to employees further down the line? Have the rank and file been involved in the master plan or do they see it as an unattainable, ivory-tower generated wish-list? Have steps been taken to deliver it? Are interim milestones in place? Are middle managers exiting in droves because they see the ship heading for an iceberg? Once stakeholders have spotted that chink in your armour, they are unlikely to let go until their concerns have been addressed.

balanced and effective board

Achieving an appropriate balance of skills, experience and personalities on a board is one of the most effective ways of controlling risks to reputation. There must first, however, be recognition of the constituencies that the board is there to serve so that they can be adequately represented.

Few today would embrace the concept of directors being in place to serve shareholders and shareholders alone. Although, the primary duty of directors is to satisfy the shareholders, they should also take into account the requirements and expectations of other major stakeholders – customers, employees, suppliers, etc. – on whom the future success of the business depends as well as impacts on the environment and on society. There is also growing pressure for boards to ensure that management act in the best *long-term* interests of the shareholders and major stakeholders; overemphasis by boards on short-term results was a key contributory factor to the US corporate scandals.

The Conference Board has argued that:

> The ultimate responsibility for good corporate governance rests with the board of directors. Only a strong, diligent and independent board of directors that understands the key issues, provides wise counsel and asks management the tough questions is capable of ensuring that the interests of shareowners as well as other constituencies are being properly served.[32]

To be 'properly served', those 'other constituencies' need first to be understood. When UK retailer Marks & Spencer reached its nadir in 2001 with customers deserting it in favour of more stylish, better value clothing elsewhere on the high street, a rival retailer observed:

> What M&S needs is someone who understand the clothing market inside out. . . . They don't have that at the top, and they have lost a lot of people further down the organisation who could do it.[33]

In this era of intense stakeholder scrutiny, businesses would be well advised to ensure that their boardrooms represent the customers they serve and the other major groups they impact. They should deliberately set out to achieve the right blend of skills and experience, the right gender and ethnic mix blend, and the right combination of personalities among their executive and non-executive directors to optimise board performance.

This involves selecting non-executive directors with the breadth and depth of skills required to oversee the business and take a dispassionate overview of the many demands upon it. Too many boards are composed of virtual clones: usually male, white, about-to-retire or just-retired former business executives. The entire UK FTSE 100 in January 2003 boasted fewer than 20 non-executives under the age of 45, only 1% from ethnic minorities, 6% women and 7% of non-British origin.[34]

Importing new talent – perhaps from outside the world of business, from the public or voluntary sector, or from academia and consultancies – could bring a fresh perspective to the boardroom, first-hand experience of the business's key constituencies and a more critical appraisal of the threats and opportunities facing it. The now-defunct UK company Railtrack, responsible for operating the UK's rail infrastructure, was the target of public outrage after a spate of fatal accidents, caused in part by shoddy maintenance. The revelation that, at the time, Railtrack did not have a qualified engineer on their board, further tarnished their image.

The process used to select non-executives is also of vital importance. Informally trawling the list of business partners, golf club cronies and tame distant relatives will not satisfy stringent independence or diversity tests. A formal, professional and transparent recruitment process, with due regard to the skills, experience and constituency gaps the business needs to plug, is more likely to win stakeholder approval and build trust. Moving away from the 'pale, frail, stale male' syndrome in the selection of non-executives and decisively ending the cronyism and clubbiness that have ill-served boards in the USA and elsewhere in recent years could prove an unexpected source of competitive advantage.

However, the focus for investors and other stakeholders is not just board diversity and the skills and experience mix, but also the balance of power and respective roles and responsibilities of the directors; stakeholders want to understand the dynamics of the boardroom. Does one individual or coterie predominate? Are the non-executives prepared to challenge their fellow executive directors?

One vexed issue is that of the separation of the roles of chairman and chief executive. Regarded as good practice in the UK for over a decade and now also advocated by the US Conference Board,[35] it is still the norm for US companies to combine the roles. It has been argued that combining the roles presents a structural block to the independent oversight of management and can undermine confidence in the business's framework of checks and balances by potentially concentrating unbridled power in the hands of one individual. That is, of course, unless that individual is truly exceptional and can fulfil two disparate functions! As Robert Monks, the renowned US shareholder activist, has observed: 'The only way you can have a good joint chairman and CEO is to have a perfectly schizophrenic person.'

Board processes should also include a robust framework for succession planning so that stakeholders can be confident that business can continue as normal, even if one or more key figures dies, has a long-term illness or resigns. Ideally succession planning should be the responsibility of an independent chairman. A common corollary of domineering and autocratic leadership is lack of proper focus on succession issues. As the CEO is patently invincible, why waste precious boardroom time discussing who should be groomed as successor? A characteristic of many recent corporate débâcles has been a gaping hole when the CEO/chairman has been ousted. In some cases where the roles of chairman and CEO are separate, the chairman – often the founder and former CEO of the company – has moved back into the top executive role. When UK travel operator MyTours chief executive Tim Byrne was forced to step down in October 2002, David Crossland, the talismanic chairman and founder, moved back as CEO until a successor could be appointed.

independent, challenging and proactive non-executives

What, besides the drawing of fees and the drinking of tea were the duties of a director?

They were all so honourable that they dared not scrutinise each other, or even their own collective policy. Worse than their dread of mistake or fraud was their dread of seeming to distrust each other.
(Musings by Soames Forsyte on the role of directors in the 1920s from *White Monkey*, the fourth book in John Galsworthy's *The Forsyte Saga*.)

Have things changed in the last century? Perhaps not in some boardrooms. But change is now inescapable as the role of non-executives is seen to be pivotal for effective corporate governance.

As the UK's Higgs report on the role of non-executive directors states unequivocally: 'Non-executives are the custodians of the governance process.'[36]

However, to make a significant and positive contribution to good corporate governance and to act as an effective counterweight to a dominant CEO, it is now recognised that non-executives should fulfil certain criteria. They should Ideally be independent and able to discharge their role effectively.

☐ INDEPENDENCE

Your business should aim to avoid complacency and the exchanging of polite banter in the boardroom; it should ensure that it has the type of directors who are prepared to get tough by proactively querying strategy and challenging the risk profile when necessary. There is growing pressure for boards to include a majority of independent directors.[37] A McKinsey survey in the USA showed that directors consider that 'more than a quarter of their "independent" colleagues are not truly independent', so there appears to be scope for improvement.[38] But what does real independence actually mean?

The Higgs report provides a useful definition:

> A non-executive is considered independent when the board determines that the director is independent and there are no relationships which could affect, or appear to affect, the director's judgement.[39]

The factors listed in Table 6-6 show where independence can be diluted.

Table 6-6. Factors influencing the independence of non-executive directors

- Employment with the company in the past five years
- Having a material business relationship in the past three years either directly or as a partner, shareholder, senior employee of a body that has such a relationship
- Family ties with any of the company's advisers, directors or senior employees
- Receiving additional remuneration apart from a director's fee
- Participating in the company's share option, performance related pay or pension scheme
- Holding cross-directorships or having significant links with other directors through involvement in other companies or bodies
- Representing a significant shareholder
- Serving on the board for more than ten years

Adapted from the Higgs report.[40]

Directors need to be squeaky clean and should avoid any whiff of conflict of interest. At the end of 2002 at least 20 US chief executives or chairmen still sat on each other's boards[41] although pressure to avoid conflict of interests and 'boardroom backscratching' was mounting. Apple Computer chief executive Steve Jobs resigned in October 2002 from his non-executive role on the Gap board, a position he had held since autumn 1999. Just four months previously, in May 1999, he had welcomed Millard 'Mickey' Drexler, then chief executive of Gap, onto the Apple board. Similarly, Citigroup chief Sandy Weill stepped down from the AT&T board, ending a four-year interlock with former chief executive Michael Armstrong who is a Citigroup director.[42] In continental Europe, interlocking shareholdings and directorships are even more prevalent than in the USA; in France and Germany there is a tradition of banks and finance company relationships being cemented with personal representation on the board.

The relevant benchmark in your own jurisdiction may differ from the new UK guidelines on independence, but it will be worth checking the details and seeing how your own non-executives compare. Recent history shows that when things start to go awry in a business, one of the first questions investors ask is 'who are the non-executives and how did they allow this to happen?' Headlines such as 'part-timers who let Cable & Wireless waste £22 billion'[43] become the norm.

The Higgs review also recommends that the chairman be independent at the time of appointment. As this would preclude former chief executives from stepping up to the role of chairman, it has met with stiff opposition. To provide oversight of management on behalf of stakeholders the board needs to be able to review the business from a truly independent and objective standpoint. To reinforce this, new corporate governance guidelines recommend that independent directors should sometimes meet in private, without the presence of the executive directors, to ensure that they are not unduly influenced by the chief executive and his acolytes.[44]

> Their job is not to nod in approval but to hold executives to account on shareholders' behalf. In private, they can better remind themselves of this and gird themselves up to keep the boss in place.[45]

☐   DISCHARGE ROLE EFFECTIVELY

Non-executives should be clear on the precise role they are expected to play and should have adequate time to carry it out to the best of their ability. The Higgs review helpfully defines the role of the non-executive director (Table 6-7) under four headings: strategy, performance, risk and people.

Higgs recommends that no individual should chair more than one major company and that full-time executives should accept no more than one non-executive role. Although no limit is set on the number of non-executive posts held by an individual, Higgs argues that it is the responsibility of that individual to ensure that sufficient time is available to fulfil his or her duties. It would be prudent for organisations to check, as part of their formal recruitment process, which other directorships a candidate already holds and whether the candidate potentially has the capacity for an additional role.

Table 6-7. Role of the non-executive director

Strategy	Constructively challenge and contribute to the development of strategy
Performance	Scrutinise the performance of management in meeting agreed goals and objectives and monitor the reporting of performance
Risk	Satisfy themselves that financial information is accurate and that financial controls and systems of risk management are robust and defensible
People	Be responsible for determining appropriate levels of remuneration of executive directors and have a prime role in appointing, and where necessary removing, senior management and in succession planning.[46]

Non-executive directors are only as good as the information given to them; if that information is inadequate, inaccurate, incomplete, late or downright misleading they cannot fulfil the role expected of them. Non-executives cannot know if the chief executive is withholding something significant; they are heavily dependent on the chief executive, company secretary and auditors to provide them with adequate information and to identify problems areas to enable them to act.

As Edward Lawler and Jay Conger have observed:

> Corporate boards are like fire departments. When the alarm bell sounds, they respond to put out the fire. If no alarm sounds, they rarely move into action. Unfortunately, by the time the alarm sounds the fire may be out of control, so that little can be done.[47]

Ensuring, usually via the chairman, supported by the company secretary, that non-executives have the data and knowledge they need to make an effective contribution and sound judgements, and that new appointees are quickly brought up to speed through a tailored induction programme,[48] will help your business to derive the maximum benefit from your investment in non-executives.

Well-informed and experienced non-executives can also potentially play a key role in helping management to decide what is material and should be reported on – both internally and externally – to build and maintain stakeholder trust. If any nasty surprises emerge when non-executives' personal details, track record and business relationships are pored over by the media, the reputation of not only the individual, but the business that hired them, can be in tatters. If this happens, and the business has not done its homework properly in screening non-executives thoroughly before appointing them, it only has itself to blame. So, do your non-executives pass muster? You may regret not finding out.

appropriate remuneration and incentives

In September 2002 Bill McDonough, president of the New York Federal Reserve, suggested that recent US executive pay increases were morally reprehensible. He cited studies showing that the average chief executive made 400 times as much as the average production worker, compared with a ratio of 42 : 1 just two decades ago.[49] Paying all executives 'top dollar' so that their package falls into the top quartile, irrespective of performance, is a highly questionable practice. Indeed the argument that remuneration is a key factor in determining whether the most sought after executives choose to join a organisation is somewhat specious; large international companies with a good reputation rarely have difficulty in attracting top talent, although remuneration may be a hurdle for smaller companies and public/not-for-profit organisations, trying to lure the best candidates from the private sector.

This widening gulf between executive and worker pay, combined with the so-called 'rewards for failure' (where, according to *Fortune* magazine, since 1999 executives in 25 companies whose stock price declined 75% or more from their peak in the period January 1999 through May 2002 'walked away' with $23 billion[50]), have resulted in a much reduced tolerance from investors, employees, unions and the general public to excessive executive remuneration packages – particularly against a backcloth of economic downturn, job losses, pension fund failures and sliding share values. CEOs even benefited personally when their companies were in the throes of collapse: Enron paid its top executives $53 million in previously deferred compensation – one of its many tax avoidance ruses – in the weeks just prior to its declaration of bankruptcy.[51]

There is a growing clamour for businesses to link the remuneration of their directors and management to the company's performance and value in the long term. The use of stock options (particularly fixed price options) and other equity-based incentives have resulted in 'an enormous incentive to manage companies for short-term stock price gains'.[52] Executive compensation had become 'too de-linked from the achievement of management's long-term performance goals'.[53] Not only were executives' compensation packages in many cases excessive, but their design entailed little downside financial risk; executives simply couldn't lose.

Emerging best practice guidance recommends that key executives and executive directors should be encouraged to hold a significant amount of a company's stock on a long-term basis to encourage them to act in the business's long-term interests. The length of contracts should be capped at 12 months to guard against excessive rewards for failure if executives resign or are forced to step down. However, recommendations on compensation for non-executives differ. In the USA, guidance from the Conference Board accepts that stock options can be an acceptable way of rewarding non-executive directors. The UK's Higgs report agrees that non-executives should have the opportunity to take part of their remuneration in shares, but argues that they should hold options over shares in their company only on an exceptional basis and with prior shareholder approval. Individual non-executives should never be in a position of overdependence on remuneration, which could compromise their independence. Higgs argues that they should be paid on the basis of what they actually contribute, comprising an annual fee, a meeting attendance fee and an additional fee for the chairmanship of committees.

There have been many examples of investors challenging and sometimes overturning proposed executive pay packages. A headline in the *Financial Times* in February 2003, 'GE and Coke bow to pressure on executive pay', reported General Electric's and Coca-Cola's agreement to phase out certain generous salary and pension benefits for top executives after pressure was brought to bear by investors. In the case of GE this was a salary scheme for the five best paid executives, which allowed them to defer annual salary and receive an above-market interest rate. For Coke it was a Key Executive Retirement Plan which offered additional pension benefits on top of the regular company retirement plan to only three executives, including the CEO.[54]

A particularly damaging public debate on executive remuneration was sparked by Glaxo SmithKline, the world's second largest pharmaceutical company, in November 2002. The company caused furore when it announced a controversial pay package for its chief executive, Jean-Pierre Garnier, which would double his shares and options, raising his remuneration to $27 million. Mr Garnier was already the third highest paid executive in the FTSE 100 at a time when GSK's performance was at best lacklustre, with a falling share price and concerns about the company's pipeline of new drugs and the success of the merger between Glaxo and SmithKline two years previously. Institutional investors were incensed that GSK attempted to justify the changes by claiming GSK needed to be in line with their pay peer group – US drugs companies such as Pfizer and Merck – without any link to increased performance hurdles. One of GSK's top shareholders commented that Mr Garnier was simply getting more shares for hitting the same targets. 'Do they really think if they paid him twice as much he would perform twice as well?'[55] Shareholder pressure finally forced GSK into an embarrassing climb-down and the company withdrew its plans. In spring 2003 GSK hit the headlines again, this time over the terms of Jean-Pierre Garnier's severance package, which would have enabled him to walk away with an estimated £22 million if he lost his job. At GSK's May AGM, a majority of shareholders voted against the company's executive pay policy. This humiliating defeat, the first in UK corporate history, marks a watershed in investor activism on remuneration.

There is a growing trend towards consulting major investors over proposed new executive remuneration deals in a bid to win their approval. After all:

> Directors who vote to reward themselves without shareholders first approving their remuneration policy are taking assets without the owner's approval – also known as theft.
> (Alastair Ross Goobey, chairman of Hermes Focus Funds[56])

UK-based mobile operator Vodafone faced damaging shareholder revolts and adverse media coverage for two years over controversial pay issues. It responded in 2002 by launching a special review of its remuneration policies, led by its chairman and the non-executive chair of its remuneration committee. Vodafone's top 20 shareholders were asked for their views on the ideal components of a remuneration package. This included such issues as performance and peer group benchmarks and the balance between basic pay, annual bonuses and long-term share options. Consultations on the resulting draft plan were then broadened beyond the initial top 20 shareholders. The final plan included biasing Vodafone's peergroup towards European companies. Although the end result still attracted criticism from some investors,[57] the process was hailed by some as a model approach to developing an executive pay package.

Stakeholders now expect total director remuneration, including stock options and performance assessment criteria, to be fully transparent so they can judge for themselves whether the performance of directors supposedly representing their interests and safeguarding their investment are doing a good job and merit their reward. In the USA and Europe there is now pressure for stock options to be expensed so that they are visible in the profit and loss account.

In the UK a Guardian–Incubon survey showed that top executive pay rose by 17% in 2001, six times higher than the national average during a period when the FTSE 100 shares index lost a third of its value.[58] Outrage about 'fat cat' salaries, 'golden hellos' and 'golden goodbyes' (excessive recruitment and termination packages) has led to new legislation in the UK, effective from 2003, requiring listed companies to provide a detailed report on directors' remuneration, explaining the links to performance.[59] The report is then put to a separate shareholder vote at the company's Annual General Meeting. While the vote is only advisory, a board facing investor opprobrium would be foolish to ignore it, as GSK has discovered.

Spring 2003 saw an unprecedented onslaught by institutional investors on excessive board-room pay and rewards for failure at UK company annual general meetings. This was fuelled partly by the new legislation – and also by the institutions' concern that if they didn't put their own house in order by challenging companies that are not acting in the interests of shareholders, they may themselves be legislated against. In the USA, too, influential investor Warren Buffett, 'the sage of Omaha', in May 2003 told shareholders of the company he chairs, Berkshire Hathaway, that there had been more misdirected compensation in corporate America in the past five years than in the previous century. He said that as the owners of companies, shareholders had to 'provide some countervailing force or you will have what we had in the last 20 years – that is, an enormous disparity in the rates of compensation between people at the top and people at the bottom, and a disconnect between people at the top and the share owners.' Hardening attitudes to excessive remuneration were summed up by a *Fortune* magazine cover in April 2003, depicting a pin-striped, cuff-linked pig and the words: 'Oink! CEO pay in the US is still out of control.'

relevant and effective board committees

The US corporate débâcles have also focused attention on the structure and function of any board committees set up to assist the board in fulfilling its responsibilities. Typically businesses have remuneration (or compensation) committees, audit or audit and risk committees and nom-ination committees. Such committees report to the board, which bears ultimate responsibility for performance, assurance and disclosure. Stakeholders interested in corporate governance are now seeking to peel back the veneer to establish which committees exist, who sits on them and what they actually do.

Does the business have the right committees in place to support what it is trying to achieve? It may be helpful to take a step back and view your board committee structure dispassionately. Do your board committees merely reflect what you have always done and the norm in your sector, or are they actually helping the board to run and monitor the business? If your biggest risks are around environmental issues or social impacts on local communities, are these being effectively addressed by existing structures? Do you have the right directorial expertise to debate the issues, understand stakeholder views and approve the forward strategic path? If not, setting up a specialist board committee and resourcing it accordingly could be beneficial.

Rob Lake, head of SRI Engagement and Corporate Governance at Henderson Global In-vestors, has argued that even strengthening the role of independent directors does not go far enough to address the host of social responsibility and ethical issues facing companies today.

Boards that fail to address effectively the particular challenges in this arena facing their business may cost the company and its investors dear through direct factors such as increased costs or damage to vital assets such as reputation.

Lake argues that having the right structure in place, such as specialist board committees on the environment or CSR (corporate social responsibility) can help to provide a focus for these issues and is good practice – although only a handful of companies currently do this.

> Setting up a committee does not solve a problem, but at least it provides a guarantee that it will be discussed. Putting people on the committee with expertise, energy and outside perspectives will help still further.[60]

Furthermore, setting up such a committee will demonstrate to the outside world that the business is getting serious about these tricky and challenging issues. Examples of such board committees include Ford Motor Company's Environment and Public Policy Committee (headed by Ford's chairman), Merck's Committee on Public Policy and Social Responsibility, Rio Tinto's Committee on Social and Environmental Accountability, Coca-Cola's Public Issues Review and Diversity Committee, McDonald's Corporate Responsibility Committee and BP's Ethics and Environment Assurance Committee. When you have decided which board committees provide the best fit for your business, you should ensure that their composition, remit and responsibilities are in line with best practice guidelines.[61]

The following joke was reportedly doing the rounds at an international audit conference in Hong Kong in November 2002[62]:

Question: What's the difference between an auditor and a supermarket trolley?
Answer: A shopping trolley has a mind of its own.

The supervision of both internal and external auditors by an independent audit committee is now seen as key to investor confidence. There are demands that audit committees be composed entirely of independent non-executive directors, or at least a majority, who would select the external auditor and oversee its terms of engagement, thus ensuring that conflicts of interest are avoided. The audit committee should also monitor and review the effectiveness of the company's internal audit function. It should review the business's systems for identifying, assessing and controlling financial and non-financial risks (unless this responsibility has been delegated to another board committee – perhaps a dedicated risk committee). Only in this way can the audit committee underpin the assurance that boards provide to shareholders and other stakeholders on the integrity of the business's audit and internal control processes.

Compensation committees have also been under attack for abdicating their responsibilities. All too often they have failed to ensure that executive remuneration policy is determined completely independently from management. They have been swayed by compensation consultants, hired by management, who have talked up packages into the top quartile of the pay league to make them 'competitive'. Ensuring that remuneration committees are composed of only fully independent directors, thus curbing the excesses of executive directors bent on feathering their own nests, is now seen as highly desirable.

Nomination committees, which lead the process for board appointments, should also ideally consist of a majority of independent non-executive directors, to ensure that they are not unduly influenced by management. It is their responsibility to evaluate the balance of skills, knowledge and experience on the board and recommend changes to it. Succession planning fits naturally within the remit of such a committee.

comprehensive and cohesive risk management and internal control systems

Investors and other stakeholders expect organisations to have a good grasp of their risks – both threats and opportunities – and to have systems in place to control them effectively. Such systems should not just focus on traditional financial and IT risks but should include social, ethical and environmental risks, relationship risks and other risks to reputation.

Does the board have clear strategies for dealing with the significant risks facing the business? Is there evidence of an all-embracing risk management system which doesn't just identify risks but actively manages them in line with the business's risk appetite? Are policies in place to support the business's approach to risk and control? Do these policies guide behaviours and decision-making throughout the organisation?

Well-informed directors whose risk management processes enable them to anticipate reputational 'hot spots' and prepare accordingly, are more likely to emerge unscathed from maulings by analysts, investors and pressure groups.

robust oversight and assurance

A crucial function of the board is to provide oversight of management on behalf of shareholders and other stakeholders and to assure them that the business is well controlled. This requires a critical appraisal of the assurances provided by management and those emanating from internal monitoring and reporting systems, in addition to the independent assurance provided by internal and external auditors. The quality of this appraisal, the ability to 'drill down' where necessary, not take things at face value and ask tough questions, is of fundamental importance if directors are to assure themselves that things are under control. Only then can the board put its name with confidence to external disclosure statements that can relied upon by stakeholders.

This oversight role is often delegated to the specialist board committees discussed above – audit, risk, remuneration, ethics, etc. – although the board retains overall responsibility.

It will stand you in good stead to be transparent about who conducts your audit work and to explain any other interests they may have.

- Are external auditors truly independent of the business? Do they provide any other services that could colour their judgement and influence their objectivity? What percentage of their fees is spent on audit and non-audit work?
- Is your internal audit work done by an in-house team or is it conducted, wholly or in part, by an external firm, perhaps one of the Big Four? Does internal audit review *all* major risks, not just financial and systems risks but those relating to social, ethical, environmental and ethical issues and reputation? Do audits cover risks relating to board activities?

Stakeholders are particularly interested in the workings of the boardroom itself. What evidence is there that the board is performing well in providing guidance and oversight for the business? New governance guidelines recommend that boards formally evaluate their own performance. The US Conference Board proposes a three-tier approach which evaluates the performance of (a) the board as a whole; (b) each board committee and (c) each director (including the CEO).[63] The UK's Higgs report advocates a similar approach carried out at least annually and followed by corrective action:

> The chairman should act on the results of the performance evaluation by recognising the strengths and weaknesses of the board and, where appropriate, appointing new members to the board or seeking the resignation of directors.[64]

full and transparent disclosure

Once you have the right elements in place, why not tell your stakeholders about the good things you are doing on corporate governance so that they can be confident that you are actually doing what you say you are doing. You might, for example, consider:

- outlining the major components of your risk and control system and the actions you are taking to further enhance it
- explaining the role of your code of conduct and other policies in setting the tone and guiding behaviours
- confirming the independence of your non-executive directors and the rationale for any board changes
- confirming that newly appointed non-executive directors have undergone an induction programme
- reporting on the remit and responsibilities of your audit committee and what it is has achieved[65]
- explaining your rationale for not having an internal audit function or for allowing your external auditors to carry out some taxation work
- confirming that you have conducted a review of board performance and summarising the actions you have taken as a result.

Building stakeholder trust in your corporate governance arrangements is not about divulging commercial secrets; it's about demonstrating to diverse stakeholder audiences that you have set an appropriate tone right from the top and that you have appropriate systems, policies, checks and balances in place to ensure full alignment throughout the organisation so that goals are more likely to be achieved.

Too often organisations miss an opportunity to bolster stakeholder confidence and enhance reputation by making only bland, minimalist statements about their corporate governance arrangements. But this may leave their practices open to question and criticism and can act as a spur for stakeholders to dig even deeper into their affairs. Being honest and open about the good things you are doing, exceeding stakeholder expectations and providing more detail and explanation than is strictly necessary can create a warm glow of confidence which leaves your stakeholders satisfied – and perhaps even extolling your virtues as an example of good practice!

Using disclosure and communications to protect and enhance reputation will be explored in more depth later in this chapter and in Chapter 9.

Sometimes, however, businesses shoot themselves in the foot by making disclosures in an effort to improve their standing, which have precisely the opposite effect. UK-based vaccines company PowderJect was the subject of much controversy during 2002. Its chairman and chief executive, Paul Drayson, attracted criticism for a personal £50 000 donation to the Labour Party early in 2002, just four months before PowderJect was awarded a £32 million government contract for smallpox vaccine. This followed an earlier £50 000 donation to Labour in 2001, shortly after winning a £17 million contract to supply schools and hospitals with BCG (tuberculosis) inoculations. Both the company and the government denied any link between the donations and contracts. The company was also dogged by product quality problems with some batches declining in potency over their three-year shelf-life. In August 2002 the company announced it was recalling all unadministered doses of its BCG tuberculosis vaccine supplied to tens of thousands of British and Irish children in the previous two years. This resulted in headlines such as 'PowderJect plant has a history of drugmaking problems', 'Ministers reject call to revaccinate children'[66] and 'Denmark supplies emergency TB vaccinations after PowderJect recall'.[67] PowderJect was accused of being slow to make a stock market announcement about the problems at its Liverpool-based plant. The unidentified chairman of a company that does business with PowderJect called for 'a strong independent chairman who will not shy away from disclosing bad news'.[68] The company's shares, which reached a high of 660p early in 2002 had fallen to 255p by October. The share price soared at the end of October, when it was revealed that PowderJect had received several bid approaches. PowderJect's decision, in November 2002, to reject a £455 million takeover bid from US drug firm Chiron, which valued PowderJect shares at about twice their market price, is believed to have been contrary to the wishes of some shareholders. It is not surprising that Paul Drayson found himself under fire from investors to separate the roles of chairman and chief executive, a combined position he had held from the company's inception in 1993, in contravention of UK corporate governance best practice guidelines. Early 2003, after the publication of the Higgs report, the pressure was set to intensify. In February 2003 Paul Drayson announced a boardroom shake-up in which he stepped down as chairman but continued as chief executive, thereby ostensibly bringing the company into line with best corporate governance practice. Closer inspection, however, revealed that he was to be replaced as chairman by his deputy chairman, Gerald Moller, who was reputed to spend much of his time running a bio-tech venture capital operation in Germany and would potentially offer little additional restraint to Mr Drayson's power. Furthermore, a newly appointed non-executive, Larry Ellberger, could not be considered fully independent as he was formerly an executive member of the board in charge of corporate development. As *The Guardian* was quick to conclude:

> This is not the appointment of a strong outsider to balance the board. It is a job-title fudge which allows PowderJect to claim it abides by the rules when in fact it is ignoring the spirit of the governance code. Mr Drayson has had much success over the past decade, turning a start-up in to a leading specialist vaccine firm. But he's missed a screaming opportunity to demonstrate the PowderJect is actually a grown-up company.[69]

availability and responsiveness

Even where disclosure is good, the top team is also expected to be available for discussion or comment, particularly when stakeholders have concerns. GSK's CEO, the French Jean-Pierre Garnier, had not endeared himself to his predominantly European shareholders by basing himself in the USA, in Philadelphia. Institutional investors had long complained about poor access to him. In the wake of his pay-deal controversy, in 2002 Mr Garnier agreed to an unprecedented series of meetings with UK analysts, shareholders and the media in a bid to repair relations.

The UK's Higgs report recommends formalisation of the role of senior independent director to provide investors with an alternative conduit for their concerns, if they feel they are not receiving an adequate hearing from the chairman or chief executive through the normal channels. Although this has met with hostile reaction from some quarters because of the potential for mixed messages and rifts between directors, it does have the merit of trying to provide a relief valve for stakeholder concern.

embracing good practice

There has been much debate post Enron on the best model for corporate governance. The UK's 'comply or explain' principles-based approach is believed by many to result in better corporate governance than a US-type rules-based approach, where it is possible to 'tick boxes' and comply minimally with the letter of the law while still acting in an irresponsible or misleading way. Part of the explanation for this is said to be that the principles-based approach embeds reforms deep into the fabric of the organisation and integrates them into its organisational culture through consensus and understanding.

Whatever the norm in your jurisdiction, there is nothing to stop you from adopting a principles-based approach to corporate governance within your own organisation – backed up of course by appropriate awareness of the letter of the law. You may find that such an approach encourages people to think through the implications of their actions and raise queries if they are uncertain, rather than mindlessly ticking a check box and moving on to the next task in hand.

Providing evidence of good corporate governance through displaying 'joined up thinking' and ensuring that your deeds are consistent with your words, which in turn are consistent with your public disclosures and communications, can help to cement your reputation. As UK utilities company Powergen stated in their Annual Report for the year 2000.

> Good corporate governance is of prime importance for the Company in demonstrating to all of those who have an interest in the Company's affairs that it is acting in accordance with, and where possible, exceeding best practice. The Company's reputation is of significant value and adherence to the principles of corporate governance is one the of the prime methods by which that reputation is supported.

One of the benefits of the Enron fall-out has been the intense activity from governments, regulators and investors to define best practice on corporate governance. While this is excellent news for businesses as the hard work has been done for you, it means that there will be little tolerance for those who fall short of the new expectations.

The list of corporate governance considerations and good practice guidelines may seem daunting, but it is critical to get the basic framework right if your business reputation is to remain untarnished and you are to retain the trust and confidence of your stakeholders. Given the importance of corporate governance and tone-setting, one would naturally expect it to be a prime focus for monitoring and auditing within organisations. Ironically, this is rarely the case as boardroom practices and processes so often remain virtually untouched by audit and assurance activities. Turning your attention to this and probing into boardroom processes may prove to be *the* most significant single step in underpinning your reputational credentials. How to win approval for this and set about doing it is discussed in Chapter 8.

To safeguard your reputation from corporate governance risk you need to understand the rules, standards and best practice guidelines relevant to your own jurisdiction – the highest standards if you are operating across national borders – and apply them to your board and boardroom processes. To recap, the major considerations are:

- compelling vision and strategy

- responsible, accountable and dynamic leadership

- balanced and effective board

- independent, challenging and proactive non-executive directors

- appropriate remuneration and incentives

- relevant and effective board committees

- comprehensive and cohesive risk management and internal control systems

- robust oversight and assurance

- full and transparent disclosure

- availability and responsiveness of directors.

Underpin these principles with clear policies, standards and procedures backed up by regular review and audit to ensure continuing compliance. Assure stakeholders that you are complying fully with relevant regulations and are, where appropriate, embracing best practice. If you choose not to, can't or can't yet, make sure you explain why.

One final tip: it's advisable to have a CEO or chairman who doesn't undermine your business's commitment to good corporate governance through some flippant remark. One prominent US chairman used to refer to his nominally independent board as his 'pet rocks'. Tiny Rowland, former head of Lonrho, once observed that boardrooms contained potted plants and non-executives – and in his experience potted plants were more useful! Rowland also famously compared non-executive directors with 'Christmas tree decorations'. A bit of fun perhaps, but not altogether helpful behaviour when you're seeking to reassure your stakeholders that their investment is safe in your hands and that their trust is most certainly not misplaced!

REGULATORY COMPLIANCE

Flouting the law or contravening regulatory standards and guidelines – either deliberately or inadvertently – can lead to costly and high-profile litigation, regulatory investigations, public censure, civil and criminal sanctions (including loss of permits or licences, unlimited fines, disqualification and imprisonment) and to harmful publicity, diminished share price, claims for damages and loss of business.[70] Furthermore, corporate reputation can be imperilled and stakeholder confidence shaken to the core. Firms supplying products and services to transgressors can also be implicated and have their reputations tarnished.

Businesses and public sector organisations are now surrounded by a raft of laws and regulations to which they are expected to adhere. Some are general laws and regulations relevant to all businesses such as tax, customs, employment, health and safety, human rights, corporate governance, data protection and contract law. Some, like environmental legislation, product liability, competition law and intellectual property regulations may vary in importance and severity, dependent on the industry sector in which the organisation operates. Others will be entirely sector specific, such as the detailed regulations and best practice codes governing financial services and gaming firms. Regulators now often have sweeping powers of investigation and unprecedented rights of prosecution. Regulators, along with investors, pressure groups and even governments, are also increasingly willing to publicly 'name and shame' wrongdoers, thereby adding to their reputational woes. And the bar is constantly being raised as new regulations and guidelines are introduced; businesses can ill afford complacency. Making sure that an organisation is fully complying with relevant existing legislation and is able to anticipate and prepare adequately for forthcoming regulations presents a major challenge – and a significant risk to reputation (Table 6-8).

Research has shown that although boards recognise the huge potential impact of regulatory risk, many are unaware of the activities that could expose them to regulatory intervention and litigation. A 2002 survey conducted by the London School of Economics (LSE) and global law firm DLA[71] showed that 96% of respondents thought that regulatory risks are growing and will continue to grow and 94% believed that directors face increased personal exposure. A massive 80% believed that institutional shareholders consider a company's management of regulatory risk to be important.

Yet, in spite of the significance attached to regulatory issues, many boards did not appear to understand the extent of their potential liability, with only 44% of respondents believing that boards were 'very aware' of activities within their company that could breach regulations and result in serious consequences; fewer than one in five of those surveyed was 'very confident' that their organisation has a risk management system that identifies and evaluates material regulatory risks effectively.

Table 6-8. Stakeholder requirements and expectations on regulatory compliance

Stakeholder group	Requirements and expectations
Regulators Governments	• Full compliance with relevant laws and regulations • Acts in the spirit of regulations
Shareholders/investors	• Full compliance with laws and regulations • Avoids regulatory investigation and litigation • Embraces good practice that mitigates risks and boosts reputation
Suppliers Customers	• Seen as law-abiding • Sufficient compliance to avoid any collateral reputational impact
NGOs/Pressure groups	• Goes beyond basic compliance to espouse relevant social, ethical and environmental issues
Communities Employees	• Seen as law-abiding and reputable employer • Goes beyond the statutory minimum in dealings with employees

Organisations operating in highly regulated areas are most at risk as, for them, failure to comply with legal and regulatory standards can literally result in loss of licence to operate. Look at what happened to Andersen as their pillars of legitimacy collapsed within a few short weeks. Examples of highly regulated sectors include financial services, mining, oil and gas, chemicals, nuclear, pharmaceuticals, utilities, airlines and railways. For such organisations the potential risk exposures – and the reputational stakes – are exceedingly high.

compliance with laws and regulation

Failure to comply with laws and regulations, particularly when this is a deliberate ploy, can prove devastating for both corporate and personal reputations. In April 2002, Alfred Taubman, former chairman of Sotheby's, one of the world's two leading auction houses, was jailed for one year and one day by a US court and fined $7.5 million. Mr Taubman was indicted for collusion with his counterpart at Christie's to fix non-negotiable commissions on articles sold at auction during the 1990s. The aim of this was to prevent discounting to gain custom and to maintain profitability at both establishments. As Sotheby's and Christie's between them control 90% of the world's live auctions of jewellery, art and furniture, this constituted a serious breach of monopoly rules. In pre-sentencing papers Mr Taubman's lawyers wrote:

> Mr Taubman's once stellar reputation, which took him decades of incredibly hard work and humanity to build, has been shattered, literally overnight.[72]

The company was also fined $45 million after Taubman's trial and faced class-action lawsuits from thousands of cheated buyers and sellers. The accusations, at the very top of the venerable 257-year-old establishment, rocked the auction house world and led to further investigations in Europe and a sharp drop in Sotheby's share price; the company's value had plunged from £1.8 billion before the scandal to £590 million by autumn 2002. In October 2002 Sotheby's was fined over £12 million (6% of turnover) by the European Commission for collusion with Christie's to rig charges, thereby defrauding clients of some £290 million. Two months after his conviction, Alfred Taubman, Sotheby's disgraced former chairman and controlling shareholder, announced that he would explore a sale, merger or selling his stake in the company, fuelling headlines that Sotheby's would itself be put 'under the hammer'.

the impact of investigations and litigation

Disenchanted and aggrieved investors, employees, regulators and other stakeholders are more likely than ever before to have recourse to the law. Although this has long been the case in the USA, litigation fever is now spreading to the UK, Europe and other economies. A survey of 600 senior executives by Corporate Reputation Watch in February 2002 found that 35% of respondents saw litigation as posing the most serious threat to reputation.[73]

One compelling reason to ensure that you are complying with relevant laws and regulations is to avoid the reputational damage that almost always ensues when there is a long drawn-out investigation by a regulator or a high-profile court case. There is nothing the media love more than the sight of chief executives shuffling uneasily in the witness box or public sector body heads being grilled by a special committee.

Lengthy investigations by regulators are extremely time-consuming for management, can sap resources and cause businesses to lose focus. Worse still, they can be extremely damaging to reputation, as findings are often drip fed to the media over a prolonged period. No one likes having their dirty linen washed in public, but being subjected to this over many months by serious-minded folk in dark suits bent on finding evidence of wrongdoing, can be a truly devastating experience for the individuals and organisations involved. Investigations by health and safety officials, environmental watchdogs, fraud investigators, competition bodies, customs, excise and tax authorities, data protection officials or industry regulators such as the SEC or FSA are best avoided as they can seriously dent stakeholder confidence, reputation and share price. Directors and officers can sometimes be held personally liable and are increasingly likely to be litigated against.

The US copier group Xerox paid a $10 million civil penalty to the Securities and Exchange Commission (SEC) in April 2002 to settle allegations that it had massaged its figures to appear more profitable. A restatement of earnings at the time showed that the company had misrecorded $6.4 billion of revenues and $1.4 billion of earnings over the five-year period from 1997 to 2001. The two-year-long SEC inquiry had had a damaging effect on Xerox's stock price, with a fall of 70% during the period of the investigation. The SEC concluded that Xerox were guilty of fraud and had used a number of accounting tricks to pull forward future revenues in order to 'meet or exceed Wall Street expectations and disguise its true operating performance from investors'. When Federal Authorities announced in September 2002 that they were launching a criminal investigation into Xerox the shares fell a further 14%.[74] An accounting firm was also caught up the investigation's path: in January 2003 it was announced that KPMG, and four of their partners, were facing a fraud suit from the SEC over their role as Xerox's auditor during the five-year period in question.[75]

Similar to the Andersen experience with Enron, KPMG's position at Xerox highlights the need for suppliers to critically appraise their customers before deciding to do business with them. Becoming embroiled in shady dealings can tar a company, its advisers and service providers with the same brush – tarnishing the reputations of all.

The questionable activities of your suppliers can also drag you blinking into the spotlight. Tyson Foods, one of the world's largest chicken producers, found itself on trial early in 2003, accused of importing illegal workers, from Mexico and other Latin American countries, to work at its plants throughout the USA. The prosecution alleged that Tyson, a company with a turnover of $23 billion, imported illegal workers into the USA so that they could be paid low wages, would not receive sickness or injury benefits and could be sacked without compensation. It was further alleged that false documents were supplied to facilitate these illegal movements of workers. The trial came in the wake of a massive five-year undercover operation by the federal authorities which claimed that up to one-third of workers at some Tyson plants were illegal immigrants.[76] Tyson claimed that the illegal hiring was carried out by three 'rogue' managers who had admitted their guilt and had since been fired. One had committed suicide. However, the company's record was not spotless: in 1997 it had pleaded guilty and paid a $6 billion fine for giving illegal gifts to the then US agriculture secretary, Mike Espy.

The perhaps more interesting corollary of the story is that Tyson are a key supplier to McDonald's of chicken McNuggets. In fact, when the story hit the papers, one headline read 'Poultry pay puts fast food giant in dock'. Whether the paper meant by this Tyson or McDonald's is a moot point, but the implications for McDonald's were clear. As the first paragraph of the article stated:

> One of the world's largest chicken producers, which is a key supplier to McDonald's, is on trial in Tennessee accused of conspiracy to import illegal workers . . . [77]

The more well-known name of McDonald's appeared in the first sentence; Tyson Foods were not featured until the second paragraph. The trial clearly raises questions over the efficacy of McDonald's controls over its supply chain. Did they only check the cost and quality of the end product, and not the conditions under which it was made or the ethical track-record of its suppliers? Food workers union activists had campaigned for two years about exploitative work practices at Tyson. The allegations against Tyson of racketeering and immigration law violations couldn't have come at a worse time for McDonald's; the company is itself faced with potential obesity lawsuits and is struggling to prove its ethical credentials. Although Tyson Foods were in March 2003 cleared by a US court of smuggling illegal immigrants from Latin America into the USA to work in its factories,[78] the potential damage to the reputations of both Tyson and McDonald's was already done.

Surely, you may be thinking, litigation is only a real threat to reputation if the business is actually found guilty of illegal conduct. Individuals and businesses are, after all, innocent until proven guilty. That may be the case in the eyes of the law, but not in the eyes of the public perception. Research shows that public opinion operates on the 'no smoke without fire' principle. In an opinion poll conducted by PR and marketing consultancy Shandwick International in 2000, 59% of respondents said they would believe a company was 'probably guilty' if they heard it was being sued. Where they heard that the company being sued refused to give any comment, the proportion thinking it was probably guilty rose to 69%.[79]

Reputations can even be sullied when a court rules in favour of the defendant and they are exonerated. This is particularly true if a large corporation is pitted against a handful of individuals, a cash-strapped pressure group or a small business. The minnows can be sympathetically portrayed by the media as the underdogs, bullied by the excessive power of the mighty conglomerate. The McDonald's 'McLibel' case, in which McDonald's sued a couple of obscure British environmental activists in 1990 for defamation, is a classic example of this. McDonald's overreaction led to the longest libel case in British legal history, a multi-million dollar lawyers' bill, adverse media coverage and the setting up in 1996 of the McSpotlight activist website[80] – which received a staggering million hits in it first month.

> The company had turned a small North London dispute into a global reputation catastophe and elevated two marginal activists into anti-capitalist icons.
>
> (Chris Genasi[81])

Their overreaction cost McDonald's dear: they ultimately won the court case, but lost the PR battle.

There is also the risk in such long drawn-out cases that key influencers, such as professional bodies and campaigners, publicly side with the plaintiff or defendant. This can strengthen the prosecution or defence case and can also help to fan the flames of media attention. During 2000, the insurance company Axa fought a case against a policyholder claiming that its proposed distribution of £1.7 billion of 'orphan' assets was inequitable. The policyholder's position was backed by the UK's influential Consumers' Association. Although the High Court found in Axa's favour, media coverage was overwhelmingly on the side of the consumers.[82]

Investigations can also bring to the public's attention weaknesses that call into question the professionalism and integrity of management. This can raise fundamental doubts about the quality of an organisation's leaders and its future prospects. A series of official inquiries into fatal rail accidents in the UK found management systems wanting at privatised rail operator Railtrack. In May 2001, when the Mitchell report into the crash at Hatfield was published, *The Guardian* commented:

> The criticism of Railtrack is familiar – chaotic lines of reporting, confused management systems and unclear lines of responsibility. Engineers reported problems with the line eight months before the crash, but the reports bogged down in the marshes of Railtrack's management.[83]

Public and investor confidence in Railtrack was at such a low ebb that bad news was almost expected; with every new revelation Railtrack's reputation – and share price – sank lower. This had an adverse multiplier effect on the company's reputation. The company was put into administration by the UK Government in October 2001.

Growing recognition of the potential damage that can be caused by lengthy legal actions has prompted many organisations in the firing line to settle out of court. In November 2000, after five months of negotiations, Coca-Cola agreed to pay $192 million to settle a class action racial discrimination lawsuit. The settlement entailed fundamental changes, including the establishment of a seven-member outside task force to oversee Coca-Cola's US diversity effort and the payment of $50 million to the Coca-Cola Foundation which arranges community support programmes.[84] It was unfortunate that Coca-Cola needed to part with the largest sum ever paid in a US discrimination case before tackling some of the diversity issues that had been apparent to insiders for some time. An effective risk management system should have flagged this as a potential reputational hot-spot.

complying with the spirit – not just the letter – of the law

The report by the US Senate's congressional joint committee on taxation, released in February 2003, found that despite reporting billions of dollars in profits between 1996 and 1999, Enron paid no income tax. At the same time that reports to investors vaunted massive profits, reports prepared for tax purposes claimed millions of dollars of losses. The various tax-avoidance schemes were concocted by an incestuous group of advisers – from the banking, accountancy and legal professions – who often served on both sides of a transaction, representing both Enron and a nominated, allegedly independent, other party. Enron's advisers were paid a staggering $88 million in fees between 1995 and the bankruptcy filing in 2001. The joint committee noted in its report that Enron made 'complexity its ally' to hoodwink the internal revenue service in the USA; it used the tax code to produce results 'contrary to its spirit'.

> Enron's behaviour illustrates that a motivated corporation can manipulate highly technical provisions of the law to achieve significant unintended benefits.[85]

Compliance with *the letter o*f the law is generally seen as a 'given' – a precondition for doing business and a fundamental component of an organisation's licence to operate. Post Enron, stakeholder expectations now go even further; businesses should act ethically and with integrity in *the spirit* of any relevant regulations, otherwise or stakeholder confidence can be shaken and reputation dented. Deciding where to position yourself on the 'basic compliance' to 'best practice' spectrum will influence your reputation.

Although many organisations are driven by fear in their approach to regulatory risk management, adopting a more positive mindset can be beneficial. Going beyond minimal compliance, moving towards best practice in some areas by being an early adopter of new regulations or voluntary codes, can create competitive advantage and strengthen reputation. It can lead to:

- being seen as a leader – not a laggard – in your sector; being regarded as an organisation that doesn't wait to be forced into embracing emerging good practice
- building positive relationships with major regulators – who are, after all, key stakeholders; and this can be particularly valuable if you operate in a highly regulated sector.

what can be done?

With the rising tide of regulation and growing appetite for litigation no longer confined to the USA, organisations need to seriously address their legal and regulatory risks. So what can be done in practice to minimise regulatory threats and create competitive advantage?

☐ CLEAR ACCOUNTABILITIES

Absolute clarity on roles and responsibilities is an essential starting point for effective regulatory risk management. The previously cited LSE/DLA survey found that many companies were unclear where the ultimate responsibility for managing regulatory risk should lie; the 'board as a whole' was seen as accountable for managing regulatory risk in only one-third of companies; indeed only 40% of respondents saw regulatory risks as 'definitely a board issue'. Consequently, 36% of respondents said that regulatory risks, which could lead to significant punitive consequences, were not discussed at board level. It is no surprise, therefore, that 60% of respondents saw 'lack of leadership at board level' as one of the four biggest obstacles to effective regulatory risk management. The other major obstacles were corporate culture, lack of knowledge and lack of resources devoted to risk management. Nearly half of the respondents felt that their business did not develop its culture and staff incentives in a way that promoted effective regulatory risk management. If people are not rewarded or recognised for managing regulatory risk, why should they bother?

Boards need to recognise that they are ultimately accountable for regulatory risk and bear shared responsibility for its effective management. They must assure themselves that exposures have been properly identified and assessed, that appropriate controls such as policies and procedures are developed and implemented, and that compliance is monitored and rewarded. They should also ensure that the business is looking ahead and is ready for new regulation when, or ideally before, it bites. Even when these responsibilities are delegated to company secretaries, risk managers, compliance officers, health and safety professionals or HR managers, the board still retains overall responsibility in the eyes of the law and the business's regulators.

☐ IDENTIFYING REGULATORY RISKS

Many organisations are developing risk-based compliance programmes to provide early indications of where they may struggle to comply with existing or planned legislation. You can use the risk identification techniques described in Chapter 4 to tease out your major regulatory exposures and opportunities, perhaps under the heading of 'compliance and governance'. What is the precise nature of your regulatory risk? Are you uneasy because you may not find out about planned regulation sufficiently early to prepare adequately for it – or even influence it? Are you concerned that you do not have the in-house expertise to interpret the new rules for your business situation? Or are you just short of resource for implementing them? Does the culture in your organisation support zero tolerance of regulatory infringement? Do you have the capability for in-house compliance checking? What are the benefits to your business of early adoption of new rules or voluntary codes of practice?

There are many situations in a business that can lead to a breach of regulations, litigation or regulatory investigations. However, these often remain unnoticed or are not acted on because the implications are underestimated or employees fear the consequences of delivering bad news to management. Examples include:

- a spate of customer complaints on product or service quality
- employee claims of bullying, stress, harassment or discrimination
- worker grumblings about unsafe workplace practices
- recurrent lapses in the agreed product specification from a supplier
- concerns about the integrity of a member of staff and their possible involvement in corrupt or fraudulent activity.

Some businesses are investing time and effort in making staff outside of their legal department more 'legal risk aware' through training and awareness raising on issues such as contract law, competition (anti-trust) law and product liability issues. The aim is for staff to understand the broader legal implications of what they are doing so that appropriate action can be taken promptly and that legal advisers can be involved at the earliest possible stage.

Empirical studies have in fact shown that a large percentage of employees are aware of inappropriate conduct in their business. A survey by KPMG covering selected US industries found that 60% of employees had observed violations of law or company standards at least 'sometimes in the previous 12 months', with 37% stating that the misconduct was so serious it could result in a significant loss of public trust if it were to become known. The same survey showed, however, that only 45% of employees polled felt they could approach management with bad news. This was presumably not unrelated to another finding – only 62% of this group was confident that senior management would not authorise illegal or unethical conduct if necessary to meet business goals.[86] If reticence to speak up is truly as endemic as it appears, an independent, non-threatening channel for employee concerns may be required. This is why so many businesses – in both the private and public sectors – have implemented whistleblowing arrangements.

☐   WHISTLEBLOWING

Whistleblowing can act as a safety valve to ensure that concerned or disgruntled employees have a means of communicating their concerns about employer malpractice – hopefully before their disquiet and frustration prompts them to tell all to the media. Even in the best run businesses, it will be prudent to have a whistleblowing policy as there may be sensitive or personal issues, perhaps involving an employee's direct superior or peers, that are difficult to discuss openly.

A whistleblowing policy should be developed in consultation with employees to ensure their cooperation and should link to the organisation's code of conduct and/or values. It should outline the procedures (with details of whom to contact) and should assure employees of confidentiality, speed of response and zero tolerance of harassment or victimisation of whistleblowers. This last point is important, given that 69% of whistleblowers in a US survey said they had lost their jobs or been forced to retire as a result.[87] In another US survey an overwhelming 87% of the public thought whistleblowers would face negative consequences at work (such as being fired or being treated poorly) 'most of the time' or 'some of the time'.[88] Employees must feel that their safety and job security will not be impacted if they blow the whistle.

US law did not protect the whistleblowers at Enron and WorldCom. However, in some jurisdictions, protection for whistleblowers against dismissal or other penalties is supported by legislation. For example, the UK's Public Interest Disclosure Act 1998, which came into force in January 1999, protects employees from being dismissed or penalised for disclosing information that they honestly and reasonably believe exposes malpractice. Under the Act, staff are expected to raise their concerns internally first or to go to a body such as a regulator. Indeed, some regulators are positively encouraging employees to expose wrongdoing by their employers; the Financial Services Authority, the UK's financial watchdog, has established a whistleblowing hotline for this purpose. The European Commission has gone still further by encouraging businesses to blow the whistle on each other. Under new leniency rules, the first company to blow the whistle on a cartel is guaranteed immunity from prosecution if members of the conspiracy can be brought to book. This is how auction house Christie's escaped prosecution in the commission-rigging scam with Sotheby's. Christie's decision to confess to the Commission and American prosecutors in January 2000, and to hand over incriminating documents detailing the secret deal, allowed it to escape without penalty.

A Work Foundation survey in 2002, three years after the UK Act came into force, found that only 32% of private sector firms surveyed had introduced formal whistleblowing policies, compared with 75% in the public sector. Most organisations, whether private or public, preferred concerns to be raised internally to designated Human Resource (62%) or senior management (61%). Only 24% encouraged whistleblowers to raise concerns with unions or staff representatives; 29% of public sector and a mere 4% of private sector respondents specifically mentioned regulatory bodies.[89]

Theo Blackwell, Chief Policy Specialist at the Work Foundation, commented at the launch of the survey that whistleblowing policies should be promoted as:

> . . . an effective tool for corporate governance. As the recent spate of scandals to hit USA Inc. reveal, employees can play a vital role in upholding good corporate governance, highlighting potential problems and maintaining organisational ethics. Transparent, well-run organisations will have nothing to fear by providing their employees with an encouraging environment in which they can raise their concerns. It is high time that organisations learnt to support, and not suppress, such participation as an early-warning against the corporate governance failings witnessed in the US.

To check that the system works, it is good practice for the audit committee to review employee whistleblowing arrangements. It can then ensure that appropriate independent investigation and follow-up takes place and that any relevant matters arising are brought to its attention.

❏   CLEARLY DOCUMENTED POLICIES

Clearly documented policies are another essential component of regulatory risk management as policies are usually the first port of call for regulators when starting an investigation. Only 36% of respondents in the LSE/DLA regulatory survey were 'very confident' that written policies were in place. The implementation of policies was another concern, with an over-whelming three-quarters of those surveyed saying that there was room for 'some or significant improvement'.

Having policies and procedures in place, as well as evidence of training, implementation and compliance monitoring, can actually act as a defence in the event of a breach. As the UK's Office of Fair Trading states in a guidance document on competition law compliance:

> The fact that a compliance programme is in place may be taken into account as a mitigating factor when calculating the level of financial penalty to impose. Careful consideration will be given as to the precise circumstances of the infringement, in particular the efforts made by management to ensure that the programme has been properly implemented.[90]

Among those policies and procedures, it will pay you to ensure that your document retention policy (a polite euphemism for a policy whose prime purpose is determining what can be destroyed and when!) would withstand scrutiny in a court of law. Such a policy should stipulate minimum retention periods which should at least meet statutory requirements. It should ensure that key documents can be retrieved if needed for defence; any documents subject to legal privilege should be carefully marked as these need not be disclosed. Destroying documents that may be required for an investigation can cause untold damage – as Andersen discovered when they were accused of obstructing justice by shredding potentially incriminating files at Enron.

In April 2002, British American Tobacco, the world's second largest cigarette firm, also found that its overzealous shredding policy proved costly when an Australian judge awarded A$700 000 in damages to the plaintiff in a tobacco litigation case who developed cancer after smoking for 40 years. The judge argued that BAT's document retention policy in Australia equated to 'a means of destroying damaging documents under the cover of an apparently innocent housekeeping arrangement' over a period of some 17 years.[91] The company's defence was therefore dismissed by the judge, who claimed that 'deliberate obliteration' of internal documents had prejudiced the case and made a fair trial impossible. BAT had literally shredded its defence.

❏   REGULATORY CRISIS MANAGEMENT

Another core component of any risk management framework is a robust crisis management plan; yet many such plans do not consider regulatory risk as a potential catalyst for a crisis. The LSE/DLA survey found that only one in four businesses incorporated the risk of regulatory intervention into their crisis management plans. One wonders how the rest would respond to a dawn raid by competition authorities or to a health and safety investigation team arriving unannounced. Would managers know their rights when questioned? Are they obliged to answer all questions fully and hand over all relevant documents? What would happen if they refused? Taking the wrong action when a regulator arrives on your doorstep can exacerbate reputational impact. Has your organisation considered regulatory risks when formulating crisis management plans? Have your staff been trained in how to respond?

in brief

In seeking to manage those regulatory risks that can impact reputation, consider the following steps:

- Establish clear ownership of regulatory risk. The board should have ultimate responsibility for this, should understand the major regulatory risks facing the business and should assure themselves that they are being managed effectively.

- Be clear where you want to be on the 'basic compliance' to 'best practice' continuum. You may wish to improve your regulatory performance in the medium term, but it is vital at any given point in time to have an unambiguous stance on what constitutes acceptable and unacceptable practice; any fuzziness could encourage non-compliance.

- Ensure that written policies are in place covering relevant legal and regulatory standards and guidelines; communicate these; make non-compliance a disciplinary offence.

- Ensure alignment between regulatory goals, culture and incentives; reward and recognise staff accordingly.

- Identify your 'hot-spots' (areas of high risk in terms of impact and likelihood) by using your risk management systems. Check through review and audit that controls in these critical areas are working properly.

- Check that you have an adequate paper trail for your defence – including evidence that reasonable measures were taken to comply, such as training and compliance reviews; make sure your document retention policy is appropriate, unequivocal and adhered to.

- Put whistleblowing arrangements in place, communicate them and check usage; your audit committee should approve and review the arrangements and outputs.

- Develop and rehearse robust crisis procedures for regulatory risks, e.g. to deal with dawn raids and regulatory investigations.

- Critically appraise your relationships with customer and suppliers: could their regulatory malfeasance put your business in the dock?

- Consider whether there are opportunities to tell your stakeholders that you are not just complying with all relevant laws and regulations, but are embracing best practice in some areas?

- Scan continuously for imminent and planned new laws and regulations; prepare adequately to ensure that you are able to comply in full.

Involving all employees in regulatory risk management can help everyone to see the 'bigger picture'; once the downside and upside implications of specific issues are understood and staff are confident that they will get a fair hearing (and that the messenger won't be shot!) it becomes much easier to involve staff in continuously identifying risks and in the design of early warning indicators that can sound alarm bells sufficiently early for a crisis to be averted. Incorporating formal whistleblowing arrangements into your risk management and governance systems can plug what is often a highly vulnerable gap and act as a relief valve for disenchanted or concerned employees.

However, irrespective of how good your risk identification processes may be, risk can still occasionally arise from unexpected quarters. Jack Welch, former chief executive of General Electric and once hailed as the world's leading business executive, found himself in the limelight after details of his apparently excessive employment and retirement contracts became public as a result of his divorce proceedings. Divorce papers filed by Mrs Welch alleged that GE paid about $80 000 a month for staff and upkeep, including food and wine, at his New York apartment; and that he used a Boeing 737 worth almost $300 000 a month while enjoying limousine services and free seats at the Metropolitan Opera, New York Yankees and Boston Red Sox baseball games.[92]

Jack Welch told the *Wall Street Journal* that the divorce papers 'grossly represented many aspects of my employment contract with GE'. Showing his customary insight, he added:

> I'm not going to get into a public fight refuting every allegation. When public confidence and trust have been shaken, I've learned the hard way that perception matters more than ever. In this environment I don't want a great company with the highest integrity dragged into a public fight because of my divorce proceedings.[93]

Mr Welch voluntarily relinquished the more controversial elements of the retirement package (worth up to $2.5 million a year) and has continued with his consulting and public-speaking engagements. Little can touch this icon of global business, whose personal reputation as an inspirational business leader is second to none. GE has, however, now become the focus of a Securities and Exchange Commission (SEC) investigation into Jack Welch's employment and retirement arrangements. This has hardly come at a good time for GE which, under the stewardship of new chief executive, Jeffrey Immelt, is striving to stave off criticism of its accounting practices and to position GE as a model of transparency and probity. In March 2003 in *Fortune* magazine's annual poll, GE slipped from five years at the top, as the most admired company in America, to the number five slot.[94] All of which serves to illustrate that in the world of reputation risk management, it pays to make sure that no skeletons get into your corporate cupboard, as they have a nasty habit of surfacing at the worst possible moment!

DELIVERING CUSTOMER PROMISE

> Today customers are far more sophisticated than they used to be. In markets where there is access to increasing levels of information there is an opportunity to disseminate more and more data.

Putting this in a business context means that greater competition and ease of technology has rendered erstwhile points of differentiation – such as price and product and service quality – today's points of parity. The battleground for differentiation is often fought at the next level up – the corporate level.

(Shailendra Kumar, senior consultant, Brand Valuation at
Interbrand Newell & Sorrell[95])

Having a good corporate reputation can tip the scales in your favour when trying to differentiate your offering in competitive markets. Price and quality are taken as 'givens' in developed economies. When choosing between similar products, the intangible reassurance and 'corporate halo' effect of a reputable company backing the offer can be the crucial deciding factor. Corporate reputation acts as a 'cohesive umbrella that provides customers with a tacit guarantee about the quality and value of a product'.[96]

Attracting customers initially is only part of the challenge; retaining them and enjoying their repeat custom is another. Customers have more information on which to make purchase decisions and more product and service choices then ever before. They may appear loyal but are notoriously fickle; if they lose confidence in you as a supplier, they are likely to transfer to an alternative supplier and you may never be able to win them back again. Delivering – and continuing to deliver – the promise to customers is paramount.

Table 6-9. Stakeholder requirements and expectations on delivering customer promise

Stakeholder group	Requirements and expectations
Customers	• Quality and fair pricing of products and services • Live up to brands • Availability and security of products and services • Responsiveness • Innovative • Responsible
Shareholders/Investors	• Strong product and corporate brands • Effective marketing • Secure customer base • Innovative: – strong new product pipeline – successful commercialisation of new products and services – growth potential
NGOs/Pressure groups Regulators Governments	• Responsible marketing and innovation • Fairness in dealings with customers
Suppliers Communities Employees	• Strong sales and secure customer base, assuring future jobs and purchases

So what do your customers want and expect of you in delivering the promise to their satis-faction? Which aspects of your compact with customers are of interest to other stakeholders? (Table 6-9)

quality and fair pricing

Good quality and fair price are regarded as 'givens' in business today; products and services are expected to be of good and consistent quality and fairly priced if they are to win over customers. But if quality slips or price is seen to be too high, customers may decamp. A spate of product defects or an unexpected price hike may find customers switching to a rival supplier. In businesses where 'value for money' – that elusive optimal blend of quality and price – *is* the business's unique selling proposition (USP), any erosion of this in the eyes of customers can have catastrophic consequences.

UK-based Marks & Spencer (M&S), in spring 1998 the second most profitable retailer in the world after Wal-Mart, witnessed a dramatic fall in sales as customers lost faith in M&S's 'value for money' promise and deserted its stores in droves. M&S's leadership had ignored research indicating that traditionally rock solid customer satisfaction was starting to wobble. The company credo – quality, value and service – was under siege; it had even been dropped after decades from the front cover of the M&S annual report.[97]

M&S's autocratic leadership, itself locked in a power battle over succession, took its eye off the ball. It allowed prices to drift upward and, in a bid to improve productivity, took actions to reduce staffing costs, including cutting training budgets. But this only alienated their loyal workforce who were renowned for helpfulness and good service.

> Customers began to notice not only the lack of sales staff but a surliness creeping into the service. Yet visiting executives, who were always expected, would always be surrounded by eager, smiling faces. Shoppers began to feel that M&S had become pricey and increasingly complained that they could not get an item on display in their size or the colour they wanted.

Stores were starting to look shabby – in stark contrast to emerging retailers Next and the Gap who were offering modern, well-designed and competitively priced clothing in brightly lit stores with a contemporary, cosy feel; their stores were a magnet for younger shoppers.

> In July and August 1998 the great British public started buying fewer clothes. Not only that, customers were unimpressed with the M&S Autumn ranges which hit the shops in early September. An attempt to woo the younger customer with a predominance of synthetic fabrics in offbeat colours misfired, while the more mature ranges were mainly black and grey. Although grey was indeed the fashion colour that autumn, the clothes looked drab and drear displayed in the vast, unbroken retail floors of the bigger M&S stores. Regular customers who had sworn by M&S for a decade could suddenly find nothing new or exciting to buy.[98]

This icon of British retailing, which for years had never put a foot wrong in the eyes of customers, investors and employees, now didn't seem able to put a foot right. When faced with plummeting sales and a 23% fall in profits, M&S's knee-jerk reaction was to cut costs by sourcing overseas (causing howls of outrage and legal challenges from their long-standing British suppliers as well as exacerbating availability problems) and closing unprofitable stores in continental Western Europe (leading to protest marches, breaches of labour law and damaging headlines). The press had a field day; thousands of column inches in the broadsheets and the tabloids were devoted to M&S's woes – for nothing sells newspapers like the mighty fallen! The latest twist in the M&S saga was the topic of conversation by the office coffee machine. M&S's demise became self-fulfilling as many customers stopped visiting their stores, no longer expecting to find anything worth buying.

M&S had broken the golden rule of reputation risk management: at a stroke they had negated all their uniqueness attributes:

- Quality/value/consistency
- Outstanding customer service
- Excellent availability
- Model employer
- Long-standing, high-quality British supply base
- Instinctive feel for what customers want.

They were even starting to chip away at the pillars of legitimacy underpinning their licence to operate. Good availability is vital for any retailer: yet on many M&S clothing lines availability was now poor.

Customers felt badly let down; they felt they could no longer trust the company that had for so long been their number one choice for a range of goods. How things had changed since the former chairman, Simon Marks, would visit stores unannounced to talk to shopfloor staff, check the quality of merchandise and witness customer reaction first hand. M&S had lost touch with their customers. It would take four years, a management shake-out, a new design team, a volte-face on acceptance of credit cards and refurbished stores to start to regain the trust of their clientele – and win back their custom.

living up to brands

Your product and service brands make a contract with your customers that must be kept. If your brand portrays you as being environmentally friendly, ethical, flexible or just plain 'fun', you must live up to the promise within your own bailiwick, in your dealings with customers and throughout your supply chain.

UK-based cosmetics and toiletries company, The Body Shop, founded by the charismatic Anita Roddick in 1976, traced its modest beginnings to a single retail outlet in Brighton, on the south coast of England. A business maverick, Roddick positioned The Body Shop as an ethical company that respected the environment and human rights, rejected testing on animals, supplied only natural products and campaigned for good causes. It proffered a new business model built on uncompromising ethical principles. The innovative concept caught the public mood and rising concern about artificially produced products and their damaging effects on the environment. Soon new stores were opened in the UK and Europe and the 1990s saw expansion into the USA and Asia. Today the company has over 1,900 retail outlets in 50 countries around the globe.

The passion of its founder is embodied in the emotive language of its Mission Statement – its 'Reason for being' – which talks about 'creatively balancing the financial and human needs' of its stakeholders, 'courageously ensuring' that the business is sustainable, 'meaningfully contributing' to the communities in which it trades, 'passionately campaigning for the protection of the environment, human and civil rights, and against animal testing within the cosmetics and toiletries industry' and 'tirelessly working to narrow the gap between practice and principle, while making fun, passion and care part of our daily lives'.[99] With its sights set so perilously high, the company inevitably attracted criticism.

A shadow was cast over the company's reputation when, in September 1994, a controversial article in the US *Business Ethics* magazine 'Shattered image: is The Body Shop too good to be true?'[100] attacked the very essence of The Body Shop. It challenged the company's green-ethical credentials: its commitment to the environment, the natural origins of its products, its record on donations to charity, the efficacy of its aid projects and business practices in its franchise operations. Other journalists jumped on the bandwagon and started to take pot shots at the company. The company refuted the charges, instituted a social audit of its supply chain and other stakeholders in 1995 and issued one of the first corporate social reports – its 'Values Report' – in the same year. In 1998 the London branch of Greenpeace, the environmental NGO, launched a new anti-Body Shop campaign with a leaflet entitled 'What's wrong with The Body Shop – a criticism of "green" consumerism', which it distributed to contacts world wide. The Body Shop was also given the McSpotlight treatment via a website containing the full text of the Greenpeace leaflet.[101] The Body Shop never fully recovered from the assaults on the integrity of its brand; it has since been the subject of close scrutiny by NGOs and the media, and its popularity and financial performance have been questioned.

Other ethically based companies were spawned in the 1970s, such as US-based ice-cream company Ben & Jerry's, founded in 1978 by Ben Cohen and Jerry Greenfield (later acquired by Unilever). Ironically, the major principles of these new business models – ethical behaviour, fair dealing with suppliers, respect for the environment – regarded as daring and unconventional at the time, have now become mainstream considerations for all businesses. However, the fundamental premise remains valid: that if you fail to strenuously uphold the promise of your brand, customer expectations may not be met and your reputation may falter.

There is also a lesson here for acquirers of businesses with unconventional brands. Although the acquired brand ethos may not entirely fit your traditional corporate philosophy, you tamper with this at your peril. If you do not respect and uphold the brand's unique promise, you may destroy brand equity – the added value generated by the brand – and the brand's good name. If you nurture the brand, as arguably Unilever have successfully done with Ben & Jerry's, it can continue to be a source of profit and reputational excellence.

Care should also be taken if you choose to extend your brand by moving into business areas with which you are unfamiliar and where you may struggle to assess the risk exposures. A baseball team that moves into merchandising, a restaurant chain that sells T-shirts and baseball caps or offers free toys to children, can face reputational difficulties when critics accuse it of labour abuses in the supply chain, unethical pricing practices or contravention of product safety regulations. These peripheral brand extensions can cause serious damage to the core product if they are not managed well. Promoting your brand in a new market or unfamiliar territory may also bring unexpected risks and difficulties – as M&S found when they overstretched themselves through rapid overseas expansion. So, before embarking on that next brand extension or foray into a new market, ask yourself:

- Do you understand the risks of moving into this new area?
- Are the exposures acceptable?
- Do you have the expertise in-house to manage these risks and put appropriate controls in place? If not, can you acquire it quickly?
- How will your key policies, processes and procedures be transferred across to the new venture so that it is bound by your values, tolerance to risk and strategic objectives?
- Are you able to monitor the effectiveness of risk controls? Do you have access to auditors with relevant skills and experience for the new area?
- How will progress be reported and integrated into your corporate risk management framework and disclosure processes?
- Think 'out of the box': how could your brand – and potentially corporate reputation – be damaged by this new venture?

availability and security

As the M&S example showed, sudden poor availability, when availability was previously taken for granted, can be highly damaging for sales and reputation. Customers had, in particular, flocked to M&S for good-quality and fairly-priced underwear and basic clothing. While in the store buying their 'basics', they would browse and purchase other higher value-added items. Now, however, their favourites were often no longer in stock. They still dropped into their local M&S store once, perhaps twice, but to no avail; and many then found an alternative source of supply which was often of comparable quality and slightly cheaper. To their surprise and delight, they found that the rival store had a range of well-designed clothing in the new fashion shades – and all at affordable prices. These customers would be difficult to win back.

Availability is an issue not just for products, but also for services. In early 2000, Barclays Bank announced the closure of 170 rural branches – a *fait accompli* that did little to endear the company to loyal, long-standing, sometimes elderly or car-less customers who relied heavily on local facilities. The fact that this hit the headlines at the same time as the CEO's generous remuneration package was revealed, and within weeks of an earlier decision to introduce charges for cash machines, proved a PR disaster. The bank found itself under siege by private and institutional shareholders, customers and NGOs. The company AGM that spring was a spirited affair to put it mildly, with the entertaining spectacle of one private shareholder, an elderly lady, threatening the board with her rolled umbrella! In October 2002, a leaked memo from the company concluded that the bank's brand name now symbolised 'a culture of greed' and consumers saw it as generating 'excessive profits', with many of its products regarded as 'substandard and expensive'.[102] The bank swiftly embarked on a plan to rebuild its battered reputation.

Another bank, Abbey National, was forced into an embarrassing climb-down in February 2003, when it abandoned attempts to persuade customers to relinquish their pass books and switch to ATM-based accounts. The bank's rationale was that account holders were using their 'Instant Saver' as a pseudo current account for cash transactions and this was creating queues in branches. The move caused a storm of protest. The bank's call centre was deluged with calls from customers threatening to close their accounts; others poured out their concerns to newspapers. Many were elderly pensioners who had banked with Abbey for decades and were nervous about being forced to use an ATM and having to retain a PIN number. *The Guardian* newspaper took up the cause and the bank's U-turn quickly followed.[103] The timing of this was unfortunate for Abbey National as, in the same week, the bank announced losses of £984 million, one of the largest deficits in UK banking history, and halved its dividend.

Availability risks are not confined to the private sector; public sector bodies are certainly not immune. The UK tax authority, the Inland Revenue, faced humiliating teething troubles with its much-vaunted online self-assessment system. Initially the new service kept crashing and denying access, causing huge frustration for users who understandably took refuge in the familiar hard-copy format. In 2002, the Internet service was suspended for 32 days following security breaches in May, which allowed some users to view other taxpayers' confidential details. The resulting headlines such as 'Online tax returns doomed, MPs warn'[104] and 'Inland Revenue red-faced as online service falters again'[105] hardly helped to inspire public confidence. The Revenue's target of 50% of self-assessments being completed online by 2005 began to look like a pipedream when it was revealed that, after almost two years, fewer than 80 000 users – less than 1% – were filing their returns electronically. The Revenue later received an embarrassing public rebuke from the Public Accounts Committee of the House of Commons. Its report, released in August 2002, criticised the Revenue for high-profile systems failures that 'sap public confidence' and called on it to 'pilot and test new systems more systematically, to minimise the teething problems experienced' and to make websites more reliable and accessible.[106] The non-availability of the new system, allied with concerns over security, tarnished the Revenue's reputation.

There are, of course, many similar examples in the private sector where availability and security problems can lead directly to bottom-line impact as disenchanted customers vote with their feet. There have been instances of insecure e-commerce sites from which customer credit card details were stolen and used for fraudulent purposes. Equally, technical problems on e-commerce websites, viruses, worms and other forms of deliberate attack have caused outages and dented customer confidence. Consumers have high expectations of e-commerce websites: they assume that a site will provide them with quick access, prompt service, good security and will be available 24/7. A major problem with a web site will affect far more customers than a computer glitch in just one of a retailer's hundred high street outlets and could lead to mass customer defections. Whether you are a private sector or public sector business, think carefully before offering customers online access as the major sales conduit for your goods and services. Focusing primarily on electronic delivery channels can hugely exacerbate your exposure: if your availability, reliability and security are not rock solid from day one, the transition may prove disastrous.

☐   THE E-PERIL

The potential of websites for inflicting serious reputational damage on businesses has not escaped the attention of pressure groups and individual activists. Some campaigners use e-savvy 'hactivists' to paralyse company websites through denial-of-service e-mail flooding attacks; to 'hijack' website users by diverting them to alternative defamatory or even salacious sites; to deface the website by changing information on it; or to expose the site's security deficiencies.

In February 2001 the animal rights activist group 'Animal Liberation-Tactical Internet Response Network' claimed to have jammed the website of Stephens Inc. – the US investment bank that saved UK-based Huntingdon Life Sciences (HLS) from liquidation. Although Stephens said the attack had failed to completely disable their site, the action linked Stephens' name publicly with beleaguered HLS and made it a focus for heightened activism.[107] Activist groups, led by Stop Huntingdon Animal Cruelty (Shac), had targeted the UK-based drug-testing company since the late 1990s, harassing, intimidating and even physically threatening HLS staff. The campaign later turned its attention to the company's backers in its continued attempts to close down HLS's operations. It was after the Royal Bank of Scotland withdrew its overdraft facility, in the face of anti-vivisection protests, that Stephens Inc. stepped into the breach as HLS's main financier. The campaigners said their next target, after Stephens, would be online share trading sites of brokers dealing in HLS shares.

HLS de-listed from the London Stock Exchange in January 2002 in an attempt to reduce the company's vulnerability. It reincorporated as Life Sciences Research, based in Maryland, USA, where shareholding rules allow the identities of investors with minor stakes to remain secret. Stephens Inc. had, just weeks prior to HLS's reincorporation, dropped its equity and debt support, following intense activism, culminating in the vandalising of the New York home of the bank's president.[108] In April 2002, US stockbroker Charles Schwab asked investors in HLS to transfer their stock to another broker. For the Royal Bank of Scotland, Stephens Inc. and Charles Schwab, the threat of being associated with HLS was simply too great. Shac's innovative campaign focus on 'tertiary targets' – third-party backers of HLS such as financiers, stockbrokers and insurers – could claim another success.

In a new twist in February 2003, HLS's auditor, Deloitte & Touche, became an activist target when a mole at Deloitte's passed to Shac the e-mail addresses, direct dial landline and mobile phone numbers of 135 managers and secretaries in the firm's life sciences team. Hailing the coup as 'the best information we've ever had from inside a company', Shac moved swiftly to bombard the e-mail addresses and disable mobile phones with jamming software capable of dialling a number 500 times a minute. This was followed by demonstrations at the managers' homes, some of which caused criminal damage and the intimidation of the wives and young children of several staff. After just a two-week Shac campaign, Deloitte announced that it would end its four-year relationship with HLS and would not offer itself for re-election after completing the company's 2002 audit.[109] It would seem that even auditors are not immune from campaigning extremists and that havoc can be wreaked by the most trusted of stakeholders – a business's employees.

The new breed of hackers is smart: in May 2001 a group of them claimed the ultimate scalp by bringing down the website of the US-government-funded CERT anti-hacking centre for three days. 'Despite boasting sophisticated defences and some of the finest minds in computer security, the CERT coordination centre . . . was left powerless as its website was engulfed by a flood of bogus e-mail data requests.'[110]

Given the sophistication of e-attacks, your security can never be 100% guaranteed. However, you can partially mitigate the threat by investing in appropriate firewalls, user training and other security measures to counter the e-peril. You can also critically appraise your customer and supplier relationships to check whether you might unwittingly become a 'tertiary target'. You can incorporate e-attacks and systems outages into your business continuity and crisis management plans. Finally, you can actively exploit the Internet to counter and even embrace your critics – an opportunity that will be explored in Chapter 9.

responsive

Customers also want their suppliers to be responsive and flexible in dealing with their requirements and concerns. This means being accessible: not leaving your customers fuming in telecommunications no-man's-land as they struggle to get through to a human being on your automated call system. It means being prepared to give customers contact details for named individuals who can help and guide them, giving your organisation a human face.

It also involves making it easy for customers to lodge complaints and dealing with their concerns swiftly and effectively; for poor complaints handling is a fertile source of customer discontent and reputational damage. Many newspapers and magazines include 'consumer watchdog' columns which give advice to aggrieved customers who have failed to obtain redress from a supplier of faulty merchandise or misleading investment advice. The media are usually only too happy to name and shame the offending business, or government department, and battle on the underdog's behalf, as in the Abbey National case cited earlier. It is usually with gloating satisfaction that one reads of the outcome: a grovelling apology, replacement product and/or financial compensation. 'Why couldn't they have done that in the first place' you chuckle.

Amusing as these piecemeal and relatively innocuous incidents may be, sometimes they can become real thorns in the flesh of a business's reputation – which can develop into running sores. If the issue is adopted by the media as a high-profile campaign cause, it can lead to the formation of an action group of wronged consumers, support from NGOs and other influencers and potentially to a mass lawsuit. The media sometimes incite aggrieved parties to unite and take action. After its acquisition of rival airline Buzz in January 2003, Irish-based Ryanair advised 100 000 Buzz passengers who had booked tickets for April that their flights would be cancelled, only the original fare would be refunded and they would have to rebook. A UK newspaper, under the catchy headline 'Don't let it tell you to Buzz off', advised those affected that they were entitled to compensation and possibly damages under contract law. The paper published details of a UK firm of solicitors who were considering launching a class action and urged irate passengers to come forward.[111]

☐   LEVERAGING COMPLAINTS

Think of your complaints system as a customer whistleblowing charter; your customers' views count and should be acted upon. As with employee whistleblowing, complaints are a relief valve for customers – possibly your final opportunity to resolve the issue just between the two of you. If you don't respond, they may take their grievances to the media or to a lawyer.

The early warning signs are almost always there: those increasingly angry phone calls, that cancellation of the long-running standing order, the spate of product quality problems or the letter threatening legal action. All too often these early indicators are not picked up and their cumulative significance is not recognised, so they are not acted upon; or legal experts are brought in too late to avert a crisis. Complaints systems, supplier non-conformances and variances in customer ordering patterns can act as crucial early warning mechanisms – allowing you to take corrective action before it is too late. But you need to make those connections and act promptly if you are to nip problems in the bud.

Actively exploit your complaints and learn all you can from them. So many complaints systems only track and report the time taken to close individual complaints against an agreed blanket target limit. There's so much more you can do with the data.

- Tag and analyse complaints by type to spot emerging trends.
- Investigate the root cause of the complaint and take steps to reduce the likelihood of it happening again (feed the risk into your risk management system to ensure it's not forgotten).
- Check movements in the absolute number of complaints. (Are they rising or falling? Why is that? What can you learn from it?)
- Ensure that summaries of complaints, conclusions and actions taken are regularly reviewed by your executive team, board and audit committee. This will help to set the tone from the top and show the organisation that complaints matter.
- Set a target for an acceptable level of complaints and monitor performance against it both in aggregate and by type – with zero tolerance for high-exposure complaints. If you want to truly delight your customers, even one complaint may be one too many!

> Those who are furthest away from head office are often closest to the customer and at the sharp-end of the intelligence gathering, and they are the ones who make the difference in determining whether the customer buys from us or not.
>
> (Geoff Armstrong, Director General, Institute of Personnel and Development, UK[112])

Using customer service departments to proactively sniff out and pre-empt trouble and to delight their customers can generate considerable goodwill and enhance reputation. The few seemingly reckless companies whose policy is to settle complaints swiftly and without question may have a point after all . . .

innovative

Customers expect their suppliers to innovate and to develop their product and service lines in line with evolving market needs. Investors also want to see innovation in the companies in their portfolio, for without this they will wither and die. Challenging a heavily research-dependent business on its ability to innovate strikes at the heart of its licence to operate, its very legitimacy and can raise doubts in the minds of investors, customers and employees.

In 2002 global pharmaceutical giant GlaxoSmithKline was under huge pressure to demonstrate to investors that it had products in the pipeline to meet future customer needs and sustain its profitability and growth. A full-page feature article in the *Financial Times* under the headline 'Sagging morale, departing scientists, a dwindling pipeline: when will GSK's research overhaul produce results?'[113] focused on the imperative for GSK to quickly bring new drugs to market. Costs savings achieved from the merger two years previously of GlaxoWellcome and Smith-Kline Beecham were starting to dry up, best-selling older drugs had lost their patent protection and shareholders were reluctant to sanction another deal when there were question marks over the company's performance and prospects. GSK's only route was to launch lucrative new products. Yet of the 125 products in clinical trials, most were still at early stages. The company was not planning an 'R&D day' – an annual display of potentially profitable new drugs – until the end of 2003. A major restructuring had taken place, morale was allegedly low and several leading scientists had defected. Chief executive Jean-Pierre Garnier refused to be drawn on which of his drug development 'children' offered the best prospects. Investors felt nervous. As the article concluded: 'Investors will certainly need to be patient: the benefits of what Mr Garnier is trying to achieve will not be apparent any time soon. Some of his children, it seems, are late developers.'

When seeking ideas for innovative new products and services that delight customers and satisfy investors, businesses often fail to tap a key source of information – their risk database.

> New and innovative products keep our stores exciting and help us meet customer desire for choice and value. As the leading retailer in many of our markets we have to be ahead of our competitors in shaping markets for new products and services.
>
> Peat free compost, energy efficient refrigeration, organic pest control – all these are products our stores did not stock until an understanding of the environmental issues led us to investigate alternatives to existing product lines.
>
> In a highly competitive retail market, it is important to be able to identify challenges and opportunities before our competitors. If we can do this we can help to shape the way the markets for our products are moving.
>
> (Kingfisher plc[114])

It was only when European retailing group Kingfisher looked at the threats posed by upcoming environmental pressures that they began to think laterally about developing innovative alternatives. These new products have provided them with a competitive edge; being first in the field with innovative offerings that consumers like and trust has also enhanced their reputation. A potential threat has been converted into a business opportunity.

So take a fresh look at your risk database and the threats and opportunities you have documented.

- Have you found time to exploit the market opportunities that you have identified? Have you listened carefully to your customers, picked up and built on their ideas for new products and services?
- Have you identified the threats to successful innovation in your business? Do you inspire your staff to think laterally, to suggest and develop ideas? What stops you from swiftly commercialising new development concepts?
- Have you critically appraised other threats – planned regulatory changes, customers complaints, environmental pressures – to see which of these could be converted into fresh ideas for new or modified products and services?

Innovation in products, services and processes form the lifeblood of any business seeking a long-term future. Businesses need to systematically identify business threats and opportunities and engage with their stakeholders to pinpoint potential areas for innovation; they then need to communicate regularly with their customers, investors and other stakeholders on the status of that innovation and ensure that it is implemented in a responsible way.

responsible

Customers and other stakeholders want their suppliers of goods and services to act responsibly in three major areas:

- Marketing and sales practices
- Supply chain practices
- Innovation.

☐   MARKETING AND SALES PRACTICES

Customers are smarter and better informed than ever before and expect to be treated fairly. Banks that fail to advise long-standing customers of better interest rate deals while promoting advantageous 'special offers' to potential new customers, can leave a sour taste in the mouths of previously loyal clients. Customers also do not like being duped by misleading marketing techniques; they will simply vote with their feet.

In April 1998, Sunny Delight, a soft drink aimed at children, was introduced into the UK by Procter & Gamble (P&G). The product's launch was a masterstroke. It was promoted as a premium-priced product that had to be refrigerated; it was packaged in frosted plastic bottles and displayed in chiller cabinets alongside fresh fruit juices. This not only gave the impression that the product was healthy, but it also meant that the product was not head-to-head with the usual soft drink rivals. A £9.2 million advertising campaign with the slogan 'the great stuff kids go for' featured children engaged in lively outdoor pursuits and depicted Sunny D as a healthier alternative to soft drinks such as colas. It was backed up with a massive direct marketing campaign to encourage people to sample it.

The launch was phenomenally successful; kids loved it and consumed it in vast quantities. By August 1999 Sunny Delight sales ranked number three in the UK's soft drinks league table.

This was in complete contrast to its profile in the USA where, available since 1964, it was marketed as a down-market product alongside squashes and other long-life drinks. But this was before P&G acquired the brand in the late 1980s.

However, Sunny D was not what it appeared. Closer analysis revealed that it contained only 5% citrus, lots of sugar and water, with vegetable oil, thickeners, vitamins, flavourings, colourings and other additives to give it the look and texture of fresh orange juice.

> It was put together with incredible care and skill, aimed at the immature taste buds of young children. They managed to get a taste that kids adore and a message that gives mums the permission to buy it.
>
> (Robert Moberly, brand consultant[115])

The backlash was fast and furious. The UK's health watchdog denounced Sunny Delight as a con, accusing its manufacturers P&G of misleading the public by putting the product in chiller cabinets. A BBC consumer affairs programme dubbed Sunny D 'the unreal thing'. P&G claimed that the UK variant *did* have to be chilled as its specification differed from the US product which was sold at ambient temperature. Then, in December 1999 a case was reported in the USA of a five-year-old girl turning orange after drinking 1.5 litres of Sunny D a day. She was overdosing on betacarotene – the additive that provides the orange colour – and pigment was being deposited in her hands and face. A new condition – Sunny Delight Syndrome – had found its way into the medical journals.[116]

As sales tumbled, P&G were forced to put a warning on its bottles: 'Like all soft drinks, Sunny Delight should be consumed in moderation.' A low-sugar version, Light Sunny Delight, was later introduced and, in March 2001, P&G announced that it was to hive off Sunny D into a new joint venture with Coca-Cola.

Consumers felt betrayed by a trusted name: P&G had promoted the product as safe and healthy for children, but they had overstretched themselves and overclaimed: a tacit promise had been made to consumers that simply could not be delivered. As Naomi Klein has observed: 'Over and over again, it is when the advertising teams creatively overreach themselves that – like Icarus – they fall.'[117]

P&G's strong individual product branding meant, however, that only Sunny D's sales dropped, its other brands were not affected, even though the corporate name was bandied about by the media. P&G have since been coy about revealing precise sales and market share figures for Sunny D. Sally Woodage, P&G's external relations manager, hinted in 2001 that lessons had, perhaps, been learned: 'In hindsight we might have wanted to make it clearer that this is a different sort of drink, i.e. a non-carbonated fruit-flavoured beverage.'[118]

Unfortunate timing can also catch businesses out – even if the message itself is seemingly innocuous. McDonald's were accused of extreme insensitivity when they launched a new hamburger called 'The McAfrika' in Norway in 2002. The launch in one of the world's most affluent economies, at a time when 12 million people were starving in Malawi, Zimbabwe and other African countries, was described as 'inappropriate and distasteful' by Norwegian Church Aid.[119] Protestors from the aid group handed out 'catastrophe crackers' – the protein-rich biscuits given to the starving – to McDonald's customers outside the firm's Oslo restaurants. McDonald's swiftly launched a damage limitation exercise, apologising in the Norwegian media for any offence caused. However, McDonald's did not agree to withdraw the offending product, but merely allowed aid agencies to leave collection boxes and fund-raising posters in the restaurants that promoted the new burger. Ever willing and able to convert a threat into an opportunity, McDonald's UK head office told a UK newspaper in August 2001:

> All of the involved parties are happy with this solution. We hope this will put a wider focus on the important job that these organisations are doing, and McDonald's in Norway is pleased to be able to support this.[120]

This local and relatively minor incident did little damage to McDonald's global brand, but it serves to illustrate that it's not just *what* you say and *how* you say it but also *when* you say it that can be important. You should ensure that your marketing message in its entirety passes the responsibility test. Even when your back is against the wall and your reputation is under threat, there may still be an opportunity to retrieve the position, if you think laterally and act promptly.

❏ SUPPLY CHAIN PRACTICES

As expectations of good corporate behaviour grow, consumers are less likely to tolerate abuses in a company's supply chain. NGOs have waged well-orchestrated campaigns against companies such as Nike, Adidas and Gap by exposing irresponsible activities in their supply networks. Damaging headlines appearing over the years such as 'Child labour scandal hits Adidas',[121] and 'Nike accused of tolerating sweatshops'[122] have maintained pressure on such companies to eliminate labour abuses. To satisfy stakeholders, these companies have had to institute comprehensive and costly auditing programmes at their suppliers' factories overseas, utilising independent third-party verifiers, to give credence to their assertions of responsible business practice.

Consumers are paying much more attention to where products are made, by whom and under what conditions. Has child labour been used? Are workers treated fairly and given a living wage – even if they are not direct employees of the retailer? Does the manufacturing process damage the environment, the health of workers or local communities? If so, where consumers have a choice they may go elsewhere; they may actively select a product or service whose credentials are assured.

As Dr Alan Knight, head of social responsibility at European retail group Kingfisher, puts it: 'If your product could tell its life story would it be embarrassing for the person who bought it – or would they be proud?'[123]

There has been a significant growth recently in the market for 'fair traded' goods – albeit from a tiny base. The concept of 'fair trade' food is that consumers pay a guaranteed price and a small social premium to groups of growers and small producers in developing countries, many of whom live in extreme poverty. Products are bought directly at a guaranteed price which covers the cost of production; this is not affected by the vagaries of world market trends and unscrupulous middle men. A small price premium enables producers to invest in their local communities and improve their living standards. The range of fair trade products now includes coffee, tea, chocolate and fruit, such as bananas. Sales of certified fair trade foods in the UK – now worth £58 million per annum – are growing exponentially and have more than tripled in three years. Retailers, such as the Co-operative Group and Safeway retail chains, which stock fair trade lines, have found that it makes good business sense. A Co-op spokesperson commented: 'We are finding growth more sustainable than organic foods. . . . Sales are growing consistently and we are switching all our own-brand chocolate to fair trade.'[124] This development, taken alongside the growth in socially responsible investment (SRI) funds discussed in Chapter 2, indicates that a rising proportion of consumers now take social, ethical and environmental criteria into account, as well as price and quality, when making purchasing decisions. The market opportunities are potentially huge. Perhaps 'fair trade' trainers or T-shirts will be the next concept to capture the imagination of ethically conscious young consumers. If that happens, the '30:3' syndrome – where a third of consumers claim to care about a product's social and ethical lineage but fewer than 3% actually buy 'ethically' – could be turned on its head.

☐ INNOVATION

Although consumers want to see innovation of products and services, they want progress to be responsible and implemented in a responsible way. As the World Business Council for Sustainable Development states:

> To preserve their freedom to innovate, corporations will have to include in their development processes an evaluation of a broader set of impacts, including the social, environmental and economic impacts of their innovations, thereby keeping themselves aligned with public expectations.
>
> In the past, firms tended to innovate in black boxes, springing results upon consumers. The world is now too transparent for this to be a viable tactic. Also, many of today's innovations come packed with moral, ethical, environmental and social controversy, as innovations occur in human, animal and plant reproduction, the production of food, and the maintenance of health. Such innovations require much discussion.
>
> Business has much to gain from transparency, except in cases where commercial confidentiality must be preserved. Thus innovation will be done in goldfish bowls. It will be stimulated by stakeholder dialogues and new partnerships. It will be best accepted coming from companies that have made their values clear and have a solid reputation for acting upon them.[125]

US conglomerate Monsanto saw its creation of genetically modified seeds as a winner; there were clear benefits to farmers, to the environment and, indirectly, to the general public. However, the technology's introduction into Europe in the late 1990s turned into a PR and reputational nightmare as Monsanto totally misjudged the public mood in a Europe battered by a string of food safety scares, such as salmonella poisoning and BSE. Monsanto had simply assumed that the technology would be broadly welcomed, as it had been in the USA.

Monsanto were vilified by the European green lobby for tampering with the laws of nature, major supermarkets banned goods containing GM ingredients and governments were forced to act – even though research indicated that GM crops could potentially benefit the environment and increase farmers' productivity. Monsanto had not invested adequately in educating and winning over its major overseas stakeholders; it mainly 'told' and hadn't engaged sufficiently in dialogue to understand and respond to concerns. As chairman, Robert B. Shapiro, candidly admitted at a conference of the NGO Greenpeace:

> The unintended result . . . has probably been that we have irritated and antagonized more people than we have persuaded. Our confidence in this technology and our enthusiasm for it has, I think, widely been seen – and understandably so – as condescension or indeed arrogance. Because we thought it was our job to persuade, too often we have forgotten to listen.[126]

Monsanto subsequently committed themselves to open dialogue with groups and individuals that have a stake in the issue and started to rebuild their battered reputation.[127]

Opposition to new and innovative ideas may come not only from customers, but also from employees and other parties who feel they may be adversely affected:

> Hurdles to adoption can come in three kinds. Employees can feel threatened by the launch of a new business because it promises to transfer the company's power and resources from them to others. Partners can feel disenfranchised by a new business – as, for example, when traditional resellers are sidestepped by a company's efforts to sell goods over the Internet. And the general public can reject a new idea, as it did with GM foods, because it is poorly understood.
>
> (W. Chan Kim and Renee Mauborgne, INSEAD[128])

When introducing and implementing an innovative new product or service it is vitally important to consult with key stakeholders and obtain their 'buy in'. Stakeholder concerns about your new product or service may pose such an overwhelming threat to your reputation that it may be unwise to proceed. Engaging with your stakeholders, addressing their anxieties, building on their ideas and carrying them with you could, on the other hand, convert your most vociferous potential critics into your most ardent advocates. Stakeholder dialogue as a reputation risk management tool will be examined in Chapter 7.

customer exposures

This section has explored the many issues to be taken into account if you are to deliver the promise to customers and protect and enhance your reputation. You also need to consider carefully whether any reputational threats could be lurking within your customer base itself.

As discussed previously, firms like Andersen and KPMG have found that their own reputations can be tarnished if they are associated with unethical or corrupt clients or clients that inhibit their ability to do a good job. Indeed, the world's largest accounting firm, PricewaterhouseCoopers (PwC), announced in December 2002 that it might decline work at companies refusing to pay for certain services, such as a risk assessments, that help the firm to conduct an effective audit. The exposure might simply be too great. PwC's global chief executive, Samuel DiPiazza, commented:

> If we have an audit client unwilling to pay what we feel are fair audit fees or that restricts our scope of services to the point where we are concerned about the quality of the audit – either of those can cause us to walk away from a relationship.[129]

It is common in the construction industry for bidders to assess the track record of a potential client as part of their project risk assessment. Does the client have a track record of on-time delivery of projects? Are they renowned for making major specification changes that can throw the project off course? Does the client act with integrity when dealing with suppliers? This type of approach is becoming more prevalent in the IT sector where the reputations of large software companies have been blemished by contracts that have gone 'belly up'. Prevarication, poor leadership, inadequate dedicated project resource or last minute changes in user requirements can all be danger signals. The right decision might be not to bid at a particular client; the potential risk exposure in terms of impact on corporate reputation may simply be too great. Even banks now have to be more cautious with whom they do business as a result of more stringent money-laundering regulations and rising investor interest in the risk-profile of projects to which they are lending. For an increasing number of businesses in different sectors, developing a good understanding of your major customers' risks is not just a 'nice to have' but a prerequisite for effective reputation risk management.

Furthermore, having an impressive list of law-abiding, highly regarded, responsible clients can enhance your reputation and help to attract additional business and investment.

> Association with reputable organisations can add value. Their presence on a list of suppliers or clients adds prestige and may help to attract other key clients and talent.
>
> (Department of Trade and Industry, UK[130])

a promise kept

There are multiple factors to take into account when delivering – and, where possible, surpassing – your promise to customers. The major considerations to mitigate threats and exploit opportunities are:

- Ensure that your product and service quality is second to none and that your pricing is fair; deal promptly with any failings that could undermine customer loyalty.

- Live up to your brands. Ensure that you uphold those unique values and attributes that embody them. Jealously guard your USP: that one unique attribute that differentiates your product or services from others in the eyes of your customers. Without it, you will lose your competitive edge.

- Be wary of brand extensions, shifts into new markets, new territories, new distribution and sales channels. Ensure that risks are understood, are acceptable and can be managed before taking the plunge.

- Don't overpromise: keep your publicists in check and don't overstretch yourself. Your organisation should be in a position to monitor and report honestly on all of its customer-related activities. If you can't, then perhaps the exposure is too great.

- Take steps to keep your products and services available and secure. Protect your systems and website through robust security measures. Integrate e-attacks and resultant system failures into your business continuity and crisis management plans. Use the Internet to counter and embrace your critics.

- Critically assess your customers and suppliers. Could any of them make you the 'tertiary target' of an activist group? Could the projects they are involved in, their values, their business practices, expose your business to reputational risk?

- Be responsive – show your human face. Regard complaints as customer whistleblowing: delight customers by dealing with them promptly and by pre-empting trouble. Learn from them, monitor them and set targets to reduce them – right from the top.

- Use your risk management systems and stakeholders to identify business threats and opportunities that could be leveraged to develop tomorrow's products and services. Innovate responsibly; and communicate progress on innovation to retain stakeholder confidence.

- Act responsibly: in your sales and marketing, in your supply chain, and when innovating – so that your customers can be confident that the products and services they buy from you do not have adverse impacts. Engage in honest and open dialogue with your customers and other major stakeholders to persuade them to 'buy in' to new developments.

Your customers' expectations and requirements will continue to evolve and the promise you make to them will need to be adapted accordingly. But you can only do this if – unlike M&S in the late 1990s – you find ways of engaging with your customers so that you pick up on their changing perceptions, wants and desires. If you get it wrong, you can be faced with customers deserting your stores, consumer boycotts, damaging NGO and media campaigns, falling sales and a tarnished reputation. If you get it right, and are able to respond to your customers in a way that doesn't just deliver the promise but exceeds it, your reputational stock can only increase.

Finally, it helps to ensure that high-profile employees in the public eye never rubbish your products – even in jest. The classic case of this is Gerald Ratner, the former chairman of the UK-based retail jewellery empire, who in 1991 described one of his firm's products, a low-priced sherry decanter with six glasses and a silver-plated tray, as 'total crap'. To thunderous laughter at an Institute of Directors conference he added, 'We sell a pair of earrings for £1 – which is cheaper than a prawn sandwich from Marks & Spencer but, I have to say, the earrings probably won't last as long.' A chairman rubbishing the quality of his own products is hardly reputation-enhancing behaviour. Ratner's jocular remarks swiftly resulted in his personal down-fall, in shattered consumer and investor confidence in the brand, and, in turn, to the demise of this long-established family business.

WORKPLACE TALENT AND CULTURE

'Human capital' is one of an organisation's most valuable intangible assets.

> The right treatment of people – human capital – is a key driver for many businesses. Investors need to know this value, human capital, is secure and is being maximised in the same way as its other assets.
>
> (Patricia Hewitt, UK Trade and Industry Secretary[131])

Human capital embraces the quality of people employed; the diversity of their backgrounds, skills and experience; their motivation and ability to innovate and create value; their job satisfaction; their enthusiasm for providing good customer service; the degree to which they feel empowered; and the organisational culture in which they operate. It is therefore understandable that shareholders, employees and others are seeking better information about the management of this critical asset before deciding whether to invest in, or work for, a business.

What, then, are the key drivers of workplace talent and culture (Table 6-10)? What threats lurk in this area that could imperil a business's standing? Where are the opportunities to boost reputation? And which aspects of employee talent and culture are of interest to which stakeholders?

Table 6-10. Stakeholder requirements and expectations on workplace talent and culture

Stakeholder group	Requirements and expectations
Employees Unions	• Good pay and conditions • Employees respected, valued and trusted • Quality training and development • Flexibility
Shareholders/Investors	• Right mix of skills and experience • Able to recruit and retain high quality staff • Appropriate incentives • Empowering culture which supports risk management and innovation
Customers Suppliers	• Competent, helpful employees • Employees take pride in their work and in the business
Regulators Governments Communities NGOs/Pressure groups	• Competent staff able to comply with regulations, keep staff and communities safe and protect the environment

'Best employer' surveys[132] are an excellent means of keeping up to date with the top concerns of employees – and of demonstrating that your business is a good employer that has what it takes to make the premier league.

One such survey, the *Sunday Times: 100 best companies to work for* in the UK, asks employees to score their business against eight factors:

- Leadership: the head of the company and senior managers
- My manager: their immediate boss and how they are managed on a day-to-day basis
- Personal growth: opportunities to learn, grow and be challenged
- Wellbeing: stress, pressure and balancing work and home life
- My team: their immediate colleagues
- Giving something back: how much their company puts back into society and the local community
- My company: the company they work for and the way it treats staff
- Fair deal: how good the pay and benefits are.[133]

Microsoft UK was voted top of the *Sunday Times* 2003 survey after being awarded second place in 2002.[134] Of its staff, 93% felt proud to work for the company, saying 'it makes a positive difference to the world we live in'; 92% were excited about where it is heading and would miss it if they left; around 90% praised Microsoft's positive and inspiring leadership, together with its high regard for customers; and 89% enjoyed working there. The company has no human resources department but a division simply called 'Great Company', whose mission is to engage staff and another linking 'people, profit and culture'.

A ringing vote of confidence from employees is the best accolade any business can wish for. It is perhaps no coincidence that Microsoft was also ranked third in *Fortune* magazine's and second in the *Financial Times* listings of the world's most admired and respected companies. Microsoft's Bill Gates was also voted the world's most respected leader by the *Financial Times* survey.[135] An interesting feature of many 'best employers' is clear senior management leadership and commitment to creating an outstanding workplace – often inspired by a charismatic and forceful CEO.

The benefit of being a great company to work for is not just a soft and intangible 'feel good' factor – there is evidence of a positive impact on the bottom line. The top 50 companies in the *Sunday Times: 100 best companies to work for* survey would have earned an investor a compounded annual return of 12.1% over the five years up to January 2003, compared with a 5.8% decline for the FTSE All-Share index overall; over the prior three years the best companies returned 3.6% compared with a 15% decline in the index; and even in the depressed trading conditions of 2002 the best had a return of −21.1% compared with −28.8% for the rest of the market.[136]

Firms that are good employers would also appear to be sound investments. As Patricia Hewitt, UK Trade and Industry Secretary, has commented:

> Many factors contribute to a company's success. Too often, however, the people factor is overlooked.... Perhaps most importantly [this listing]... shows how these businesses benefit from their investment in people. Companies that respect, value and invest in staff are more productive

and significantly more profitable . . . high levels of employee satisfaction have a corresponding link to high levels of customer satisfaction.[137]

pay and conditions

Employees want to be fairly rewarded for their efforts and expect fair treatment, unambiguous terms of employment, clear disciplinary, grievance and termination procedures, a safe and healthy working environment, freedom of association and the right to collective bargaining. The unions that represent them have similar goals. Investors, too, want to be sure that these basic building blocks of good human resources practice are in place – or their investment could suffer.

The effect of directors' pay schemes on their behaviour and motivation was discussed in the corporate governance section of this chapter. The same principle applies to other employees in the organisation; short-term incentivisation can result in short-term thinking but long-term reputational damage. Poorly designed compensation schemes can even undermine a business's ethical code by manifestly providing incentives for misconduct; schemes with a short-term focus, particularly those that are earnings related, can entice less scrupulous employees into focusing exclusively on the financial ends, while paying scant regard to the means of achieving them. The case of Nick Leeson, the rogue trader who caused the downfall of Barings Bank through his self-serving activities in their Singapore branch, is a classic example of this.

Remuneration and incentive schemes should support your business goals while concurrently embracing your business principles. If your reputation is to remain intact, alignment is essential. Some forward-thinking companies are starting to use their appraisal and remuneration systems to encourage responsible behaviour that can protect and enhance their reputations.

Hill & Knowlton's Corporate Reputation Watch survey 2002, conducted by Harris Interactive, found that there is a growing tendency for CEOs to be remunerated in part according to their ability to impact corporate reputation. This ranged from 12% of CEOs in Germany to 44% in Italy, with 26% in the UK and 29% in the USA. The cash received for corporate kudos can be significant: in the UK and Germany it was over 40% and in the USA it was just of a third of total compensation.[138] Nine per cent of the companies surveyed by Sustainable Assets Management (SAM) in 2002 for the Dow Jones sustainability indices reported that more than 3% of their overall workforce received variable remuneration and compensation linked to their environmental and corporate responsibility performance. Of the companies polled, 18% had integrated compliance with codes of conduct into their employee performance appraisal systems.[139]

Non-financial assessment criteria can be in the form of key performance indicators (Diageo), through individual balanced scorecards (Statoil) or through leadership principles and desired competencies (Siemens and Merck), according to a World Economic Forum Report.[140] Other companies starting to develop specific non-financial measures and targets include Coca-Cola, McDonald's, Anglo American, Electricité de France, UBS, WMC and Rio Tinto. Most commonly such targets include employee safety and diversity, followed by ethical and environmental performance. Companies such as Coca-Cola are seeking to include broader measures such as how well they manage people and look after the company's reputation, as well as environmental and diversity matters. BP include non-financial criteria in performance contracts throughout the business and expect managers to provide ongoing assurance that company policies on ethical conduct, employees, external relationships, health, safety and environment as well as finance and control are complied with.

Identifying and measuring appropriate performance indicators for non-tangible criteria is a challenging task, with tools and thinking still at an early stage. Although only a relatively small number of leading-edge organisations have to date embarked on this path, the trend is set to continue. Since alignment between corporate values, goals and corporate behaviour is so crucial in building and retaining stakeholder trust and safeguarding reputation, it makes good business sense to reinforce and promote the desired behaviours through reward and recognition systems. The old axiom 'what gets measured gets managed' certainly applies here.

Employees are looking for good pay, fair conditions and incentives. Investors will be checking that the pay is appropriate, with additional awards only for superior performance that are fully aligned with the business's values and goals. So make it easy for them: don't force them to speculate and possibly draw the wrong conclusion. Spell out your remuneration policies and principles and summarise them in your annual report – perhaps providing further detail on the employee or vacancies sections of your website.

valued, trusted and respected

The basic requirements in treating employees with respect are taken as givens: employees expect not only fair pay and conditions but open and honest communication (particularly at times of major change and possible redundancy), respect for diversity, lack of discrimination on grounds of sex, race or religion and protection from harassment and bullying. Employees also expect to have formal channels for dialogue with their employers to discuss and shape policies on workplace issues and to resolve grievances. In most developed countries these basic human rights are enshrined in law. If things go wrong there can be fines, penalties, public censure and, perhaps more importantly, potential for significant reputational damage. Headlines such as 'Sexist Schroder pays out £1.4m in compensation' are hardly a good advertisement for potential recruits. When Marks & Spencer announced the closure of stores in continental Western Europe early in 2001, embittered employees took to the streets in protest. There was panic buying by shocked customers, keen to show solidarity with workers, at M&S's flagship store on the Boulevard Haussman in Paris. A window display at M&S's store in Nice, in southern France, depicted a coffin draped with an M&S flag, surrounded by chained, blindfolded and hooded mannequins dressed in black, presumably destined for the gallows. Employee disaffection in action! The images graphically depicting a once revered employer apparently disregarding its employees' basic rights were more damaging to the company than any alleged breaches of employment legislation.

If direct action fails, employees are more willing than ever to take legal action against their employers. The American-style compensation culture has spread to Europe and beyond. Employees are very aware of their rights and will take employers to court for unfair dismissal, work-induced stress, discrimination, bullying and other workplace grievances. A series of industrial tribunals and high-profile court cases can sap business resources, tie up senior management and result in damaging headlines, adverse publicity and significant fines.

If employees don't feel valued, or worse, if they feel exploited and are not being listened to, they may resort to even more damaging tactics. In October 2002, international law firm Clifford Chance hit the headlines when a leaked internal memo from junior lawyers in the USA thrust the firm's questionable employment and business practices under the global media spotlight. The 13-page memo, sent by a group of six of Clifford Chance's 430 junior lawyers in the USA to the firm's New York partners, alleged that so much pressure was put on juniors that they were encouraged to over-record the time spent on clients' affairs. An extract from the memo stated:

> ... associates found the stress on billable hours dehumanising and verging on an abdication of our professional responsibilities insofar as the requirement ignores pro bono work and encourages 'padding' of hours, inefficient work, repetition of tasks and other problems.[141]

Other choice sound-bites from the memo included concerns about 'being yelled at' and told 'we own you' and the billable hours requirements making 'me feel that management cares exceedingly about hours billed but gives no thought to the quality of my work, let alone my career development'. The memo had been prompted by a job satisfaction survey in *American Lawyer* magazine that ranked Clifford Chance 132nd of 132 firms. The fundamental complaint was the firm's requirement that junior lawyers bill 2420 hours a year; this not only encouraged padding and inefficiency but created an incentive to put expensive senior associates on jobs that less expensive lawyers could do, if a shortfall on target hours was predicted. Damaging headlines such as 'top law firm hit by "padding" claims' and 'stress put on billable hours "dehumanising": explosive staff memo from Clifford Chance lawyers certain to make eye-popping reading for clients'[142] inevitably resulted. The affair focused attention on charging practices not only at Clifford Chance but in the legal profession as a whole. Other legal firms were hit by the collateral fall-out, as their clients started to take a closer and more informed look at their invoices.

Clifford Chance management moved swiftly to make changes but the damage had already been done. A taskforce was set up to deal with the morale problem and, in December 2002, incoming US managing partner, John Carroll, announced a complete policy revamp that would replace the punishing 2420 hour target with rewards and promotions based on seven categories: respect and monitoring; quality of work; excellence in client service; integrity; contribution to the community; commitment to diversity; and contribution to the firm as an institution. In his Christmas 2002 message to employees John Carroll said:

> The associates who wrote the memo were really just speaking for others. As odd as this may seem, a year from now they will be viewed as the heroes of this process ... One never likes bad press but it certainly creates a challenge and an opportunity to have a lot of dialogue that has been very useful for the firm.[143]

But this isn't all about downside; survey after survey reveals the major upsides for bosses, employees, customers and ultimately the bottom line if staff are not just respected but valued, nurtured, trusted and empowered. Employees of 'best employer' businesses talk about feeling valued and motivated; about being treated as important contributors rather than as hired hands;

about relishing going to work; about loyalty to and pride in their organisation. To achieve this involves going beyond the legal minimum and responding flexibly to staff concerns, expectations and preferences by:

- respecting the individual's work/life balance – perhaps by offering family-friendly policies such as job sharing, part-time working, home working, term-time working
- valuing the individual's contribution – whether it be a novel idea for a new product or a concern about a supplier's activities that could threaten the reputation of the business and, above all
- trusting all individuals to give of their best.

Stakeholder dialogue doesn't just apply to external stakeholders: your employees are also stakeholders. Carrying out employee surveys and taking heed of the results, listening to your employees and acting on their concerns will be time well spent. And having a whistleblowing process to act as a relief valve may, in extremis, prevent employees from feeling that they will never get satisfaction unless they air their grievances externally.

Maybe there's a potential uniqueness attribute lurking among the employee feedback that could help you to differentiate yourself in your market as the 'most flexible' or 'most caring' employer, the 'employer that promotes diversity' – or another epithet enabling you to attract and retain the best staff. UK retailer B&Q (part of the Kingfisher Group) has made a virtue of its acceptance of older workers. As an experiment in 1989, B&Q opened a store in Macclesfield, in north-west England, staffed entirely by people over the age of 50. An independent survey, conducted two years later, showed that Macclesfield out-performed other stores against a number of assessment criteria, including customer service, staff turnover and sales. The company subsequently modified its country-wide recruitment practices to attract older workers.[144] In 2001 B&Q removed all age qualification for recruitment, promotion and training. In 2002 its most mature member of staff was 89 years old![145]

rights skills: recruitment, retention, training and development

Job security, although still a consideration, is for many employees not of prime importance. Most employees today don't expect to stay with the same business until retirement. They know they will probably move several times during their career and therefore seek an employer that will add value to their curriculum vitae – a business with a poor reputation could damage their career prospects. The last thing bright new graduates want is a potential stain on their CV because they have opted to work for an organisation that has a poor record on human rights or is found guilty of unethical business practices. In today's fluid job market employees are much more prepared to move on if they are not satisfied and if their expectations of fair treatment and enhancement of career prospects are not met.

> Employees expect some degree of security but they recognise that they cannot be given a career for life. So they treat an employer as a candidate for their services, not as someone to whom they are beholden.
> (Geoff Armstrong, Director General, Institute of Personnel and Development, UK[146])

Having the right skills for the job to meet both current and future requirements is a major challenge for all organisations – and of interest to many of a business's stakeholders. Employees want to work in an environment that will stimulate and challenge them and prepare them for more demanding, better paid roles in the future; a business's reputation will be a consideration in choosing an employer.

A survey in 2000 by the UK's Industrial Society[147] found that 82% of UK professionals would not work for a company whose values they did not believe in; 59% select an employer because they believe in what it does and what it stands for; and 73% take social and ethical considerations into account when selecting a job. It seems that in this new millennium employees are likely to consider whether an organisation matches their own personal values and self-image before applying. Younger people increasingly want to be associated with an organisation that makes a real difference so that they can take pride in their work. Having a good reputation, clear values and principles, can be a magnet for young graduates.

Employees have come to expect good training and development opportunities that will improve their prospects, increase their contribution and enhance their earnings. They want their chosen employer to offer them individual tailored development programmes to maximise their career potential and opportunities for promotion.

Investors too want to be sure that their investment is in competent hands – confident that a business recognises what blend of people, skills and experience it needs to grow and innovate as it rolls out its strategy, and is able to recruit and retain the right talent. Investors will be avidly reading your annual reports and other communications to check that you are successfully filling vacancies, and are investing adequately in training so that your employees acquire the necessary skills to meet the needs of tomorrow's business. Any reduction in staff development budgets or sudden increase in staff turnover at middle management levels could signal problems ahead.

Regulators and local communities want reassurance that your staff are competent and will comply with safety and environmental regulations. Your customers and suppliers want to deal with knowledgeable and helpful staff who take pride in their work.

So tell your prospective employees, investors and other stakeholders what you have to offer, how training and development are structured, how much you invest in it and what the prospects are for career progression within the business. Tell them about your targets to increase diversity, attract older workers and recruit researchers to boost your new product pipeline. Describe to them your plans to hone the telephone skills of your customer service staff and train your warehouse personnel on new systems. Give your stakeholders confidence in you as an employer and as a nurturer of workplace talent.

organisational culture

The best defence against 'infectious greed'[148] is a healthy corporate culture.
(The Economist, 27 July 2002)

Mention has been made many times already of the importance of organisational culture – or 'the way we do things around here'. Put another way, corporate culture is how employees behave when no one is looking. If your organisational climate is seen to inadequately support – or even thwart – the achievement of business objectives and effective risk management, it may arouse stakeholder concern and result in loss of confidence. And the single biggest influence on culture is the business's CEO, who sets the tone for the entire organisation.

As the US Conference Board observes:

> A major challenge to corporations and their leaders it to create a 'tone at the top' and a corporate culture that promotes ethical conduct on the part of the organization and its employees. Improvement in systems of governance alone will not restore the public's trust. Corporations should work to support responsible behavior and build environments in which employees take the initiative to address misconduct rather than waiting until after the damage is done.[149]

Employees are your first line of defence in managing risks, particularly risks to reputation. So often the early indications of an impending crisis are visible to those with the knowledge to spot and interpret them; employees are frequently aware of inappropriate conduct but choose to do nothing about it because of cultural issues. The previously cited KPMG study, in which 37% of employees claimed to have observed misconduct in the previous year that could result in a significant loss of public trust if it were exposed, also threw some light on the reasons for misconduct. It found that employees believe misconduct is caused, in descending order of importance by: cynicism/low morale/indifference; pressure to meet schedules; pressure to hit unrealistic earnings goals; desire to succeed or advance careers; lack of knowledge of standards; and desire to steal from or harm the company.[150] The majority of these are organisational 'hygiene' factors.

Being able to rely on employees to speak up if they have concerns is your best possible early warning system of potential threats to reputation. You stifle or ignore this at your peril. Autocratic 'command and control' cultures, where mistakes are personalised and blame readily apportioned, are fertile breeding grounds for undeclared risks and employee discontent. The top team may only received a sanitised version of reality and may profess genuine disbelief when a crisis strikes – although the crisis may have been long predicted by those lower down the organisation. When investigators rake over the debris of corporate catastrophes, they often conclude that alarm bells were ringing but were ignored, not heard or cleansed out of the 'truth' presented to senior management. Marks & Spencer and Clifford Chance are good examples of this: management allowed themselves to become isolated and preoccupied with other issues – they were deaf to the early rustlings of the gathering storm.

To support reputation risk management, you should aim to promote the type of culture where employees will swiftly take action at the first hint of a threat materialising – not one where problems are left to fester and escalate until some exalted superhero steps in to rescue the business from the brink of disaster. Staff should be recognised for prompt problem prevention as well as for taking calculated risks to benefit the business.

At Enron, the organisational culture is widely believed to have contributed to the company's downfall. The culture was one of 'sink or swim'. Enron paid well and recruited from America's top universities, but worked its staff hard and expected much of them. The climate was hardly conducive to airing concerns and nipping problems in the bud:

Twice a year, 15% of the workforce was ritually sacked, to be replaced by new arrivals, and a further 30% warned to improve. Employees were usually young, inexperienced and lacking in job options, since they lived in Houston, where Enron had few rivals. The company's cut-throat working culture destroyed morale and internal cohesion but also made workers afraid to question their superiors, let alone blow the whistle on sharp practices.[151]

Organisational culture can sometimes be a direct threat to the safety and well-being of employees themselves. In August 1999 operators at British Nuclear Fuels Ltd (BNFL) were found to be falsifying records at the Mox demonstration facility at Sellafield in north-west England. A subsequent report from the Nuclear Installations Inspectorate, published in February 2000, accused BNFL of 'systematic management failure' and having a 'serious safety culture problem'. The report was unequivocal in pointing the finger of blame of at BNFL's management:

Behind any deficiency in an individual's performance was often a trail of poor standards which had been tolerated by management. Responsibility must start at the top.

Evidence of lax standards in such a high-risk, high-profile industry severely tarnished BNFL's already fragile reputation and raised questions about its reliability as a supplier. In the ensuing months, BNFL replaced much of its senior management team and embarked on a crusade to change its culture and implement a policy of zero tolerance on compliance issues. The company lost business in Japan; its financial position deteriorated and the company had to defer indefinitely its planned transition to a Public Private Partnership. In 2000, the newly appointed chairman, Hugh Collum, articulated the scale of the problem then facing the company: 'My goal over the next two years is to rebuild BNFL and trust amongst our key stakeholders, particularly our customers.'[152]

Tokyo Electric Power (Tepco), the Japanese utility company, faced similar problems to BNFL in August 2002 when the company was found to have been faking safety reports and interfering with equipment to pass regulatory checks. Several reactors were shut down for inspection as a result of safety fears, with local communities living near its three nuclear power plants housing a total of 17 reactors, calling for the other reactors to be closed for re-inspection. In November 2002, Tepco warned residents of Tokyo and surrounding areas that they could face black-outs during the summer of 2003 – a phenomenon virtually unheard of since the 1950s. In an attempt to avert this, Tepco launched an advertising campaign over the winter to encourage consumers to conserve electricity. Tepco's president, Teruaki Masumoto, spent much of the latter part of 2002 travelling around Japan apologising on behalf of his company. He commented: 'All I do these days in bow in apology. You have to count how long the bow takes. It's important to get it right.'[153] Mr Masumoto's mission was to win back public confidence over nuclear power at a time when the industry's reputation for safety was tarnished and the company's credibility as an electricity supplier was at stake. 'It will take five to ten years for Tepco to regain the public's trust in our company,' Mr Masumoto stated. Warren Buffett's famous comment, 'It takes twenty years to build a reputation and five minutes to destroy it', certainly rings true.

Your organisational culture should support risk management by creating good awareness of sources of threats and opportunities to the business, by creating a climate in which employees are prepared to voice any concerns and by establishing a clear 'freedom to act' hierarchy so that all employees know what level of risk they are empowered to take on behalf of the business and do not overstep the mark.

Care should also be taken in making acquisitions – bringing into your ambit an unfamiliar set of values and lines of communication that can cause staff morale problems and lead to inappropriate actions or decisions by the acquired subsidiary. Partners at Clifford Chance admitted that there had been a crisis of confidence at the firm since the mergers with US-based Rogers & Wells and Germany's Punder, Volhard, Weber & Axster in 2000, which made Clifford Chance the world's largest law firm. The level of staff dissatisfaction had not been helped by trying to amalgamate firms with such differing cultures. Stuart Popham, a senior partner, admitted that insufficient attention had been given to personnel issues in the USA after the merger with Rogers & Wells, saying: 'I think we spent a little too much time forging the merger at certain levels without noticing some of the, shall we say, softer elements.'[154]

If you are planning an acquisition, consider the following questions:

- Does the acquisition target share your values and ethos?
- If not, how quickly could your company impose its values and culture? Where are the major exposures? Would the transition require sweeping management changes? How long would it take? Is it prudent for you to tolerate this level of exposure in the interim? If not, should you proceed?
- Could staff morale in your core business be adversely affected by the deal?

An appropriate organisational culture isn't just about nipping threats in the bud, it's also about spotting and exploiting opportunities and creating the right climate for innovation to flourish. Recruiting, developing and retaining people with the right skills for today's – and tomorrow's – business is a vital prerequisite to having the sort of culture in which technical innovation and entrepreneurship can thrive. Corporate reputation is both a draw and motivator for high-quality staff, their continuing commitment, and the competitive edge it generates.

A 2002 survey of European business leaders conducted by MORI on behalf of the UK-based Business in the Community cited the top issues affecting performance in the next five years as: attracting and retaining talented staff, ability to innovate and corporate reputation.[155] The three issues are inextricably intertwined.

The ability to innovate technically is vital, but so also is the need for complementary skills to bring the new offering swiftly to market. Knowing how to leverage skills internally and to combine those with the requisite skills in key stakeholders groups, is fundamental to successful innovation:

> Companies increasingly need strong, distinctive internal capabilities. But their distinctive know-how has to be combined with complementary assets, resources and skills provided by partners, investors and suppliers. A bright idea for a new product has to attract finance to research and develop it; skills and investment will be required to make it and different capabilities will be needed to market it effectively. Intellectual capital on its own is never enough. The job of senior

management is increasingly to orchestrate this dynamic combination of complementary skills and assets to generate and then realise innovative ideas and product improvements.

(Charles Leadbeatter [156])

The impact of organisational culture on employee behaviour is very powerful; it is little wonder the topic is attracting increasing attention from investors, regulators and other stakeholder groups. Post Enron, stakeholders are keen to peel back the corporate veneer and dig deep into the culture of a business in an attempt to understand its dynamics: its DNA.

achieving the right balance

To sum up, you can help safeguard and enhance your reputation by treating your employees well and creating a working environment that allows them to give of their best. To achieve this consider the following issues:

- Ensure that your pay, conditions, incentive schemes and performance management systems are fully aligned with your business values and goals.

- Show employees that they are trusted, valued and respected and that you are prepared to be flexible to allow them to achieve an appropriate work/life balance.

- Ensure that you have the right blend of people, skills and experience for both today's and tomorrow's business. Nurture and develop individual employees to allow them to achieve their full potential. Only then will you be maximising your human resources asset.

- Develop an organisational culture in which employees can thrive – one that supports staff, promotes risk management and sparks innovation.

- Constantly communicate what you are doing both to your employees and your external stakeholders. Tell them about your successes and your plans for the future on HR issues. Your investors will see you as lower risk if you are able to demonstrate that you are managing your 'human capital' effectively. Get yourself on a 'best companies to work for' list, publish the summary findings of your employee surveys, include data on staff turnover, training and development budgets and staff involvement in community projects.

- Ensure that communication is two-way: engage in genuine dialogue with your employees, listen to their concerns and act on them.

Contact with an 'insider'– an employee of the organisation – is one of the most persuasive influences on corporate reputation. The business's ethos influences the way employees think and feel about it and the way in which they communicate these feelings to external parties. Creating a culture in which your employees are proud of the organisation they work for, and emit the right vibes to customers and other stakeholders can be a great fillip to reputation.

Businesses that create a supportive and dynamic organisational culture with the right blend of skills, experience, trust, passion and pride, reap many benefits: their profile as a 'good'

Q   *Which comes closest to your opinion of your company as an employer?*

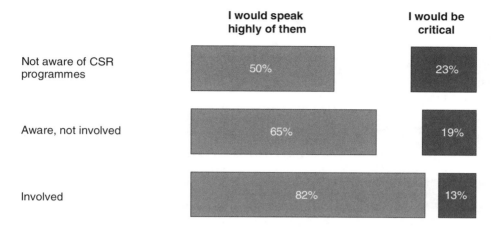

Base: c. 2 000 employees across six companies, March–May 2000   *Source:* MORI

Figure 6-3   Impact of CSR programmes on employees. (Reproduced by permission of MORI (Market & Opinion Research International))

employer wins the confidence of analysts and investors, creates a climate where innovation can flourish, retains the loyalty of existing employees, delights customers and helps to attract the most talented new recruits to contribute to the business's future growth and prosperity. Your employees become your reputational ambassadors and a virtuous circle is created which can continuously bolster your standing in the eyes of your stakeholders.

As an interesting aside, and a lead into the next section on corporate social responsibility (CSR), research has shown that one of the most powerful influences on employees to speak highly of their businesses, is commitment to CSR and community investment initiatives (Figure 6-3). Involving employees directly in such projects can be an excellent team-building activity and can increase pride in the business and its achievements.

MORI's research shows that looking at the views of employees across a range of companies, among those unaware of their company having CSR initiatives, 50% would speak highly of the company and 23% critically – a net balance of +27. The net balance leaps to +46 among those aware of schemes but not personally involved and to +69 among those personally involved. This is a compelling argument indeed for taking the time to communicate to employees the good things you are doing – and to start doing some good things, if you're not doing them already!

CORPORATE SOCIAL RESPONSIBILITY

Corporate social responsibility (CSR; or corporate citizenship as it is often known) is not a new phenomenon – it is the natural extension of traditional concepts of customer care, supplier management and corporate philanthropy to investors, local communities, pressure groups and the general public. Businesses are, and always have been, dependent on their stakeholders for their livelihood and their continuing 'licence to operate'. Companies have often known instinctively that it makes sense to take these wider relationships into account in managing business risk. That is why, without specifically mentioning corporate social responsibility, CSR-related topics such as transparency of financial reporting, boardroom ethics, marketing practices and treatment of employees have arisen naturally in the discussions about reputation risk earlier in this chapter.

To recap on what is meant by CSR, here is a reminder of the WBCSD definition used when the topic was first introduced in Chapter 2:

> Corporate social responsibility is the commitment of business to contribute to sustainable economic development working with employees, their families, the local community and society at large to improve their quality of life.[157]

By behaving responsibly businesses can contribute to sustainable development: i.e. 'forms of progress that meet the needs of the present without compromising the ability of future generations to meet their needs'.[158]

CSR is about a business placing the core values of ethics, integrity, fairness, accountability and transparency at the heart of all its activities.

In practice, this involves the business:

- considering its wider impacts on and contributions to society and the environment: finding ways of minimising negative impacts and maximising positive impacts
- identifying, assessing and addressing its social, environmental and ethical (SEE) risks
- displaying responsibility, fair dealing and respect for human rights in its relationships with employees, local communities, customers, suppliers and other business partners
- taking into account and responding to the needs and expectations of the diverse stakeholder groups on which its future success depends
- adopting responsible approaches and behaviours that go beyond basic legal compliance and permeate all areas of operation – from the board downwards
- balancing all those factors and integrating them into decision-making, strategy, corporate governance, management and reporting systems.

This final point is the most significant: it's what differentiates the holistic CSR programmes of today from isolated acts of corporate philanthropy in the past. A cup of corporate kindness here, a dash of largesse there, was once sufficient for a business to be seen as a good corporate citizen. These days the definition of a responsible organisation embraces so much more than this. As Lord Holme of Rio Tinto has colourfully put it:

> ...if companies behave irresponsibly, in social or environmental terms, then no amount of good-cause giving will tilt their overall contribution to society back from the negative to the positive. . . . A pirate throwing a few doubloons to a beggar may claim to be a philanthropist, but that hardly makes him a responsible businessman.[159]

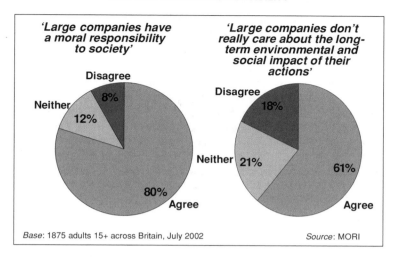

Figure 6-4   British public attitudes, July 2002. (Reproduced by permission of MORI (Market & Opinion Research International))

Today the expectation is that companies don't just pay lip service to CSR and wear it as a badge of honour, but embed socially responsible thinking into strategy, decisions and behaviours throughout their operations. Embracing CSR and communicating your stance and progress to all those with a stake in your business, is now seen as good business practice. Getting it right can result in growth, improved performance and competitive advantage; getting it wrong can damage the reputation not only of the perpetrator, but of the sector as a whole.

> Many multinational enterprises have demonstrated that respect for high standards of business conduct can enhance growth. Today's competitive forces are intense and multinational enterprises may be tempted to neglect appropriate standards and principles of conduct in an attempt to gain undue competitive advantage. Such practices by the few may call into question the reputation of the many and may give rise to public concerns.
> (Organisation for Economic Co-operation and Development (OECD)[160])

Almost all organisations will have pockets of CSR-related activity, such as cause-related marketing, charitable donations, employee surveys and waste reduction targets. However, if there is no integrated approach and the business's overall position on CSR is potentially ambiguous, it may be vulnerable to attack.

This is particularly true in the post Enron era, when the public has heightened expectations of businesses' obligations to society. Research (Figure 6-4) has shown that the public now expects businesses to behave with integrity, and respect the rights and concerns of employees, customers and other stakeholder groups, almost as a precondition of doing business.

Although adoption of CSR remains largely voluntary, a number of issues forming part of the CSR agenda are covered by legislation in many countries. These include employment issues, human rights, money laundering, bribery and corruption, anti-competitive activity and, increasingly, reporting on non-financial risks and performance. In some areas, as discussed in Chapter 2, self-regulation against voluntary codes of practice is encouraged, and governments and regulators are threatening legislation if businesses fail to conform.

A burgeoning interest in social, ethical and environmental risks from investors (increasing investor activism, growth in socially responsible investment funds), a more socially and environmentally aware consumer base, public intolerance of malfeasance and powerful pressure groups all contribute to a compelling business case for adopting CSR principles. There is growing recognition that CSR is no longer a 'nice to have' but a 'must have' if businesses are to succeed in the longer term and enjoy a good reputation.

> CSR is . . . recognised as strategically important in terms of brand, reputation and customer and employee satisfaction. Critically, it is also being realised by companies that demonstrating an appropriate response to CSR throughout the business is becoming necessary to obtain, and maintain, a licence to operate from investors, employees, customers and wider stakeholders.
> (FORGE II Guidance on Corporate Social Responsibility Management and Reporting[161])

The belief that CSR can make good business sense is backed up by research. A 2002 PricewaterhouseCoopers (PwC) survey of 1161 CEOs across 33 countries found 70% agreeing that 'corporate social responsibility is vital to the profitability of any company'.[162] In another survey by Business in the Community (BITC), 78% of corporate European executives agreed that 'integrating responsible business practices makes a company more competitive' and 73% agreed that it can 'significantly improve profitability'.[163] As for motivation in embracing CSR, a further PwC study conducted in the USA in 2002 found that 90% of US corporations committed to sustainability were doing so to enhance or protect their reputations.[164] In this same survey, an overwhelming 89% of companies thought the next five years would see more emphasis on sustainability, citing reputation enhancement (53%), followed by customer/consumer demand (40%) and industry trends (39%) as the top three drivers for future action.

In a 2002 World Economic Forum survey, when asked to list the three most important factors in making the business case for their companies' corporate citizenship activities, CEOs most commonly cited:

- Managing reputation and brand equity (78%)
- Attracting, motivating and retaining talented employees (58%)
- Protecting licence to operate (48%)
- Enhancing competitiveness and market positioning (48%).[165]

Although much healthy scepticism remains, there is growing evidence that being a good corporate citizen can help to build reputation as well as saving costs, increasing revenues, reducing risk exposure, cutting the cost of capital and increasing shareholder value. Many major investors certainly seem to think so.

> Shareholders still want financial returns. But investors see that it has become more important to take account of the views of other interest groups – ranging from employees to

campaigners – because meeting their needs can be beneficial for companies, whilst failing to do so can have a substantial negative impact on shareholder value.

(Association of British Insurers[166])

In these turbulent economic times, investors are increasingly looking for sound, well-run businesses that will provide 'safe havens' in the longer term. As Keith Jones, CEO of Morley Fund Management, stated at the launch of Morley's new Sustainability Index in May 2002:

> Morley increasingly believes that companies operating in a socially and environmentally responsible manner will be most likely to succeed over time.... By encouraging companies to improve their sustainability rating we aim to protect and enhance shareholder value. [167]

What, then, do these diverse interest groups require of businesses under the CSR banner (Table 6-11)?

Table 6-11. Stakeholder requirements and expectations on corporate social responsibility

Stakeholder group	Requirements and expectations
All stakeholders	• Clear tone set from the top on ethics, integrity, fairness, accountability and transparency • Responsiveness to stakeholder needs and concerns
Employees	• Good employer: treats staff fairly and with respect • Has reputation for being a responsible business
Customers	• Responsible sales, marketing and innovation • SEE risks managed well so customers not exposed
Suppliers	• Fair dealing • SEE risks managed well so suppliers not exposed
Communities	• SEE exposures managed well so local communities safe and jobs secure
Shareholders/Investors	• Internal and external SEE risks managed effectively • Evidence of commitment to CSR and improving performance • Shareholder CSR concerns addressed • Meets criteria for sustainability/CSR league tables and relevant SRI funds
Regulators Governments	• Goes beyond basic legal compliance to embrace good practice
NGOs/Pressure groups	• Comprehensive appraisal of material impacts and risks, backed up by policies, action plans, improvement targets, monitoring and reporting.

Stakeholder special interests and their strength of feeling on specific CSR issues will vary according to the nature of the business, its products and services, its market sector and the countries in which it manufactures and trades. Businesses operating in emerging economies face particular corporate citizenship challenges – and potentially high exposure to reputational risk. Issues such as bribery and corruption, human rights violations, poverty and disease, inadequate educational and public health infrastructures are daily challenges. These businesses face a barrage of questions from investors, pressure groups and the media.

- What is their attitude to worker rights in contractor-owned factories?
- Do they employ children and, if so, on what terms?
- Are they prepared to provide their HIV-infected workers with free anti-retroviral drugs?
- Do they pay 'sweeteners' to get the job done?
- Are political donations prohibited?
- Will they allow their facilities to be guarded by the local militia?
- Why do they continue to operate in a country blacklisted for human rights abuses?

Any reticence in answering their critics may lead to a shareholder resolution at the next AGM.

The set of issues coming under the CSR banner is hugely diverse. It would require another hefty tome entitled 'corporate social responsibility risks to reputation'[168] to do justice to this multifaceted topic and to outline all the conceivable CSR impacts, issues and risks that can affect reputation. Many such risks have been alluded to earlier in this chapter. Some, such as ethics and integrity in the boardroom and employment practices, will be applicable to all businesses, others – such as the digital divide,[169] GM technology, political lobbying and globalisation – may be sector- or business-specific. There is no 'one size fits all' approach to the management of CSR risks to reputation. However, it may be useful to outline the basic framework for identifying and managing CSR risks; indeed some risks to reputation can arise from the chosen approach itself. The major steps are:

- Making the business case: CSR strategy and positioning
- Identifying impacts, issues, threats and opportunities
- Making it happen: integrating with management and reporting systems
- Communicating goals and progress.

The first two steps are usually iterative. Organisations state their commitment to embracing CSR internally and then explore what this means for their business by defining the key stakeholders, issues, impacts, threats and opportunities relevant to their circumstances. They then assess the issues, agree priorities and integrate the conclusions into their business strategy.

making the business case: CSR strategy and positioning

The first step is to make the business case for adopting a holistic approach to CSR appropriate for your organisation. A key element of this is to have a clear vision for CSR within your business. Do you want to be a leader or a follower in your sector or territory? Do you want to be seen as proactive beacon of CSR excellence or as a reactive passive complier with legislation? Your positioning is important because, whatever stance you take, you will need to fully align the organisation behind you and support your position with a raft of policies, procedures, monitoring and reporting mechanisms. Only by having full alignment can you ensure that no gap emerges between your avowed aims and what you are seen to be doing in practice. Any such gap could severely damage your reputation. The higher you aim, the further you can fall unless your CSR credentials are rock solid.

Businesses often make the mistake of going for a 'big bang' on CSR, announcing that they are now enthusiastically embracing CSR and plan to tackle it simultaneously on all fronts. This is neither necessary nor desirable, and may expose you to reputational damage. CSR can and generally should be adopted stepwise; once the organisation has achieved some early successes it will have the confidence to build on these initial foundations. You will need to communicate your intentions clearly and manage the expectations of your stakeholders by explaining the precise status of this 'work in progress' and what remains to be done – or your reputation for fair play and responsible business practice could be damaged. Pin your colours to the mast: state clearly why you are embracing CSR and articulate the business case for your unique set of circumstances:

> Statoil's commitment to sustainable development rests on a moral obligation to do what is right. However, principles here go hand in hand with commercial interests. Actively adapting our business operations to our social surroundings reduces risk, enhances reputation and thereby improves profitability. By contributing to sustainable development, we can strengthen our position in labour, capital and consumer markets.
>
> (Olav Fjell, President and CEO, Statoil[170])

The CSR vision of European retailer Kingfisher, developed by its Social Responsibility Committee in May 2001, was simply: 'To improve the quality of life of all the people we touch.'

You will also need to link CSR with your values and business principles and embed them into your overall vision and business policies. The CSR-related values may overlap with the pillars of legitimacy and uniqueness attributes you were urged to consider at the start of this chapter: concepts of trust, dependability, integrity, good relationships with regulators and other stakeholders often feature. Once you've articulated those values, you will need to live and breathe them and communicate them clearly to employees, suppliers and other business partners. Any attack on your values could dent your credibility and your reputation.

identifying impacts, issues, threats and opportunities

As there are a large number of potential CSR issues, some generic, many business-specific, you need to devise a means of identifying the major issues that are relevant to your particular business. Many of the techniques for risk identification discussed in Chapter 4 can be used to tease out CSR risks, either as a separate exercise or as an integral part of an enterprise-wide risk identification process. If conducted as a separate exercise, the threats and opportunities emerging should be fed back into the overall business risk management process so that material CSR risks to the business are visible at board level.

UK-based *Business in the Community*[171] has a four-quadrant approach for CSR impacts (Figure 6-5) which can act as a useful prompt.

Figure 6-6 shows how this basic approach can be tailored for a particular industry or business sector. It is an extract from the FORGE consortium's guidance on CSR management and reporting for the UK financial services sector.[172]

MARKETPLACE	WORKPLACE
▪ Impact of core products and services ▪ Product safety ▪ Full and reliable customer information ▪ Provision for customers with special needs ▪ Anti-competitive or unfair practices ▪ Prompt and fair payment of suppliers ▪ Fair and honest advertising and direct sales	▪ Fairness and honesty in overall employee relations ▪ Fair pay and conditions ▪ Health and safety ▪ Diversity – achieving it and managing it ▪ Ensuring fundamental human rights respected in all areas of operation ▪ Training and life-long learning ▪ Work–life balance
ENVIRONMENT	COMMUNITY
▪ Environmental impact of core products in use ▪ Energy and water consumption ▪ Emissions to air, land and water ▪ Solid waste production ▪ Risk of accidents impacting upon the environment ▪ Raw materials sourcing ▪ Impacts upon biodiversity	▪ Impact on the community of day-to-day operations (such as nuisance, noise, visual amenity, traffic congestion) ▪ Impact on the local community of positive community involvement (employee volunteering, charitable support, mentoring partnerships, etc.) ▪ Impact on national society, for example through lobbying activities designed to influence or initiate legislation

© Business in the Community

Figure 6-5   Potential CSR impacts by area. (Reproduced by permission of Business in the Community)

FORGE concluded that, for the UK financial services sector, the 'marketplace' category presented the greatest challenge to develop, deliver and demonstrate a response. This category is therefore the greatest source of CSR risks to reputation.

The World Economic Forum promotes a similar approach (Figure 6-7) that puts corporate governance and ethics at the heart of corporate citizenship.[173]

Your discussions will need to cover both direct and indirect impacts if a good reputation is to be sustained. CSR principles need to be extended beyond business boundaries, into the supply chain and the customer base to ensure that no major risks to reputation are being unwittingly 'imported' through business partnerships.

When UK-based fund manager Morley launched their Sustainability Matrix in May 2002 they surprised the markets by initially excluding two financial services groups: HBSC and

WORKPLACE	MARKETPLACE
▪ Disciplinary practices	▪ Access to products and services
▪ Work/life balance	▪ Advertising and pricing
▪ Health and safety	▪ Business ethics
▪ Learning and development	▪ Customer service
▪ Diversity and equal opportunities	▪ Privacy
▪ Freedom of association/collective bargaining	▪ Terms of trade
	▪ Supplier relationships
▪ Forced and child labour	▪ Value of products and services
▪ Bullying and harassment	
ENVIRONMENT	**COMMUNITY**
▪ Materials consumption (energy use, water, office consumables)	▪ Involvement with the community
	▪ Investment in the local community
▪ Waste management	▪ Exposure to human rights risks for investment activities arising from third party activities, e.g. governments
▪ Transport	
▪ Property design and management	
▪ Indirect impacts	▪ Indigenous rights
	FORGE II

Figure 6-6   CSR issues for the UK financial services sector. (Reproduced by permission of the Forge Group)

Standard Chartered Bank. Morley explained this by saying: 'These are not smoke-stack in-dustries. . . . But there is a lot of corporate lending to projects with environmental and social risks'.[174] Morley's stance heralds an interesting shift in approach: investors are starting to look beyond the obvious risks to a business from activities within its own bailiwick, to social, environmental and ethical risks in its supply chain and the risks run by the customers for its services. For these risks too can adversely impact reputation and hence shareholder value. Per-haps the acronym KYC – know your customer – coined to combat money laundering, should be expanded to KYCR – know your customers' risks to safeguard lenders' reputations. It is clear that even if companies haven't taken the trouble to properly investigate the uses to which their services or products are being put, there is increasing likelihood that an institutional investor, rating agency, NGO or over-zealous investigative journalist will do the job for you and gleefully print the results for public consumption.

In 1995 Royal Dutch/Shell, the multinational oil and gas company, was vilified by environ-mental pressure groups and the media when they announced plans to sink the redundant Brent

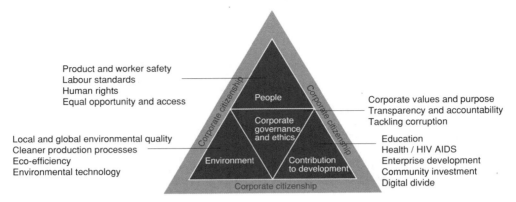

Figure 6-7   Key corporate citizenship issues. (Reproduced by permission of World Economic Forum)
Source: "Global Corporate Citizenship: The Leadership Challenge for CEOs and Boards," World Economic Forum Global Corporate Citizenship Initiative and the Prince of Wales International Business Leaders Forum, January 2002.

Spa oil drilling platform in the North Sea. Substantial research and consultation had shown this to be the most environmentally friendly and, as it happened, lowest cost alternative. Shell secured backing for their plan from the governments of the UK and other countries bordering the North Sea. But Shell had reckoned without the force of outraged public opinion, stirred up by pressure groups. A high-profile campaign was mounted by NGO Greenpeace, accusing Shell of being greedy and irresponsible in plumping for a cheap disposal option that could wreak environmental havoc. Television images showed Shell using water cannons to prevent Greenpeace protestors from boarding the platform as it was towed out to sea. The vision of a ruthless corporate machine pitted against defenceless and legitimate protestors in a wild and dangerous ocean caught the public imagination. Mass boycotts of Shell fuel stations in Germany followed and the company's reputation was severely tarnished. In June 1995 Shell backed down and towed the rig back to shore where it was later cut up and recycled to build a Norwegian dock.

In the same year, Shell suffered another reputational crisis arising from its activities in Nigeria. Shell was extracting oil from reserves in Nigeria under a joint venture agreement with the Nigerian government. Shell stood accused of political dealing with the ruling military junta, of human rights abuses and of ignoring the claims of the indigenous Ogoni people for a share of the oil profits. The Ogoni case was articulated by environmental activist Ken Saro Wiwa who, in November 1995, was tried and executed by the brutal regime alongside fellow dissidents. Shell was depicted as having blood on its hands; its share price fluctuated wildly and its reputation suffered another hit.

Shell were chastened by the experience and shocked by the raw emotion of the public response. Similar to the Monsanto GM seeds example, Shell learned that with Brent Spa they should have considered a wider range of stakeholder groups in their consultation process, including NGOs. Like Monsanto, Shell had been so convinced by the legitimacy and power of their technical arguments that they had failed to engage in genuine two-way dialogue, using language that NGOs and the general public would understand. They had made little attempt to win over their key audiences by educating them before the event – chiefly because they did not expect the public or media to show any interest in the fate of an ancient rig. They had failed to recognise society's changing expectations. In Nigeria too, Shell was bewildered that a local operation in a far-flung land could attract the attention – and wrath – of the world's media.

> [Shell] has attracted a lot of activism as a result of the profile it generated for itself with Brent Spa and also its activities in Nigeria. Shell's misfortune is a good lesson to other corporations to show how long it can take to recover from a pubic relations backlash. Whether the publicity is deserved or not does not matter. The lesson is that your reputation is extremely vulnerable if you don't reflect the values of society in the way you run your business.
>
> (Tony Juniper, Policy and Campaigns Director, Friends of the Earth[175])

Shell was forced to acknowledge that its financial performance was heavily dependent on relationships with customers, investors, NGOs, the general public and the media. In 1996 Shell set about trying systematically to rebuild their battered reputation. Part of their task was to address the requirements and expectations of a much broader ranger of stakeholders than previously to gain a better understanding of society's changing expectations and what it would take for Shell to be admired. This led Shell to re-examine and recalibrate its core purpose, values and business principles. In 1998 Shell issued a report entitled *Profits and Principles – Does there have to be a choice?*[176] which outlined what Shell had done to respond to stakeholder concerns about environmental and human rights issues and to demonstrate Shell's accountability to a broader range of stakeholders. It stated Shell's belief that 'fundamentally... there does not have to be a choice between profits and principles in a responsibly run enterprise'.[177]

Today Shell is seen as one of the world's most admired companies: it was ranked 18th in the Financial Times 2002 World's Most Respected Companies survey[178] and wins accolades for its performance and reporting on corporate social responsibility issues. Sustainable development principles now sit at the very heart of the business.

As Phil Watts, chairman of the Committee of Managing Directors Royal Dutch/Shell Group and chairman of the WBCSD, argued in a paper launched at the Johannesburg World Summit on Sustainable Development in August 2002:

> ... business should embrace sustainable development and CSR not just as a 'force for good', but because it is to your clear competitive advantage. And this trend can only increase as society's expectations of business continue to change. The fact is, CSR has moved beyond a simple equation of profitability + compliance + philanthropy. It's now more about understanding the societies in which we operate. And that means dealing with a range of issues – from workplace ethics and corporate governance codes, to stakeholder management and sustainability strategies.... If the risks of neglecting the needs of sustainable development are big, so are the rewards of responding to them – improved reputation, brand value, staff loyalty and revenue generation, particularly in

large, undeveloped markets. Sustainability thinking also promotes innovation – through responding to new challenges and changing wants.[179]

As many CSR risks can inflict serious damage on reputation, it is essential to take soundings from external interest groups who can inform the internal debate on risks and open your eyes and ears to impacts and issues you may never have considered. So often businesses have 'blind spots' about potential risks; they dismiss even the possibility of a seemingly unlikely risk occurring and so fail to spot the warning signs of an impending crisis. This is what happened to Shell in the mid-1990s. Capturing CSR threats and opportunities requires you to think 'out of the box', to think the unthinkable. Dialogue with stakeholders can often facilitate this.

> CSR risks fall outside most managers' usual areas of experience and expertise, which is why it is necessary to engage with outsiders. Dialogue is about stepping back from corporate preconceptions, going beyond the company's own values and norms to discover those of the stakeholders. The process is about managers talking to people they would not normally engage with about subjects they would not normally discuss.
>
> (Association of British Insurers[180])

Using scenario planning techniques, as discussed in Chapter 4, can also assist as it can enable connections to be made between apparently unconnected events and sets of circumstances. Scenarios can also explore the impact of potential alliances between ostensibly disparate stakeholder groups.

CSR is also about upside: about tapping a rich seam of opportunities to enhance reputation, strengthen brands, bolster stakeholder loyalty and create value. A business could, for example, improve brand awareness, sales and corporate reputation by embarking on a cause-related marketing programme. Cause-related marketing is defined by the UK's Business in the Community as 'a commercial activity by which businesses and charities or causes form a partnership with each other to market an image, product or service for mutual benefit'.[181] Supermarket chain Tesco's 'computers for schools' programme is a good example of cause-related marketing in action. The programme encourages consumers to shop at Tesco during an 8–10-week period each spring. They are rewarded by a voucher for every £10 spent, which can be donated to their chosen school and redeemed against a wide range of IT equipment. From the programme's inception in 1991 to the end of 2002 some £70 million of equipment had been distributed to schools nationwide and teachers had received around £100 000 of IT training. Tesco not only improved sales but found their reputation as a responsible retailer enhanced through association with an innovative programme that benefited the community.[182]

As mentioned at the end of the 'workplace talent and culture' section, community projects, as well as 'doing good' can act as an excellent employee motivator and team-builder and can make staff feel proud to work for a business – in turn helping to build corporate reputation. The Lattice Group (now merged with the National Grid Group to form National Grid Transco) runs gas pipelines and utility infrastructure in the UK. Lattice employees are involved in programmes to train and provide apprenticeships and employment for young offenders and young people excluded from school. This has not only solved a recruitment problem in some geographical areas by developing skills to make young people more employable, but has generated positive media coverage and boosted staff morale.

> ...we are dedicated to finding solutions to some of the most pressing of the social problems faced within diverse communities where we operate and where our employees live. Everyone benefits. The company gains a credible reputation and builds shareholder value. Local people and communities thrive. We all gain from the continuing sharing of knowledge and expertise.
>
> (Dr John Parker, chairman, Lattice[183])

making it happen: integrating with management and reporting systems

Once CSR risks have been identified, they should be integrated into mainstream management and reporting systems – including the corporate governance and risk management frameworks – not managed separately by a PR or a specialist CSR team. However, this would appear to be more easily said than done.

The same PwC survey that found 90% of businesses committed to sustainability to enhance or protect their reputations, also found that only one-third of respondents actually incorporated the associated risks (threats and opportunities) into their internal risk assessment processes or business strategies.[184] CSR risks should be handled in the same way as other risks: they should be assessed by likelihood and impact, with impact measured both financially and in terms of reputation. Suitable action plans to control the risks should then be agreed, in line with the business's risk appetite.

Using existing governance structures – such as the board, the audit or risk committee – to manage CSR risks can also help to achieve the right focus. A growing number of companies are choosing to put in place specialist committees to oversee CSR issues, such as Merck's Committee on Public Policy and Social Responsibility and McDonald's Corporate Responsibility Committee.[185]

Develop supporting policies and principles such as codes of business conduct[186] and policies on environmental and social issues that spell out your stance on key CSR issues such as human rights, bribery, child labour and political donations. Communicate these to your employees and make compliance with them an integral part of performance assessment so that they guide behaviours and decision-making throughout the business. Extend these over time to your suppliers and contractors so that they, too, abide by the same principles and do not expose you indirectly to adverse reputational impacts.

The European retailer, Kingfisher Group, has an environmental and ethical code of conduct for suppliers. Its opening vision statement demonstrates Kingfisher's commitment to working with factories to help them to improve, rather than boycotting them:

> It is Kingfisher's policy to buy from factories that are committed to improving worker welfare conditions and reducing their impact on the environment.
> Kingfisher believes that every link of the supply chain should benefit from the trade of the product. It is Kingfisher's vision to enable people to enjoy their home and lifestyle better than any

other retailer in the world. This enjoyment would be undermined if it was at the expense of the quality of life of the people making our products.

The code goes on to enumerate clear minimum standards that must be met by partner factories. Kingfisher will not buy from factories whose working practices fall within any of its Critical Failure Points. The factory fails if:

- The factory employs children below the local legal minimum age, and/or a minimum age of 14.
- The factory uses forced, bonded or involuntary labour.
- Workers are forced to lodge 'unreasonable' deposits or their identity papers with their employers, so they are not free to leave after reasonable notice.
- Workers are subjected to physical abuse, the threat of physical abuse, or intimidating verbal abuse.
- Accommodation, if provided, is not clearly segregated from the factory or production area.
- An adequate number of safe, unblocked fire escape routes are not accessible to workers from each floor or area of the factory and accommodation if provided.
- The factory knowingly and continually contravenes local or national environmental legislation without being able to demonstrate a plan of action to improve.
- The factory management does not demonstrate a willingness to improve on any significant areas of concern identified during the audit.

Factories that pass the Critical Failure Points are then assessed against the Kingfisher Standards for labour and welfare conditions, health and safety and environmental management and are awarded a performance grade accordingly.[187] By setting clear standards of engagement for their operations, Kingfisher are able to adopt a globally consistent approach which that ensures minimum standards are met, while promoting continuous improvement.

You will need to develop performance indicators against each of your CSR objectives. These will enable you to monitor progress while ensuring that risks are well managed and that you remain on track. Publication of progress against these indicators also demonstrates to your stakeholders that you are taking your responsibilities seriously and are committed to improvement. A growing number of businesses around the world are now basing their monitoring and reporting in whole or in part on the framework of indicators developed by the Global Reporting Initiative in their *Sustainability Reporting Guidelines*.[188] The use of this framework will be discussed more fully in Chapter 9.

communicating goals and progress

The issues involved in CSR – integrity, child labour, worker health and safety, pollution – often involve subjective judgements and qualitative assessments, and are therefore often open to misinterpretation. These are the same emotionally laden issues that could spark damaging headlines across the front pages if your intentions are misunderstood. In this area, more than any other, you cannot communicate enough. Articulating your stance on a particular issue, reiterating it unequivocally time and again, enshrining your approach in policies and procedures and providing incontrovertible evidence that you are doing what you say you are doing, will be effort well spent.

> ... business is increasingly being held to account not only for what it does, but how it does it. Companies therefore need to be able to demonstrate, more quickly and with increasing levels of detail, that their operations enhance economic development, ensure environmental protection and promote social equity. Gone are the days of 'trust me'. People want proof in the 'show me' world.
> (World Business Council for Sustainable Development[189])

Demonstrating 'accountability' should be one of the fundamental aims of your reporting and communications in this area. Accountability is the preparedness of a business or individuals to justify their actions and decisions and to be answerable to those with a legitimate interest in the business, i.e. the business's stakeholders. It requires a business to:

- give a transparent, full and honest account of the its social, environmental and ethical impacts and the challenges it is facing
- show that it is complying with relevant laws and regulations and is acting in the spirit of them
- demonstrate that it is responsive to the needs, concerns and expectations of its stakeholders and is taking these into account in formulating future strategy, developing targets and enhancing processes to improve the organisation's future performance.[190]

You must not just *act* responsibly but also be *seen to be acting* responsibly. Paying lip service to CSR concepts, PR spin and 'greenwashing' will soon be gleefully exposed by your critics. You must be able to substantiate your assertions with evidence of what you are doing in practice.

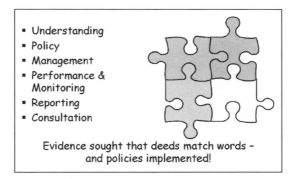

- Understanding
- Policy
- Management
- Performance & Monitoring
- Reporting
- Consultation

Evidence sought that deeds match words – and policies implemented!

Figure 6-8   FTSE4Good Model of best governance practice for CSR.

When the FTSE4Good UK ethical index was first launched in July 2001 the exclusion of household names such as retail giants Tesco and Safeway and the Royal Bank of Scotland caused outcry. However, some exclusions were simply because the companies had not made available sufficient information to enable an accurate judgement to be made. The FTSE4Good methodology is revealing in terms of what companies actually need to do to satisfy the socially responsible investment screening criteria (Figure 6-8). Businesses need to demonstrate that

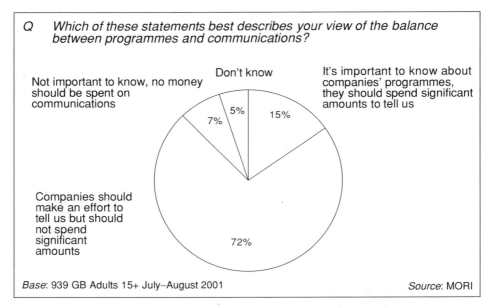

Figure 6-9   Communication of CSR activities. (Reproduced by permission of MORI (Market & Opinion Research International))

they understand the issues, have policies in place to deal with them, monitoring systems to track performance, evidence of consultation with key stakeholders (to inform the debate and avoid surprises) and robust reporting and communications.

Stating that you comply with voluntary guidelines and standards on CSR such as the Global Compact[191]; the OECD Guidelines for Multinational Enterprises[192]; the Universal Declaration of Human Rights[193]; the AA1000[194] standard on social, and ethical accounting, auditing and reporting; SA8000 on workplace conditions[195]; the CERES principles on sustainability[196]; the Ethical Trading Initiative base code[197]; the GoodCorporation charter[198]; the International Labour Organisation (ILO) Conventions[199]; or the Global Reporting Initiative[200] will provide evidence to your stakeholders of your serious intent.

Research has shown that the public positively wishes to be given information on businesses' CSR activities. As Figure 6-9 illustrates, only a very small proportion of respondents wanted no money to be spent on communications; 15% wanted spending to be significant.

Companies are addressing this through fuller and more transparent reporting on the full range of their activities across the 'triple bottom line' (Figure 6-10) to demonstrate that they have struck an appropriate socioeconomic balance. To make these 'triple bottom line', 'sustainability' environmental and social reports credible in the eyes of stakeholders, an increasing number of businesses are using the services of a fully independent, third party to verify that the position is as claimed – particularly in sensitive areas such as human rights in developing countries.

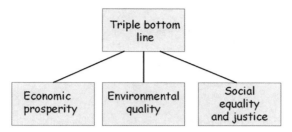

Figure 6-10   Triple bottom line reporting.

Following adverse publicity over sweatshop labour, Nike and Gap have made extensive use of third-party verifiers to investigate local conditions in supplier factories and to check local compliance with their codes of conduct.[201]

But beware! Once you have declared your hand on CSR, any perceived change in stance may damage your reputation and attract unwelcome criticism and greater scrutiny.

British clothing retailer and mail order firm Littlewoods hit the headlines when it was announced in February 2003 that the company would be scrapping all charitable donations and dropping its membership of the Ethical Trading Initiative, following its acquisition the previous October by the Barclay brothers, billionaire owners of the Scotsman newspaper and the Ritz hotel. Littlewoods had been a founder member of the Ethical Trading Initiative, set up in 1998 to promote a voluntary code of conduct on responsible labour practices in the supply chain. The business had enjoyed a long-standing reputation for corporate philanthropy under its previous founder owners, the Moores family, with around 1% of profits being donated to charity each year. As part of the Barclay brothers' cost-cutting rationalisation programme, ten employees responsible for checking that the group's suppliers meet labour standards were also to be sacked.[202]

An open letter to the *Financial Times* jointly written by 18 individuals representing trades unions and NGOs commented:

> ... we considered Littlewoods to be a leading corporate light in the promotion of ethical trade and of social dialogue between employers and free trades unions. It is short-sighted and irresponsible of the new owners to undermine this work and the reputation of the company at a time when consumers, investors and the workers employed by Littlewoods and throughout their supply chains see corporate social responsibility as an integral part of business operations.[203]

Although the company was quick to counter that it was not abandoning ethical standards, merely integrating them into the roles of departmental directors and buying teams, the damage was done. Littlewood's supply chain performance will undoubtedly now be dissected by a number of sceptical NGOs. With delicious irony, later that same month, the Office of Fair Trading slapped a £5.4 million fine on Littlewoods for price-fixing on toys between 1999 and 2001 – a period prior to the takeover.[204]

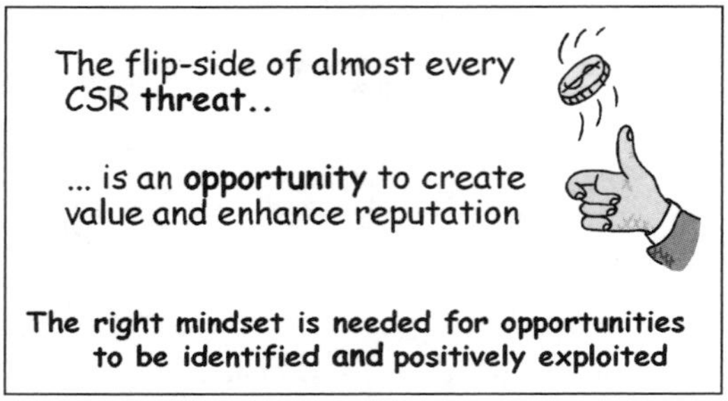

Figure 6-11   Downsides . . . and upsides.

CSR: threat or opportunity?

Although there can be downsides from CSR-related impacts, there is often upside of opportunity (Figure 6-11). In fact, in this area, perhaps more than any other of the seven drivers of reputation, there is frequently scope to convert a potential threat into an opportunity, to:

- forge close relationships with your stakeholders so that you are the first to spot that market opportunity or to hear about that emerging issue
- boost stakeholder confidence, trust and loyalty
- differentiate yourself by making a difference
- display the human face of business
- reduce raw material and energy costs
- cut the cost of fines, investigations, clean-ups, lost sales and lost personnel.

In a graphic example of this, Kingfisher has chosen to manage CSR by asking operating companies to rank their current position on a four-rung ladder against 12 trends identified as being of critical importance to Kingfisher's business. The trends include:

- The way we treat people is becoming more important than ever
- Every product will soon be telling a story – and they all need to be good
- Communities will reject businesses who are not good neighbours.[205]

The rungs represent a spectrum from managing the risk (in the sense of downside threat), through managing the issues, to creating an opportunity and finally proactive social leadership. Operating companies are asked not only to assess their current position, but to establish their target position and the timescale for achieving it, and to produce an action plan for discussion with the Kingfisher Social Responsibility Team. This allows Kingfisher to monitor and report on progress across the group (Figure 6-12).

For example, against the 'respect for people' trend, operating companies just 'managing the risk' and protecting against downsides will be complying with all relevant legislation, ensuring that robust health and safety procedures are in place to comply with current and pending regulations and catering for the needs of disabled customers. Contrast this with behaviour on the 'creating an opportunity' rung which might involve:

Table 6-12. Kingfisher's four-rung ladder (Reproduction by permission of Kingfisher)

1. **Leadership**
   Companies on this rung will be actively involved in the debate on that particular trend or issues. They will be recognised as 'best in class' and making a significant contribution to the overall discussion in society.
2. **Creating an opportunity**
   Companies on this rung will have used the trend to create a business opportunity whether from cost savings, an improved marketing position or in some other way.
3. **Managing the issues**
   Companies on this rung will be managing the trend in a positive and comprehensive manner. They will have a good understanding of how the trend will affect their products, processes and people and be willing to discuss the issues with interested parties.
4. **Managing the risk**
   Companies on this rung will take a reactive approach, implementing only those actions which are essential to protect their business from current trends.[206]

- stocking a range of products and services to meet the needs of everyone
- being recognised as an employer of choice in its sector as a result of career development and strategies tackling issues such as disability, cultural diversity, age and gender.[207]

To monitor progress, Kingfisher uses relevant performance indicators such as the proportion of women employed as senior executives and senior managers and the proportion of employees with a disability. The same data are relayed to external stakeholders to enable them to track the company's performance against its stated objectives.

Managing CSR threats will enable you to safeguard your reputation; and proactively converting some of those threats into opportunities can go further by enhancing your standing and boosting stakeholder confidence.

no longer an optional extra

Although the jury is still out in terms of the financial performance of socially responsible businesses compared with the rest of the market, there is a growing body of opinion that companies showing a true commitment to CSR and active management of their social, environmental and ethical impacts and risks tend to be better run and therefore present lower risk exposure and better long-term prospects. Such businesses offer better quality, less volatile earnings and are seen as a 'safe bet' in the longer term.

As retailer Kingfisher has argued, doing nothing is no longer a viable option. The potential benefits of embracing CSR far outweigh the consequences of maintaining the status quo, as shown in Table 6-13.

Whether your major impacts and risks are about genetic testing, e-mail monitoring, child labour, political donations, deforestation, use of pesticides or pollution from oil spills, it will be in your long-term interests to actively monitor and manage them as they evolve over time.

Table 6-13. CSR: doing nothing is not an option (Reproduced by permission of Kingfisher)

Consequences of inaction	Benefits of success
Staff embarrassed/ashamed	Proud staff
Staff discomfort with job	Confidence in job
Poor staff recruitment	Quality recruitment
Poor retention of staff	Higher retention
Detachment of staff	Involvement
Customers reject shops	Preferred choice for customers
Customers reject products	We are a trusted brand
Mistrust from customers	Respect and loyalty
Disappointment	A story that adds value
Low-quality/cynical suppliers	High calibre suppliers
Ignorance about the supply chain	Buyers understand supply base
Skeletons in the cupboard	Good PR about our supply base
Issues manage us	We manage issues
Not ready for the future	Ready for future
Business strategy undermined	Strategy reinforced by our action
We become defensive to outside world	Outside world celebrates our success
Planners reject our stores	Planners accept, even welcome us
Uncompetitive	Better than our competitors[208]

Directors are just as likely to be challenged about their business's human rights record, policy on bribery or climate change, attitude to animal testing or their own personal ethics as they are about the business's financial performance, value drivers and future strategy. Concerned investors and other stakeholders will pressurise and penalise businesses that pay lip service to CSR and will reward those that take their responsibilities, and CSR risks, seriously.

> Damage to reputation occurs when there is a perceived gap between corporate performance and stakeholder expectation. The key to successful reputation management is the early identification of such gaps and closing them quickly. Corporate responsibility programmes play a crucial role in keeping them closed.
>
> (Michael Regester[209])

CSR has now entered the business mainstream: it's no longer an optional extra but an integral part of doing business in the twenty-first century, a major component of corporate governance, a core competency for business leaders and a key element of a sound risk management system. Being – and being seen to be – a good corporate citizen is also vital for the health and well-being of a business, its self-esteem and the esteem in which it is held by its stakeholders. Even if you're sceptical about the bottom-line business benefits of CSR, the fact remains that the corporate graveyard is littered with companies broken by losing their reputations – so often because of social, environmental or ethical risks that were ignored.

> It is now widely recognised that improved social and environmental performance is an increasingly important driver in the long-term creation of value . . . [As a result] organisations are moving to

establish strategic and operational management processes that will assist in learning about the impacts of their activities, in identifying, evaluating and better managing the risks arising from those impacts, in meeting the needs of stakeholders for information about the social and ethical impacts of an organisation's activities, and in building competitive advantage through the projection of a defined stance on social, ethical and environmental issues.

(Simon Zadek, chief executive, Institute of Social and Ethical Accountability[210])

What, then, are the key steps businesses need to take if they wish to protect themselves (and their reputations) from CSR-related threats and seek to tap the opportunities that proactive CSR management can bring?

- Set the scene for CSR by articulating a clear business-wide stance on ethics, integrity, fairness, accountability and transparency, set clear CSR goals and delineate the boundaries of your responsibility. Reinforce this through your vision, values and policies.

- Use all available techniques (such as stakeholder dialogue and scenario planning) to think 'out of the box' and identify CSR-related trends, impacts and risks that affect your business. Refresh this regularly to take into account changing socioeconomic factors and to respond to emerging stakeholder wishes and concerns. Remember that CSR risks can arise not just from within the business itself, but from your customer base, supply chain, acquisitions, other business partnerships and new ventures.

- Integrate the CSR threats and opportunities identified with your risk management and corporate governance frameworks to ensure focus at the right level in your business.

- Establish and adapt policies, procedures, working practices and performance management criteria to ensure complete alignment with your stance on CSR throughout the organisation, as any disconnect could impact reputation.

- Set clear time-phased targets for your CSR goals. Develop appropriate performance indicators to monitor whether you are on track – and provide early warning if not.

- Communicate your overall approach to CSR, its limitations and progress over time to your stakeholders, providing them with the performance information they require and expect to monitor your progress. Be clear on which voluntary standards and guidelines you are complying with; consider 'triple bottom line' reporting, perhaps using the GRI sustainability guidelines, to allow stakeholders to benchmark your performance against your peers.

- Use independent external verification where necessary to assure your stakeholders that your deeds match your fine words, remembering that any credibility gap could undermine your reputation.

- Be honest and open about where you stand, where you have fallen short of the mark and what remains to be done.

COMMUNICATIONS AND CRISIS MANAGEMENT

Communications can take many forms, including annual financial, environmental or sustainability reports; prospectuses; issue documents; website information; press releases; analyst meetings; investor briefings; stakeholder forums; annual general meetings; and media interviews. Some of these are statutory disclosure obligations, others are required or expected by stakeholders and many are discretionary. Whatever form communications take, stakeholders expect them to be honest, accurate, complete (with no significant omissions), transparent and made promptly; they also expect businesses to be responsive to their changing information needs (Table 6-14). The previous sections in this chapter have stressed the need for businesses to communicate clearly what they are doing against each reputation driver and to back up their assertions with hard evidence of action; otherwise credibility and reputation may suffer.

the case for transparency

The challenge for all companies is . . . to look beyond their existing financial statements which provide historic 'accounting' records of tangible assets and to consider the wider perspective of how to invest in and make best use of all the assets of the business, tangible and intangible. Ultimately, the ability of your organisation to meet not only its current goals and objectives, but also to grasp future opportunities, will depend on its ability to create value from the intangible assets. It is only by identifying, managing and developing the full spectrum of intangibles that you will be able to unlock your full potential.

(UK Department of Trade and Industry[211])

There is a compelling rationale for the provision of broader and better information to stakeholders on intangible assets, as these are the assets – including reputation – that are so often the real barometer of a business's future prospects.

Table 6-14. Stakeholder requirements and expectations on communications and crisis management

Stakeholder group	Requirements and expectations
All stakeholders	• Transparency • Honesty • Clarity and consistency • Accuracy and completeness • Timeliness • Responsiveness (to stakeholders and to crises)
Shareholders/Investors	• No surprises • Equal treatment with other shareholders • Accessibility and openness
The media	• Accessibility and openness

Setting aside for a moment the 'sticks' wielded by governments, regulators and investors to force business to provide yet more data, there are some attractive 'carrots' that reward transparent reporting. Businesses that voluntarily provide additional information on their real value drivers and the associated risks – their employee talent, their capacity to innovate, their workplace culture, their product and service brands, their business relationships and their response to social and environmental impacts – will find that they are valued more accurately in the market, command a higher stock price and see stakeholder trust and their reputations enhanced.

A 2002 study by Standard & Poors (S&P) found that companies with greater transparency and disclosure rankings had lower market risk and a higher stock price. It follows that companies can lower their cost of capital by improving transparency and disclosure. The study found that although the disclosure of non-financial information in annual reports generally needed improvement, those companies ranking highest in the study were the ones that 'practice a greater level of non-financial disclosure along with full financial disclosure'.[212]

Once a business has clearly established what its stakeholders are concerned about and what data they require to monitor their 'stake', the business can respond to stakeholder needs by providing the requisite information and corroborative data. As new trends and issues emerge, stakeholders naturally want to be kept informed. The rate of HIV infection in the workforce and policies on greenhouse gas emissions did not even appear on the risk radar screen as potentially material business issues five years ago; now they are hot topics for investors and NGOs – topics that those companies affected would be unwise to disregard in their communications. And yet businesses still often choose to ignore even the burning issues of the day in their disclosures. The S&P study found that, even post Enron, most US companies failed to respond to stakeholder concerns about potential conflicts of interest for external auditors conducting both audit and consultancy work and did not disclose the amount paid in audit and non-audit fees in their annual reports. Discussion of, or reference to, a corporate governance charter or code of best practices was also one of the least commonly disclosed items.[213]

Reluctance to disclose more than the legally required minimum can result in businesses missing opportunities to enhance their reputations and market value. It has been suggested that a business's audit committee should be restyled 'transparency committee', which is not a bad idea given the emphasis now put on the accuracy and completeness of written and verbal disclosures and the role of communications in underpinning corporate reputation. Perhaps a restyled 'transparency committee' should have a clear accountability, enshrined in its terms of reference, to oversee public statements and ensure that they meet the needs of major stakeholders.

It is not just the content of communications, but also the style with which they are conveyed, that need to satisfy the 'transparency' test. In August 2002, Phil Watts, Shell's executive chairman, was fiercely criticised by shareholders complaining he was one of the 'poorest communicators running a FTSE 100 company'.[214] A number of shareholders claimed that their relations with the Anglo-Dutch oil conglomerate had hit a low, citing Mr Watt's style as a primary cause. They attacked Mr Watts for his 'brusque' manner, poor ability to communicate strategy and defensiveness when handling difficult questions. One of Shell's top five shareholders said 'he seems to show a complete disdain for communication with the City'.[215] This was in stark contrast with his predecessor, the well-regarded Sir Mark Moody-Stuart, who devoted considerable time to investor relations. He was once described thus by the *Financial Times:* 'with his thick white hair and eyebrows, and a way of speaking that suggests every word has been weighed judiciously, [Sir Mark] comes across as a wise and palpably decent doctor'.[216] An aura of honesty and integrity in communication counts for a lot. Mr Watts, describing himself as 'perplexed, frankly' vowed to learn from the criticism.

CEOs and chairmen beware! Your personal style of communication can influence your business's reputation.

> The argument that a chief executive's style reflects his or her personality, or that they are too busy to bother with all that tiresome investor relations stuff, is misguided. In a bear market, where dozens of executives have proved to be liars and crooks, investors are increasingly vigilant and naturally suspicious of defensive or evasive executives. . . . As the value of their investments dwindle, investors are in no mood to be trifled with. Business people who explain themselves in a clear and friendly way and who own up when they make mistakes . . . create tremendous goodwill. Those who fail will pay the consequences. As one analyst says: 'It's not a question of style over substance, but the substance needs to be put over with style and consistency.'
>
> (Jane Simms [217])

no surprises

Investors want stability and minimum volatility – eleventh hour profits warnings and other unwelcome surprises are anathema to them. However, this poses some tricky dilemmas. At what point do you decide to break bad news to the market, with the loss of market confidence and reduction in share price that can ensue. Should you announce that downbeat forecast if you still have a fighting chance of getting earnings back on track? There are no easy answers here but, as a rule of thumb, if further bad news may follow the initial bad news it could be prudent to disclose early. Bad news may actually prove better than no news at all. Research conducted by the UK's Institute of Chartered Accountants of England and Wales found that:

> A number of analysts and fund managers asserted that bad news is punished, but many investors will give the management the 'benefit of the doubt' as long as they are kept informed of developments. If bad news is covered up, until it is impossible to hide it any longer, the reputation of the management for honesty and integrity will be permanently damaged.
> So bad news is bad, but no news followed by bad news that had been covered up is worse. No news makes investors nervous.[218]

This is illustrated by the case of MyTravel, discussed earlier in this chapter. MyTravel had to give three profits warnings in a period of just five months. The day after MyTravel gave its third profits warning and axed its dividend, one incensed major investor complained that the statement was 'absurdly short on detail', that there was no conference call or meeting and that the company hadn't returned their calls'.[219] Investors and analysts were furious about MyTravel's cavalier attitude to them:

The content and the style of [the] statement infuriated investors and analysts. Though rumours of a further warning had been circulating, most analysts were stunned by MyTravel's admission that full-year profits could take a further hit, this time of up to £50m. Equally controversial was the company's decision to publish as few details as possible – a move made worse by the fact that not a single MyTravel executive was available for comment. Even the powerful investment banks were scrambling for details, and many analysts were left bewildered by the breakdown of an otherwise well-oiled PR machine.[220]

A failure to warn the markets is often interpreted as a symptom of inadequate management control – which in turn can hit investor confidence and damage reputation. Information vacuums that leave organisations open to accusations of arrogance or incompetence can be equally damaging. Misleading statements or the deliberate withholding of information can prove catastrophic.

In June 2002 Samuel Waksal, former CEO of US biotechnology group ImClone, was arrested on illegal insider trading, fraud and perjury charges, relating to the sale of shares on 27 December 2001, the day before the US Food and Drugs Administration (FDA) rejected the company's promising new cancer drug Erbitux. It is alleged that he attempted to sell his own shares and tipped off family members who, between them, sold $10 million of ImClone stock. When the information was finally disclosed to the markets, ImClone's stock price plummeted.[221] The pharmaceutical and biotechnology industry had long been accused by investors, regulators and doctors of suppressing or delaying the results of clinical trials if market reaction was likely to be negative and only disclosing information that would put them in a good light. But the ImClone case went further: the CEO stood to benefit personally by acting on price-sensitive information that had not been provided to the markets, so that he and his family could cash in shares before ImClone's stock price fell.

In a twist of fate, an icon of American business – Martha Stewart – was dragged into the murky affair and her company was severely damaged by the collateral fall-out. Martha Stewart, America's lifestyle queen and chief executive of Martha Stewart Living Omnimedia and friend of Sam Waksal, stood accused of selling her holding in ImClone for $227 000 on the same day as Waksal's family, after being tipped off by insiders about the impending FDA rejection. By the end of June 2002, her company's share price had fallen to $9.90, almost half of its close of $19.01 earlier that month just before the allegation became public. This was amidst concerns that the brand would be sullied by the suggestion of wrongdoing; the Martha Stewart image was one of home-loving, finger lickin' 'apple pie' goodness – scarcely more at odds with the insider trading allegations.[222] Martha Stewart continued to maintain her innocence, claiming that she had an agreement with her broker to sell if the ImClone share price fell below $60.

In October 2002 Sam Waksal pleaded guilty to insider trading charges and US securities regulators announced their intention to bring a civil action against Martha Stewart.[223] In June 2003 Sam Waksal was jailed for seven years and fined $4.3m. Martha Stewart was charged with several counts of criminal behaviour and resigned from the company she founded.

striking the right balance

It is no easy task to strike the right balance between quantity, quality, timeliness and relevance of communications so that reputation is enhanced, not tarnished. The challenge is to communicate sufficient high-quality and relevant information to maintain and boost the trust and confidence of stakeholders. Providing too little information may suggest that the business is secretive, opaque, even underhand; providing too much inconsequential detail or burying key material deep within a mass of trivia may irritate and confuse investors and other stakeholders.

> Companies which get it right ... have a head-start when it comes to tapping into the burgeoning liquidity of global capital markets. These companies have grasped that the guardians of that liquidity, the global fund management and analyst communities, are basing investment strategies increasingly on 'soft' focused information rather than hard, top-line figures. ... The companies in the upper reaches of the World's Most Respected survey have not got there by chance, but by examining their business on a continual basis, and telling the outside world what it needs to know.
>
> (Kieran Poynter, UK senior partner, PricewaterhouseCoopers[224])

The challenge is also to use every communication, both written and verbal, as an opportunity to bolster reputation and trust. Using your risk management systems to anticipate the issues can help you to deflect criticism and appear fully in control, not on the defensive. An example of this is Shell UK's Annual General Meeting in May 2001 when the charismatic Sir Mark Moody-Stuart was at the helm as chairman. When faced with difficult questioning, the chairman tackled three 'hot potatoes' head on. He told a Friends of the Earth activist that the company had no intention of exploring for oil in the Sundarbans Reserved Forest in Bangladesh, haunt of the rare Bengal tiger. He confirmed to another questioner that the company would endeavour to ensure that its aviation fuel was not used for bombing raids in southern Sudan. A third person was assured that the company's social works in the oil region of southern Nigeria were producing worthwhile results. The Friends of the Earth questioner later praised Shell for aspects of their approach to environmental matters – a dramatic turnaround from the opprobrium heaped on Shell in the mid-1990s over Brent Spa and Nigeria! Since then Shell has:

> ... thought through its approach to social issues, engaged its critics and accepted its wider responsibilities. The AGM reflected its confidence in this area and the grudging respect it has won from some activists.[225]

potential pitfalls

When communicating with stakeholders, take care over the timing of your various announcements; consider carefully whether the impact of several separate and unrelated announcements (perhaps generated by different departments) could deliver an unintended message to stakeholders. In the previously cited Barclays Bank example, the almost simultaneous communications early in 2000 about levying new charges, closing branches and excessive executive pay, had a very different effect on customers from that intended. As a leaked Barclays report on their *annus horribilis* concluded: 'The almost contemporaneous set of events resulted in a media feeding frenzy... the group is seen by many ... as the ringleader of anti-consumer measures.'[226]

Sometimes, communications to improve a company's image can backfire. In the wake of the US corporate accounting scandals, PricewaterhouseCoopers (PwC) ran full-page advertisements in the US press. These were presumably designed to reassure investors by asserting that the firm's role was to 'ask the tough questions and tackle the tough answers'. The ads also stressed that 'in any case where we cannot resolve concerns about the quality of the information we are receiving or about the integrity of the management teams we are working with, we will resign'.[227] One cannot help but surmise that the ads may have had precisely the opposite effect on some investors. As the *Financial Times* observed:

> Investors might have assumed and hoped that accounting firms always worked that way. PwC's attempt to gain the moral high ground through these advertisements simply draws attention to the awful laxness of the bubble years.[228]

managing the media

The media can often be utilised to disseminate news stories in an attempt to stem reputational damage, and to restore or even enhance reputation. The ability to track media activity, judge the public mood and make the right communication at the right time is crucial.

Following its mauling by Europe's media over the GM seeds débâcle, biotechnology firm Monsanto at first maintained a low media profile. In spring 2000 the company generated positive copy by making its research data on the genetic make-up of rice freely available to the International Rice Genome Sequencing Project, a publicly funded international consortium established to decode the rice genome. Monsanto's gesture was described as 'giving a huge boost to research on new varieties of high-yielding rice, needed to feed a burgeoning world population'.[229]

In this era of intense stakeholder scrutiny and low public trust in business, it's not just the story that needs to be good; if the 'spin' is not backed up by fact and by robust management, monitoring and reporting systems, your good news may rebound negatively on your reputation.

managing the Internet

The Internet has brought with a new set of challenges for reputation risk management. The Internet allows a website set up by lone protestors to attract the same number of hits as a well-orchestrated mainstream NGO campaign; it allows a disaffected employee to post scurrilous information about an organisation; it allows 'rumours' about a company's performance and future prospects to be aired in public. Knowing whether and how to intervene via an appropriate communication can be crucial if problems – and potential crises – are to be averted.

The tools employed by Internet 'activists', in addition to the attacks on website/service availability and security discussed in the 'delivering customer promise' section above, include:

❐   SPOOF WEBSITES

Spoof websites – or 'sucker sites' as they are known in North America where they were
originally launched by consumers to let people know that a particular product 'sucks' – aim
to draw public attention to issues or problems surrounding a business and its products. The
idea of a sucker site is to pillory a product, service or entire business as publicly as possible, by deliberately locating the site's web address so close to the genuine one that search
engines will bring up the sucker site inadvertently. Hence Chase Manhattan Bank receives the
www.chasebanksucks treatment, along with countless others. Cable company NTL in 2002
found itself the focus of www.nthellworld.com 'a renegade forum set up to allow disgruntled
staff, subscribers, shareholders and suppliers to vent their spleens by taking verbal pot shots
at the company'.[230] The site was established by a single customer who had endured persistent
problems with his cable modem. Tim Ryan, NTL corporate communications director, in April
2002, described the site as 'a thermometer which told us the temperature of our customers in
terms of satisfaction'.[231] By all accounts, it was white hot at the time. NTL took the unusual
step of buying the troublesome website and putting its founder on their payroll. The company
vowed, however, to keep it open so that they could continue to 'learn from it', although the
site has since lost some of its bite.

   Such sites are often a harmless and amusing means of disgruntled consumers letting off
steam, although they can develop into a more sinister focus for activism. Allowing the site
to continue in existence, but monitoring it as closely as a source of valuable intelligence on
stakeholder perceptions is usually the best option.

   Sometimes businesses store up trouble for themselves by not being sufficiently 'e-savvy'.
In mid-2002 the consulting arm of PricewaterhouseCoopers relaunched itself under the name
Monday and set about communicating its new image. The company faced considerable flak
from employees, clients, investors and the media who were baffled by the meaningless and
costly rebranding. To them it smacked more of hung-over Monday mornings and start-of-the-
week blues, than the intended upbeat message of fresh thinking, doughnuts and hot coffee.
To add to PwC's embarrassment, they had failed to register the 'co.uk' domain name for
the 'Introducing Monday' site. It was quickly 'snapped up by a prankster who filled it with
animation that flicks the v-sign at Monday and laughs "ha ha ha ... we've got your name".'[232]
PwC had certainly not anticipated that their new 'fresh' image would alienate stakeholders
to such an extent; their failure to register all relevant domain names exacerbated the situation
by inviting ridicule. It highlights the dangers of rebranding which, as opposed to injecting
'freshness and dynamism' can also 'alienate employees, confuse clients, devalue brand equity
and even be an open invitation for ridicule'.[233] The Monday name was mercifully short-lived
and was dropped when the consulting group was later acquired by IBM.

❐   ACTIVIST WEBSITES

With increasing frequency, websites now provide a focal point for campaigns by activists and
NGOs. These are usually websites established by or affiliated with campaigning groups. They

usually include, or are close to, the name of the target business. The www.McSpotlight.org campaign against McDonald's and www.campaignexxonmobil.org and www.stopesso.org against ExxonMobil are examples of this.

Monitoring activity on sites where you are targeted will provide you with critical information on shifting perceptions and the changing mood. It could also give you vital advance warning of changed tactics and an impending crisis.

❐   DISCUSSION BOARDS

Internet discussion boards are constantly changing e-notice boards, packed with the most up-do-date information, which allow Internet users to interact and exchange views. This can result in malicious rumours, leaks and misinformation about businesses that can damage their reputation. For example, the charmingly named website www.fuckedcompany.com devotes itself to assessing likely corporate failures, based in part on insider comment. Other sites form a rallying point for staff who have been laid off, giving them the opportunity to hit back at their former employers.

Dangers do not only lurk in unofficial sites and discussion board postings; damage can also be done by well-established sites. The Motley Fool is the longest established of a number of discussion boards focused on shares and shareholders. Its UK website[234] alone has a regular readership of around 250 000 internet users, of whom 100 000 regularly visit the discussion board area of the website. Between 5000 and 10 000 people regularly post messages on the boards, giving a participation level of 1 : 200 of those who visit the discussion boards.[235] The vast majority of visitors are employees, customers and investors, although activists and campaigners also have a presence. Risks on such sites can be both from 'outsiders' and 'insiders' and include:

- 'rampers' outside a business who seek to influence the share price for short-term advantage, perhaps by manipulating news, by claiming to have insider knowledge or via outright fraud (such as faking a Regulatory News Service report)
- attacks on a business's reputation by competitors, ex-members of staff, disgruntled customers or campaigners
- deliberate leaks from a disgruntled employee
- inadvertent leaks from an over-enthusiastic insider who posts confidential or 'on subscription' only material in a bid to be helpful.[236]

Although the targeted firms would often dearly love to take legal action to curb these activities and bring the culprits to book, the anonymous nature of postings make this extremely difficult. So how should you respond?

If a message is defamatory or breaches confidentiality you can report it to the discussion board administrators who will usually remove it, although the damage may, of course, already be done. Some web hosts argue that as the site is promoted as a 'gossip' site, with content clearly based on rumour, users are forewarned and therefore no action is justified. However, if the message is simply the expression of an unfavourable opinion, you will have to consider your response carefully. An appropriate balance will need to be struck to nip the problem in the bud, while avoiding inflaming the situation. A simple factual response is often best. To do this, and to guard against Internet threats, businesses should have staff designated and authorised to deal with Internet posting risks. They also need to have formal Internet policies in place and clarity on what business information is confidential, so that employees know where to draw the line.

However incensed you are about defamatory comments posted about your business on the web, it will never be a good idea to threaten to sue the perpetrators – especially if they happen to be your shareholders. In October 2002, a UK company 10 Group started legal proceedings against ten shareholders over postings in an online chat room. The company, furious about offending messages that it claimed contained untrue statements, took the action after obtaining a High Court order against the chat room host, forcing it to disclose the names of the participants. The ensuing headline 'Leisure company sues group of shareholders for defamation'[237] was hardly reputation enhancing!

❐   WEBLOGS

A relatively new, but growing, Internet phenomenon is that of weblogs. These are sites where Internet users can post links to other content on the web, along with their own individual commentary. The typical layout for an information item on a weblog is a link, an explanation and a space for commentary by others.[238] The sites of greatest concern for reputation are those often termed 'metalogs'[239] as a wide community of users can post to them, in contrast with the millions of personal weblogs that do not allow posting submissions. Their appeal – and their danger – lies in the way in which they can create a consensus view of an issue, a sense of community among users and can identify the stories that really matter to people.

One example of this is the case of Matt Haughey, the founder of metalog www.metafiler.com. Aggrieved by the business practices of information security company, Critical IP, he posted on his site a suggestion that anyone agreeing with him should post a link to his page on their website.

> Within days, the number of people linking in to this 'Critical IP Sucks' message drove the page to the top of Google's research results list for Critical IP – above the company's own Web site. The long-term impact of this kind of campaign (called 'google-bombing') should not be overstated – the effect on Google only lasts a matter of weeks – but it is an importing illustration of the potential power of weblogs.[240]

Direct business intervention in a weblog can easily backfire if it is seen as not in the spirit of the weblog community. The best tactic, therefore, is merely to observe and soak up the invaluable and free market research provided on reaction to new products, services and other business activities.

Many large businesses already regularly monitor relevant websites, discussion boards and other web activity related to their company and sector. If Internet activity is a potential threat to your business, you should ensure that systematic monitoring is carried out either in-house or by using an Internet research and monitoring service.[241] The intelligence gathered can be fed into your risk management process and used as an input for risk assessment, risk action planning and future strategy development. The Internet is where the first stirrings of an impending reputational crisis may occur: if you're oblivious to web activity relating to your business, you may miss those vital early warning signs.

Although the Internet can pose a serious threat, it also offers a fertile opportunity by which businesses can engage and influence their critics. This will be explored further in Chapter 9.

crisis management

You may have done everything possible to anticipate and guard against reputational threats, but if a crisis strikes and you are caught unprepared or respond inappropriately, your reputation may still be in tatters. Crisis management these days is seen as an integral part of business continuity management – ensuring that the business can operate 365 days a year, 24 hours a day, 7 days a week if required. It's much more than just guarding against fires, floods and power failures.

> An event can become a crisis because it threatens a company's short-term prospects and, if the event is mismanaged, its long-term survival. Companies rely on delicate interrelationships for their mandate to operate. When these relationships are jolted – and profitability threatened – by an internally or externally generated disaster, companies with a strong reputation that act quickly to maintain stakeholder confidence, underpin sales, protect their market position and communicate with regulators will be the companies that go furthest toward guarding shareholder value.
>
> (Michael L. Sherman, chief operating officer, AIG Europe (UK) Limited[242])

The immediate impact of a crisis is almost always reduced share price, but other insidious and more deleterious consequences often ensue. Johnson & Johnson's market value fell by $1 billion, or 14%, after some of its Tylenol bottles were contaminated with cyanide by an extortionist in 1982. Exxon's stock was devalued by $3 billion, or 5%, the week after the 1989 oil spill from the Exxon Valdez in Alaska. Motorola saw its capitalisation fall $6 billion, or 16%, after scientists in 1995 hinted at a link between cell phones and brain cancer.[243]

Share price adjustments at the time of a crisis will incorporate market expectations of damages, clean-up costs, legal costs and fines, many of which can be covered by insurance. Factored into this are the anticipated indirect effects of damaged reputation on customer buying patterns, employee loyalty and productivity, and the attitude of regulators and communities; these can be even more harmful long-term and are generally not insurable risks. The good news is that managing a crisis well can actually enhance reputation and shareholder value in the longer term.

> Over time, some companies recover lost value quickly and the crisis fades. Others experience more extended damage. Research suggests that the difference lies in how the crisis was handled and in what the reputation of the company was beforehand. Good reputations have considerable

hidden value as a form of insurance – they act as a 'reservoir of goodwill'. The insurance value of reputation derives from its ability to buffer well-regarded companies from problems.

(Professor Charles J. Fombrun[244])

This is borne out by research at Templeton College, Oxford[245] which focused on the consequences of corporate catastrophes and the impact on the company's share price. Where share price fell, this resulted from a market re-evaluation of managerial ability resulting from their handling of the crisis. Conversely, if the crisis was handled well, management's reputation was enhanced and shareholder value rose – mainly as a result of increased confidence in future cash flows.

UK rail infrastructure operator Railtrack saw its reputation spiral downwards as it attempted to defend itself during a series of rail disasters.

> Railtrack has been weakened by the steep fall in its share price since the autumn of 1998 and by rising debt since the Hatfield crash in October 2000. The company's panicky reaction to the accident, the revelation of its poor maintenance record and the serious fall in passenger numbers further eroded its prestige.[246]

Railtrack's poor handling of each crisis, and the subsequent revelation of a litany of previously unknown errors of judgement, cover-ups and non-conformances, shook public and investor confidence. Unguarded and insensitive remarks made by Railtrack chairman Gerald Corbett, when he likened the pursuit of rail safety to a journey in which 'you never arrive at your destination' were seized on by the media as further proof of Railtrack's incompetence. The company's reputation had been fatally wounded: Gerald Corbett resigned and the company was later put into administration by the UK government, to be replaced by Network Rail.

In 1999 Coca-Cola was slow to respond to a drinks contamination scare in Belgium and France, involving mainly children suffering from upset stomachs, nausea and headaches after drinking Coke. The conglomerate's dilatory response to the crisis did little to allay public fears, with consumer confidence in Europe already battered by BSE, salmonella and other food scares. Coca-Cola seemed blissfully unaware that the Belgium government had fallen just days prior to the crisis, due to criticism over its handling of the discovery of the carcinogen dioxin in a range of meats, eggs and dairy products.[247] Coca-Cola responded inappropriately by putting out unconvincing statements from its Atlanta headquarters in the USA, thereby reinforcing the impression of a distant, uncaring, profit-hungry corporation. Coca-Cola's contention that the contamination might be related to two separate chemical problems at different plants but that 'no health and safety problems were found' was simply not credible. The company's insistence on calling the affected product 'substandard' also smacked of arrogance. The Belgian Health Minister was quoted as saying, 'It's a bit disturbing that a big firm with worldwide fame . . . did not take far reaching measures more spontaneously.'[248] The Belgian, French and Luxembourg governments forced Coca-Cola to withdraw their products; only in the Netherlands did the company take the lead in the product recall.

> Without a convincing explanation, consumers are left to be concerned about the true nature and extent of the problem. They are likely to conclude that the company has something serious to hide.

What might have been a minor issue becomes a major crisis through hesitation and inaction. The sentiment expressed by a Coca-Cola France spokesman becomes merely retrospective wishful thinking. 'This is not a scandal. It is not an "affaire". It is simply an issue.'

(Professor Andrew Chambers[249])

Scandal or not, the crisis proved very costly for Coca-Cola. Its profits dropped by 31% and its share price fell. The total cost to the company was put at some $103 million.[250]

Coca-Cola might have acted more swiftly and decisively to limit the damage if it had picked up from its risk radar systems that the impact would be magnified as a result of the sensitive environment pertaining in northern Europe at the time. Nevertheless, it would probably not have managed to avert the crisis altogether as the source was totally unexpected and without precedent.

However good you believe your risk management systems to be, you will never be completely immune to crises. It will therefore be prudent to develop and rehearse crisis plans and to integrate these into your overall business continuity management arrangements. You may not be inclined to plan for a crisis because of the time, effort and expense involved, but if you think crisis management is expensive – try a real crisis for size! Contingency plans should be considered for those 'very low likelihood, catastrophic impact' risks discussed in Chapter 4 that you documented during your risk identification exercise – including collateral damage risks from competitors in your sector.[251]

Your choice of crisis team and spokesperson will be crucial. As discussed above, the communication style of the CEO or chairman contributes to reputation on a day-to-day basis; but the characteristics of that style will be under even more intense scrutiny when he or she utters the first words after a tragedy or incident. Their tone, style of dress, the appropriateness of their empathy with the victims, their praise (if any) for the support services and their willingness to take responsibility and learn from the incident, will be pored over by the media. Woe betide the spokesperson who has not undergone media training to prepare for this eventuality and appears uncaring, reticent or defensive. Any sniff of shirking responsibility and 'passing the buck' will be frowned upon. The heartfelt, compassionate yet purposeful tone struck by New York Major Rudolf Giuliani in the hours after the 9/11 atrocities is something to aspire to.

Once a crisis strikes, openness and honesty are prerequisites for allaying stakeholder fears and maintaining the confidence of the public:

Being open is one of the axioms of crisis management. Openness tells people that you are trustworthy and honest. Research and experience indicates that a brisk 'no comment' will suggest that you and your company have something to hide. It may also suggest that you do not care, or are not competent to deal with the problem that you have created.

(Mike Seymour and Simon Moore[252])

Use your risk management system, your early warning indicators, your risk identification techniques, such as scenario planning, to try to anticipate possible crises. Make sure you are continuously tracking any unresolved stakeholder concerns that could suddenly erupt,

- Develop scenarios: what could happen?
- Establish response: how should we react?
- Challenge: what could go wrong?
- Define roles: who should do what?
- Raise awareness: do they know what to do?
- Train: can they do it under pressure?

Plan, test, learn and re-plan

Figure 6-12   Rules of effective crisis management.

emerging stakeholder alliances that could overnight present a powerful, united front and web activity that could act as a rallying point for protestors. Know how to spot the early signs of a gathering storm such as increased noise from pressure groups, heightened media interest and rising public awareness. Be clear about how it would look and feel when a risk starts to crystallise into a crisis, so that you can invoke your crisis plan without delay and maintain the upper hand.

Be ready for the crisis by having a response team in place whose members understand their respective roles and have been trained to carry them out – even under intense pressure (Figure 6-12).

Make sure that, as the crisis unfolds, you communicate early, communicate and communicate again, never leaving a void that can be filled by rumour and speculation. Don't forget to include, in your crisis plan, clarity on who is to act as the media spokesperson(s); regular media and online updates (your website is likely to be the first port of a call for the media, NGOs, investors and the general public – hungry for news and reassurance); comprehensive product recall arrangements (if applicable to your business); and your response to regulatory dawn raids and investigations. When the storm has abated, take time out to learn from what happened. Did you get it right? Could damage have been reduced if you had acted differently? What changes could you make to improve your response? Build the learning into a modified crisis plan for future use.

A text book case of effective crisis management in action was, in fact, one of the very first deliberate product contaminations – the Tylenol tablet crisis in 1982 at US Healthcare company Johnson & Johnson. J&J's gut reaction was exactly right: the company promptly recalled all product nationwide; established a toll-free hotline; placed full-page advertisements in newspapers; sent over 450 000 electronic messages to the medical community to explain the position; and arranged executive interviews in the media. J&J's sincere, honest and sure-footed reaction to the crisis enhanced their reputation.

It may be pure coincidence, but at the heart of J&J's business lies the company's 'credo': a one-page document introduced by Robert Wood Johnson Jr when he was chairman of J&J

during the period 1932 to 1963. It is a values-based, stakeholder-focused business philosophy which states that:

> ...our first responsibility is to our customers, to give them high-quality products at fair prices. Our second responsibility is to our employees, to treat them with dignity and respect and pay them fairly. Our third responsibility is to the communities in which we operate, to be good corporate citizens and protect the environment... our final responsibility is to our shareholders, to give them a fair return.
>
> (Ralph S. Larsen, former chairman and CEO, Johnson & Johnson[253])

J&J's instinctive reaction to the Tylenol crisis was the right one: it satisfied the company's customers and quickly restored their confidence and trust. The business has consistently been ranked among the best in 'most admired' and 'most respected' company surveys in the USA and globally. J&J were also ranked eighth globally in 2002 in a 'wealth added index', devised by US-based consultancy Stern Stewart, which ranked companies according to the amount of wealth they had created in the five years up to December 2001, based on total shareholder return.[254]

In 2003, in the wake of the US corporate scandals, Ralph Larsen, ex J&J chairman and CEO and a member of the Conference Board's Commission on Public Trust and Private Enterprise commented on the importance of tone setting and values in guiding behaviours:

> If I've learnt anything over the last few years, then it's that for a large organisation to conduct itself properly, the tone has to be set at the top. It's not the big decisions, it's how you do the everyday things. How do you talk to the lady in the cafeteria, do you treat them with dignity? Do the small things right and when crisis hits, you instinctively do what's right.[255]

Despite their obvious importance, many businesses do not have formal crisis plans. Such plans should not just cater for product contamination scares, oil slicks and NGO campaigns, but should also ensure that the business can continue to operate and maintain stakeholder confidence when faced by a disruption caused by a terrorist attack, a major system or website collapse or a failure in the supply chain. Businesses in some sectors, such as financial services and travel, are particularly vulnerable; for them a systems outage of even an hour could result in customer defections and dented reputation. Not having an up-to-date and well-rehearsed business continuity plan, including crisis management and disaster recovery procedures, can, itself constitute a risk to reputation.

A KPMG survey found that nearly half of US companies did not have firm plans to cope with a crisis, despite concerns over the business disruption caused by the 11 September attacks in 2001. Of the 135 senior executives contacted in August 2002, 5% said a crisis plan was not a priority, 10% said they had no plan in place and acknowledged their vulnerability, a further 31% said that although some preparations had been made, their plans were 'on the backburner'.[256] Figures released by UK regulator, the Financial Service Authority, stated that '30 to 40% [of the 11 500 firms the FSA regulates] haven't got any sort of back-up plan at all'.[257] From a reputation risk management viewpoint, not having a crisis plan is a downright dereliction of duty.

It could be argued that failing to invest in reputation by building good long-term relationships with stakeholders is also negligent, as this is a crucial means of safeguarding your business from the effects of a crisis.

> The best defence is not only to be prepared, but also to have built up a bank of goodwill with each stakeholder group over time. This can be powerful enough to secure a second chance for companies even after a catastrophe.
> (Michael L. Sherman, chief operating officer, AIG Europe (UK) Limited[258])

Oil and gas group BP, a company consistently highly ranked in 'most respected company' league tables and whose trusted CEO, Lord John Browne, was for four consecutive years awarded the prestigious 'most admired business leader' by *Management Today*, was subject to a number of body blows in the latter half of 2002. The company had downgraded oil production targets three times in two months (causing an estimated £7 billion to be wiped off the value of shares in a single day[259]), financial performance was disappointing compared to industry rivals and the company's safety record in Alaska was under attack. The headline 'Tarnished Lord Browne loses the pixie dust' summed up the mood of investors: here was an iconic leader, known as the 'Sun King', who previously couldn't put a foot wrong, suddenly finding himself beleaguered. In spite of the press having a field day (nothing sells papers quite like a fallen hero!), the mood was sombre, bewildered and questioning. This, after all, was BP, a company – once described as another arm of the British civil service – that had been plucked from obscurity and transformed into a global giant worth over £90 billion. This was the company that had first introduced environmental thinking to the oil and gas industry and had received accolades for its stance on social and environmental issues. Lord Browne was a charismatic business leader of the greatest integrity, who inspired confidence; a leader for whom many business people and investors would privately love to work. The accumulated goodwill had created an expectation that the company would emerge from the crisis chastened but somehow stronger. As one paper quipped 'the halo may have slipped a little, but the shine may yet be restored on the Sun King'.[260] The company didn't disappoint. Lord Browne was immediately available for comment and spoke with his customary candour; internal investigations were launched. In February 2003 Lord Browne again demonstrated his ability to surprise and delight the markets by announcing his new strategy one month early: the pursuit of a more balanced set of targets and a series of portfolio changes, including a major new investment in Russia. Headlines such as 'BP hits bull's-eye on banishing targets'[261] and 'Browne polishes up BP's tarnished credibility'[262] suggest that the sun is yet to set on the empire of the Sun King.

Stakeholder goodwill is indeed so critical that businesses should take the greatest care not to abuse it. If reputational capital starts to wear thin, the tide of stakeholder opinion can quickly turn, which was illustrated in the case of Sir Richard Branson, head of the global Virgin group. In late 2000 Virgin decided not to appeal against the final decision to allow the lottery operator Camelot to continue to run the UK's National Lottery – a position Virgin had lobbied long and hard to secure. This came in the wake of a series of other problems, including failure of the bid to run the east coast mainline railway and poor performance on Virgin Rail's west coast service.

Recent events had eaten away at the goodwill Sir Richard had built up for the Virgin name. . . . The brand was in danger of reaching a 'tipping point' where another setback could send its reputation tumbling.

(Rita Clifton, chief executive of Interbrand brand consultancy[263])

Knowing your organisation's reputational 'tipping point' by carefully monitoring stakeholder reactions is a key element in effective reputation management. Do you know yours?

in a nutshell

What, then, are the key considerations for effective communication and crisis management?

- Ensure that communications are fully transparent and include all material issues of interest to stakeholders; information should be accurate, prompt, honest and consistent; where possible go beyond the statutory minimum to build confidence and goodwill.

- Put your communications across in an accessible, jargon-free style; and ensure that the person delivering any verbal communication adopts an appropriate tone and approach – particularly during a crisis. Provide media training to key personnel; be honest and sincere; commit to learning from any mistakes; and don't try to 'pass the buck'.

- Try at all times to strike an appropriate balance between quantity, quality, timeliness and relevance. Tailor your communications to individual stakeholder group audiences to ensure that their information needs are met.

- Avoid surprises: convey bad news as soon as practicably possible. Never put yourself in a position where you could benefit personally by withholding it.

- Monitor media activity and manage the media with care: 'Good news' stories must be backed up by solid fact and evidence – pure PR spin will swiftly be exposed. Beware of trying to take the moral high ground as it often backfires.

- Monitor Internet activity relating to your business. Intervene only when strictly necessary to correct a factual inaccuracy. The best tactic is usually to observe and soak up the flow of free intelligence on stakeholder perceptions and expectations.

- Be accessible and available for comment – particularly during a crisis.

- Carefully consider the timing of communications, particularly of multiple statements over a relatively short period, to ensure that messages are consistent and cannot be misconstrued.

- Utilise your risk management systems to anticipate issues – ideally to head off a crisis but at least to be prepared for it. Ensure that contingencies have been considered for all 'very low likelihood, very high impact' threats.

- Have detailed and well-rehearsed crisis management arrangements in place. Know when issues and risks cross the line and become a crisis, and act swiftly and decisively.

- Seek to build stakeholder goodwill whenever possible and never abuse it. Know your reputational 'tipping point' and act accordingly.

The irony is that you can take all possible steps to protect and enhance your reputation, but if you don't communicate what you are doing in a credible way, or don't respond well to a crisis, your reputation may still suffer major impairment. In many ways, this final driver of reputation is the most important. That is why Chapter 9 is dedicated to exploring innovative ways of bolstering reputation by leveraging reporting and communications.

MAKING A START

If you feel baffled and bamboozled – or just plain overwhelmed – by the diversity of issues covered in this chapter, take heart. It doesn't all need to be done at once, but can be approached stepwise over a period. If you want to make a swift start, consider the following:

- Go back to your pillars of legitimacy and uniqueness attributes discussed at the beginning of Chapter 6. If the major threats to these are not under control, your reputation, competitive advantage and even licence to operate could be in jeopardy.

- If you are looking for a first set of priorities to target, complete the reputation risk driver/stakeholder matrix in Figure 6.3 for your business circumstances. Which are your most critical stakeholders? Where are your reputational hot spots?

- If you are planning to accept orders via your website, are launching an innovative product, acquiring a new business, or using suppliers in a new territory for the first time, all these changes will be teaming with potential risks to reputation. Carrying out a risk assessment as part of the change project will tease out the major threats – and also some opportunities that may otherwise remain buried.

- Check out your crisis response plans. Are they as robust are they should be? Do they cater for scenarios such as an e-attack on your website, a regulatory dawn-raid or a virulent NGO campaign?

Also, don't neglect those opportunities: not only are missed opportunities potential threats to the success of your business, but well-exploited opportunities can create real sustainable value. If you want to go further than just protecting your reputation and seek to bolster it, try to adopt a mindset that regards opportunity as the flip side of threat and sees risk as a continuum ranging from negative downside threat to positive upside opportunity. A well- managed threat can often be converted into an opportunity. Seek out that silver lining and leverage it (Figure 6-13).

The following chapters will examine in more detail how reputation can be continuously assessed, so that you know where you stand (Chapter 7) and how to gain the peace of mind

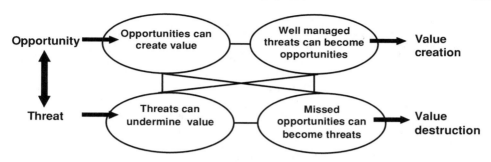

Figure 6-13 Threats and opportunities (adapted from FORGE II[264]).

through audit and assurance (Chapter 8) that will enable you to report to your stakeholders with confidence (Chapter 9) – another means of further enhancing your reputation.

NOTES AND REFERENCES

1. Reported in *The Guardian*, 25 May 2002.
2. Reported in the *Financial Times*, 31 August 2002.
3. Lucinda Kemeny writing in *The Observer*, 4 August 2002.
4. Reported in *Business Week*, 8 April 2002.
5. This methodology, albeit fairly rough and ready, provides you with a starting point for thinking about the impact of various stakeholders and their specific areas of interest. A much more sophisticated stakeholder audit or analysis can be carried out either in-house or using a specialist PR or market research consultancy to elicit stakeholder views by conducting structured interviews with them. Going beyond merely collecting data to active two-way engagement with key stakeholders thorough meaningful dialogue is discussed in Chapter 7.
6. Financial principles reproduced by permission of Hermes Pensions Ltd. See also Appendix A for details of the ten Hermes Principles. The document can be downloaded in full at www.hermes.co.uk.
7. *No Surprises: The Case for Better Risk Reporting* (1999). London: ICAEW, p. 36.
8. Reported in the *Financial Times*, 29 June 2002.
9. *Financial Times*, 27 June 2002.
10. Reported in the *Financial Times*, 10 August 2002.
11. Reported in *Business Week*, 5–12 August 2002.
12. Findings of a report by the US General Accounting Office, 23 October 2002.
13. As reported in the *Financial Times*, 18 and 21 October 2002.
14. MyTravel's chief development officer, Richard Carrick, as reported in the *Financial Times*, 21 October 2002.
15. It was announced in March 2003 that Tim Byrne would receive a pay-off of £1.2 million. The company argued that the settlement 'resulted in a better outcome for the company than was likely to be achieved through a process of protracted litigation' (*The Guardian*, 21 March 2003). By this time, the MyTravel's share price stood at 12.75p (compared to 283.5p before the crisis), bookings were down but the company seemed set to survive.
16. Reported in the *Sunday Times*, 20 October 2002.
17. As reported in the *Financial Times*, 27 February 2003.

18. As reported in the *Financial Times*, 1 March 2003.
19. McKinsey and Company's Global Investor Opinion Survey was undertaken between April and May 2002 in cooperation with the Global Corporate Governance Forum. The survey was based on responses from over 200 institutional investors, collectively responsible for some USD 2 trillion of assets under management. See www.mckinsey.com/governance for further details.
20. The Cadbury report (1992) *Report of the Committee on the Financial Aspects of Corporate Governance*. London, para. 2.5.
21. OECD (April 1999) *Principles of Corporate Goverance*. See www.oecd.org.
22. As reported in the *Financial Times*, 30 January 2003.
23. McKinsey and Company's Global Investor Opinion Survey was undertaken between April and May 2002 in cooperation with the Global Corporate Governance Forum. The survey was based on responses from over 200 institutional investors, collectively responsible for some USD 2 trillion of assets under management. See www.mckinsey.com/governance for further details.
24. *The Responsibilities of Institutional Shareholders and Agents* issued by the UK's Institutional Shareholders' Committee (ISC), October 2002. The ISC's membership includes the Association of British Insurers (ABI), the Association of Investment Trust Companies (AITC), the Investment Management Association (IMA) and the National Association of Pension Funds (NAPF). It speaks for a membership that controls the vast majority of institutional funds in the UK.
25. From *The Guardian*, 23 March 2001.
26. Reported in the *Financial Times*, 4 July 2002.
27. Robert Bruce writing in the *Financial Times*, 15 August 2002.
28. John Argenti, UK business consultant, designer of the A-Score (a predictor of corporate failure) quoted in the *Financial Times*, 11 October 2002.
29. Findings from the fourth annual Corporate Reputation Watch survey of 600 US executives conducted in February 2002 by Harris Interactive on behalf of international public relations and public affairs firm Hill & Knowlton.
30. CNN/USA Today/Gallup poll July 2002 as cited in *The Conference Board Commission on Public Trust and Private Enterprise – Findings and Recommendations Part 2: Corporate Governance*, pp. 4–5 released on 9 January 2003 (available for download from www.conference-board.org).
31. *The Conference Board Commission on Public Trust and Private Enterprise – Findings and Recommendations Part 2: Corporate Governance*, p. 25, released on 9 January 2003 (available for download from www.conference-board.org).
32. *The Conference Board Commission on Public Trust and Private Enterprise – Findings and Recommendations Part 2: Corporate Governance*, p. 6, released on 9 January 2003 (available for download from www.conference-board.org).
33. A rival retailer, quoted in the *Financial Times*, 24 February 2001.
34. *Financial Times*, 21 January 2003.
35. The US Conference Board recommends that the roles of chairman of the board and CEO be split and that the chairman be an independent director. See *The Conference Board Commission on Public Trust and Private Enterprise – Findings and Recommendations Part 2: Corporate Governance*, p. 8, released on 9 January 2003 (available for download from www.conference-board.org).
36. Higgs, D. (January 2003) *Review of the Role and Effectiveness of Non-executive Directors*. London: The Stationery Office, p. 11, para. 1.6. The report is available for download from the UK's Department of Trade and Industry website at www.dti.gov.uk/cld/non_exec_review.
37. In the USA under the new 2002. NASDAQ and NYSE listing rules a majority of the board should be independent. In France the Bouton report, *Promoting better corporate governance in listed*

companies (September 2002), recommends that half the board be independent. The UK's Higgs review, published January 2003, recommends that at least half of the members of the board, excluding the chairman, should be independent.

38. Findings of McKinsey survey *Inside the Boardroom* based on discussions with 200 directors who collectively sit on some 500 US boards and 50 directors, governance experts and investors conducted during April–May 2002. Available from the McKinsey website www.mckinsey.com.

39. *The Role and Effectiveness of Non-executive Directors*, by Derek Higgs, published 20 January 2003, proposed code provision A.3.4, p. 81. The full text of the Higgs report can be downloaded from www.dti.gov.uk/cld/non_exec_review.

40. Adapted from *The Role and Effectiveness of Non-executive Directors*, by Derek Higgs, published 20 January 2003, proposed code provision A.3.4, p. 81.

41. Data from The Corporate Library, a US-based corporate governance research website which, in November 2002, launched a database tool allowing subscribers to track connections between directors, as reported in the *Financial Times*, 25 November 2002. See also www.thecorporatelibrary.com.

42. As reported in the *Financial Times*, 25 November 2002.

43. *The Sunday Times*, 15 December 2002. This headline relates to the demise of telecommunications company Cable & Wireless and the squandering of the proceeds of disposals it made after 1999.

44. The New York Stock Exchange (NYSE) listing rules published in 2002 require independent directors to meet regularly at scheduled sessions without management present. The UK Higgs review recommends that non-executives should meet at least once a year without the chairman or executive directors present and should state in the annual report whether such meetings have taken place.

45. *The Economist*, 13 July 2002.

46. From the Role and Effectiveness of Non-executive Directors, by Derek Higgs, published 20 January 2003, p. 27.

47. Edward Lawler, professor at the Marshall School of Business at the University of Southern California and Jay Conger, professor at the Marshall school and the London Business School, in an article in the *Financial Times*, on 1 April 2002.

48. The Higgs report includes a useful induction programme for newly appointed directors (Higgs, D. (January 2003) *Review of the Role and Effectiveness of Non-executive Directors*. London: The Stationery Office, Annexe. The full text of the Higgs report can be downloaded from www.dti.gov.uk/cld/non_exec_review).

49. As reported in the *Financial Times*, 18 September 2002.

50. From an article in the US *Fortune* magazine 'You Bought, They Sold', 2 September 2002.

51. Noted in the report of the US congressional Joint Committee on Taxation, February 2003.

52. *The Conference Board Commission on Public Trust and Private Enterprise – Findings and Recommendations Part 1: Executive Compensation*, p. 4, released on 17 September 2002 (available for download from www.conference-board.org).

53. *The Conference Board Commission on Public Trust and Private Enterprise – Findings and Recommendations Part 1: Executive Compensation*, p. 7, released on 17 September 2002 (available for download from www.conference-board.org).

54. Reported in the *Financial Times*, 12 February 2003.

55. Major investor in GSK quoted anonymously in the *Financial Times*, 22 November 2002.

56. Alastair Ross Goobey, chairman of Hermes Focus Funds and Governor of the Wellcome Trust, writing in the UK's *Director* magazine, August 2002.

57. At Vodafone's AGM in July 2002, 9.5% of shareholders voted against its pay policy and further 6% abstained. This compared with 39% who voted against or abstained the previous year.

58. Findings of Guardian–Incubon survey reported in *The Guardian*, 4 October 2002. Top executive pay had risen 28% in 2000 and 16.5% in 1991.

59. The Directors Remuneration Report Regulations 2002 (which amend the 1985 Companies Act) will apply to annual reports from 2002 year end. Although the incorporation of a remuneration report in the annual report is already required for listed companies, more detailed disclosures will be needed under the new legislation including details of individual directors' remuneration; the rationale for any compensation packages the previous year; membership of the remuneration committee; details of any consultants used; and a 'forward looking statement' on company pay policy, explaining how this is linked to performance.

60. Rob Lake, Head of SRI Engagement and Corporate Governance at Henderson Global Investors in a letter to the *Financial Times*, 22 January 2003.

61. For example, sample duties for Remuneration and Nomination Committees are provided as appendices to the Higgs report (Higgs, D. (January 2003) *Review of the Role and Effectiveness of Non-executive Directors*. London: The Stationery Office, Annexes E and F). The full text of the Higgs report can be downloaded from www.dti.gov.uk/cld/non_exec_review); a specimen terms of reference for an audit committee is provided as an appendix to the Smith report (Smith, R. (January 2003) *Audit Committees Combined Code Guidance*. London: Financial Reporting Council, Appendix 1). The full text of the Smith report is available for download from the Financial Reporting Council website at www.frc.org.uk/publications.

62. Reported in the *Financial Times*, 22 November 2002 as related by Desmond Pearson, audit-general for Western Australia.

63. *The Conference Board Commission on Public Trust and Private Enterprise – Findings and Recommendations Part 2: Corporate Governance*, pp. 10–11 and 24, released on 9 January 2003 (available for download from www.conference-board.org).

64. *The Role and Effectiveness of Non-executive Directors*, by Derek Higgs, published 20 January 2003, Code provision A.6.1, p. 84. Annex J to the report 'Performance and Evaluation Guidance' is a useful checklist for evaluating the performance of the board and its non-executives directors. The report can be downloaded from www.dti.gov.uk/cld/non_exec_review.

65. The UK government-sponsored Smith report makes it a requirement for UK listed companies to include in the directors' report within the annual report 'a separate section that describes the role and responsibilities of the audit committee and the actions taken by the audit committee to discharge those responsibilities'. Smith, R. (January 2003) *Audit Committees Combined Code Guidance*. London: Financial Reporting Council, p. 17, para. 6.1. The full text of the Smith report is available for download from the Financial Reporting Council website at www.frc.org.uk/publications.

66. Headline from the *Financial Times*, 17 August 2002.

67. Headline from the *Financial Times*, 9 October 2002.

68. As reported in the *Financial Times*, 17 August 2002.

69. *The Guardian*, 8 February 2003. PowderJect's acquisition by Chiron was finally agreed in May 2003.

70. According to a Hill & Knowlton/Opinion Research Corporation Litigation Survey (published July 2002), 51% of US respondents said they would be less likely to buy the products of a company accused of misconduct. See www.hillandknowlton.com.

71. From the report *Rethinking Regulatory Risk* (published October 2002) by Professor Robert Baldwin or the London School of Economics and Richard Anderson of DLA. The report was based on structured interviews with 50 FTSE 250 companies or equivalents and discussions with regulators, analysts and commentators. See www.dla.com/regulation.

72. As reported in *The Guardian*, 23 April 2002.

73. From February 2002, Corporate Reputation Watch survey, as reported in a press release on the Hill & Knowlton website (www.hillandknowlton.com). Global public relations firm Hill & Knowlton jointly sponsored the survey in conjunction with *Chief Executive* magazine.

74. Reported in *The Guardian*, 25 September 2002. In June 2003 six former Xerox executives agreed to pay a total of $22m to settle their allegations.

75. As reported in the *Financial Times*, 20 January 2003.

76. As reported in *The Guardian*, 8 February 2003.

77. Headline in *The Guardian*, 8 February 2003.

78. As reported in *The Guardian*, 28 March 2003.

79. Shandwick International survey of 1000 respondents as reported in the *Financial Times*, 29 January 2001.

80. The anti-McDonald's website is still going strong at www.McSpotlight.org. A blow-by-blow account of the McLibel proceedings is available on the site.

81. Genasi, C. (2002) *Winning Reputations: How to be Your Own Spin Doctor*. Palgrave: Basingstoke, p. 144.

82. Reported in the *Financial Times*, 29 January 2001.

83. As reported in *The Guardian*, 9 May 2001.

84. As reported in *The Guardian*, 17 November 2000.

85. Report of the US congressional Joint Committee on Taxation, February 2003.

86. KPMG Integrity Management Services (2000) *Organisational Integrity Survey* as reported in the Conference Board's *Commission on Public Trust and Private Enterprise – Findings and Recommendations Part 2: Corporate Governance*, p. 11, released on 9 January 2003 (available for download from www.conference-board.org).

87. Rothschild, J. and Miethe, T. D. (February 1999) 'Whistle-Blower Disclosures and Management Retaliation', *Work and Occupations*, volume 26, No. 1, p. 120.

88. Time/CNN Survey/Harris Interactive December 2002.

89. Findings of a Work Foundation (previously known as the Industrial Society) survey published July 2002. See www.theworkfoundation.com.

90. From the Office of Fair Trading guidance note *How your Business can Achieve Compliance: A guide to achieving compliance with the Competition Act 1998* (August 1999), p. 13. The guidance is available from www.oft.gov.uk.

91. As reported in the *Financial Times*, 29 April 2002.

92. Reported in *The Guardian*, 17 September 2002.

93. As reported in *The Guardian*, 17 September 2002.

94. As reported in the 3 March 2003 edition of *Fortune* magazine. See also www.fortune.com/fortune/mostadmired.

95. Quoted in the Institute of Directors' Guide *Reputation Management: Strategies for protecting companies their brands and their directors* (1999). London: Director Publications, pp. 25–26.

96. From an article by Michael L. Sherman, chief operating officer AIG Europe (UK) Limited in the Institute of Directors' Guide *Reputation Management: Strategies for protecting companies their brands and their directors* (1999). London: Director Publications, p. 12.

97. Bevan, J. (2001) *The Rise and Fall of Marks and Spencer*. London: Profile Books, p. 4.

98. Bevan, J. (2001) *The Rise and Fall of Marks and Spencer*. London: Profile Books, p. 6.

99. Mission statement is available on The Body Shop's website at www.thebodyshop.com.

100. The article, by Jon Entine, appeared in the September 1994 edition of *Business Ethics* magazine.

101. See www.mcspotlight.org/beyond/companies/bodyshop. The McSpotlight website has, over the years, also targeted other companies such as Wal-Mart and Nestlé.

102. Extracts from the leaked Barclay's memo as reported in the *Sunday Times*, 8 October 2000.

103. As reported in *The Guardian*, 1 March 2003.

104. *The Guardian*, 29 August 2002.

105. *Financial Times*, 27 September 2002.

106. Reported in the *Financial Times*, 29 August 2002.

107. As reported in the *Financial Times*, 28 February 2001.

108. As reported in the *Financial Times*, 5 June 2002.

109. As reported in the *Financial Times* and *The Guardian*, 1 March 2003.

110. As reported in *The Guardian*, 25 May 2001.

111. *The Guardian*, 1 March 2003.

112. From an article by Geoff Armstrong (2000) 'People practices make a difference' in *Human Capital and Corporate Reputation: Setting the Boardroom Agenda*. London, ICAEW Centre for Business Performance, p. 9.

113. Article in the *Financial Times*, 24 October 2002.

114. Extract from *Kingfisher's plan for corporate social responsibility* (October 2001). The plan can be downloaded from www.kingfisher.co.uk. Reproduced by permission of Kingfisher plc.

115. Quoted in *The Guardian*, 11 April 2001.

116. As reported in *The Guardian*, 11 April 2001.

117. Klein, N. (2000) *No Logo*. London: Flamingo, p. 361.

118. Quoted in *The Guardian*, 11 April 2001.

119. As reported in *The Guardian*, 24 August 2002.

120. As reported in *The Guardian*, 24 August 2002.

121. *The Observer*, 19 November 2000.

122. *The Observer*, 20 May 2001.

123. Dr Alan Knight, Head of Social Responsibility, Kingfisher plc, speaking at the Institute of Directors' Corporate Social Responsibility Conference, London, 25 September 2002. Reproduced by permission of Kingfisher plc.

124. As reported in *The Guardian*, 26 February 2003. See also the website of the Fairtrade Foundation (www.fairtrade.org.uk) for further details.

125. *The Business Case for Sustainable Development: Making a Difference Towards the Johannesburg Summit 2002 and Beyond* (2002). Geneva: WBCSD, p. 12.

126. Extract from the address of Robert B. Shapiro, Chairman, Monsanto, to the 4th Annual Greenpeace Business Global Conference, 6 October 1999.

127. This case study is adapted from one which first appeared in Rayner, J. (2001) *Risky Business: Towards Best Practice in Managing Reputation Risk*. London: Institute of Business Ethics, p. 24.

128. As quoted in the *Financial Times*, 25 January 2001.

129. Reported in the *Financial Times*, 12 December 2002.

130. From Department of Trade and Industry Study (May 2001) *Creating value from your intangibles*, p. 23. Can be downloaded from www.dti.gov.uk.

131. Extract from a speech by Patricia Hewitt, UK Trade and Industry Secretary, in Cambridge, as reported in the *Financial Times*, 6 July 2002.

132. A number of such surveys exist. In addition to the *Sunday Times* survey, they include *Fortune* magazine ('America's 100 best companies to work for': The listing for 2002 was published in *Fortune* on 20 January 2003; see www.fortune.com/fortune/bestcompanies); and the *Financial*

Times listing of 'Best workplaces' in the UK and European Union (the listing for 2003 was published on 28 March 2003; see www.ft.com/euplaces.2003).

133. As reported in *The Sunday Times: 100 best companies to work for*, 2 March 2003. The survey was based on the opinions of 47 000 employees across over 200 companies.

134. Microsoft was ranked 20th in *Fortune* magazine's 'America's 100 best companies to work for' survey, published 20 January 2003, up from 28th position in 2002.

135. *Fortune's* 2003 Most Admired Company listing published in the 3 March 2003 issue (see also www.fortune.com/fortune/globaladmired) and the *Financial Times*, Most Respected Company listing published 20 January 2003 (see also www.ft.com/wmr2002).

136. Financial performance comparisons carried out by financial services company, Frank Russell, for the *The Sunday Times: 100 best companies to work for* survey, published 2 March 2003.

137. Patricia Hewitt, quoted in *The Sunday Times: 100 best companies to work for*, 2 March 2003.

138. From an article by Andrew Pharoah, managing director, Public and Corporate Affairs, Hill & Knowlton, *Financial Times*, 16 September 2002.

139. SAM survey based on 336 companies polled in 2002, reported in *Responding to the Leadership Challenge: Findings of a CEO survey on global corporate citizenship* (2003). World Economic Forum, p. 23 Can be downloaded from www.weforum.org/corporatecitizenship.

140. *Responding to the Leadership Challenge: Findings of a CEO survey on global corporate citizenship*. (2003) World Economic Forum, p. 24.

141. As quoted in the *Financial Times*, 26 October 2002.

142. *Financial Times*, 26 October 2002.

143. As reported in the *Financial Times*, 24 December 2002.

144. As reported in *Ethical Corporation* magazine, March–April 2002.

145. As reported in *How Green is my Kitchen? Kingfisher's update on the social and environmental trends that affect our business (2002)*. p. 33. The report can be downloaded from www.kingfisher.com. Reproduced by permission of Kingfisher plc.

146. From an article by Geoff Armstrong (2000) 'People practices make a difference', in *Human Capital and Corporate Reputation: Setting the Boardroom Agenda*. London, ICAEW Centre for Business Performance, p. 9.

147. *Corporate Nirvana – Is the Future Socially Responsible?* (2000) London: Industrial Society.

148. 'Infectious greed' is the term used by Alan Greenspan, chairman of the US Federal Reserve in 2002 to describe the earnings and growth frenzy that gripped much of American business pre Enron and Worldcom.

149. *The Conference Board Commission on Public Trust and Private Enterprise – Findings and Recommendations Part 2: Corporate Governance*, p. 11, released on 9 January 2003 (available for download from www.conference-board.org).

150. KPMG Integrity Management Services '2000 Organizational Integrity Survey', cited in *The Conference Board Commission on Public Trust and Private Enterprise – Findings and Recommendations Part 2: Corporate Governance*, pp. 11–12, released on 9 January 2003 (available for download from www.conference-board.org).

151. *The Observer*, 28 July 2002.

152. Extract from the chairman's statement in BNFL's 2000 annual report and accounts.

153. As reported in the *Financial Times*, 27 December 2002.

154. As reported in the *Financial Times*, 26 October 2002.

155. See www.bitc.co.uk.

156. Leadbeatter, C. (2000) *New Measures for the New Economy*. London: ICAEW Centre for Business Performance.

157. Definition used the World Business Council for Sustainable Development in *Corporate Social Responsibility: Making Good Business Sense*, January 2000, WBCSD, Geneva, p. 10.

158. *Corporate Social Responsibility: Making a Difference Towards the Johannesburg Summit* (2002). WBCSD, Geneva, p. 4.

159. Lord Holme, special adviser to the chairman, Rio Tinto plc, *quoted in Corporate Social Responsibility: Making Good Business Sense* (2000) Geneva: WBCSD, back cover.

160. OECD Guidelines for Multinational Enterprises (2000). Can be downloaded from www.oecd.org.

161. *Guidance on Corporate Social Responsibility Management and Reporting for the Financial Services Sector* (2002), p. 15. Can be downloaded from the websites of the British Bankers Association (www.bba.org.uk) and the Association of British Insurers (www.abi.org.uk).

162. *CEO survey Uncertain Times, Abundant Opportunities*, 5th Annual Global CEO Survey, PricewaterhouseCoopers, 2002 (see also www.pwcglobal.com).

163. *FastForward Research: Setting the New Agenda for Business*, Business in the Community, 2002. See www.bitc.org.uk.

164. *2002 Sustainability Survey Report* (August 2002) PriceWaterhouseCoopers, p. 7 which surveyed senior executives and mangers of 140 large US-based companies to determine their attitudes and approaches towards sustainability. The report can be downloaded from www.pwc.global.com.

165. *Responding to the Leadership Challenge: Findings of a CEO survey on global corporate citizenship* (2003). World Economic Forum, p. 14. Can be downloaded from www.weforum.org/corporatecitizenship.

166. *Investing in Social Responsibility: Risks and Opportunities* (2001) London, Association of British Insurers, p. 6. Can be downloaded from www.abi.org.uk.

167. Morley press release, 13 May 2002.

168. There are many publications on the subject of Corporate Social Responsibility. The author is joint editor of the *Corporate Social Responsibility Monitor* (2002). London: Gee Publishing: a one-stop reference guide on CSR available in updateable loose-leaf and online format, supplemented with quarterly e-briefings on emerging CSR risks and developments.

169. The digital divide is the gulf between developed and developing nations on telecommunications and access to the Internet.

170. Quoted in *Responding to the Leadership Challenge: Findings of a CEO survey on global corporate citizenship* (2003) World Economic Forum, p. 14.

171. Business in the Community's aim is the continued improvement of the impact of business society. Its members commit to integrate responsible practice throughout their business. The new index on Corporate Responsibility, launched March 2003, enables companies to assess the extent to which responsible practice is integrated in the management of four key areas: community, environment, marketplace and workplace (see also www.bitc.org.uk).

172. *Guidance on Corporate Social Responsibility Management and Reporting for the Financial Services Sector* (2002), p. 11. The practical guidance, known as FORGE II, launched in November 2002, was developed by the UK FORGE consortium including eight major financial services companies. It follows the FORGE I *Guidelines on Environmental Management and Reporting for the Financial Services Sector*, launched in November 2002. Both sets of guidance can be downloaded from the websites of the British Bankers Association (www.bba.org.uk) and the Association of British Insurers (www.abi.org.uk).

173. From '*Global Corporate Citizenship: The Leadership Challenge for CEOs and Boards*' World Economic Forum Global Corporate Citizenship Initiative and the Prince of Wales International Business Leaders Forum, January 2002, p. 6. Can be downloaded from www.weforum.org/corporatecitizenship. Figure reproduced by permission of the WEF.

174. Jo Johnston, analyst at Morley, quoted in the *Financial Times*, 13 May 2002.

175. Quoted in *Internal Auditing and Business Risk*, February 2001.

176. See Shell's website www.Shell.com for downloadable versions of this and subsequent Shell reports, more recently entitled: *Shell Report: People, Planet and Profits*.

177. Then chairman of the Committee of Managing Directors, Cor Herkstroter, quoted in the 1998 Shell report.

178. Published in the *Financial Times*, 20 January 2003. Also available from www.ft.com/wmr2002.

179. Watt, P.: Walking the Talk: The Business Case for Sustainable Development. A speech to the World Summit on Sustainable Development, Johannesburg, 31 August 2002. The full text of Phil Watt's speech can be downloaded from Shell's website at www.Shell.com.

180. *Investing in Social Responsibility: Risks and opportunities* (2001). London, Association of British Insurers, p. 39. Can be downloaded from www.abi.org.uk.

181. See the Business in the Community website www.bitc.org.uk and visit BITC's dedicated Cause Related Marketing Campaign website for case studies, guidelines and other resources

182. This and other examples of cause-related marketing can be found on the dedicated Business in the Community site at www.crm.org.uk.

183. Quoted in the Lattice Foundation's *Linking People . . . Linking Lives*. See also www.lattice-foundation.com.

184. *2002 Sustainability Survey Report* (August 2002). PriceWaterhouseCoopers, p. 10, which surveyed senior executives and mangers of 140 large US-based companies to determine their attitudes and approaches towards sustainability. The report can be downloaded from www.pwc.global. com.

185. See the piece on Relevant and Effective Board Committees in the Corporate Governance section of Chapter 6 for further examples of specialist CSR committees.

186. See BP's policy on ethical conduct in Appendix C.

187. See *Kingfisher's Plan for Social Responsibility*, October 2001, pp. 52–54 for details of Kingfisher's standards on labour and welfare conditions, health and safety and environmental management for sourcing from factories. The plan and Kingfisher's update for 2002 can be downloaded from www.kingfisher.com. Extract reproduced by permission of Kingfisher plc.

188. The Global Reporting Initiative (GRI) is a long-term, multi-stakeholder, international process whose mission is to develop and disseminate globally applicable sustainability reporting guidelines. The guidelines are for voluntary use by organisations reporting on the economic, environmental and social dimensions of their activities, products and services. This includes private, public sector and non-governmental organisations. GRI was launched in 1997 and produced its first set of guidelines in 2000. These were substantially updated and re-issued in 2002. See www.globalreporting.org for further information and to download the *Sustainability Reporting Guidelines*.

189. *Corporate Social Responsibility: Making Good Business Sense* (2000). Switzerland: WBCSD, p. 16.

190. This is based on *Accountability 1000 (AA1000)* framework's definition of accountability as comprising transparency, responsiveness and compliance (p. 8). See the website of the UK-based Institute of Social and Ethical Accountability for further details of the framework www.accountability. co.uk.

191. The Global Compact is a compact between the United Nations and signatory multinational businesses to uphold nine principles in the areas of human rights, labour standards and environmental practices.

192. The OECD Guidelines, revised in June 2000, have been adopted by 37 countries. They are based on 11 principles relating to a wide range of corporate governance and CSR issues. They can be downloaded from www.oecd.org.

193. The Declaration, made by the United Nations in 1948, on political, civil, economic, social and cultural rights has provided the foundation of all subsequent human rights agreements. See www.unhchr.ch/udhr/index.

194. See the AccountAbility website at www.accountability.org.uk. AA1000 comprises principles and a set of process standards covering the stages of planning; accounting; auditing and reporting; embedding; and stakeholder engagement.

195. Social Accountability 8000 (SA8000). See www.sa-intl.org for details.

196. See www.ceres.org.

197. See www.eti.org.uk.

198. A 21-point global charter for social responsibility available from www.goodcorporation.com.

199. The ILO is an inter-governmental organisation linked to the UN which specialises in employment matters. It issues conventions setting basic standards for worker welfare. See www.ilo.org.

200. See www.globalreporting.org from which the GRI reporting guidelines can be downloaded.

201. The role of independent verification will be examined further in Chapter 8.

202. As reported in *The Guardian*, 1 and 5 February 2003.

203. *Financial Times*, 12 February 2003.

204. As reported in the *Financial Times*, 20 February 2003.

205. For details of the further nine trends see *Kingfisher's Plan for Social Responsibility*, October 2001, pp. 34–39. The plan and Kingfisher's update for 2002 showing how operating companies rated themselves against the 12 trends can be downloaded from www.kingfisher.com. Reproduced by permission of Kingfisher plc.

206. *Kingfisher's Plan for Social Responsibility*, October 2001, pp. 40–41. Reproduced by permission of Kingfisher plc.

207. *How Green is my Kitchen? Kingfisher's update on the social and environmental trends that affect our business*. (2002), p. 23. Can be downloaded from www.kingfisher.com. Reproduced by permission of Kingfisher plc.

208. *Kingfisher's Plan for Social Responsibility*, October 2001, p. 33. Reproduced by permission of Kingfisher plc.

209. Michael Regester, Founding Director of Regester Larkin Ltd, writing in *Ethical Corporation* magazine March–April 2002.

210. Simon Zadek quoted in the UK journal *Business Standards*, February/March 2001. The Institute of Social and Ethical Accountability (ISEA – otherwise known as AccountAbility, a UK-based organisation operating internationally which aims to enhance social, ethical and overall organisational performance by developing and promoting effective tools and enabling techniques. See www.accountability.org.uk.

211. *Creating Value from Your Intangibles* (2001). London: Department of Trade and Industry, p. 1.

212. *Transparency and Disclosure: Overview of Methodology and Study Results – United States* (October 2002). Standard & Poor's, p. 4. The report can be downloaded from the Standard & Poor's website at www.standardandpoors.com.

213. *Transparency and Disclosure: Overview of Methodology and Study Results – United States* (October 2002). Standard & Poor's, p. 10. The report can be downloaded from the Standard & Poor's website at www.standardandpoors.com.

214. As reported in the *Financial Times*, 22 August 2002.

215. As reported in the *Financial Times*, 22 August 2002.

216. As reported in the *Financial Times*, 19 May 2001.

217. Jane Simms, freelance journalist and former editor of Financial Director and Marketing Business writing in *Director* magazine January 2003.
218. Vance, Dr Caroline (2001) *Valuing Intangibles*. London: ICAEW Centre for Business Performance (a discussion paper summarised from research undertaken by Paul Ormerod, Jeremy Holland and Helen Lucas).
219. Jamie Rollo of Morgan Stanley, as quoted in a morning research note, reported in the *Financial Times*, 18 October 2002.
220. Reported in the *Financial Times*, 18 October 2002.
221. As reported in the *Financial Times*, 28 June 2002.
222. As reported in the *Financial Times*, 28 June 2002.
223. As reported in the *Financial Times*, 16 and 22 October 2002.
224. Quoted in the *Financial Times World's Most Respected Companies* survey, 15 December 2000.
225. *Financial Times*, 10 May 2001.
226. Extracts from the leaked Barclay's memo as reported in the *Sunday Times*, 8 October 2000.
227. As reported in the *Financial Times*, 9 January 2003.
228. *Financial Times*, 9 January 2003.
229. As reported in the *Financial Times*, 5 April 2000.
230. As reported in *The Guardian*, 29 April 2002.
231. As reported in *The Guardian*, 29 April 2002.
232. *Reputation Impact*, July 2002.
233. *Reputation Impact*, July 2002.
234. See www.fool.co.uk established in 1997. See also www.fool.com established in 1993.
235. From 'The Risks of the Web', an article by George Row of The Motley Fool in *Strategic Risk*, June 2002, p. 75.
236. From 'The Risks of the Web', an article by George Row of The Motley Fool in *Strategic Risk*, June 2002, pp. 76–79.
237. *Financial Times*, 7 October 2002.
238. *Reputation Impact*, August 2002.
239. Examples of metalogs are www.metafilter.com, www.slashdot.com, www.kuro5hin.org and www.plastic.com.
240. *Reputation Impact*, August 2002, p. 9.
241. Infonic (www.infonic.com) is one of a number of providers of such a service.
242. Michael L. Sherman, chief operating officer, AIG Europe (UK) Limited quoted in the Institute of Directors' Guide *Reputation Management: Strategies for protecting companies their brands and their directors* (1999). London: Director Publications, p. 13.
243. From article entitled 'The value to be found in corporate reputation' by Professor Charles J. Fombrun, of the Stern School of Business of New York University in the *Financial Times*, 4 December 2000.
244. From article entitled 'The value to be found in corporate reputation' by Professor Charles J. Fombrun, of the Stern School of Business of New York University, in the *Financial Times*, 4 December 2000.
245. Pretty, D. (1996) *The Impact of Catastrophes on Shareholder Value*. Templeton College, Oxford.
246. *Financial Times*, 2 February 2001.
247. As reported in an article by Michael Regester in *Ethical Corporation* magazine March–April 2002, p. 23.

248. Quoted in 'Managing reputational risk' by Professor A.D. Chambers, which appears in *Business Risk Management* (2000). London: Gee Publishing, Chapter 9.

249. Chambers, A.D. (2000) 'Managing reputational risk', *Business Risk Management*. London: Gee Publishing, Chapter 9.

250. As reported in an article by Michael Regester in *Ethical Corporation* magazine, March–April 2002, p. 23.

251. As discussed at the start of Chapter 6

252. Seymour, M. and Moore, S. (2000) *Effective Crisis Management: Worldwide Principles and Practice*. London: Continuum, p. 40.

253. Ralph Larsen, then chairman and CEO, Johnson & Johnson, addressing the BSR/CSR Europe Network Conference, 9 November 2000.

254. As reported in the *Financial Times*, 9 October 2002.

255. Quoted in the *Sunday Times*, 12 January 2003.

256. As reported in the *Financial Times*, 11 September 2002.

257. As reported in the *Financial Times*, 16 August 2002.

258. From an article by Michael L. Sherman, chief operating officer AIG Europe (UK) Limited in the Institute of Directors' Guide *Reputation Management: Strategies for protecting companies their brands and their directors* (1999). London: Director Publications, p. 13.

259. As reported in the *Sunday Times*, 3 November 2002.

260. As reported in the *Sunday Times*, 3 November 2002.

261. *Financial Times*, 12 February 2003.

262. *The Guardian*, 12 February 2003.

263. Quoted in the *Financial Times*, 24 December 2000.

264. *Guidance on Corporate Social Responsibility Management and Reporting for the Financial Services Sector* (2002), p. 16. Can be downloaded from www.bba.org.uk or www.abi.org.uk.

seven

reputation in the spotlight

WHAT GETS MEASURED GETS MANAGED

You have now used the tools described in Chapters 3 and 4 to identify your risks to reputation. Many of these threats and opportunities will arise from the seven drivers of reputation discussed in Chapter 6. You have mobilised your managers and employees across all sections of your business to identify and assess that set of reputational risks unique to your business, its markets and areas of operation (Chapter 5). You have documented the data gathered (perhaps in the form of a risk register or risk profile) and have decided whether the exposure each threat and opportunity presents is compatible with your business's risk appetite. Finally, you have decided on a plan of action to tolerate, terminate, transfer or treat the risks to your business's reputation.

Can you now afford to rest on your laurels? Sadly not; there is still much work to be done. Successfully managing risks to reputation requires not only recognising the uncertainties surrounding your business, but continuously monitoring the ever-changing status of those that could impact stakeholder perception, and tracking stakeholder perception itself. Only by having a tight grip on the factors that drive your reputation, and having a deep understanding of how your stakeholders perceive your business and of their shifting concerns, will you be able to assess accurately the likelihood and impact of the reputational risks facing you and formulate winning responses.

According to the 2002 Corporate Watch survey, more than 75% of international companies measure their corporate reputation, either formally or informally. In the USA and the UK the figure is over 80%. The most favoured methods are word of mouth (over 70%) and custom research (50% of international companies). Other forms of measurement include company financial performance (the higher the price/earnings ratio the more positive the market), media coverage, and published industry rankings and analyst commentary.[1]

223

What does your organisation do to understand how it is perceived by its stakeholders? Given the crucial importance of reputation as a key intangible asset, are you doing enough? Do you have a sufficiently balanced view of how you are regarded by the key groups upon whom your future success depends?

The old maxim holds as true for reputational risk management as for other areas of business life: what gets measured usually *does* get managed. In so many organisations, the right data are not collected, the right measures are not monitored and crucial early signs are missed. You have done the groundwork on threats and opportunities to your reputation. You now need to build a robust and comprehensive reputation risk-monitoring system that will confirm whether you are on target for success and will provide the earliest possible indication of emerging threats and opportunities, to enable you to respond swiftly to uphold and enhance your reputation.

This chapter will summarise the numerous and diverse sources of available information, alluded to earlier in the book, that will enable you to track your reputation and respond appropriately to the risks facing it. You won't have to start with a blank sheet of paper; you will quickly find that you already possess, or can readily obtain, much of the necessary data.

IN-HOUSE INFORMATION

A significant amount of information on what stakeholders are thinking and saying about you and your risks already resides in your business. However, you may need to think laterally to establish the many sources of data on stakeholder attitudes, gripes, wishes and concerns that lie scattered around your operations. These might include:

- Employee surveys
- Customer surveys
- Vendor surveys
- Investor and analyst questionnaires and requests for information
- Investor corporate governance and disclosure codes and guidelines
- Rating agency questionnaires
- Shareholder resolutions
- Staff turnover trends
- Customer buying patterns
- Customer complaints
- Exit interviews for employees who have resigned
- Staff appraisal feedback
- Internal and external audit reports
- Benchmarking surveys
- Recommendations and observations from consultants' reports
- Stakeholder/reputation surveys conducted by external consultants
- Learning points from internal project and incident reviews
- Safety near misses
- Issues raised by the internal whistleblowing process.

These pockets of data will be the preserve of a variety of individual departments: customer service, sales, procurement, HR, company secretariat, PR/investor relations, health and safety, internal audit and finance. This highly valuable and often underutilised information needs to be pooled across the entire business and evaluated with a risk management mindset. Personnel from individual departments will need to work together to unlock the many clues, trends, symptoms, connections and innovative ideas that could otherwise lie buried. These can then be embedded into the risk management process as formal controls or assurance measures to provide the business with a continuous flow of risk-relevant data to inform its decisions.

For example, a 'near miss' on a manufacturing plant is potentially an early warning that there are weaknesses in safety procedures. Learn from it and put it right before calamity strikes. Build 'near misses' as a key indicator into your reporting systems so that alarm bells will ring and prompt action can be taken. Similarly, thoughtful analysis of customer complaints could provide the earliest possible indication of an impending slump in sales or a damaging product liability claim.

Think laterally about how the stakeholder data you currently possess can best be sifted and analysed to protect and enhance your reputation. What embedded monitors and early warning indicators can be introduced into your internal monitoring and reporting systems to help you track the status of risks to reputation? How, over time, can you influence the data content to improve the quality of information: perhaps by including specific questions in employee, customer and vendor surveys relating to the threats and opportunities to your business? How can you raise the risk awareness of your staff so that they recognise the significance of those early signs and take prompt action?

WHAT THEY ARE SAYING ABOUT YOU

Outside your business – in the media, on the Internet – there are a host of other reputational indicators. A Hill & Knowlton[2] study in 2002 found that 49% of executives saw negative press in the print and broadcast media as posing a significant threat to reputation. A surprisingly low 13% saw Internet criticism in the same light – perhaps indicative of the lack of awareness of the potential power of Internet activism. These reputation health indicators, both negative and positive, are there to be found, although 'finding' in a systematic and efficient way may have a cost attached to it.

the media

What are people writing and saying about your business in newspapers, magazines, trade journals, television and radio? How are their sentiments evolving over time? Is their attitude positive or negative? Has the number of mentions on the media suddenly increased? Could a negative press turn into a media-fuelled, NGO-backed campaign and spark a crisis?

In this e-enabled era, the traditional corporate 'cuttings service', which at one time provided all published information on your business, is somewhat redundant. Businesses can now set up their own tailored profiles of keywords with Internet-based news services to provide a continuous flow of information on the relevant business(es), sector(s), products and services.[3] If you don't have the resource to do this efficiently in-house, media monitoring services are offered by many PR consultancies and other providers.

internet activity

Do you have formal processes to monitor activity by your critics, detractors and opponents on the Internet? As discussed in Chapter 6, these may include:

- Spoof websites
- Activist websites
- Discussion boards
- Weblogs.

Do you know where to look? Are you picking up activity sufficiently early to take pre-emptive action? If not, why not? What can you learn from occurrences that have slipped through the net? Do you have staff in place with the knowledge and authority to intervene at the right time and in the right way so that the situation is not inflamed? Where you have decided not to intervene directly, what intelligence have you been able to glean through observation? If you are likely to be the focus of Internet attention, systematically monitoring all relevant sites could yield vital clues about stakeholder perceptions. Again, if you do not have the capability or resource to do this in-house, there are a number of communications and PR consultants that offer e-monitoring services.

league tables and indices

Are you aware of all relevant global, national and sector surveys that might include your business? Are you keeping track of where you rank – if at all – in the raft of league tables and indices spawned by rating agencies, institutional investors, PR firms and the media? Are you in the upper quartile or struggling in the bottom ten? What does this tell you? Perhaps you are not communicating well and have a low ranking because the relevant information is not made freely available. Have you taken the necessary actions to correct this? Do you include this type of independent assessment as a component of your risk assurance activities?

Examples of league tables and indices include:

- Most Respected and Most Admired company surveys by country and sector[4]
- Best employer surveys[5]
- Institutional investor league tables of the most 'sustainable' companies, most 'green' lenders, etc.
- Ethical indices such as the Dow Jones Sustainability Index and FTSE4Good.

How does your ranking impact your reputation? Could it influence the behaviour of one or more of your key stakeholder groups? Could you perhaps enhance your standing by taking steps to move up a few notches? Is being number one feasible and desirable with effort and determination, or is it just a pipe dream?

LEARNING FROM OTHERS' EXPERIENCE

How closely do you track the fortunes and adventures of your competitors? Do you actively seek to learn from their mistakes, or do your stick your head in the sand saying, 'it couldn't happen here'? Do you keep an eye on the media coverage your competitors are receiving – as well as your own? Do you take steps to protect yourself from sectoral collateral damage if a competitor gets into difficulties? Have you built early warning indicators of an impending collateral damage crisis into your risk management systems so that you can swiftly invoke your contingency plan if needed?

If you work for a legal firm, have you reviewed your processes for charging clients and setting internal targets for staff as a result of the Clifford Chance débâcle? If you are in the food-processing business, have you tightened up your supplier contracts and factory audit procedures in the light of Tyson Foods' alleged importing of illegal labour into the USA, embarrassing its key customer, McDonald's? Even though Tyson were later exonerated by the USA courts, the investigation and court case damaged their reputation and potentially that of their major customer. Could this happen to you?

DIALOGUE WITH STAKEHOLDERS

Stakeholder dialogue, as discussed in Chapter 4, is a central plank of successful reputation risk management. It is a process in which organisations and their stakeholders work together to develop mutually beneficial solutions by striking a balance between the needs and expectations of the different parties. It involves frank and honest discussion of perceptions, issues, concerns, requirements and expectations and can be a vital source of both threats and opportunities to reputation.[6]

When Monsanto were faced with a PR disaster after their ill-considered introduction of GM technology in Europe, their chairman, Robert Shapiro, admitted that the company had forgotten to listen to its stakeholders and had engaged in debate – not real dialogue. He drew a distinction between the two when addressing a Greenpeace conference in 1999. In his opening remarks he described debate as a:

'... win/lose process, in which the antagonists defend their position and attack the positions of their opponents and in which they try to score as many rhetorical points as they can' and dialogue as 'a search for answers ... a search for common ground; for constructive solutions that work with a wide range of people'. Debate tends to be either/or and dialogue tends to be both/and.[7]

Monsanto's clear conviction that biotechnology was good, safe, useful and valuable had resulted almost exclusively in debate. To restore their battered reputation they started to embrace their critics and work towards meaningful dialogue.

What processes do you have in place for active dialogue with your stakeholders? In addition to 'one-way' surveys and questionnaires, does 'two-way' engagement take place? Do you organise one-to-one or group interviews, focus groups, workshops and seminars? Are surveys conducted by phone, or in person to enable informal feedback and nuances of mood to be collected? Are you sufficiently accessible: can stakeholders contact you easily to voice any concerns? Before launching an innovative new product or service, or before embarking on a new construction project, or before announcing a new executive pay package, do you consult with the relevant stakeholders to harvest their feedback and ideas?

Given the importance of effective stakeholder dialogue in managing risks to reputation, it is no surprise that emerging good practice models include stakeholder consultation as a core element. Investors see a hit to reputation as a hit to shareholder value, and stakeholder engagement is a means of anticipating and avoiding this. The FTSE4Good ethical index includes consultation with stakeholders as an integral part of its best governance practice model:

> **Consultation:** Companies should consult with key stakeholders about the company's activities and impacts. Stakeholder concerns and priorities should be incorporated into the decision making process.[8]

Once you have engaged with you stakeholders, the threats and opportunities arising should be incorporated into your risk management systems, managed actively and used to inform decision-making and planning throughout the organisation.

Your stakeholders will also be looking to you to be transparent and accountable. Ask them, as part of your engagement process, what data they would like from you to inform their opinion and hold you to account so that they can have confidence in you. Integrating the indicators and measures your stakeholders want and need into your monitoring and reporting systems has a double benefit: you can be sure that the information you supply is fully aligned with stakeholder needs and expectations and will build trust; you will also have gained invaluable insights into stakeholder perceptions and likely future requirements to enable you to continue to keep pace with them and respond to them.

PUTTING IT ALL TOGETHER: THE REPUTATION RISK BAROMETER

Once you have identified all useful indicators of your reputation and the risks to it, you will need to evaluate each indicator carefully:

- Does it provide you with information on the changing status of an existing risk? If so, it could be integrated into your risk reporting system as an *embedded monitor*, to update you continuously on evolving risk exposure as your controls take effect and circumstances change. (For example: customer satisfaction survey feedback trends; the number of suppliers whose facilities and labour practices have been audited; the number of women in management roles.)

- Could it provide you with advance warning that a risk may be materialising? If so, could it be developed into an *early warning indicator* that would sound alarm bells sufficiently early for corrective action to be taken? (For example: a significant missed milestone on the critical path of a project; a major code of conduct breach; a sudden increase in customer complaints or a step change in pressure group Internet activity.) Often an early warning indicator can be created by inserting a more sensitive threshold into an existing performance measure that will trigger management attention.

Many of these potential embedded monitors and early warning indicators will have been picked up in your earlier discussions of risk descriptions, root causes and existing controls and assurance measures. Now you need to take a step back and evaluate them dispassionately; you need to narrow them down to a manageable number of critical indicators that can be incorporated into your management and monitoring systems and be updated regularly. As a final sanity check, and to ensure that you are reaping maximum benefit from the selected indicators, ask yourself the following questions about them:

- Individually could they be improved and enhanced to furnish you with more accurate, detailed or more timely information?
- Taken together, do they give you sufficient information to know precisely how a specific stakeholder group perceives you, what it wants and expects of you and how its attitude is evolving over time?
- Overall, does the system of reputation monitors and indicators – your reputation risk barometer – give you an accurate snapshot of your reputation at any given point? Would it alert you if you were approaching your reputational 'tipping point' – that point at which stakeholder goodwill is running thin and the tide of opinion could turn against you?
- Will the data you are collecting and reporting in-house also serve to keep stakeholders informed on your progress and performance?

If your reputation risk barometer falls short of expectations, use all available expertise and experience across the business to improve your existing indicators and, if necessary, to devise new ones, in order to deliver the accuracy and detail you need to be fully in control – and to demonstrate your prowess to your stakeholders.

As there are a number of useful documents and sets of guidelines detailing effective indicators that meet both internal and external needs, you won't need to reinvent the wheel.[9] Some of these are quantitative, others are qualitative. Examining the data reported by others in your sector, in annual reports and on websites, can tell you whether you are a leader or a laggard. Looking at the indicators reported by businesses that receive accolades for transparent reporting can be a useful guide to best practice.[10] Table 7-1 provides some examples of reputation-related indicators.

You will probably find that some of the indicators in Table 7-1 are pertinent to several of your business risks. Well-constructed employee surveys can, for example, provide a wealth of feedback on a range of risks such as job satisfaction and motivation, discrimination and bullying, 'buy in' to business strategy and trust in management.

Table 7-1. Reputation-related indicators

Reputation driver	Indicator
Financial performance and long-term investment value	• Price/earnings (P/E) ratio • Intangible assets (ratio of market capitalisation to book value) • Investment in research or innovation • Investment in staff training
Corporate governance and leadership	• Boardroom diversity • Number of fully independent directors • Rating in 'most admired company' survey
Regulatory compliance	• Number of non-conformances against standards or regulations • Number of claims or cases of litigation • Uses of whistleblowing system
Delivering customer promise	• On time in full (OTIF) delivery level • Number and type of customer complaints • Customer satisfaction levels • Customer retention levels
Workplace talent and culture	• Staff turnover • Ratio of jobs offered to jobs accepted • Employee satisfaction levels • Breakdown of workforce by race, gender, disability and age • Ranking in 'best employer' survey
Corporate social responsibility	• Complaints from local communities regarding operations • Energy consumption • Recycling rates • Value of cash/staff time/in kind donations as percentage of pre-tax profit. • Number of suppliers and contractors screened against labour conditions and other business standards
Communications and crisis management	• Number and type of media mentions • Internet activity • Ranking in sustainability reporting survey

SUMMING UP

What gets measured does tend to get managed, but data can only be managed effectively if those receiving the data:

- are able to interpret them and understand their significance
- are prepared, willing and able to take prompt and appropriate action.

Raising risk awareness throughout your organisation, involving everyone in moulding and upholding your reputation and recognising and rewarding them for their efforts is vital. Setting the right tone from the top and promoting an organisational culture that supports your reputation risk management activities will provide the right environment for success.

The range of reputation indicators you have developed as an integral part of your risk management system can serve a dual purpose. They can:

- provide you with a gauge of your reputational standing and progress in managing associated risks; and
- furnish your stakeholders with the relevant data they need to monitor your performance in their specific areas of interest.

Disclosing all of the information you have gathered internally to stakeholders may, of course, not always be desirable, as some of it may be commercially sensitive, too detailed or technically complex. However, having all relevant information to hand when preparing for investor briefings, the annual general meeting, media interviews or encounters with NGOs, will enable your top team to feel confident that they are unlikely to be out-manoeuvred or wrong-footed.

In extremis, your reputation risk barometer should give you adequate warning that your reputation is approaching a 'tipping point' and is in jeopardy. If this occurs, there may still be time to change tactics and avert disaster.

Having developed relevant indicators, gathered the data and integrated them into your risk management process, you may be satisfied that your reputation is fully under control. However, given the importance of reputation as a critical intangible asset, it may be wise to invest further resources to verify that your position on reputation is as robust as you believe it to be. You can then confidently use some of the data gathered to report to your stakeholders, without fear of challenge or reprisal. Various means of obtaining this additional assurance are discussed in Chapter 8.

NOTES AND REFERENCES

1. Findings from the fourth annual Corporate Reputation Watch survey of more than 800 CEOs and senior managers in nine countries, conducted in February 2002 by Harris Interactive on behalf of Hill & Knowlton, as reported in the *Financial Times*, 16 September 2002.
2. From the February 2002 Corporate Reputation Watch survey, as reported in a press release on the Hill & Knowlton website www.hillandknowlton.com. The global public relations firm Hill & Knowlton jointly sponsored the survey in conjunction with *Chief Executive* magazine.
3. The UK's Financial Times provides such a service, which allows users to build a tailored individual profile and to access a large archive of historic information. See www.ft.com.
4. Such as the listings drawn up annually by *Fortune* magazine, the *Financial Times* and *Management Today*. See Chapter 1 for details.
5. See Chapter 6, section on 'workplace talent and culture' for details of the *Sunday Times best companies to work for* survey. Similar surveys are published by *Fortune* magazine ('America's 100 best companies to work for': The listing for 2002 was published in *Fortune*
   on 20 January 2003; see www.fortune.com/fortune/bestcompanies) and the *Financial Times* listing of 'Best workplaces' in the UK and European Union (the listing for 2003 was published on 28 March 2003; see www.ft.com/euplaces2003).

6. A model for stakeholder engagement is provided by the AccountAbiltiy1000 (AA1000) framework for social and ethical accounting, auditing and reporting. See www.accountability.org.

7. From the address of Robert B. Shapiro, chairman, Monsanto, to the 4th Annual Greenpeace Glboal Conference, 6 October 1999.

8. See www.ftse4good.com.

9. Examples include: The Global Reporting Initiative, *Sustainability Reporting Guidelines* (2002) (available from www.globalreporting.org), CSR Europe 2000 social reporting guidelines (available from www.csreurope.org) and Business in the Community's CSR indicator framework (available from www.bitc.org.uk).

10. For example the annual awards for sustainability, environmental and social reporting and electronic media reporting run by the Association of Chartered Certified Accountants (ACCA). See www.accaglobal.com/sustainability. Also the bi-annual *Global Reporters* survey conducted by the United National Environment Programme (UNEP) and consultancy and think-tank SustainAbility. See www.sustainability.co.uk.

eight

peace of mind through audit and assurance

WHAT IS AUDIT AND ASSURANCE?

Assurance is a positive declaration intended to give confidence and enhance credibility. In a business context it refers to the confidence of one party (all/part of a business or its stakeholders) in the assertions of another party (all/part of a business, its management and/or auditors). Providing assurance goes beyond mere verification that stated facts and figures are accurate; it implies a more qualitative check that controls and actions to manage risk are operating as intended. Assurance can come from an organisation's monitoring and reporting system, self- or peer assessment and internal or external audits, inspections and reviews.

Oil and gas company BP currently (2003) defines assurance as follows:

Assurance is the justified confidence that controls are operating and risks are being managed as intended.

Audit is just one form of assurance. An audit examines systems, procedures and ways of working to ensure that the right controls are in place and that they are having the desired effect.

This chapter focuses on the need for robust and comprehensive assurance to give a business confidence that its key risks to reputation are being effectively controlled, so that it can provide meaningful and accurate information to its stakeholders. As transparent and open communication is one of the major means of gaining and maintaining stakeholder trust and confidence, that assurance must not only be adequate for internal purposes, but should, where required, also pass the stakeholder credibility test.

The US corporate scandals have resulted in calls around the globe for more relevant, honest and accurate business reporting. But improved and expanded reporting in turn requires more comprehensive risk management, better performance monitoring and robust, wider-ranging

233

assurance. Remember that directors can be liable for misleading or inaccurate information in annual reports and other formal disclosure documents, so their ability to place reliance on the information furnished by the business is crucial. One of the challenges in risk management is to determine where existing controls and assurance are adequate and where more rigorous, perhaps independent third-party assurance is desirable to satisfy both business and stakeholder requirements.

WHAT NEEDS TO BE DONE?

Through your reputation risk assurance activities, you are seeking answers to the questions: 'How can the business be confident that. . . ':

- no major threats or opportunities to reputation remain unidentified?
- responses to control the identified risks are appropriate, have been implemented and are having the desired effect?
- a process is in place to provide early warning of potential risks starting to materialise so that they can be dealt with before a crisis erupts or an opportunity is lost?
- it is unlikely to be wrong-footed by pressure groups, investors, the media and other stakeholders on an issue of which it is unaware? Avoiding surprises, being seen to have a solid grasp of the latest issues and being 'in control' can enhance your reputation.
- it can report externally on what it is doing in a way that will pass muster with stakeholders so that they, too, can feel confident that risks are well managed?
- the risk management process remains dynamic, that changing risk exposures are monitored and that emerging threats and opportunities to reputation are picked up and acted on promptly? This involves having an effective reputation risk barometer that will signal emerging risks and provide up-to-date information on the status of existing ones.

Prime candidates for additional assurance will not only be those 'red zone' risks identified in your risk register that need urgent management attention. Those risks where controls are uncertain and need to be validated are also potential targets. So, too, are those where exposure is currently deemed acceptable, with low or medium likelihood, because controls are seen as adequate, although potential impact would be extremely high if the risk actually materialised. If the critical controls on those very high impact risks stop operating, the consequences for reputation could be disastrous. So it will be prudent to periodically check that controls are continuing to work as intended.

Different types of assurance activities that can assist with the management of risks to reputation are shown in Table 8-1. These are all activities that may feature in the final column of your risk register as existing or planned means of providing assurance against specific reputational risks. Generally speaking, the greater the independence of the person or group providing the assurance, the greater the likely credibility of their findings, both internally and with external stakeholders. You should consider who the ultimate audience for the assurance will be – just internal or a challenging external stakeholder such as an NGO? – when deciding who is best placed to provide the assurance and the form it should take.

Table 8-1. Examples of assurance activities

Type of assurance activity	Description/example
Self-audit/self-assessment	This can take many forms, e.g. positive confirmation that business risks have been identified and assessed and appropriate controls are in place via an annual certificate or letter of assurance; confirmation of compliance with business policies, procedures or codes of conduct; responding to a questionnaire on the existence and effectiveness of controls in a given area.
Control risk self-assessment (CRSA) or control self-assessment (CSA)	Individual line managers and staff themselves reviewing the adequacy of existing controls and implementing any necessary improvements.
Supervisory oversight	Review and challenge of the effectiveness of controls by a more senior individual, group, the board or a board committee.
Peer review	Review of the effectiveness of controls by a peer manager, employee, another department or business unit.
Audit	A review (usually by a third party) of systems, procedures and ways of working to ensure that the right controls are in place and that they are having the desired effect.
The social (or stakeholder) audit	A social (or stakeholder) audit measures how an organisation's external stakeholders and its employees perceive the organisation, to what extent it is seen to meet its goals and work within its own values statements. Social auditing assesses the social impact and ethical behaviour of a business.[1]
The ethical audit	An ethical audit is generally regarded as an internal management tool that tests the consistency of the application of values throughout an organisation by examining its systems and the behaviours of its employees. This can be combined with a social audit as a social and ethical audit.[2]
The environmental audit	An environmental audit assesses the effectiveness of business policies and procedures in complying with relevant regulations and managing environmental impacts in a way that minimises negative effects.
Benchmarking study	A review (usually by a third party) that compares given parameters across businesses within a sector and/or across sectors to show whether a specific business is a leader or a laggard and where it might improve.
Inspection and compliance reviews.	Reviews by regulatory and government bodies to check compliance with laws, regulations, standards and guidelines, e.g. on health and safety, customs and excise.

Table 8-1. Examples of assurance activities (*cont.*)

Type of assurance activity	Description/example
Reporting assurance	Assessment of the quality and completeness of an organisation's external reporting/communications and the systems, processes and competencies underlying its performance. This is of particular relevance to social, ethical, environmental and 'triple bottom line' sustainability reports.[3]

There are, however, a host of other measures that can also provide some assurance. These include many of the indicators discussed in Chapter 7, such as:

- Results of customer, employee and vendor surveys
- Performance data on environmental emissions, staff turnover, etc, from in-house reporting systems
- External league tables and indices.

Their value in bridging the credibility gap will again largely depend on the independence, integrity and consistency of their source. For example, a key performance indicator such as OTIF (on time in full delivery) can help to gauge customer satisfaction. A group-wide definition of OTIF that is consistently applied across an entire business could be a strong independent source of assurance. However, an OTIF measure that is interpreted differently by the various operating companies would be an inadequate form of assurance at group level. The acid test is whether the assurance gives you justified confidence that the risk is under control. Would you be prepared to pin your colours to the mast and state publicly that delivery performance is meeting customer expectations on the basis of this measure?

WHO DOES WHAT?

The board has ultimate responsibility for the effectiveness of internal control in managing risks to the business and hence for the overall risk management system. Management is accountable to the board for managing risks, for monitoring the system of internal control and for providing assurances on the effectiveness of controls.

The board needs to form its own view of effectiveness after considering the information and assurances given to it, so it can provide meaningful and transparent disclosure to stakeholders. One interesting feature of the Sarbanes–Oxley Act is the requirement for the management of listed companies to publicly state their responsibility for internal control and to provide an assessment of the effectiveness of the overall internal control system. This will undoubtedly highlight the importance of robust and 'fit for purpose' assurance. In contrast, in the UK, the board merely needs to confirm that an effectiveness review has taken place. No opinion is required.

Board directors and managers often call on the services of internal auditors or other internal or external assurance providers to assist them with the task of providing and evaluating assurance. Dependent on the nature of the business and the degree of regulation these assurance providers may include:

Internal

- Internal auditors (from the internal audit department)
- Compliance officers (particularly in the financial services sector)
- Health and safety auditors
- Quality auditors.

External

- External (financial) auditors
- Consultancies offering specialist audit and benchmarking services, e.g. environmental, social and ethical audits
- Regulators and inspectors from government departments (whose reports and communications are virtually guaranteed legitimacy in the eyes of stakeholders!)

Selecting the right assurer for the job in hand is fundamental if the output is to convince your diverse target audiences.

THE CRUCIAL ROLE OF INTERNAL AUDIT

It was an obscure internal auditor, Cynthia Cooper, who uncovered the initial $3.8 billion accounting fraud at WorldCom. She was to:

> . . . join the ranks of women who have blown the whistle on a 'good ole boy network' employer – and shaken corporate America's foundation along the way. Like Sherron Watkins of Enron and Colleen Rowley of the Federal Bureau of Investigations, Ms Cooper was working within a male-dominated system that rewarded unquestioning loyalty and shut out those who did not follow the rules.[4]

Cynthia Cooper first took her discovery of the fraud to the chief financial officer, Scott Sullivan, then to Max Bobbitt, head of internal audit, and finally to the company's external auditors. Her actions demonstrate the unique position of the internal audit department. If properly positioned and staffed with auditors possessing the right mindset, it can act independently of management and blow the whistle if necessary.

Calls for greater transparency in the wake of corporate scandals, and the recent heightened focus on risk management, have bestowed on internal audit a broader and more demanding potential remit.

internal audit's changing role

This broader remit is reflected in the revised definition of internal auditing, which was approved by the global Institute of Internal Auditors in June 1999.

> Internal Audit is an independent, objective assurance and consulting activity designed to add value and improve an organisation's operations. It helps an organisation accomplish its objectives by bringing a systematic and disciplined approach to evaluate and improve the effectiveness of risk management, control and governance processes.
>
> (Institute of Internal Auditors)

Although a wide range of interpretations and applications are possible, the revised definition encourages internal audit to broaden the scope of their activities and influence by:

- providing independent assurance to the board and its committees that the organisation is managing its risks effectively
- raising business awareness on risk and control matters to improve the management of risk in the business
- coordinating risk reporting to the board and its audit/risk committees.

However, in discharging its role, Internal Audit must take great pains not to compromise its independence and objectivity – or it may undermine the credibility of the assurance it seeks to provide.

independence and objectivity

Although internal audit's primary purpose is to provide independent assurance, it is not the servant of or a substitute for, management. As a guidance note from the Institute of Internal Auditors (IIA) clearly states:

> Primary responsibility for risk management lies with line management. Internal audit's involvement should stop short of responsibility and accountability for risk management across the organisation and of managing risks on management's behalf. However, in order to add value, it is often beneficial for internal audit to give proactive advice or to coach management on embedding risk management processes into business activities.[5]

Internal audit can and should, therefore, facilitate, challenge, cajole, coach, train, test and suggest to help management to discharge their responsibilities for assurance and improve risk management practice, but should never cross the 'independence line' and be seen as management's lackey.

The IIA offers further clarification in a bulletin on independence and objectivity by defining the two terms as follows:

> **Independence** [i.e. relating to the internal audit function as a whole] – Free from interference in determining the scope of internal auditing, performing work and communicating results.

Objectivity [i.e. a personal trait that refers to the frame of mind of the individual internal auditor] – An unbiased mental attitude that requires internal auditors to perform engagements in such a manner that they have an honest belief in their work product and that no significant quality compromises are made. Objectivity requires internal auditors not to subordinate their judgement on audit matters to others.[6]

Provided that the internal audit department, and the people within it, continue to meet these two criteria, the function has huge scope to develop its activities, add value to the risk management process and assist in the effective management of reputational and other risks.

the challenge for internal audit

This means that internal audit must redefine its role, not just in the traditional areas of finance and IT, but also in areas that could impact reputation: corporate governance risks; legal risks; social, environmental and ethical risks; and risks to the relationships with employees and external stakeholders.

Internal auditors must be equipped to meet these new challenges if they are to satisfy the expectations of both the board and external stakeholders, such as investors, regulators and NGOs. To provide effective assurance on risks to reputation they must think and act strategically, be prepared to ask tough questions and challenge the most senior managers on sensitive topics. They need to systematically assess the organisation's climate (or control environment). Do clear values and policies exist? Are they appropriate for the organisation and the risks it faces? Do the board and/or employees merely pay lip service to them or do they truly determine how people think and act? Are there potential conflicts of interest at the highest level of the organisation?

Internal audit now faces a three-pronged challenge on assurance:

- The control environment
- The risk management framework
- The management of key risks.

Recent reputational catastrophes have highlighted the importance of a robust **control environment**, where an appropriate tone is set and a suitable organisational culture is promoted by the top team. So many reputational crises result from lack of congruence between an organisation's avowed aims and values and what it says and does in practice.

Internal audit needs to confirm that:

- an appropriate ethical tone is set by the board and permeates the entire organisation
- directors (both executive and non-executive) take an inclusive view of, and have an understanding of, the key risks to reputation including social, environmental and ethical threats and opportunities
- the organisation is fully aligned behind up-to-date, relevant and appropriate values, policies and codes of conduct which help to guide behaviours and decision-making in all areas of operation. Are these policies modified in the light of experience? Is there evidence of

understanding, implementation and compliance? Are goals, roles and rewards aligned from top to bottom throughout the business?

- there is constructive challenge at board level and that (a) one or two executive directors do not dominate board proceedings and (b) non-executive directors are 'fit for purpose' and are discharging their responsibilities effectively. How many are truly independent? Are they actively involved in the board-level risk identification and assessment process? Do they challenge the risk register for completeness? Do they test risk impact and likelihood rankings?
- there is clarity on freedom to act throughout the organisation and a climate where employees feel able to raise any concerns. Is there a well-publicised whistle blowing policy? Is the process used?
- disclosure in the annual report and elsewhere is sufficiently transparent. Does it meet the requirements and expectations of key stakeholders? Are appropriate performance indicators and benchmarks being utilised? Is good use being made of the company website as a means of communicating with stakeholders? Is there a robust audit trial – tracking back through the major data-generating systems – that would withstand external scrutiny? Do performance indicators show year-on-year improvement? Are the measures detailed keeping pace with reporting developments and stakeholder expectations?

Secondly, internal audit should play a key role in providing assurance on the robustness of the **risk management framework** in identifying and managing risks to reputation. The following questions should be considered:

- Is the risk definition all-embracing? Does it imply or explicitly refer to stakeholder issues and reputational impacts?
- Is risk capture sufficiently comprehensive? Are the demands and expectations of stakeholders taken into account? Has the organisation specifically considered threats and opportunities to reputation – past, present and future? Does this analysis extend to key third parties in the supply chain and customers?
- Is the business's reputation risk barometer effective? Is there a comprehensive framework of performance measures, embedded monitors and other indicators that continuously provide the business with information on the status of risks to reputation and the perceptions, needs and expectations of major stakeholder groups? Are appropriate early warning indicators in place?
- Are threats and opportunities to reputation integrated into the forward strategic planning process so that resources are effectively deployed to mitigate and exploit them?
- Are the range and depth of assurance activities and reporting to stakeholders adequate to meet or exceed their expectations and build trust? Are key issues material to the business's reputation covered in the annual report?
- Does the business have adequate and well-rehearsed crisis management plans?

Finally, internal audit should check the **management of key risks – i.e. how well individual major reputational risks are being managed.**

- Is management's response appropriate?
- Is all relevant information sought and utilised in formulating a response (e.g. employee surveys, investor and rating agency questionnaires, output from stakeholder dialogue)?
- Are key controls in place and working as intended?
- Are there appropriate early warning indicators and embedded monitors?
- Are opportunities identified and exploited?
- How adequate are management's assurances on the management of risks to reputation? Do they, combined with any other assurance activities, form a solid bank of assurance on which the business and its stakeholders can rely?

This changed focus may require internal audit to tackle areas with which it has previously not been involved – such as the boardroom itself. Setting the right tone from the top and boardroom dynamics are crucial to effective reputation risk management, yet so often organisations do not allow internal audit to review those board processes and policies that define the culture, ethics, tone and strategy of the entire organisation. Probing into boardroom processes may prove to be *the* most significant single step you take in underpinning your business's reputational credentials. Conducting an organisational alignment review by checking the consistency of strategic corporate goals with departmental and individual goals, and confirming that they have been rolled out and are being implemented, could throw up alarming divergences of approach which, if left unchecked, could harm reputation. Checking throughout business operations that the code of business conduct is understood, implemented and complied with, may highlight reputational black spots. Confirming that, in each area of operation, business goals are consistent with allocated roles, and that rewards and incentives are appropriate in supporting their delivery, should guard against the threat of a self-serving rogue trader or 'fat cat' accusations.

Winning support for internal audit's engagement in these new activities may not prove easy, but could be helped by the emerging requirement for a 'board effectiveness review' in the USA, the UK and elsewhere[7] and the current investor focus on 'tone-setting' and boardroom ethics. These types of review are essential if reputation is to be safeguarded. If internal audit does not have the resource, capability or backing to carry out the work, an external party should be brought in to deliver it.

As part of its consulting role to enhance the business's risk and control systems, internal audit can also advise on changing corporate governance and regulatory requirements and on the use of emerging codes and guidelines on risk management, stakeholder dialogue, assurance and reporting. Anything internal audit can do to improve reputation risk assurance and its credibility in the eyes of the business's stakeholders will increase reputational capital.

having the right team

To carry out the new 'dual' role required of internal auditors – a seamless blend of assurance and consultancy – may require different skills. You will need people who can both think 'in' and 'out of' the box; people who are good communicators, are not afraid to drill down when required and ask penetrating, even uncomfortable, questions of senior managers; people who are prepared to blow the whistle even if their job might depend on it. And finally, people who are prepared to admit to the limitations of their own skills, knowledge and experience and to pull in expertise from within their own organisation or externally.

Do internal audit have the skills to provide effective assurance in all of the business's operations, including those new-fangled and intellectually challenging areas of derivatives trading and off-balance-sheet special-purpose entities where killer risks may lurk? Does internal audit have the right skill-sets, tools, knowledge, experience and sheer chutzpah to tackle all these areas? If not it should be brave enough to say so and bring in the requisite expertise before the quality of assurance is jeopardised. There is nothing less valuable – and potentially more lethal – than a 'satisfactory' audit opinion, when the audit has been conducted by people lacking the necessary competence. The false sense of security you have been lulled into may receive a sharp jolt when crisis strikes.

The special-purpose entities set up by Enron were approved by the board of directors even though it was clear that the chief financial officer, Andrew Fastow, was involved in both sides of the transactions. Although this patently contravened Enron's own code of ethics which prohibited self-dealing, neither the board, nor the audit committee, nor Enron's internal or external auditors acted on this blatant conflict of interests at the very top of the company.

added value on risk assurance

Some internal audit departments have already risen to the challenge and have adapted in order to provide significantly more added value for the business. A 2002 survey conducted in the UK by Deloitte & Touche Enterprise Risk Services and IIA – UK and Ireland compared the views of heads of internal audit with those of their key customers – board directors, chief executives, chief financial officers and chairs of audit committees.[8]

Board directors and heads of internal audit agreed that internal audit adds most value by providing assurance that the main business risks are being managed and that the general internal control framework is operating effectively.

Another interest finding of the survey was that heads of audit believe that when a company is hit by a 'surprise', it is usually the result of procedures not being followed. Board directors begged to differ, claiming that the reason was more frequently that the risk had never been identified in the first place! This speaks volumes for the importance of rigorous and comprehensive risk identification – a process in which internal audit can play a key role: reviewing and challenging.

Perhaps internal audit should rename itself: 'internal' is now a misnomer. If audit is to do its job properly, be effective and add value, particularly in the area of reputation risk management, it needs to look externally – to the business's customers, deep into its supply chain, at the expectations of stakeholders, at socioeconomic and political influences, at corporate governance and regulatory developments and at developments in assurance and reporting. 'Audit', too, is a loaded term, with connotations of secret police and box-ticking. Audit's fundamental role is to assure the assurance process, those critical assurances provided by management and the business's systems on the basis of which the board will make its external

Less of:	More of:
▪ Conformance checking	▪ Performance enhancing
▪ Knowledge hoarding	▪ Knowledge sharing
▪ Policing	▪ Coaching and facilitating
▪ Low profile	▪ High profile
▪ Activity auditing	▪ Risk based auditing
▪ Criticism	▪ Constructive challenge
▪ 'Watch out-the auditors are about!'	▪ Credible and valued

Figure 8-1   Business reassurance: shifting the internal audit focus.

disclosures to stakeholders. Perhaps 'business reassurance' would be a more apposite epithet, as suggested in Figure 8-1.

the boundaries of credibility

In those sensitive 'hot spot' areas – such as environmental impact analysis, use of child labour in the supply chain, diversity and discrimination – even an independently positioned and objective internal audit function may not be sufficiently independent to satisfy some stakeholders. Stakeholders are increasingly likely to require confirmation from a fully independent source that the vaunted claims are not PR spin, but a genuine attempt to identify and actively manage impacts and risks. This credibility gap may need to be bridged by external third-party verification – an approach adopted by a growing number of businesses.

However, internal audit can still provide a single-point contact for the board – a 'one-stop-shop' – on assurance by recommending areas where a third-party external review is desirable, by engaging a suitable third party and by collating the outputs in a manageable form for the audit or risk committee. This should be seen not as a threat, but as an opportunity for internal audit to fully meet board and stakeholder assurance requirements while not overstretching their own capabilities.

THE ROLE OF EXTERNAL INDEPENDENT VERIFICATION

Independent verification of business claims in sensitive areas such as social, ethical and environmental risks and stakeholder dialogue is a growing feature of the overall assurance package for many organisations. Arranging for an external, fully independent third party to conduct your social/stakeholder, ethical or environmental audit, or to verify the claims in your sustainability report through 'reporting assurance', may be crucial if you are to satisfy your critics and persuade your stakeholders that your fine words really are matched by your deeds.

Your challenge now will be to ensure that your supposedly independent assurer has the right credentials and is as independent as they appear. If they are seen to be unduly influenced by you, their report could lose all credibility.[9]

BEEFING UP BOARD COMMITTEES

Oversight of assurance on the risk and control system should come from the board's audit or risk committee. As discussed in Chapter 6, you may consider creating a new committee or adding to the remit of an existing one, to ensure that the softer risks to reputation receive adequate attention at board level. Setting up an 'ethics and environment' committee or a 'social responsibility committee' will at least ensure that the issues are discussed. Staffing such committees with knowledgeable and experienced non-executive directors who sanity check the risk profile, challenge assumptions and drill down for substantiation when not satisfied, could provide an additional and value-adding layer of assurance. Establishing such specialist committees also sends a clear message to your stakeholders that you are sincere in seeking to manage effectively these key risks to reputation.

OPTIMISING THE OVERALL ASSURANCE EFFORT

In optimising the overall assurance effort, the trick is to match the right type of assurance and the right assurance provider to each risk. Your risk register could be the opportunity you have been waiting for to turn current assurance arrangements on their head and get more 'bang for your buck'. It will allow you to focus audit attention where it is most needed: on the areas of greatest business exposure and uncertainty. This should provide a more value-adding assurance focus than traditional audits of the petty cash! Against each risk earmarked for additional assurance, consider the following:

- Will the information be used internally only or is it to be communicated externally, either now or in the future?
- What degree of independence is required, given the sensitivity of the issues and expectations of the intended audience(s)? Is external third-party verification necessary?
- What is the prime and most credible source of assurance for a given risk? If assurance is duplicated elsewhere, can this be eliminated and reliance placed on the prime source, thereby saving costs and resource?
- Where more than one audit is necessary, can assurance providers cooperate more closely to avoid overlap and wasted effort? Perhaps internal audit could coordinate the various assurance activities, providing the board with a 'one-stop-shop' on assurance.
- Does the business have a risk blind spot, perhaps on risks inherent in boardroom processes, in the supply chain or in the customer base? If so, it may be advantageous to bring in specialist external consultants to 'rattle cages' and raise awareness by conducting a focused review.

It could make good business sense to conduct a social (or stakeholder) audit near the start of your reputation risk management journey, to assess objectively what stakeholders think about your business and whether your long-held assumptions about them are valid. This type of comprehensive, multistakeholder audit, could, at a stroke, provide you with invaluable information on the quality of your stakeholder relationships and risks to them. It could also yield vital data about threats and opportunities to populate your risk management system and generate useful indicators for your performance monitoring processes.

THE BENEFITS

The greatest benefit of a well-thought-through assurance programme is giving you confidence that you truly are in control, and the confidence to make accurate, meaningful and transparent disclosures to your stakeholders which meet their expectations, boost their trust in you and enhance your reputation.

Effective assurance can also surface weaknesses and inadequacies that might otherwise have remained hidden. It is surely preferable for an organisation to detect and correct a chink in its corporate armour before a pressure group, institutional investor or tabloid newspaper exposes it for you.

Assurance can also yield some welcome, yet unexpected, opportunities, as UK-based insurance company CIS has found. Although CIS originally conducted a social audit to 'check that our perception of ourselves was matched by that of our stakeholders', the process threw up large groups of potential customers who had not previously been accessed.[10] Added to this, the beneficial PR coverage received by winning an Association of Chartered Certified Accountants' Award for social reporting, would have cost an estimated £2 million in advertising. CIS use a three-tier process for the audit in which their social accountability manager writes the report, the factual data are checked by the company's internal and external auditors, and an independent third-party auditor audits the report and the auditors' approach. For CIS this form of assurance has proved a real winner.

Once you are confident that your assurance processes are effective and can be relied on, you can start thinking innovatively about using the data generated to bolster reputation through transparent reporting and communications to your stakeholders.

NOTES AND REFERENCES

1. The AA1000 standard (1999) provides a framework for social and ethical auditing, accounting and reporting. See www.accountability.org.
2. The AA1000 standard (1999) provides a framework for social and ethical auditing, accounting and reporting. See www.accountability.org.
3. See the AccountAbility Assurance Standard (launched March 2003) downloadable from www.accountability.org. It outlines a framework for evaluating the credibility of published reports.
4. *Financial Times*, 4 July 2002.
5. *The Role of Internal Audit in Risk Management Position Statement* (June 2002). Institute of Internal Auditors UK and Ireland, p. 1. See www.iia.org.uk.
6. *Independence and Objectivity – The New Challenge for Internal Auditors? Professional Issues Bulletin* (January 2003). Institute of Internal Auditors UK and Ireland, p. 1. See www.iia.org.uk
7. See the corporate governance section in Chapter 6.

8. The study comprised detailed questionnaires completed by heads of internal audit and by one-to-one interviews with board directors of 97 companies, including over three-fifths of the FTSE 100. Summary findings were reported in *Internal Auditing and Business Risk,* December 2002. The full survey report is available from www.iia.org.uk/knowledgecentre/practicescentre/research.cfm.
9. The AA1000 Assurance Standard provides some useful guidance on selection criteria for assurance providers. It can be downloaded from www.accountability.org.
10. Paul Burke, CIS's social accountability manager, as reported in *The Guardian*, 19 August 2002.

nine

bolstering reputation through transparent reporting

Image is reality. It is the result of your actions. If the image is false and our performance is good, it's our fault for being bad communicators. If the image is true and reflects our bad performance, it's our fault for being bad managers. Unless we know our image we can neither communicate nor manage.

(B. Bernstein[1])

THE COMMUNICATIONS IMPERATIVE

Business is increasingly held to account not only for what it does, but how it does it. Stakeholders want evidence that a business is doing what it says in this 'I don't trust you – show me – prove it to me' era. They also want that evidence to be credible and, where necessary, backed up third-party independent verification. If you don't tell people about the good things you are doing (Figure 9-1), how can you expect them to know?

Analysts, investors, journalists and others will be looking for cracks in the corporate veneer and for indications of non-alignment between what you *say* you are doing and what you actually *are* doing in practice. The first place they will look is in your public statements. Are they consistent? Are there any telling gaps? Have you actually done this year what you planned to do last year? Are your targets being met? Have you set more challenging targets for the forthcoming period?

Annual reports are generally put together by a number of different departments within an organisation. Has anyone in your business done a quick sanity check for consistency? Mixed

What's the point of doing it if you don't tell anyone?

The key to a sustainable reputation is not just doing it–but being *seen* to be doing it!

Figure 9-1   Spreading the good news.

messages can be as damaging as no message at all! What might you unintentionally be giving away or raising concerns about?

Institutional investors and analysts will pore over the small print in your annual reports and press statements searching for clues. Perhaps they will spot, from your published data on human resources, that there has been an increase in staff turnover at middle management level – a sure sign that all is not well. Environmental activists will scrutinise your disclosure on environmental impacts to see if you are living up to your policies and if you are meeting the targets you have set yourself. If they have concerns, they may demand an audience with your leaders – or simply leak their concerns to the press. Corporate governance rating agencies will check whether you are following or flouting best practice guidelines. They will scrutinise your choice of directors to check whether there are any interlocking directorships and potential conflicts of interest.[2]

Chapter 6 explored growing stakeholder expectations of transparency, honesty, completeness and timeliness in communications. It examined the threats to reputation from opaque or late disclosures and the need to track and manage media and Internet activity. It underlined the pivotal role of communications in shaping perceptions of a business: you may be devoting considerable resource to protecting and enhance your reputation, but if you fail to communicate your performance in a way that is credible and convincing to your major stakeholders, your reputation could still be in jeopardy. In areas that drive your reputation, you can't communicate enough. You should always strive to:

- say what you are going to do
- then do precisely as you have said and, finally,
- confirm that you have done it.

On issues that count, there should be no need for stakeholders to second guess you or to make assumptions to fill a communications vacuum. Your position should be unequivocal and clearly stated. Exercising shrewd judgement in determining not only content and timing but also the most appropriate communication medium is essential.

This chapter will suggest some innovative ways of bolstering reputation through transparent reporting and communications, using available and emerging tools including reporting guidelines, the Internet and other media.

As discussed in Chapter 6, stakeholders want a balanced and complete picture of a business's activities. They want information on strategic direction and goals, future prospects, value drivers, tangible and intangible assets and business risks. They want all material relevant factors and risks to be included so that they can evaluate the company's true performance and prospects for themselves. They want the information-gathering process to be efficient: they won't thank you for bombarding them with so much information that they can't see the wood for the trees.

The Global Reporting Initiative (Table 9-1) suggests 11 reporting principles that will enable businesses to present a balanced view of all aspects of their performance, will allow comparisons over time across organisations and will address the major issues of concern to stakeholders.

THE BENEFITS OF TRANSPARENT REPORTING

A commitment to report externally on a particular issue in itself provides an impetus to improve data collection and monitoring systems. For example, in order to report from January 2004 on non-conformances against agreed labour standards in the supply chain, processes would have had to be put in place by the end of 2002 to allow auditing and data collection during 2003 for reporting in 2004. The lead-time for new indicators requiring data collection and assurance is a minimum of 18 months. There are, however, many benefits to be derived from setting up such systems. As the GRI guidelines on sustainability reporting argue:

> The process of developing a sustainability report provides a warning of trouble spots – and unanticipated opportunities – in supply chains, in communities, among regulators, and in reputation and in brand management. Reporting helps management evaluate potentially damaging developments before they develop into unwelcome surprises.[4]

Committing to providing stakeholders with data on risks can also force the discipline of tracking evolving risk exposures and sharing information on the actions taken to control them. A 1999 report by the Institute of Chartered Accountants in England and Wales, *No surprises: the case for better risk reporting*, argues that 'better risk reporting is a key that can unlock capital from public markets'.[5] The report asserts that providing information on risks can help investors and others to judge the quality of a business's earnings:

> Knowing how the directors of a business see its riskiness and what they do to manage its risks helps outside investors to assess the volatility of its returns. The more they know, the more accurately investors will be able to determine a company's cost of capital and value.[6]

This, in turn, can help to minimise the cost of capital and maximise shareholder value. The ICAEW research has shown that companies present far more detailed information on risks and strategies in the prospectuses they produce when they first float. The breadth and depth of information provided in annual reports never quite matches up to the initial effort when

Table 9-1. Global Reporting Initiative reporting principles (Reproduced by permission of Global Reporting Initiative)

Transparency	Full disclosure of the processes, procedures and assumptions in report preparation are essential to its credibility.
Inclusiveness	The reporting organisation should systematically engage its stakeholders to help focus and continually enhance the quality of its reports.
Auditability	Reported data and information should be recorded, compiled, analysed, and disclosed in a way that would enable internal auditors or external assurance providers to attest to its reliability.
Completeness	All information that is material to users for assessing the reporting organisation's economic, environmental, and social performance should appear in the report in a manner consistent with the declared boundaries, scope, and time period.
Relevance	Relevance is the degree of importance assigned to a particular aspect, indicator, or piece of information, and represents the threshold at which information becomes significant enough to be reported.
Sustainability context	The reporting organisation should seek to place its performance in the larger context of ecological, social, or other limits or constraints, where such context adds significant meaning to the reporting information.
Accuracy	The accuracy principle refers to achieving the degree of exactness and low margin of error in reported information necessary for users to make decisions with a high degree of confidence.
Neutrality	Reports should avoid bias in selection and presentation of information and should strive to provide a balanced account of the reporting organisation's performance.
Comparability	The reporting organisation should maintain consistency in the boundary and scope of its reports, disclose any changes, and re-state previously reported information.
Clarity	The reporting organisation should remain cognizant of the diverse needs and backgrounds of its stakeholder groups and should make information available in a manner that is responsive to the maximum number of users while still maintaining a suitable level of detail.
Timeliness	Reports should provide information on a regular schedule that meets user needs and comports with the nature of the information itself.

Sustainability Reporting Guidelines[3] © 2002 GRI.

companies are trying to win the confidence of prospective investors. And yet, continuously updating and refreshing this same information could help to retain and boost stakeholder confidence and maintain a business's licence to operate.

Some investors are now pushing for unambiguous disclosure of the biggest risks to a business in its annual report. 'Boilerplate' statements on internal control that regurgitate minimal corporate governance requirements or key risks buried in masses of data in a separate environmental or sustainability report are of little use to those striving to inform their investment decisions.[7]

In some jurisdictions there are also government and regulatory pressures to make the Operating and Financial Review more relevant and meaningful and to include information on material

- Managing stakeholder expectations and building confidence
- More accurate market valuation
- Lowering the cost of capital and increasing shareholder value
- Forcing a discipline of robust internal management and monitoring systems
- Providing you with the information to anticipate and fend off your critics
- Enabling differentiation and the creation of competitive advantage

Figure 9-2   The upsides of transparent disclosure.

factors and risks in company annual reports. These developments add impetus to the calls for improved risk reporting. Why not pre-empt them by providing more meaningful information on major risks *before* you are forced to do so? Being the first in your sector to provide more transparent reporting on a particular topic may win you competitive advantage.

The actual process of reporting – and the data gathering and internal and external discussions it necessitates – can enhance the effectiveness of the risk management process itself, as well as provide the business with a continuous flow of information that will help it to anticipate and pre-empt emerging issues (Figure 9-2).

There are, of course, also potential downsides such as potential leakage of commercially sensitive information; raising doubts that could lead to a loss of confidence and a fall in share price; or setting a precedent that may be difficult to sustain. An appropriate balance must therefore be struck. However, given the current degree of external scrutiny of business communications and behaviour, deliberately withholding relevant information on the strategies and risks that could impact your reputation and future prospects in the hope that no one will find out, is unlikely to prove successful in the long run.

AVAILABLE TOOLS

A number of principles, guidelines and tools are emerging which can help you get the message right and respond promptly using the most appropriate communication medium every time.

statutory vs discretionary communications

You already have the opportunity to make more meaningful and transparent disclosure in your statutory annual report, prospectuses, proxy statements, Annual General Meetings, 10k filings (in the USA) or other legal or regulatory requirements imposed by your sector and jurisdiction. You also have a wide range of discretionary opportunities to communicate with stakeholders such as press releases, newsletters, articles and letters to newspapers and journals, voluntary 'triple bottom line' sustainability, environmental or social reporting, your business intranet, extranet and corporate website, investor and analyst briefings and other forms of stakeholder dialogue, speeches and interviews. A large proportion of the information you need to communicate effectively will already exist or be readily available – you are probably just not choosing to communicate it or are not yet in a position to marshal the data in a way that will be accessible, credible and convincing. You might consider whether you are currently optimising the impact of your statutory and voluntary communications.

Have you derived the maximum reputational benefit from your statutory communications?

- Have you packed as much useful and relevant information as possible into the corporate governance and internal control sections of your annual report?
- Have you gone beyond the minimum requirements in outlining your corporate governance arrangements and your risk management framework? Have you explained their importance in setting the right tone from the top and in promoting an appropriate organisational culture?
- Are your investors starting to ask you about your underlying group policies, whether you take an inclusive approach to non-shareholder stakeholders, the precise role of your board committees or what proportion of your non-executive directors are truly independent? Pre-empt them and tell them – before they either force you to make a statement or draw the wrong conclusions.
- What level of detail do your stakeholders require on board remuneration? Do they want to know how your senior executives are incentivised and how this links to business performance? Are you meeting their expectations?

Have you considered the range of voluntary communications and the scope to tailor responses to meet the information needs of specific stakeholder groups?

- Are you informing stakeholders of your business and what it stands for? Have you communicated the values and business principles by which you operate?
- Are your code of conduct and major business policies readily available – ideally on your website – for all to see? Do you explain how these have been adjusted over time in response to changing circumstances and stakeholder expectations?
- Have you communicated forward-looking information about strategic goals, risks and value drivers? A bi-annual global study of company disclosure to investors conducted by Shelley Taylor & Associates found that only 44% of chairmen mentioned corporate strategies in their letter to shareholders, just 36% of annual reports provided clearly stated objectives and only 44% described the challenges, risks and uncertainties ahead.[8]
- Are you capitalising on areas where you have voluntarily gone beyond minimal legal compliance to embrace best practice?
- Have you established what issues are of current or potential future concern to your stakeholders? What is your stance? Have you bothered to communicate it?
- Are you prepared to tackle the most contentious 'hot issues' head on, even if you don't yet have all the answers? US healthcare company Baxter International's sustainability report for 2001 comes across as refreshingly honest and transparent by including a 'sustainability

report card'. This details areas of strength, areas where significant progress has been made and 'developmental areas' which still need further attention. For 2001 these included product stewardship, social responsibility measurements and verification and supplier diversity.[9]

- Are you keeping your internal stakeholders – your employees – fully informed on the good things you are doing and the way in which you are proactively managing your reputation, to ensure that they can continue to be proud of the organisation they work for? It would be a shame if the first knowledge employees have of breaking news about your business is via their daily newspaper. They could be wrong-footed when a concerned customer rings at 8.30am seeking reassurance. Your employees do, after all, have the potential to become your most effective reputational ambassadors, but they can only fulfil this role if they are kept fully informed. Your intranet is an excellent means of keeping everyone up to date.

- Are you voluntarily using reporting templates provided by organisations such as the Global Reporting Initiative (GRI), CSR Europe, DEFRA (environmental reporting guidelines) and the GoodCorporation charter?[10] Have you made clear where and how these are utilised? It is interesting to note that 60% of the top 50 sustainability reports from around the world were based on GRI, according to a 2003 SustainAbility/UNEP survey. Fifty-two per cent of first time reporters, many of whom were ranked in the top 50, had utilised GRI. The study noted that 'these reporters have tended to enter the game at a higher level than many of their predecessors, which we think speaks volumes for the quality and robustness of GRI as a reporting framework'.[11] There also appears to a growing correlation between use of GRI to aid reporting transparency and being a respected company. Among the 2003 CEO generated list in the *Financial Times'* world's most respected companies survey, two-fifths of the top 50, including Shell, Ricoh and Johnson & Johnson, are GRI reporters.[12]

- Does the process you use for your social reporting and stakeholder dialogue conform to any standard, such as AA1000? If so, have you stated this?

- With which other voluntary codes and standards have you chosen to comply? Have you received a high rating in a 'most respected company', 'best employer', or 'best reporter' league table or some other award or commendation? If so, let your stakeholders know. You should consider inserting hot links from your website to the sites of the organisations involved, to enable your stakeholders to check out the credentials of organisations whose norms you espouse and which bestow accolades upon you. Baxter International's sustainability report does this very effectively.[13]

- Are you utilising opportunities to further enhance the credibility of your reports by using independent third party verification? Have you spelled out where this is done? Have you confirmed the credentials of the verifier?

As Roger Adams, technical director of the Association of Chartered Certified Accountants (ACCA) and a Global Reporting Initiative (GRI) board member has stated:

> All organisations want to show themselves in the best possible light. ACCA believes that independent external assurance is a vital part of the credibility and trust building process. The role of independent assurance is to ensure that the reporter presents an account that is fair complete, unbiased and relevant.[14]

The use of third-party verification is growing as businesses strive to bridge the credibility gap and restore stakeholder trust. The SustainAbilty/UNEP 2002 survey found that a full 68% of the top sustainability reports (34 of the top 50) were independently verified; this had grown from 50% at the time of the previous survey in 2000.[15]

- Are you using some of the reporting tools and performance indicators used by leading edge reporters? Take a look at what they are doing; see what you can learn from them or borrow to benefit your own business.

Two useful surveys are the previously cited bi-annual SustainAbility/UNEP *Trust Us: the 2002 Global Reporters Survey of Corporate Sustainability Reporting* and the Association of Chartered Certified Accountants' (ACCA) annual UK awards for sustainability reporting.[16] For 2002, in both these surveys, UK's Co-operative Bank was ranked number one. The Co-operative Bank's report is entitled 'Our impact: partnership report 2001'.[17] It details the priorities and performance measures used to respond to the needs and expectations of seven partners (or stakeholders): shareholders; customers; staff and their families; suppliers; local communities; national and international society; and past and future generations of cooperators.

Other global leading edge sustainability reporters in the SustainAbility/UNEP survey whose reports provide useful insights include:

(2nd) Novo Nordisk – pharmaceuticals, Denmark; (3rd) BAA – airport management, UK; (4th) BT Group – IT and telecommunications, UK; (5th) Rio Tinto – mining, UK; (6th) Royal Dutch/Shell Group – oil, gas and renewables, UK; (7th) BP – oil, gas and renewables, UK; (8th) Bristol-Myers Squibb – pharmaceuticals, USA; (joint 9th) ITT Flygt – fluid technology, Sweden; South African Breweries – beverages and leisure, South Africa; and BASF – chemicals, Germany.

leveraging the Internet

As discussed in Chapter 6, although the Internet can pose a major threat to businesses, it is also potentially a powerful tool for countering and persuading your critics, gathering intelligence and building stakeholder trust. Your website allows you to regularly update performance data and to provide stakeholders with a constant stream of information that is potentially more focused, detailed and relevant than your standard annual or six-monthly reports.

Many organisations now have sections of their websites devoted to individual stakeholder groups such as investors, prospective employees, suppliers, customers, communities and the media. Your website provides an unrivalled opportunity to communicate effectively with your stakeholders. Via your website you can tailor material for the various stakeholder audiences to enable you to provide lively and interesting content in appropriate depth; show your leaders in action through webcasts; allow users to sift and sort information to suit their own needs and enter into live dialogue with you. Via the Internet you can not only passively track the activities of your detractors and intervene as appropriate to correct factual inaccuracies and negative perceptions, but you can also engage in real-time dialogue with those interested in your business.

The Internet, exploited as it often is as a rallying point for pressure groups and hostile campaigns, certainly presents a threat to many businesses, but it also offers an unparalleled direct channel of communication with individual stakeholder groups, a first-class opportunity to engage with your critics and the ability to personalise your communications and display the human face of your business. *As Reputation Impact* magazine argues:

> ...the reality is that the same tools used by protestors to attack companies can be harnessed by those companies to counter their criticism.... Even more significantly, it is possible to build up a network of advocates in exactly the same way that protester networks are built up. A content-rich Web site will attract visitors including potential customers; hosted forums and discussion groups will keep them engaged; and a responsive attitude to their opinions and concerns will make them feel valued.... Using the Web it is even possible to boost customers' loyalty and get some effective market research done at the same time. Using the Net to ask for opinions on a new product will encourage customers to buy into the concept, even buy the product, providing a valuable insight into what the market wants. The Net also gives stakeholders, including shareholders and influential opinion formers a powerful channel to make their voices heard. Using the Net it is possible, in an instant, to respond to any concerns that any of these groups might have, and silence a whisper of criticism before it becomes a shout.[18]

The range of possibilities for building trust and countering criticism offered by the Internet are simply too numerous to detail, but here are some examples to help to change your mindset and start you thinking about innovative ways of bolstering your business's reputation through e-communication. Have a look at the websites of some of the best e-communicators mentioned here, analyse the sites of your competitors and other organisations in your sector to see what they are doing and what you can learn from them. Where does your business stand in the e-communications league table?

- Do you have a website that contains useful and relevant information for all interested users? Have you divided up your website into specific portions for individual stakeholder groups? Is it easily navigable?
- Do the tailored portions contain sufficient breadth and depth of detail and comparable performance data to allow users to track your progress? Is it easy for users to 'drill down' to obtain the detail they require? Remember that your website allows you to provide a high level of detail at relatively low cost.

> ...a typical website goes beyond being a simple reputation development and protection mechanism. A modern site is an order taker, information provider, database, archive, electronic HR department, library and talking point.
>
> (Chris Genasi[19])

Perhaps you enable users to create their own customised websites so that they can readily access the precise information they need to monitor your performance. BP's DataDesk facility enables users to click checkboxes online to select the information they require for their customised site. BP also offer an 'off the shelf' DataDesk geared to the specific information needs of socially responsible investors. The BP website, like many others, also allows users to register to enable them to be automatically e-mailed news and information about the business.[20]

- Do you have a 'frequently asked questions' section? Are you using it to clarify your stance on issues of interest to your stakeholders?
- Do you positively encourage your stakeholders to debate with you and other interested parties online? Shell has created 'Tell Shell' – a portion of its corporate website that it describes as follows:

> Tell Shell is an area for global discussion on topics and issues relating to us. We are committed to open and transparent dialogue with our stakeholders, so come on in and join the debate.[21]

Previous 'popular topics' have included potentially controversial subjects such as 'Our recent performance: what do you think?'; 'How far can multinationals' activities be a "force for good" in developing countries?'; and 'What will be the dominant energy form by 2050?'

- Ask yourself whether a stakeholder would feel more – or less – confident about your business after visiting your website?
- Do you have an intranet that disseminates news and information to employees? Is it actively used for sharing knowledge and best practice?
- Do you have an extranet site (a password-protected site for your most influential stakeholder audiences and opinion formers such as key customers, relevant NGOs, major investors, analysts, rating agencies, regulators and journalists)? Do you use it to e-mail your key contacts preferentially about your stance on specific hot topics, new products and services and new performance data? Do you populate it with information that will meet their specific needs?
- Do you participate in online discussions to challenge negative perceptions of your business?

> ...companies that are prepared to venture into this public arena are seen to be making active efforts to listen to their customers, investors and external critics. The personal 'one-to-one' nature of interaction on online discussion boards reinforces this.[22]

Even if you currently see yourself as a leader in communications, ignoring the power – and perils – of the Internet will quickly turn you into a laggard. It is not surprising that a number of the companies who regularly feature at the top of 'most respected company' league tables – such as Shell and BP – proactively exploit the power of the Internet to bring them closer to their stakeholders and to help them to track the vagaries of public opinion.

SIMPLY THE BEST

first mover advantage

Deciding to pre-empt planned legislation and regulation and announcing that you will comply prior to the official implementation date, can be a useful means of creating goodwill and building stakeholder confidence. Voluntarily adopting new best practice codes and guidelines on, for example, corporate governance, remuneration or labour practices, can also have a positive impact on reputation. An astute choice of the issue that will maximise reputational capital is also important.

In the midst of the furore over indecent executive remuneration in the USA, largely as a result of stock options, Coca-Cola broke ranks and announced on 14 July 2002 that it would start to deduct the cost of stock options for executives and other employees from profits. The *Economist* magazine commented that, not only was Coca-Cola's timing 'spot on' but:

> Coca-Cola's choice of reform is also clever. Although other initiatives are beginning to take shape in Congress, efforts to make it compulsory to charge the cost of stock options as an expense have fallen foul of the high-tech business lobby. That has turned options-expensing into a pressing issue among those Americans who feel their government is doing too little.[23]

Other companies such as Heinz, Delta Airlines and Citigroup quickly followed Coca-Cola's lead, but it was the first mover that generated the greatest quantity of positive media coverage.

In the wake of Enron, Philips, the Dutch electronics group, announced in July 2003 that it was to introduce a comprehensive policy covering auditor independence. It planned to spell out the difference between audit and non-audit work; all non-audit work worth more than 250 000 euros would be put out to tender; any non-audit work (including tax and consulting services) that would generate fees of more than 2 million euros would require the approval of the company's supervisory board. Key audit personnel would be rotated after set periods and external auditors would be appointed for only three years.[24] Philips' chief financial officer, Jan Hommen, commented:

> 'Philips is taking a pioneering role in establishing an unambiguous policy with regard to the role of our external auditor on a global basis'.[25]

Phillips' speed and confidence in arriving at this best practice position, while many of their peers were still gazing at the tea leaves hoping the whole unhappy saga would just go away, earned them stakeholder and media approval.

The UK's Co-operative Insurance Society announced in October 2002 that it would publish on its website full details of how it has voted on resolutions at the companies in which it invests. The move, pre-empting the government's company law review recommendations that institutional investors publicly reveal how they have voted in respect of their shareholdings, was welcomed by John McFall, chairman of the Treasury select committee who said: 'The corporate world needs to show more transparency and accountability to all its stakeholders.'[26] Ian Jones, CIS's head of corporate governance, commented:

> By making this information publicly available, we hope to encourage other investors to empower themselves by using their votes and their voices to effect positive change within the companies in which they invest.[27]

What opportunities does your business have to create first-mover advantage by complying early with new regulations or by voluntarily adopting emerging best practice before others in your sector?

emerging good practice

Once you have selected the issue on which you plan to take action, make sure that you do what you said you were going to do, and then confirm that you have done it.

Shell, in common with many present-day businesses, require their suppliers and contractors to meet minimum standards of behaviour if the business relationship is to continue. The Shell report for 2001 confirmed that 100 contracts had been cancelled during the year (compared with 106 in 2000) because of 'operations incompatible with our Principles mostly relating to safety and environmental performance and business integrity'.[28] Confirming that compliance with your policies is monitored and non-compliance is dealt with can increase your credibility. Shell International, whose 2001 sustainability report was joint runner up with BT Group plc in the ACCA sustainability reporting category, was commended for being 'honest about the dilemmas the company faces, both now and in the future' and for including 'detailed information on hard issues such as bribery and integrity'.[29] Shell's 2001 report shows the number, type and value of reported cases of bribery of/by Shell employees, intermediaries and contractor employees during the period 1998 to 2001.

The UK's Co-operative Bank revealed in its 'partnership report' for 2001 that it turned down 52 finance opportunities on ethical grounds. The breakdown of rejections showed that 41% of projects were rejected because of potential damage to the environment and 15% because the company involved did not have a satisfactory animal-testing policy or engaged in intensive farming.[30]

What opportunities do you have to demonstrate that your policies are not just hollow documents, but that you police them and are prepared to make difficult decisions in order to uphold them? Emerging good practice requires businesses to use every available opportunity to communicate that they really do practice what they preach.

being a winner

Having a slick risk radar system that keeps you fully apprised of stakeholder perceptions and potential vulnerabilities will also help you to maintain the upper hand when communicating, to have the answers before even being asked the questions – to avoid being embarrassed and put on the defensive. The assured performance of former Shell chairman, Sir Mark Moody-Stuart at the company's 2001 AGM, described in the communications section of Chapter 6, is a good example of this.

The UN Global Compact[31] is often criticised because businesses that voluntarily sign up to it do not have to comply fully with the guidelines as a condition of membership. Therefore, as soon as a company announces it has joined, it should prepare itself for a barrage of questions from critics on its level of compliance. A business aware of this potential Achilles heel, can turn the situation to its advantage by ensuring that it complies fully with all aspects of the guidelines *before* announcing its membership. Pushing the good news out through traditional channels such as press releases and the corporate website as, well as via discussion groups and directly, via e-mail, to investors, NGOs and relevant pressure groups, will not only obviate criticism but should create a warm glow of confidence amongst your stake-holders.

A firm grasp of the issues that concern and excite your stakeholders will also allow you to surprise them pleasantly on occasion, and steal a march on your competitors. In June 2002, BP unveiled plans to specifically target gays and lesbians, by offering equal benefits for partners in same-sex relationships, as part of a drive to recruit and retain the best. Speaking at a 'Women in Leadership' conference in Berlin, BP CEO Lord Browne asserted that 'human capital' was more important than all the plants and equipment needed for oil and gas exploitation. He explained:

> If we can get a disproportionate share of the most talented people in the world, we have a chance of holding a competitive edge ... That is the simple strategic logic behind our commitment to diversity and to the inclusion of individuals – men and women regardless of background, religion, ethnic origin, nationality or sexual orientation. We want to employ the best people everywhere, on the single criteria of merit.[32]

One commentator seized on this by suggesting that old-style British Petroleum, which had restyled itself as 'beyond petroleum', was now seeking to go 'beyond prejudice'. The media was generally receptive to Lord Browne's determinations to rid BP of the 'golf club culture' and commended Lord Browne for his confident and enlightened stance.

What opportunities does your business have to pre-empt public opinion and gain competitive advantage by signalling your intention to act?

THE KEY TO UNLOCKING REPUTATIONAL CAPITAL

The quality of your reputation will depend to a large extent on the quality of your reporting and communications. Your ability to meet the information needs and expectations of your stakeholders is the key to unlocking your reputational capital.

> In an uncertain world, the natural response is a flight to quality. And the markets can only judge quality on the basis of what they can see. So companies need to start from an assumption of transparency, both for financial and non-financial information, and give external investors and other stakeholders the raw material they need to make an informed choice. More and more corporations are taking these facts on board – and building reputational value as a result.
> (Kieran Poynter, chairman, PricewaterhouseCoopers LLP[33])

To communicate well, to build trust and to enhance your reputation, you will need to use all the tools and techniques at your disposal – both traditional and new – to provide your stakeholders with the right quantity and quality of relevant, timely and credible information about your performance and future plans.

The issue of 'relevance' has particular resonance at present. There has been something of a backlash against bulky sustainability and environmental reports which smack of 'greenwash-ing' and at times seem designed to conceal key facts within a mass of insignificant data. The new challenge for reporters is one of *materiality*. The key question is this:

Have all relevant issues and risks been included to enable stakeholders to have sufficient understanding of the current performance and future prospects of the business to inform their decision on whether to retain, relinquish or take a 'stake' in it?

If your reporting fails in this single crucial respect, it is not 'fit for purpose'. However, if you get it right, and your communications are deemed by your stakeholders to be transparent (Figure 9-3), complete and fully credible, you can successfully build trust and bolster your reputation.

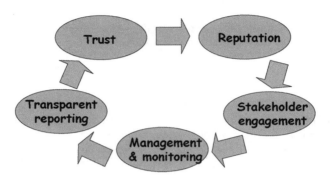

Figure 9-3   The virtuous circle of transparent disclosure.

Even when you are under attack and your back is against the wall, communication is the key to maintaining stakeholder trust. A Hill & Knowlton/Opinion Research Company survey conducted mid 2002 showed that the public is often prepared to give organisations the benefit of the doubt as long as they explain themselves properly.[34] There is nothing worse than silence or a 'no comment' when accusations of wrongdoing start to fly.

Eighty-one per cent of survey respondents said they would be willing to suspend their judgement over the guilt or innocence of a company involved in court action if the company were to provide a clear and timely explanation of its actions. All too often organisations under siege adopt a bunker mentality and either refuse to comment publicly or communicate very sparingly. Such an attitude feeds the media frenzy and allows the imagination of stakeholder to run wild.

> The reputation of business in this country [the US] is now under siege. More than ever companies must realize that the only way to combat negative perception about them is to communicate with the public in a forthright, unambiguous and comprehensive manner.. . . The courage to communicate actively can change the course for an organization. Silence only accelerates the reputation free-fall.
>   (Harlan Loeb, Director of Litigation Support, Hill & Knowlton)

A wide range of individuals and departments in a business play their part in oiling the wheels of the reporting and communications process. There are those who design and implement performance indicators and reporting mechanisms; those who collate and input data; those who monitor trends; those who provide assurance that the information is accurate and the collection methods robust; those who decide what information should be disseminated outside the business and when and how this should be done; and those who are responsible for presenting the information in an accessible format for external consumption. All these players, from data inputters on manufacturing plants, to internal auditors in the field through to PR professionals and board directors, have an important role to play in this most vital aspect of your reputation risk management framework.

NOTES AND REFERENCES

1. Bernstein, B. (1980). *Company Image and Reality*. Continuum, Preface.
2. The Corporate Library, a US-based corporate governance research website in November 2002 launched a database tool allowing subscribers to track connections between directors: www.thecorporatelibrary.com.
3. *Sustainability Reporting Guidelines* (2002). Global Reporting Initiative, pp. 22–30. The guidelines can be downloaded from www.globalreporting.org. Reproduced by permission of the GRI.
4. *Sustainability Reporting Guidelines* (2002). Global Reporting Initiative, p. 4. The guidelines can be downloaded from www.globalreporting.org.
5. *No Surprises: The Case for Better Risk Reporting* (1999). London: ICAEW, p. 4.
6. *No Surprises: The Case for Better Risk Reporting* (1999). London: ICAEW, p. 11.
7. *Trust Us: the 2002 Global Reporters Survey of Corporate Sustainability Reporting*, issued by SustainAbility and the United Nations Environment Programme (UNEP) in November 2002, found that the overall size of reports had increased significantly, with the average page length of printed reports in 2002 standing at 86 pages, a 45% increase over the 2000 level. This highlights a concern expressed by some stakeholders – that key messages can be buried in a mass of data thereby impeding transparency. See www.sustainability.com/trust-us for further information.
8. As reported in the *Financial Times*, 6 February 2003. Further details of Shelley Taylor Associates, *Full Disclosure* report for 2002 are available from www.infofarm.com.
9. Baxter's sustainability report can be downloaded from www.baxter.com. The report ranks 15th in the Sustainability/UNEP survey: *Trust Us: The 2002 Global Reporters Survey of Corporate Sustainability Reporting*.
10. See www.globalreporting.org, www.csreurope.org, www.defra.gov.uk and www.goodcorporation.com for further details.
11. *Trust Us: The 2002 Global Reporters Survey of Corporate Sustainability Reporting* (2002), Sustain-Ability/UNEP, p. 15. The report follows the first *Global Reporters* survey, released in 2000.
12. According to a letter in the *Financial Times* on 23 January 2003 from Ernst Ligteringen, chief executive, Global Reporting Initiative, Amsterdam. For details of all organisations that use the GRI reporting guidelines, see the GRI website at www.globalreporting.org.
13. See www.baxter.com.
14. Quoted in *AccountAbility Quarterly*, second quarter 2002.
15. *Trust Us: The 2002 Global Reporters Survey of Corporate Sustainability Reporting* (2002). Sustain-Ability/UNEP. The report follows the first *Global Reporters* survey, released in 2000.
16. See www.accaglobal/sustainability for full details of the winners in the sustainability, environmental, social and electronic media categories and to download the judges' report which contains useful recommendations for further improvement.

17. See www.co-operativebank.co.uk from which the full report can be downloaded.

18. Extract from an article entitled 'The Net Effect of Reputation Management' which first appeared in *Reputation Impact* magazine in 2002. The full text of the article can be downloaded from www.infonic.com.

19. Genasi, C. (2002) *Winning Reputations: How to be Your Own Spin Doctor*. London/New York: Palgrave, p. 135.

20. See www.bp.com.

21. Visit www.shell.com/tellshell.

22. *Reputation Impact*, May 2002, p. 8.

23. *The Economist*, 20 July 2002.

24. As reported in *The Guardian*, 17 July 2002.

25. Quoted in *The Guardian*, 17 July 2002.

26. As reported in the *Financial Times*, 8 October 2002.

27. Quoted in the *Financial Times*, 8 October 2002.

28. See the relevant Shell reports at www.shell.com.

29. *ACCA UK Awards for Sustainability Reporting 2002: Report of the Judges* (2003), London: ACCA, p. 13. The report can be downloaded from www.accaglobal/sustainability.

30. Reported in the *Financial Times*, 15 May 2002. See also the full report which can be downloaded from www.co-operativebank.co.uk.

31. The UN Global Compact is a voluntary compact between the UN and businesses to uphold nine principles in the areas of human rights, labour standards and environmental practices. For details see www.unglobalcompact.com.

32. As reported in *The Guardian*, 20 June 2002.

33. *Financial Times*, 20 January 2003.

34. From a Hill & Knowlton/Opinion Research Corporation Litigation Survey, launched July 2002. It was conducted June/July 2002 to probe the public's expectations of how American business and organisational leaders should respond to allegations of corporate misconduct. See www.hillandknowlton.com.

ten

maintaining momentum

CONTINUOUS IMPROVEMENT

So, is that *finally* it? You've systematically identified and assessed your risks to reputation, put in systems to monitor whether your risk response plans are having the desired effect, established your reputation risk barometer to track changes in how you are perceived, carried out audits just to be certain, and have communicated the good news to your major stakeholder groups. It would seem that your reputation is now safe for the next decade. Or is it?

Reputation is subject to ever-shifting sands of stakeholder opinion. What is perceived as good practice today may be bad practice tomorrow. Public interest in specific issues waxes and wanes. Research in the UK has found, for example, that the public is now relatively less concerned about animal welfare and more concerned about fair trade and the effects of global warming and genetically modified crops.[1] Tolerance of excessive executive pay packages for poor company performance has reduced significantly in the wake of Enron and other scandals, while expectations of integrity, honesty and transparency have grown exponentially.

What are the forthcoming 'burning issues' of your major stakeholder groups likely to be? Isn't it better that you find out and pre-empt any concerns before you are exposed in the media and forced onto the defensive? You need to keep those antennae alert, pick up on new trends and requirements before your competitors, update the risk profile and respond rapidly to those changing market, regulatory and environmental demands and opportunities. Only by doing this will you be able to spot those early stirrings of an impending crisis and act swiftly to avert disaster. Only by doing this will you be able to stay ahead of the pack, retain competitive advantage and sustain your reputation in the longer term.

You should regard reputation risk management as a journey of continuous improvement on which you endeavour to plug any emerging gaps in information or alignment that might cause you to miss an important clue or misjudge a relationship. It involves regularly reviewing and refreshing your risk profile and embedding risk management thinking fully and seamlessly into management processes and working practices, so that it becomes a natural reaction – an unconscious competence.

Although reputations are often referred to as 'solid' or 'robust', they are in fact ever shifting and potentially transient

> Reputation is the product, at any particular moment, of a fermenting mix of behaviour, communication and expectation.
>
> (Stewart Lewis, Market & Opinion Research International (MORI)[2])

If you are not constantly scanning the horizons for new threats and opportunities, new stakeholder issues and concerns, you can be sure that someone out there will be. An agile competitor will seize the moment and beat you to the spoils. An investor, journalist or pressure group will be looking for that new 'hot topic' to protect their investment, sell newspapers, change business behaviour or attract new funding.

How, then, can you sustain the interest of the board, senior management and other employees in updating your reputation risk profile? How can you persuade them that reviewing and refreshing the risk profile is a worthwhile activity? How can you maintain momentum, keep the risk management process alive and continue to improve it?

REVIEWING, REFRESHING – AND DIFFERENTIATING

If managers and staff are indifferent to continuing the good work, you might try some of the following tactics:

❐   TRAINING AND AWARENESS RAISING

- Remind them of the value of a strong reputation and what drives it.
- Demonstrate the business benefits of having your finger firmly on the reputational pulse of your business so that you can swiftly detect and respond to changes in stakeholder perceptions, wants and desires and know your 'tipping point'.
- Show how acting early to meet emerging stakeholder expectations can help to differentiate your business and create competitive advantage – as well as bolstering reputation.

❐   ILLUSTRATING THE PERSONAL BENEFITS

- Tell employees that it will be worth their while. Not only will they feel more in control of their own remits and those of their departments, but they will be personally recognised and rewarded for curbing threats, leveraging opportunities and nipping problems in the bud – assuming, of course, that your performance management system has first been adapted to cater for this!

- Show how effective risk management can make individual roles more satisfying – by enabling people to spend less time 'fire-fighting' and more time innovating and leveraging value-adding opportunities.

☐   CAGE RATTLING

- Get them worried by bringing to their attention nascent risks and emerging best practice.
- Describe the fate of organisations whose reputation risk barometer has not been effective – perhaps those in your sector that have failed to spot the warning signs of an impending crisis or have responded inappropriately;
- Remind them that in some areas, such as forthcoming regulation, they will *have* to do something, whether they want to or not. Isn't it better to prepare for and pre-empt regulation, rather than being caught out?

To add value, your risk register should be reviewed and refreshed regularly. Risk management should not be seen as a 'once a year exercise'. Dusting off the results of last year's efforts and giving them a quick 'once over' just in time for the annual report, is unlikely to be effective. Although some of the risks to your tangible risks may have remained static, it is doubtful that your risks to reputation will be unchanged in a twelve-, six- or even three-month period. A new pressure group target issue, an incident at one of your competitors' factories, a high-profile investigation into a fellow government body, will have subtly changed public perceptions and the expectations of your stakeholders. Or perhaps stakeholders have banded together to thrust into the media spotlight an issue affecting you.

Pharmaceutical multinationals have been under pressure for some time regarding their blocking the poor in developing countries from access to life-saving drugs at affordable prices. The potential exposure from this risk moved up a notch when, in March 2003, a group of Europe's biggest investors warned that they believed that the profitability and reputation of the drug groups could ultimately be harmed by this stance. The investor coalition wrote to 20 of the world's leading pharmaceutical companies outlining the actions they believe are required to tackle the threat and demonstrate a commitment to improving access to medicines for the poor. Although most companies had reduced the price of their Aids drugs following the embarrassing collapse of the South African patent trial in 2001,[3] many were still under attack for their pricing policies on other drugs. Investors expressed concern that the bad publicity could adversely impact public opinion in the developed world and could become an impediment to the recruitment of top staff. It could therefore affect the quality of the business and the long-term value of investors' assets.

The investors' code called on drugs companies to introduce differential pricing between rich and poor countries and to display 'sensitivity to local circumstances' when enforcing patents or giving licences to local generic manufacturers. It also called upon them to use their

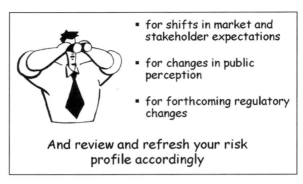

- for shifts in market and stakeholder expectations
- for changes in public perception
- for forthcoming regulatory changes

And review and refresh your risk profile accordingly

Figure 10-1   You need to scan the horizons....

'influence with governments to address the public health crisis in emerging markets'[4] and to provide details of their approach to the problem in their annual report. This joint action has increased both the impact and the likelihood of this risk materialising and will now require urgent management attention and a well-considered response.

Your risk register should be reviewed at least every six months, and perhaps more regularly dependent on the pace of change in your sector. There should be a more formal review by your Board/Audit Committee prior to the year end to allow an appropriate and accurate statement to be made in the corporate governance and internal control section of your annual report. As part of your review you should verify the status of your key risks: not only whether the actions you have taken are being effective, but whether something has changed that alters the impact and/or likelihood of the risk itself.

Once you have gained people's attention, *focus on what has changed since the last review* and how this might affect your risk profile. Consider in particular *upcoming changes*, so that steps can be taken sufficiently early to deal with the risks arising. Questions to ask might include:

❑   LOOKING INSIDE THE BUSINESS

- Have there been any organisational, personnel or systems changes that might impact reputation or change the impact and/or likelihood of existing risks to reputation?
- If you have restructured or set new strategic goals have you realigned operational and individual roles and goals accordingly? Have performance measures been adjusted to track progress towards your new goals?
- Have you just reorganised your customer service department or started selling via the Internet? Are you planning to move into a new market? Are you embarking on a project to build a warehouse or retail outlet in a rural area? Are you about to launch a new technically innovative product? Could these ventures attract opposition from local communities, NGOs and customers?

❏   LOOKING AT YOUR BUSINESS BOUNDARIES

- Have your business boundaries changed? Are they about to change?
- Have you recently entered into a new joint venture? Are you in the throes of acquiring a new business? Has your due diligence been adequate in teasing out potential risks to reputation which could be unwittingly imported?[5]
- Are you planning to outsource your IT department or manufacturing facilities? Who is legally responsible if things go wrong? How would your stakeholders and the media view a lapse in business behaviour or product quality resulting from the activities of your new business partner?

❏   LOOKING OUTSIDE THE BUSINESS

- Has the business taken on any new customers or suppliers? Could any of these pose a threat to the organisation's reputation?
- Have there been any reputational crises in your industry or market sector? Are you concerned about the unethical behaviour of one of your competitors? Could you be vulnerable to collateral reputational damage?
- Has there been any change in the stance of regulators in your sector? Are any new laws or regulations under discussion that could affect you?
- Are investors, NGOs or other stakeholder groups showing concern about a new issue that impacts you? Could this become a coordinated campaign?
- Is there a new best practice standard, guideline or league table against which your performance may be measured by analysts, rating agencies and investors? How do you match up?

❏   TAKING AN OVERVIEW

- How dynamic is your risk profile? A profile that remains unchanged over a 12-month period indicates that the process is not working properly. Risks exposures should change over time as your action plans take effect; some risks should drop off as other emerging, higher priority risks are introduced.
- Have you had any unexpected surprises that affected your reputation? Were these risks included in your risk profile? What can you learn from them and how can learning be disseminated for the benefit of the entire organisation? How can the risk management process be improved to plug the gap?
- Consider those risks that were seen as having a high reputational impact but a low likelihood. Critically assess whether anything has changed internally or in the external environment that could increase the likelihood of the risk occurring, e.g. an action group has been formed on a specific issue, the government or a regulator is considering new or more stringent standards, scientific opinion is querying the safety of an ingredient or raw material that you use. Could any of these influences also increase the impact of the risks to reputation that you have defined? Could exposure therefore be greater than you first thought?

- Are the steps you have taken to control risks having the desired effect? If the intent was to reduce the likelihood of the risk occurring from 'high' to 'medium', has this happened? If not, why not? What can be done to correct this? Are there lessons from this that might be applicable to other parts of the business?

LEADER OR LAGGARD?

How good are your processes for maintaining momentum, reviewing and refreshing your reputation risk profile? You may wish to benchmark your business against best practice as a means of driving continuous improvement. See how your organisation measures up against this six-point checklist:

- You have considered *all* significant risks to your business's reputation. You strive at all times to learn proactively from the past, examine the present and scan for future shifts in market and stakeholder perceptions and expectations which could impact your reputation. You have regular, honest and open dialogue with your major stakeholders and have in place a robust reputation risk barometer which taps all relevant information sources and enables you to keep your finger on the pulse of your reputation. Your risk register is refreshed regularly to incorporate any changes.

- You actively and continuously monitor the status of reputational risks, using embedded monitors and early warning indicators as an integral part of your business reporting systems. You receive early warning of major problems *before* they arise and take corrective action.

- You regularly check the effectiveness of the risk management process. You confirm that exposures are being reduced as intended and that opportunities are being exploited. You make adjustments if necessary.

- You proactively seek out the flip-side of opportunity in each risk to reputation and endeavour to leverage the upsides to differentiate your business and create competitive advantage.

- Major risks to reputation are given adequate airtime at board level. Progress in managing them is reviewed by the board and/or a board committee at least six-monthly. There is a formal and systematic review at year end prior to external disclosure in your annual report.

- Continuous constructive challenge of your risk profile is encouraged throughout the organisation. In particular you make good use of those experienced and independently-minded 'conscience prickers' within your organisation – your non-executive directors, internal auditors and risk managers – to help you to tease out potential new risks and changed exposures.

SUCCESSFUL EMBEDDING

To maintain momentum in the longer term your best chance of success will be to fully integrate the controls and assurance measures relevant to reputation risk management into your business management, monitoring and reporting systems. This will put responsibility for day-to-day management of risks to reputation where it rightfully belongs – with management. The following techniques may prove useful:

- Modify the strategic planning process so that discussion of threats and opportunities to reputation is required for all key objectives. Each strategic objective could have, attached to it, documented upside and downside risks and risk response plans. These can then be challenged by the board and executive management as an integral part of the strategy approval process. In a complex organisation, this can be cascaded down to business unit level to make it a feature of second-tier strategies.
- Include a compulsory risk identification step for all new projects such as new manufacturing facilities, new products or services, acquisitions and forays into new territories. Risks should, as a minimum, be assessed for financial and reputational impact. This will help to promote a 'risk conscious mindset' throughout the business. In a 2002 UK survey conducted by Deloitte & Touche Enterprise Risk Services,[6] this attribute was rated by board directors as the most valuable embedded risk management component in their organisation.
- Build mandatory stakeholder dialogue into major initiatives such as construction projects and the launches of new and innovative products and services. This will provide you with the opportunity to make the change with stakeholder support and to pick up the first whispers of any opposition.
- Integrate the monitoring of all key risks, including those to reputation, into a standard set of Key Performance Measures (KPMs), perhaps using a balanced scorecard[7] or EFQM model.[8]
- Ensure that all threats to reputation with a certain exposure level (say, high impact/high likelihood and high impact/medium likelihood) have built-in early warning mechanisms that provide red flags to management if things start to go awry. These triggers can often be built into KPMs by inserting a threshold above which alarm bells are activated. Examples could include mandatory upwards reporting of safety near misses, internal breaches of codes of conduct, missed critical project milestones or a sudden increase in customer complaints or pressure group activity.
- Incorporate specific accountabilities for risk management – including non-financial risks that could impact reputation – into the job descriptions of directors and managers. Ensure that everyone in the organisation is aware of their personal ongoing responsibility for identifying and controlling risks so that objectives – whether individual, departmental or corporate – can be achieved and the business's reputation is upheld.
- Give a specific board committee responsibility for tracking trends and factors that could impact reputation. This could be your audit committee, risk committee or a specialist committee such as an ethics and social responsibility committee.
- Reinforce risk management as a core competency by supporting staff with risk management training; include risk management in organisational value statements and job descriptions;

Table 10-1. The risk management embedding continuum

Embryonic	Fully integrated
• Driven by business strategy but not directly linked	• Drives business strategy, priorities and resource allocation
• Management focus – limited employee involvement	• All employees actively manage risks to achieve business goals • Recognised by reward and performance management systems
• Compliance risks dominate	• Dynamic and comprehensive
• Stand-alone system	• Integrated into management processes, procedures and KPIs
• Minimal assurance and disclosure	• Comprehensive assurance enables meaningful discclosure

establish reward and recognition systems that encourage risk-taking and problem prevention; recruit risk-takers; and ensure that board directors and management 'walk the talk'!

- Encourage employees to participate actively in risk identification and assessment and in developing risk responses. They are more likely to feel ownership for implementation if they have been involved from the outset.
- Regularly assess and recalibrate performance indicators. Are they sufficiently forward looking? Are they 'fit for purpose' in managing reputational risks to the achievement of tomorrow's goals? Will they provide the necessary early warning of impending problems?
- Promote sharing of learning from the business's successes and failures; encourage open and honest appraisals of projects that foundered and new product launches that bombed. Decide what actions could have averted the crisis, or which indicators might have provided an early warning, and build that learning into your risk management systems.
- Encourage constructive challenge as a key component of your organisational culture so that all employees are willing and able to speak up if they have a concern.
- 'Let go' once the top team has confidence that risks are being adequately controlled. Re-define the 'red, amber, green' risk zones on the risk profile, thereby relaxing risk appetite as the business's competence in managing risks grows. Such a move underlines that risk management is the rightful responsibility of the managers and employees within the business: it is their actions and behaviours that provide the board with justified confidence that major risks are under control.

Once reputation risk management processes (as suggested in Table 10-1) are embedded, become part of the organisation's DNA, and are simply part of 'the way we do things around here', you will be well on your way to creating a sustainable reputation.

NOTES AND REFERENCES

1. Based on research conducted by the UK's Co-operative bank of its two million customers on its ethical stance. Reported in *The Guardian*, 1 May 2002. As a result of the research, the bank included a section on genetic modification in its revised ethical policy.
2. Lewis, S. (2001) *Corporate Communications: An International Journal*, Volume 6, Number 1. MCB University Press, p. 31.
3. Discussed in Chapter 2.
4. As reported in *The Guardian*, 25 March 2003.
5. For example, a quarter of FTSE 350 companies claimed that significant environmental problems emerged after the completion of deals, according to a 2003 KPMG survey of UK health, safety and environmental managers. This was in spite of four out of five having undertaken environmental due diligence. As reported in *Accountancy* magazine, April 2003, p. 10.
6. The study comprised detailed questionnaires completed by heads of internal audit and by one-to-one interviews with board directors of 97 companies, including over three-fifths of the UK's FTSE 100. Summary findings were reported in *Internal Auditing and Business Risk*, December 2002. The full survey report is available from www.iia.org.uk/knowledgecentre/practicescentre/research.cfm.
7. The 'balanced scorecard' aims to balance **financial** measures of performance (such as cash flow, return on investment, return on capital employed, etc.) with measures of **innovation** and renewal (e.g. proportion of revenues from new products, research and development successes, etc.), measures of **internal processes** (such as cycle times, quality and productivity) with measures of **customer satisfaction** and retention (such as on time in full deliveries, customer turnover, etc.) in order to present a balanced picture of a business. The balanced scorecard was first described by Robert Kaplan and David Norton in a *Harvard Business Review* article in 1992 and a subsequent book.
8. The European Foundation for Quality Management Model (EFQM) is based on the US Malcolm Baldridge award for quality. It relates to a wide range of weighted non-financial measures of business performance and aims to provide a comprehensive picture of the processes an organisation uses to set strategy and manage its assets to achieve its business goals.

eleven

towards a sustainable reputation

The way to gain a good reputation is to endeavour to be what you desire to appear.

(Socrates, 469–399 BC)

REPUTATION, REPUTATION . . . AND REPUTATION

When seeking to purchase a house with long-term potential and enduring value, there are said to be just three main considerations: location, location and location. When running a business that will have a sustainable future in the globalised, technologically enabled, stakeholder-aware twenty-first century, the key considerations are: reputation, reputation and reputation.

Managing your reputation – by curbing the threats and leveraging the opportunities that impact it – will encourage your stakeholders to think and act positively towards you. A good reputation will help to ensure that they continue to buy your products and services; continue to hold your shares; come to work for you and are content to stay; partner with you long-term to supply products and services; adopt a 'lighter touch' in regulatory oversight; and will respect you and feel goodwill towards you. Stakeholders' trust and confidence in you will be boosted and this will, in turn, increase your stock of reputational capital. A virtuous circle (Figure 11-1) is thereby established which, if nurtured, can create enormous value for the business.

Reputation matters, not just because of its impact on stakeholder behaviour which ultimately impacts the bottom line, but also because of its protective effect. A good reputation can give you that vital second chance when a crisis strikes.

- Building stakeholder trust
- Continued 'licence to operate'
- Maintaining customer and supplier loyalty
- Attracting investment
- More accurate valuation
- Bolstering competitiveness
- Recruiting and retaining the best
- Barrier to entry for new competitors

Virtuous Circle

Figure 11-1   The benefits of active reputation risk management.

> Researchers ... suggest two ways in which reputations matter. On the one hand, reputations are valuable: they have bottom line effects on firms. On the other hand, reputations buffer firms from the immediate reactions of stakeholders in their environments when controversial events occur. Reputation management is, therefore, justified on both economic and strategic grounds.
>
> (Charles F Fombrun and Violina P. Rindova[1])

The corporate scandals in the USA have demonstrated that the major threats to an organisation and its reputation are not only external: they can be part and parcel of the fabric of business, embedded into every nook and cranny. If the business is inadequately controlled and is not actively managing its risks, disaster may strike and opportunities can be overlooked. It is now recognised that a strong, sustainable and reputable business is not just about financial targets and complying with laws and regulations. It's also about the right behaviours and actions permeating the entire organisation, starting with its leadership. If the leadership contains a few bad apples, the whole crop is likely to be tainted. The right tone must be set from the top. The right values, standards and policies must be in place and observed.

The US scandals and the growth of CSR have resulted in unprecedented interest not just in *what* profits businesses have made but *how* those profits were made. Was it at the expense of employees, contract workers, local communities or the environment? Was it the result of earnings manipulation, bribes or other dubious business practices? Businesses need to be accountable for their impacts and must demonstrate transparently that they are doing their utmost to maximise positive impacts and minimise negative ones if their reputations are to remain intact.

Investors and other stakeholders are aware of the huge value contained in a business's intangible assets and expect more active management of the threats and opportunities surrounding them. There is increasing recognition that businesses will only be able to unlock their full potential if they have a tight grip on these critical value drivers – including their reputation.

The management of reputation and its associated risks is fast becoming a major challenge for the boardroom. A good reputation can transform a business's fortunes, act as a critical differentiator in an increasingly competitive marketplace and afford protection against the occasional ill wind. Reputation is now seen as an indicator not only of past performance, but of future promise.

What, then, is the secret of a sustainable reputation? What enables the reputations of some businesses to grow and endure while others falter, wither and die? The answer lies in a business's success in taking both an 'inside out' and 'outside in' approach to reputation risk management.

AN 'INSIDE OUT' AND 'OUTSIDE IN' TASK

'inside out'

Building a sustainable reputation is primarily an 'inside out' job. Educating people with glossy PR, advertising and self-promotion may gain a short-term improvement in reputation, but will not convince a sceptical press and increasingly sophisticated investors, customers and employees. A sustainable reputation needs to be built from inside, starting with who we are, what our business is here to do and how we go about it: our purpose and values.

(Oonagh Mary Harpur[2])

The 'inside out' component of reputation risk management requires the organisation's leaders to established a vision, values and strategic goals that set the right tone, will permeate the entire organisation and guide actions and behaviours throughout all its operations, creating a culture where responsible and ethical conduct is the norm.

These should be supported by policies and codes of conduct; a robust framework for identifying and managing threats and opportunities to reputation; and roles and reward systems that are fully aligned with the objectives and ethos of the business. The business's approach to governance should consider the needs and expectations not only of shareholders, but of other partners who have a stake in the business.

A compelling vision, based on unambiguous values, is essential. A study conducted by Collins and Porras, two researchers at Stanford University,[3] found that the 18 companies deemed to be 'most admired' when the study began in 1989, outperformed the US stock market average by 15 times during the period 1926–1990. What distinguished these 'built to last' companies from their peers was that they all had a purpose beyond making a profit. As a result, they were sometimes prepared to act in a way that could adversely affect short-term profitability but allowed them to adhere to their business philosophy. Although some of the original 18 companies, such as Hewlett Packard, Ford and Walt Disney, have since experienced difficulties, others, such as General Electric, Procter & Gamble and Wal-Mart have endured and are still widely respected. In living by their values, these visionary businesses have often succeeded in generating higher long-term shareholder returns. Refusing to compromise their principles has not, it seems, resulted in compromising profits. Wal-Mart ranked first and General Electric fourth in a Stern Stewart 2002 survey of companies that created the most wealth for their shareholders in the five years to December 2001.[4] Another visionary company, Johnson & Johnson, which has lived by its values-based 'Credo' since 1943, ranked eighth in the same survey.

The 2003 *Fortune* World's Most Admired Companies survey[5] observed that the most admired are more focused on strategic issues and are more successful at maintaining employee morale, even in difficult trading circumstances. Research in late 2002 showed that the highest ranked companies 'have been more focused on addressing critical strategic issues and more successful in maintaining the capability and commitment of their workforces. These companies have capitalized on the challenges that face them, creating momentum that has helped sustain them through tough times.' A review of the survey research carried out by the Hay Group over a six-year period shows that most admired companies:

- focus more on selecting, developing and rewarding top talent
- encourage teamwork and collaboration, especially within the executive team
- refuse to compromise their long-term objectives for short-term demands.

Refusal to compromise long-term objectives for short-term gains and investment in people are recurrent 'inside out' themes that earn respect and admiration outside the business.

'outside in'

Socrates was quite right: the way to gain a good reputation certainly *is* 'to endeavour to be what you desire to appear'. But this tackles only the 'inside out' perspective of reputation. You also need to scan external impacts and influences, canvass stakeholder opinion and understand future trends to ensure that the business you are seeking to be is the business your stakeholders want you to be – both now and in the future.

> A good reputation depends on keeping the respect, trust and goodwill of not only our customers and shareholders, but all the people who have an influence over our ability to run a successful business: employees, suppliers, investors, politicians, campaign groups, local communities across our supply chain – to name but a few. Our ability to manage our perceived impact on the issues important to our stakeholders will be fundamental to gaining the trust of our customers.
>
> (Kingfisher plc[6])

To gain a real understanding of those impacts and issues, to truly grasp what will earn the respect and trust of your stakeholders, to fathom what might spark conflict, and where new business opportunities may lie, requires frank and open dialogue with your stakeholders.

> it is essential to widen the sphere of understanding by engaging with others who can present 'outside-in' thinking to complement the 'inside-out' mentality of company staff. Dialogue with campaigners and others who can present provocative view of existing and imminent developments should not be rushed into thoughtlessly. Inappropriate dialogue may be worse than none at all. But at the right time, and managed well, it may be the only way to understand the kind of risks which stem from societal changes.
>
> (Association of British Insurers[7])

These are the very risks that may creep up unexpectedly on a business over a period – the ones least likely to be captured by in-house risk identification exercises.

Trust me   Show me   Prove it   Engage with me

Figure 11-2   Engaging with stakeholders.

Stakeholders now expect and often want to participate in frank dialogue and be consulted. Many stakeholders no longer trust business (Figure 11-2): being shown selected evidence of good behaviour or even external independently verified reports may no longer suffice. Stakeholders now often want to engage directly with businesses to bring about change, and will respect those businesses that respond positively.

a winning combination

What is needed is both an 'inside out' approach that enshrines the business's values in policies, integrates them with strategy and examines internally generated risks – and an 'outside in' approach that appraises the business from the perspective of its stakeholders and its external impacts on society and the environment, and seeks to minimise threats and maximise opportunities.

Only through this winning combination can full alignment be achieved between the way a business sees itself 'inside out' and the way its stakeholders see it 'outside in'. This continuing alignment is crucial if reputation is to be sustained.

Just five companies have managed to stay in the top ten of the *Financial Times'* World's Most Respected Companies during the five years it has operated since 1998. They are General Electric and Microsoft (first and second respectively in each of the five years), followed by IBM, Coca-Cola and Toyota. The one striking attribute they have in common is integrity. The five most respected companies over the years dominated the special 2002 league table of 'companies displaying the most integrity': GE first, Toyota second, Microsoft third, IBM fourth and Coca-Cola sixth (fifth place was taken by Wal-Mart). The link between being admired and being seen as ethical is clear.'[8] These are the same companies that ranked first (Wal-Mart), second (Microsoft), third (IBM) and fourth (GE) in the Stern Stewart wealth generation index.[9]

Research by the UK's Institute of Business Ethics (IBE),[10] comparing companies in the FTSE 350, has provided further evidence that businesses clearly committed to responsible and ethical behaviour perform better over the longer term than those without such a commitment. Companies were chosen that had had a code of ethics/conduct/business principles in place for at least five years; their financial performance was compared with companies who explicitly stated they had no such code. The two groups of companies were also measured against two external non-financial benchmarks: ratings for managing social, ethical and environmental risks and the 'Britain's most admired company' rankings published annually by *Management Today*. The companies with ethical codes not only appeared to be better at risk management, but were also more frequently rated as 'most admired' during the four-year survey study period (1997–2001). When rated against four parameters of financial performance, those companies with codes performed significantly more strongly on three measures (Economic Value Added – EVA; Market Value Added – MVA; and stability of price/earnings (P/E) ratio) than their uncommitted peers. This lower P/E volatility suggests that the ethical group may present a more secure long-term investment and will tend to attract capital at below average cost. On the fourth measure, return on capital employed (ROCE), the evidence was less clear-cut, with the ethical companies displaying lower ROCE than their peers until the stock market collapse began in 2000, after which they outperformed them. The IBE have suggested that this might be because 'well run, ethical companies have been able to wring more productivity from staff during the downturn'.[11] In 1998 and 1999, the ethically committed group also had an average 18% higher profit/turnover ratio than their non-committed peers. The study lends weight to the argument that acting ethically and responsibly can boost shareholder value in the longer-term and help to create the conditions for a business that will endure.

The steps you need to take to achieve a sustainable reputation are akin to those required to create a sustainable business and be a good corporate citizen. It involves taking a 'balanced scorecard' approach to the impacts of and influences on your business.

> Movement towards corporate concern for the 'triple bottom line' – financial, social and economic performance – requires radical change throughout the corporation. It is not 'either or'. The new paradigm is 'and also'. A sustainable business excels on the traditional scorecard of return on financial assets and shareholder and customer value creation. It also embraces community and stakeholder success. It holds its natural and cultural environments to be as precious as its technology portfolio and its employees' skills.
>
> (World Business Council for Sustainable Development[12])

INVESTING IN REPUTATION

The 'virtuous circle' described above is not necessarily self-perpetuating. It needs to be monitored and requires investment if it is to continue to turn.

As reputation is a key intangible asset – 'the corporate brand' – it needs investment in the same way as other assets. Although fragile if not looked after, it can continue to grow in value and importance if nurtured. So why wouldn't you invest in it as you would in assets such as people, research, product brands, buildings, plant and equipment?

A study by the UK's Department of Trade and Industry clearly articulates the case for investing in reputation:

> Successful companies recognise the key role reputation and trust play in their ability to compete effectively and therefore invest significant effort in constantly seeking to enhance their reputation and to develop trust both within the organisation and externally. In addition they also seek to

recognise issues which could damage these key intangible assets and take steps to reduce this risk as far as practicable.[13]

Taking time to build a reputation risk management system and to engage actively with your employees and external stakeholders will pay dividends.

BUILDING A SUSTAINABLE REPUTATION

A good reputation requires full alignment between an organisation's:

- vision and values (what it says it is)
- conduct and actions (what it actually does and how its stakeholders experience it) and
- stakeholders expectations.

When a business lives up to its vision and values and strives to meet the evolving needs of its stakeholders, at times even exceeding their expectations, its reputation will be enhanced. When a business's performance falls short of its assertions, or the experience of its stakeholders falls short of their expectations, reputation may be damaged.

Sophisticated media campaigns can go some way towards creating a responsible and reputable image for a 'non-aligned' business, but, if built on hollow truths or shaky foundations, the truth ultimately emerges – with potentially disastrous consequences.

> . . . presentation cannot transform an irresponsible company into one which is widely admired and respected. Worse still, when the veneer of responsibility is penetrated, as it surely will be, the backlash from disillusioned customers, employees and others will be doubly fierce.
>
> (Association of British Insurers[14])

Businesses enjoying strong reputations know instinctively that by putting the balanced interests of their stakeholders at the heart of business activities, they will optimise the likelihood of success and of building shareholder value in the longer term. Such businesses create an environment where valued and trusted employees can thrive and innovate. These are organisations that engage actively with stakeholders to respond to their concerns and expectations and set the tone internally in a way that encourages employees to do and say the right thing all of the time. The previously cited Ralph Larsen quotation is most apt.

> Reputations reflect the behaviour you exhibit day in and day out through a hundred small things. The way you manage your reputation is by always thinking and trying to do the right thing every day.
>
> (Ralph Larsen, former chairman and chief executive, Johnson & Johnson, in the wake of the Tylenol contamination in 1982.)

To bridge the alignment gap between goals and values, practical experience and stakeholder expectations, businesses have three options:

- to improve business practice so that stakeholders' experience matches or exceeds their expectations
- to recalibrate vision and values to match stakeholder expectations

- to educate stakeholders to moderate their expectations so that they are realistic and achievable.

Only a combined 'inside out' and 'outside in' approach can deliver that complete alignment of vision, values and performance with stakeholder expectations that is a prerequisite for a good reputation. Businesses consistently at the top of the 'most admired' league tables have systematically adopted this type of inclusive, two-pronged approach in a deliberate attempt to build and safeguard their reputations.

The key components of effective reputation risk management are:

1. *Unequivocal vision and values* that set the tone for the entire organisation and delineate accountability.
2. *Supporting policies and codes of conduct* that guide employee behaviours and decision-making so that goals are achieved in accordance with organisational values.
3. *Inclusive approach to governance* that is accountable to stakeholders other than share-holders.
4. *Understanding of/responsiveness to shifting stakeholder requirements and expectations* that seeks balanced solutions
5. *A robust and comprehensive risk management system* that is able to curb threats and leverage opportunities to reputation and deliver credible assurance.
6. *Willingness to learn, adapt and recalibrate* in response to new issues, impacts, threats and opportunities.
7. *An open and empowering organisational culture* where employees feel valued, trusted and able to express their views.
8. *Alignment of goals, roles and rewards* so that employees throughout the business are aligned in pursuit of business goals and are recognised and rewarded in accordance with its values and ethos.
9. *Extension of values and policies to business partners* who participate in safeguarding and enhancing the business's reputation.
10. *Transparent and credible reporting and communications* that meet stakeholder requirements and build trust and confidence.

unequivocal vision and values

The business's vision and values – what the business stands for and is there to do, how it will achieve this, what the business is and is not prepared to be held responsible for – are all important features. The vision and values, and the strategic goals that cascade from them, provide the backcloth for employees to go about their daily work and engage in the myriad interactions with stakeholders that will mould the business's reputation. Awareness of the risks to those objectives and to the reputation of the business as a whole will enable staff and business partners to detect and act on those emerging threats and opportunities that can influence the business's fortunes and standing.

The business should be clear about what it is – and is not – prepared to be held accountable for. In defining your vision it is vital to state both what you do, and do not, stand for. Any failure to delineate the boundaries of your role and responsibilities can result in attack and reputational damage. Do you see it as the role of your business to save the Bengali tiger from extinction? Is it your job to encourage despotic regimes to desist from torture and respect human rights? If you leave gaps unfilled in describing what you stand for and are prepared to answer to, others will move in to tell you what you should do. An unequivocal statement of your vision and values establishes what the WBCSD terms your 'corporate magnetic north'.[15]

Shell faced a dilemma in the mid-1990s over the fate of the Ogoni people in Nigeria. Should they intervene against a ruthless military junta? If they were a responsible company, where did their responsibilities start and end? As the boundaries between government and business have blurred, and businesses have gradually taken on societal roles, the expectations of those societies on the role of business has grown. Are you unwittingly creating expectations that you cannot possibly fulfil?

Karen de Segundo, Shell's senior manager for Group External Affairs, commented in 1997 on the surprisingly high expectations of Shell, revealed in widespread stakeholder consultations following the Brent Spa and Nigeria débâcles in 1995.

> We found that many rational and intelligent people thought that it was a reasonable proposition that companies such as Shell should mediate to reduce tensions between different levels of government, or that they should take positions on social policy matters.... Activities such as these are not within the normal, legitimate role of a business. Therefore, we cannot meet such expectations. However, the fact is that they do exist ... And there is no doubt in our view that – to the extent that unfulfilled expectations persist – they detract from corporate reputation.[16]

This was a lesson well learned. Shell UK's chairman, Sir Mark Moody Stuart, generated positive reputational capital for the company at its AGM in May 2001 by tackling NGO and shareholder concerns head on. However, when drawn by NGO Friends of the Earth, he wisely refused to give a blanket assurance that Shell would never drill in the world's 'most precious protected areas'.[17] Shell had learned that clearly articulating the boundaries of your responsibility and then consistently respecting them is a key plank of reputation risk management; over-promising and then failing can have a disastrous impact on corporate standing.

Vision and values are the corporate glue that can help to keep all aspects of business life in alignment and perspective. The importance of clear values in guiding behaviours and decision-making throughout the organisation (both at collegiate board level and for each individual) cannot be overemphasised.

Even the most vociferous of business critics recognise the pivotal role of values:

> If you are going to minimise risks to your company, you need to do it in a way where you take a broad view based on values. You can't just think what might be risky and what isn't and think about where you might be caught out. You need to be more philosophical than that. If you take a non-negotiable stance, based on values, you can defend yourself.
> (Tony Juniper, Policy and Campaigns Director, Friends of the Earth[18])

There is little point in having a well-formulated vision and values if you don't communicate them internally and to your external partners. Indeed, positively communicating them can, in itself, enhance reputation by demonstrating that the business seeks to act responsibly. A 2002 World Economic Forum survey found that communicating values internally was ranked by CEOs as the single most effective means of embedding corporate citizenship values and policies throughout the organisation's management structure.

> Perhaps more than anything we do, furthering our company's values and standards will have the greatest effect on the future success of our company.
>
> (Ray Gilmartin, CEO of Merck[19])

A business's values should be lived and breathed by everyone in the organisation, become embedded in the corporate fabric and form a natural part of the corporate culture: 'the way we do things around here'. Having leaders who patently 'walk the talk', act responsibly and embody the business's values in all that they say and do, is the best possible means of reinforcing their importance.

> Good leadership means doing the right thing when no one's watching. Values governing the boardroom should be no different from the values guiding the shop floor.
>
> (Carly Fiorina, CEO, Hewlett Packard[20])

supporting policies and codes of conduct

Your vision and values should be underpinned by appropriate policies, codes of conducts, guidelines and procedures. As discussed in Chapter 3, these should:

- define expected and undesirable behaviours
- set out the boundaries of acceptable risk exposure by defining the 'thou shalt not' and 'thou may if due process is followed' areas of the business
- ensure that goals are achieved in accordance with the business's vision and values.

Compliance should be checked as part of your assurance programme. A code of ethics or business conduct should be central to your policy framework. A sample ethical conduct policy (from BP) can be found in Appendix C. Guidance from the Institute of Business Ethics on implementing a code is included as Appendix D.

Your policies should not be hefty, intimidating tomes that sit yellowing in the sun on your office window ledge. They should be succinct accessible documents, available to all on your intranet and corporate website. They should be regularly reviewed and updated in the light of changing circumstances and stakeholder expectations. In short, they must be living, credible documents if they are to be relevant to today's business and capable of guiding the behaviours and decisions of employees, wherever they operate.

inclusive approach to governance

There is an emerging consensus between governments, regulators, investors and other stake-holders around the globe that shareholders are just one of a number of stakeholder groups whose interests and concerns need to be taken into account if a business is to flourish and enjoy long-term success.

Organisations need to incorporate their obligations and accountability to major stakeholders into their overall corporate governance approach. This will involve reviewing the status of relationships with stakeholders and the risks to them. As discussed in the corporate governance section of Chapter 6, it may also involve new independent director appointments or the establishment of board committees to improve representation of the main stakeholder groups.

understanding of/responsiveness to shifting stakeholder requirements and expectations

To align its business practices with the reasonable current and future expectations of its stakeholders, a business needs to consult and engage with them. If it fails to do this its licence to operate could be jeopardised, its cost of capital may increase and its reputation may be impaired.

> We ... highlight the need for organisations to improve the quality of dialogue with a variety of stakeholders, in communicating risks and uncertainties. Ultimately the quality of the dialogue affects both 'licence to operate', which includes consent to and support for activities from non-financial stakeholders, and 'cost of capital' which is influenced by the attractiveness of the overall business proposition for financial stakeholders. ...
>
> For your company to reach its full potential ... it is essential that you not only consider how you can develop and improve your current relationships, but that you also carefully consider how you can develop and improve the relationships necessary for your future success.
>
> (UK Department of Trade and Industry[21])

As discussed in Chapter 4, stakeholder engagement has the potential to highlight current and upcoming issues and threats – and to flag exciting new opportunities. This central plank of the 'outside in' approach can also help to close the gap between business vision and stakeholder expectations. It can assist in:

- correcting misconceptions
- modifying the beliefs that inform stakeholders' expectations about how a business should act
- raising stakeholders' awareness of the conflicting demands of stakeholder groups, perhaps moderating extreme views
- developing compromise multi-stakeholder balanced solutions.

Investing in stakeholder relationships is a form of enlightened self-interest; it can help to build strong long-term partnerships that will underpin the legitimacy and future success of the business.

a robust and comprehensive risk management system

The risk management system should be embedded in the operations of the company and form part of its culture. It should be capable of detecting and responding swiftly to new and emerging threats and opportunities. It should monitor the changing status of risks and provide early warning of potential problems to enable corrective action to be taken. It should provide credible assurance that risks are under control so that the business can communicate with confidence to its stakeholders.

Risk management thinking should be an unconscious competence, part of the corporate DNA. All individuals should take responsibility for the risks in their own area and for identifying and acting on reputational risks to the business as a whole. Everyone, from the board down, should adopt a risk-based mindset when making a decision, embarking on a new project or formulating a new strategy. When faced with a task or decision, each individual should ask:

- What am I expected to deliver?
- What are the risks to achieving it?
  - what events and circumstances could hinder my achievement of the goal (the threats); and
  - what might help me to achieve my goal faster and more efficiently – or even exceed it (the opportunities).
- What are the reputational and financial impacts of those risks?
- How can they best be managed?
- What can I do to ensure that things stay on track?
- How can I be confident that everything is working as intended?

An effective risk management system that successfully curbs threats and leverages opportunities to reputation will create value and improve business performance over time. Furthermore, it can provide the top team with the justified confidence to make increasingly meaningful and transparent disclosures to their stakeholders – internal (employees) and external – that will bolster trust and further enhance the reputation of the business.

willingness to learn, adapt and recalibrate

This requires a business to learn continuously, by utilising all the information from its engagement with stakeholders, from its risk management, monitoring and assurance systems. It requires a business to be willing to learn from its mistakes and to listen to those employees and other business partners, who may be more sensitive to the perceptions and concerns of customers and other stakeholders. Managers should welcome news – whether it be good, bad, challenging or uncomfortable – without succumbing to the temptation to 'shoot the messenger'.

The business should be prepared, if necessary, to adapt to changing circumstances, to recalibrate its vision, values, strategic goals and supporting policies to keep in step with evolving stakeholder requirements and expectations.

an open and empowering organisational culture

Effective management of risks, and of reputational risks in particular, is highly dependent on an organisational culture which supports the risk management process. The business should promote constructive challenge throughout all areas of operation and encourage honesty and openness. Employees should feel valued, trusted and able to express their views, with a clear 'freedom to act' that empowers and enables them.

The culture should welcome criticism, spark debate and value innovation and new ideas. Integrity, responsible and ethical behaviour should be the norm – with the tone set right from the top.

alignment of goals, roles and rewards

Employees should be aligned in the pursuit of the business's strategic goals, have the account-ability and authority to deliver them, and be recognised and rewarded in accordance with its values and ethos. The reward system should encourage appropriate behaviour throughout the organisation – behaviour that will safeguard and enhance reputation.[22]

extension of values and policies to business partners

Business partners – such as joint venture and outsource partners, suppliers and contractors – should be expected to progress towards compliance with the business's values and relevant policies and standards. They, too, have a role to play in upholding the reputation of the business.

transparent and credible reporting and communications

Communications should be based on ethics, integrity, transparency and strong corporate governance.

> These qualities form the only route to public trust – and it can be followed only through the use of a reporting model that embodies these values. This in turn means abandoning the 'earnings game', which in recent years has seen managements and analysts locked into a cycle of massaged expectations, whispered numbers and an obsession with one reported measure, namely earnings.
> (Kieran Poynter, chairman, PricewaterhouseCoopers LLP[23])

Communications should be clear, consistent, accurate and complete – containing all material issues of interest to stakeholders. They should fully meet stakeholder information requirements and should, where necessary, be tailored to meet the needs of particular groups. The credibility of external reporting should be enhanced, where appropriate, by the use of independent verification.

TO CONCLUDE

As the opening quote in the Preface to this book suggested:

> Warning signs that suggest a patient may not be suitable for cosmetic surgery include: expectations of an appearance enhanced beyond possibility; unrealistic expectations of lifestyle/career/relationship effects; an unwillingness to change the behaviour that led to the problem.
> (Plastic Surgery Information Service)

A good reputation cannot be achieved by cosmetic surgery and spin alone. It hinges on a business living by the values it claims to espouse so that reality matches perception and stakeholder expectations match their experience. It is no longer sufficient to assert that there is a match, but to continuously demonstrate that this is so through transparent communications and effective stakeholder engagement. Only in this way can a business continue to enjoy the trust, confidence, loyalty and goodwill of its stakeholders.

A values-based 'inside out' and 'outside in' approach to reputation risk management can generate a good reputation that will endure. Businesses that stay in tune with their stakeholders' evolving needs and expectations will be more successful in the longer term by being able to maintain their legitimacy, attract the best employees, customers, investors and business partners to support future growth, innovation and prosperity. Such businesses will manage their reputational risks well, curbing threats and leveraging opportunities to create value, bolster competitiveness and assure a sustainable future.

NOTES AND REFERENCES

1. Fombrun, C.J. and Rindova, V.P. (2000). 'The Road to Transparency: reputation management at Royal Dutch/Shell' in *The Expressive Organisation: Linking Identify, Reputation and the Corporate Brand*. Oxford: Oxford University Press, p. 79.
2. Harpur, O.M. (2001) writing in C. Moon and C. Bonny (Eds), *Business Ethics: Facing up to the Issues*. London: Profile Books Ltd, p. 102.
3. See Collins, J. and Porras, J. (1995). *Built to Last*. London: Century.
4. Reported in the *Financial Times*, 9 October 2002. Stern Stewart Wealth Added Index (WAI) which aims to measure corporate performance from the shareholder perspective. WAI builds on Total Shareholder Return. The WAI 2002 index ranks wealth generation by companies for the five year period ending December 2001.
5. *Fortune*, World's Most Admired Companies survey, 3 March 2003, p. 35.
6. Extract from *Kingfisher's Plan for Corporate Social Responsibility*, October 2001. The plan can be downloaded from www.kingfisher.co.uk.
7. Investing in Social Responsibility: Risks and Opportunities (2001). London: Association of British Insurers, p. 38. Can be downloaded from www.www.abi.org.uk.
8. From the 2002 World's Most Respected Companies survey, *Financial Times*, 20 January 2003. See also www.ft.com/wmr2002.
9. Reported in the *Financial Times*, 9 October 2002.
10. Webley, S. and More, E. (2003). *Does Business Ethics Pay? Ethics and Financial Performance*. London: IBE.
11. Philippa Foster Back, IBE Director, quoted in the *Financial Times*, 3 April 2003.
12. *The Business Case for Sustainable Development: Making a Difference Towards the Johannesburg Summit 2002 and Beyond* (2002). Geneva: WBCSD.
13. *Creating Value from Your Intangibles* (2001). London: Department of Trade and Industry, p. 23. The complete study can be downloaded from www.dti.gov.uk.
14. *Investing in Social Responsibility: Risks and Opportunities* (2001). London: Association of British Insurers, p. 7. Can be downloaded from www.abi.org.uk.
15. From The Business Case for sustainable development: making a difference towards the Johannesburg Summit 2002 and beyond (2002). Geneva: WBCSD p. 8.
16. de Segundo, K. (1997). 'Meeting Society's Changing Expectations'. *Corporate Reputation Review*, **1**, pp. 16–19.

17. As reported in the *Financial Times*, 19 May 2001.

18. Quoted in *Internal Auditing and Business Risk*, February 2001, p. 25.

19. As quoted in *Responding to the Leadership Challenge: Findings of a CEO survey on global corporate citizenship* (2003). World Economic Forum, p. 22.

20. Carly Fiorina, CEO, Hewlett Packard in an address to the Confederation of British Industry (CBI) conference, Manchester, UK, 25 November 2002.

21. *Creating Value from Your Intangibles* (2001). London: Department of Trade and Industry Study, p. 5. The complete study can be downloaded from www.dti.gov.uk.

22. Hill & Knowlton's Corporate Reputation Watch survey 2002, conducted by Harris Interactive, found that there is a growing tendency for CEOs to be remunerated in part according to their ability to impact corporate reputation. This ranged from 12% of CEOs in Germany to 44% in Italy, with 26% in the UK and 29% in the USA. And cash received for corporate kudos can be significant: in the UK and Germany it was over 40% and in the USA just a third of total compensation. This was reported in an article by Andrew Pharoah, managing director, Public and Corporate Affairs, Hill & Knowlton, *Financial Times*, 16 September 2002.

23. *Financial Times*, 30 January 2003.

twelve

future challenges and opportunities

THE WAY AHEAD

Business has had a rocky ride: the economic downturn and the fall-out from the US corporate scandals have seen public trust in business plummet. Yet, this gaping hole in public trust presents a huge opportunity for individual organisations to differentiate themselves from the pack, to forge ahead and to create competitive advantage.

> Rarely have business leaders faced such a complex and challenging set of economic pressures, political uncertainties and societal expectations. Regardless of their industry sector, country of origin, or corporate ownership structure, they are under growing pressure to demonstrate outstanding performance not only in terms of competitiveness and market growth, but also in their corporate governance and their corporate citizenship.
>
> (World Economic Forum, 2003[1])

Six strands of challenge and opportunity are emerging:

- High self-esteem
- Values driven and value driven
- Visionary and ethical leadership
- The new governance
- Safe havens
- Reputation: the cornerstone of business strategy.

high self-esteem

Stakeholders want and need the businesses they deal with to have high self-esteem, to have total clarity on where they are going and how they plan to get there, to have unambiguous values and standards that will guide their behaviour along the way, and to unequivocally set out the boundaries of their accountability. In order to succeed, organisations need to think well of themselves.

As Sue Slipman, chairman of the board of the UK's Financial Ombudsman Service and formerly Director External Relations and Compliance of UK lottery operator Camelot, has said:

> Given the terrain that business now occupies and the myriad expectations upon it, it would be unwise for business not to scope its proportionate responsibilities on all fronts. Its legitimacy, its morale, purpose, drive and success all depend upon the business understanding all the issues it confronts from all sources and being in a position to make decisions and plan its course of action to create honest relationships and trust. Succeeding in the modern world requires the business to think well of itself, to have high self-esteem. It is unlikely to retain all this unless it engages with its stakeholders, comes to terms with criticism and deals with the legitimate demands upon it. Indeed, the proponents of old fashioned 'shareholder value' as the only purpose of business seem like 'flat-earthers', unable to come to terms with an altered universe.[2]

This self-esteem is not arrogance; it is born of a confidence that derives from adopting a systematic 'inside out' and 'outside in' approach to reputation, by engaging actively with stakeholders and responding to their needs and expectations and recalibrating values and realigning vision and strategic goals as necessary.

Businesses that swiftly restore their self-esteem and demonstrate their new-found confidence to their stakeholders, will be well placed to meet the challenges and leverage the opportunities that lie ahead.

values and value driven

In the wake of the Enron and WorldCom scandals, the expectations of employees, investors, customers, suppliers, regulators, pressure groups and the general public on business behaviour have increased exponentially. The mood of the times is captured by the US *Time* magazine nominating three whistleblowers as its 'Person of the Year' for 2002. This highlights the new imperative for business leaders: to be both 'values driven *and* value driven'.[3]

- *Values driven* in the sense of putting unambiguous values of ethics, integrity, transparency and accountability at the heart of the business – and ensuring that those values are never compromised.
- *Value driven* in the sense of creating increased value for shareholders, improved products and services for customers and more empowering and economically sound environments for employees and communities.

A number of values-based material social, environmental and ethical (SEE) concerns are now an integral part of the mainstream investment agenda, as shareholders recognise that traditional financial analysis only portrays a small proportion of the threats and opportunities facing a business, its true value, and real future prospects. There is rising investor interest in a business's values and its performance in managing its softer, CSR-related issues and impacts, as this can provide insights into its overall strategic management capability, governance approach, organisational climate and key relationships.

Businesses that fail to appreciate their real value drivers – so often their intangible assets and corporate culture – and to leverage them through their strategy and disclosures, will miss opportunities to be valued accurately by the markets and to build increased value through innovation, rapid response and resourcefulness.

> The greater the discrepancy between share prices and the values foreseeable from relevant, reliable disclosure, the less effective our capital markets. The greater the discrepancy between managers' appreciation of the sources of value and the real sources, the less sure their strategies.
> (Robert K. Elliott, chairman, American Institute of Certified Public Accountants[4])

It is a business's intangible assets that are their most fertile source of potential value creation – and of value destruction:

> The combined impacts of globalisation, new technology and increased competition means that all companies are facing the prospect of continual incremental and, occasionally, radical change. In practice, there are few sources of competitive advantage that cannot be duplicated and matched by competitors. Ultimately a company's ability to flourish in this environment will depend on its ability to create value from intangibles. Irrespective of sector, innovative companies recognise that to maintain their competitive advantage they must continually seek to identify, develop and make best use of all their available resources so that they can continue to offer new and improved products and services.
> (UK Department of Trade and Industry[5])

Businesses that demonstrate an in-depth understanding of the power and potential of the values/value combination and succeed in marrying the two harmoniously, are more likely to attract investment and flourish.

visionary and ethical leadership

Businesses today operate in a very different environment from those of our forebears. The CEO of a large national or multinational concern is often a household name, appearing on chat shows, panel games and often quoted in the media. The personal values, ethics and lifestyle of the individual executive can come under intense scrutiny. The image of the CEO can play a key role in shaping the reputation of the organisation he or she heads and stakeholders' confidence in its products, services and prospects. As Harlan Teller of Harris Interactive commented when the results of the 2002 Corporate Reputation Watch survey were unveiled, 'Our research plainly shows that the CEO is now the "chief customer satisfaction officer" and that corporate names are brands in their own right which endorse a company's entire line of product brands.'[6]

The battering the 'cult of CEO' concept has received in the aftermath of the US corporate débâcles has given business leaders an unprecedented opportunity to reinvent themselves in a new mould – and to make a real difference. Leaders can re-establish their personal reputations and credibility by promoting themselves – and their businesses – as responsible. They can aim to position themselves on that top rung of the Kingfisher threat/opportunity ladder[7] and provide ethical and social leadership. Here they will be shaping policy and practice on selected issues, be proactively engaged in debate and be seen to exemplify best practice.

> Business leaders have the most to do. The good news is, it'll be good for your business. You *can* help yourself by helping society. But you'll need to develop a new maturity in the way you operate in society: not afraid to take on a leadership role in those areas where you can bring about social change; comfortable in helping to tackle the serious issues that your customers and employees care about.
>
> (Steve Hilton and Giles Gibbons[8])

Professor Warren Bennis and Robert Thomas of Havard University pinpoint in a recent book[9] the traits that enable some leaders to thrive, even during testing times:

- *Adaptive capacity* – the ability to adapt to changing circumstances. The authors argue that most failures in business leadership are the result of failure to adapt.
- *The ability to create shared meaning* – the ability to motivate people behind a common goal even in difficult circumstances. Tolerating and even encouraging dissent is an important component of this.
- *Personal voice* – character and genuineness underpinned by a strong set of principles about how people should be treated.
- *Integrity* – defined as the delicate balance of ambition (personal or some greater goal), competence and moral compass.[10]

It was arguably 'ambition' and 'competence' without 'moral compass' that led to the US corporate scandals! These qualities of principled purpose, integrity, genuineness and responsiveness are a perfect fit for the ethical leadership mantle.

Perhaps the time has come for leadership to be redefined as visionary and ethical: leadership that not only sets a tone that keeps a business in tune with its stakeholders, but exceeds stakeholder expectations by positively seeking to resolve some of the broader social issues that concern them.

the new governance

The 'new governance' does not regard non-shareholder stakeholders as peripheral groups, whose interests will only be taken into account after the short-term shareholder value needs of the business's 'owners' have been met. The new governance puts all stakeholders on an equal footing and requires businesses to seek balanced solutions to meet their diverse interests and concerns.

The new governance acknowledges that sustainable success can only be achieved by responding to the evolving requirements and expectations of *all* key stakeholders groups and by aligning internal values, behaviours and targets accordingly. The new governance is not just about curbing threats to short-term shareholder value, but also about leveraging opportunities to provide long-term benefits for investors, employees, customers, the environment and society as a whole.

The new governance could lead to a board model where all the major constituencies served by the business are represented at board level – 'the stakeholder corporation'. What better way of involving your key stakeholders than one that enables them to shape your future strategy and influence tone-setting and decision-making?

safe havens

In these uncertain times, with stock markets under pressure, pensions in jeopardy, and trust in businesses and their leaders at a low, it is no surprise to find investors desperately seeking 'safe havens' for their depreciating assets.

In the rising bull market there was never any question that long-term investors for pension funds would be able to honour their commitments – but now, with markets tumbling and in turmoil around the globe, there are serious doubts over whether these long-term liabilities can be met. Investors have had their fill of short-termism. It is not only risky but costly. In the UK alone as much as £2.5 billion is spent on actively trading UK equity portfolios – often just to meet short-term performance objectives.[11] In the 'growth hungry' bull market, managers would go to any lengths to maintain the illusion of growth – and their generous stock options. Earnings management, fraudulent bookkeeping, and a string of worthless acquisitions were all *de rigueur*.

> The growth imperative led companies to seek market share at all costs, often destroying the profitability of their entire industry. It also drove diversification into questionable new fields and encouraged acquisitions that create no economic value, while providing opportunities to manipulate reported earnings.
>
> (Professor Michael Porter, Harvard Business School[12])

Now that the bubble has burst and investors have come to their senses, they no longer value short-term wins; they are seeking long-term stability and a higher quality of earnings. The management skills lauded in the bull market are not appropriate for a bear market. Those gung-ho business leaders who continually led their troops into promising but uncharted new territories are no longer revered as heroes. The markets are looking for a firm, responsible and steady hand on the tiller that will steer a straight course through clear blue waters, avoiding the rocks and other unwelcome surprises. Investors are turning to low-risk 'safe havens' that will be steady, perhaps unexciting long-term performers and will return cash to shareholders through regular dividends – a stark contrast to the thrilling roller-coaster ride of the bull-era 'Growth Mountain'.

In March 2003 a consortium of large investors in pensions, led by the UK's Universities Superannuation Scheme (USS) and including the Ontario Teachers' Pension Plan and Hewitt, Bacon & Woodrow, threw out a challenge to fund managers, whose mode of investment decision-making had latterly focused on 'relative outperformance over the short term'.[13] A competition was launched to find fund managers who could devise a scheme to manage 30 billion euros of pension assets over the long term in a genuinely responsible manner. Part of the challenge, according to Peter Moon, Chief Investment Officer of USS, was to ensure that: '... our funds are not delivering returns at the expense of undermining the quality of life for our members and their children'.[14]

It seems likely that responsible, reputable businesses, known for their enlightened governance approach, strong stakeholder relationships, integrity and credible earnings, will be those favoured by the winners as safe investment havens.

reputation: the cornerstone of business strategy

It can be argued that the management of reputation and its associated risks is so critical to business success and sustainability that it should be a central plank of corporate strategy as it can help businesses to:

> ...cope with the changing expectations of their many audiences, to manage the interpretations those audiences make, and to build favorable regard. In so doing, they are enhancing their ability to exploit a new source of competitive advantage that derives from cognitive assets – their reputational capital.... Stakeholder expectations should be routinely monitored to ensure that performance results are not jeopardized by shifting expectations. A corollary of this idea is that reputation management should be a cornerstone of strategic analysis because it addresses how firms position themselves in changing environments. It also follows that changes in strategy should be conceived and evaluated in terms of their possible reputational consequences.
>
> (Charles J. Fombrun and Violina P. Rindova[15])

The paths of good corporate governance, risk management, reputation management and corporate social responsibility are not discrete and separate but are inextricably intertwined and must move forward in harmony if businesses are to succeed and prosper in the longer term. The convergence of these agendas, and increasing cooperation between those who drive and respond to them, will be a feature of business life for the foreseeable future. Reputation risk management can act as a useful bridge between these agendas.

Businesses that invest positively in their reputation by positioning reputation risk management centre stage will reap the benefits of better informed strategy development, stronger stakeholder relationships and more credible communications. These will, in turn, further enhance their standing and prospects.

TOWARDS A BRIGHTER FUTURE

Trust in business has been severely dented by US corporate scandals and by business leaders compromising values to achieve short-term financial targets. This gulf between public expectation and perceived business practice presents an unprecedented opportunity to restore trust, build confidence, create competitive advantage and enhance personal and business reputations.

A risk-based 'inside out' and 'outside in' approach to reputation, which takes into account the perceptions, needs and expectations of major stakeholders can help to rebuild that trust. A systematic assessment of the risks to reputation from financial performance, corporate governance and leadership, regulation, customer relations, workplace talent and culture, corporate social responsibility and from reporting and communications, will equip businesses to respond appropriately to the ever-changing impacts and issues that face them. By adopting such an approach, they will automatically meet the exigencies of the evolving corporate governance, CSR, risk management and reputation agendas.

Those businesses that act swiftly can reap the benefits of first mover advantage, reinforce their legitimacy and create unique differentiators that will enable them to compete, grow and thrive. Those that lag behind and ignore these new imperatives may see their performance and their reputations dwindle.

Positioning reputation risk management at the heart of your business activities, proactively seeking to curb the threats and leverage the opportunities that arise, will provide you with the confidence and the sureness of touch to respond swiftly and decisively to the challenges and opportunities that lie ahead. A prosperous and sustainable future beckons.

NOTES AND REFERENCES

1. *Responding to the Leadership Challenge: Findings of a CEO survey on global corporate citizenship* (2003). World Economic Forum, p. 1.
2. From 'Making the business case for CSR: the Camelot Experience' in the *Corporate Social Responsibility Monitor* (2002). London: Gee Publishing, Chapter A2. www.gee.co.uk.
3. *Responding to the Leadership Challenge: Findings of a CEO survey on global corporate citizenship* (2003). World Economic Forum, p. 17.
4. Adriessen, D. and Tissen, R. (2000). *Weightless Wealth: Find your real value in a future of intangible assets*. Financial Times/Prentice Hall/Pearson Education London, Foreword.
5. *Creating Value from your Intangibles* (2001). London: Department of Trade and Industry Study, p. 1. The complete study can be downloaded from www.dti.gov.uk.
6. Harlan Teller, president of Harris Interactive's corporate practice and chief client officer commenting on findings from the fourth annual Corporate Reputation Watch survey of 600 US executives conducted in February 2002 by Harris Interactive.
7. See Table 6-12 in Chapter 6.
8. Hilton, S. and Gibbons, G. (2002). *Good Business: Your World Needs You*. London: Texere.

9. Bennis, W. and Thomas, R. (2002). *Geeks and Geezers: How Era, Values and Defining Moments Shape Leaders*. Harvard Business School.
10. Summarised from Bennis, W. and Thomas, R. (2002). *Geeks and Geezers: How Era, Values and Defining Moments Shape Leaders*. Harvard Business School in the *Financial Times*, 17 September 2002.
11. As reported in the *Financial Times*, 3 March 2003.
12. Quoted in the *Financial Times*, 17 February 2003.
13. Peter Moon, Chief Investment Officer, USS, quoted in the *Financial Times*, 3 March 2003.
14. Quoted in the *Financial Times*, 3 March 2003.
15. Fombrun, C.J. and Findova, V.P. (2002). 'The Road to Transparency: reputation management at Royal Dutch/Shell' in *The Expressive Organization: Linking Identify, Reputation and the Corporate Brand*. Oxford: Oxford University Press, p. 95.

appendix A

the Hermes Principles

what shareholders expect of public companies – and what companies should expect of shareholders

Hermes' overriding requirement is that companies be run in the long-term interest of shareholders. Companies adhering to this principle will not only benefit their shareholders, but also we would argue, the wider economy in which the company and its shareholders participate. We believe a company run in the long-term interest of shareholders will need to manage effectively relationships with its employees, suppliers and customers, to behave ethically and to have regard for the environment and society as a whole.

communication

Principle 1 'Companies should seek an honest, open and ongoing dialogue with shareholders. They should clearly communicate the plans they are pursuing and the likely financial and wider consequences of those plans. Ideally goals, plans and progress should be discussed in the annual report and accounts.'

financial

Principle 2 'Companies should have appropriate measures and systems in place to ensure that they know which activities and competencies contribute most to maximising shareholder value.'

Principle 3   'Companies should ensure all investment plans have been honestly and critically tested in terms of their ability to deliver long-term shareholder value.'

Principle 4   'Companies should allocate capital for investment by seeking fully and creatively to exploit opportunities for growth within their core businesses rather than seeking unrelated diversification. This is particularly true when considering acquisitive growth.'

Principle 5   'Companies should have performance evaluation and incentive systems designed cost-effectively to incentivise managers to deliver long-term shareholder value.'

Principle 6   'Companies should have an efficient capital structure which will minimise the long-term cost of capital.'

strategic

Principle 7   'Companies should have and continue to develop coherent strategies for each business unit. These should ideally be expressed in terms of market prospects and of the competitive advantage the business has in exploiting these prospects. The company should understand the factors which drive market growth, and the particular strengths which underpin its competitive position.'

Principle 8   'Companies should be able to explain why they are the 'best parent' of the businesses they run. Where they are not best parent they should be developing plans to resolve the issue.'

social, ethical and environmental

Principle 9   'Companies should manage effectively relationships with their employees, suppliers and customers and with others who have a legitimate interest in the company's activities. Companies should behave ethically and have regard for the environment and society as a whole.'

Principle 10   'Companies should support voluntary and statutory measures which minimise the externalisation of costs to the detriment of society at large.'

appendix B

appendix to the Turnbull report

ASSESSING THE EFFECTIVENESS OF THE COMPANY'S RISK AND CONTROL PROCESSES

Some questions which the board may wish to consider and discuss with management when regularly reviewing reports on internal control and carrying out its annual assessment are set out below. The questions are not intended to be exhaustive and will need to be tailored to the particular circumstances of the company.

This Appendix should be read in conjunction with the guidance set out in this document.

1. *Risk assessment*

- Does the company have clear objectives and have they been communicated so as to provide effective direction to employees on risk assessment and control issues? For example, do objectives and related plans include measurable performance targets and indicators?

- Are the significant internal and external operational, financial, compliance and other risks identified and assessed on an ongoing basis? (Significant risks may, for example, include those related to market, credit, liquidity, technological, legal, health, safety and environmental, reputation, and business probity issues.)

- Is there a clear understanding by management and others within the company of what risks are acceptable to the board?

2. *Control environment and control activities*

- Does the board have clear strategies for dealing with the significant risks that have been identified? Is there a policy on how to manage these risks?

- Do the company's culture, code of conduct, human resource policies and performance reward systems support the business objectives and risk management and internal control system?

- Does senior management demonstrate, through its actions as well as its policies, the necessary commitment to competence, integrity and fostering a climate of trust within the company?

- Are authority, responsibility and accountability defined clearly such that decisions are made and actions taken by the appropriate people? Are the decisions and actions of different parts of the company appropriately coordinated?

- Does the company communicate to its employees what is expected of them and the scope of their freedom to act? This may apply to areas such as customer relations; service levels for both internal and outsourced activities; health, safety and environmental protection; security of tangible and intangible assets; business continuity issues; expenditure matters; accounting; and financial and other reporting.

- Do people in the company (and in its providers of outsourced services) have the knowledge, skills and tools to support the achievement of the company's objectives and to manage effectively risks to their achievement?

- How are processes/controls adjusted to reflect new or changing risks; or operational deficiencies?

3. *Information and communication*

- Do management and the board receive timely, relevant and reliable reports on progress against business objectives and the related risks that provide them with the information, from inside and outside the company, needed for decision-making and management review purposes? This could include performance reports and indicators of change, together with qualitative information such as on customer satisfaction, employee attitudes, etc.

- Are information needs and related information systems reassessed as objectives and related risks change or as reporting deficiencies are identified?

- Are periodic reporting procedures, including half-yearly and annual reporting, effective in communicating a balanced and understandable account of the company's position and prospects?

- Are there established channels of communication for individuals to report suspected breaches of laws or regulations or other improprieties?

4. *Monitoring*

- Are there ongoing processes embedded within the company's overall business operations, and addressed by senior management, which monitor the effective application of the policies, processes and activities related to internal control risk management? (Such processes may include control self-assessment, confirmation by personnel of compliance with policies and codes of conduct, internal audit reviews or other management reviews.)

- Do these processes monitor the company's ability to re-evaluate risks and adjust controls effectively in response to changes in its objectives, its business, and its external environment?

- Are there effective follow-up procedures to ensure that appropriate change or action occurs in response to changes in risk and control assessments?

- Is there appropriate communication to the board (or board committees) on the effectiveness of the ongoing monitoring processes on risk and control matters? This should include reporting any significant failings or weaknesses on a timely basis.

- Are there specific arrangements for management monitoring and reporting to the board on risk and control matters of particular importance? These could include, for example, actual or suspected fraud and other illegal or irregular acts, or matters that could adversely affect the company's reputation or financial position?

appendix C

BP's policy commitment on ethical conduct

We will pursue our business with integrity, respecting the different cultures and the dignity and rights of individuals in all the countries where we operate.

BP supports the belief that human rights are universal. They are enshrined in the UN Universal Declaration of Human Rights (UDHR), which we support. The UDHR sets out the obligations to promote universal respect for and observance of human rights and fundamental freedoms for all, without distinction as to race, gender, language or religion. The promotion and protection of all human rights is a legitimate concern of business.

In our actions and our dealings with others, we will:

- Respect the rule of law
- Promise only what we expect to deliver, make only commitments we intend to keep, not knowingly mislead others and not participate in or condone corrupt or unacceptable business practices
- Fulfil our obligations and commitments, treat people according to merit and contribution, refrain from coercion and never deliberately do harm to anyone.
- Act in good faith, use company assets only for furthering company business and not seek personal gain through abuse of position in the company.

We expect the same commitments from third parties directly acting on BP's behalf.

BPS POLICY EXPECTATIONS SUPPORTING THE ETHICAL CONDUCT POLICY COMMITMENT

Many ethical decisions involve dilemmas and require judgement in order to arrive at the best way forward. In cases of uncertainty, everyone working for BP is expected to raise the issues within an open environment with their management and colleagues to obtain clarification. All employees have the right to make confidential reports directly to the helpline.

In deciding whether or where to do business, it will be a precondition that we can implement our policy commitments in all our operations.

We will respect the law in the countries and communities in which we operate

This will include competition and antitrust laws and the Foreign and Corrupt Practices Act. Where the law is unclear or conflicting, we will take expert advice but will always seek to act in accordance with these commitments.

BP will never offer, pay, solicit or accept bribes in any form, either directly or indirectly

This includes those transactions formerly known as facilitation payments. Any demand for or offer of a bribe in whatever form to any BP employee must be rejected and reported immediately to line management.

We will hold no secret or unrecorded funds of money or assets.

We will only give or accept gifts and entertainment that are for business purposes and are not material or frequent.

In consultation with Regional and Country Presidents, Business Unit Leaders should put in place local rules to cover the giving and acceptance of gifts and entertainment which reflect this expectation and local custom. We will never accept gifts or entertainment during the process of a competitive bid or tender exercise.

We will avoid situations where loyalty to the company may come into conflict with personal interests or loyalties

If such a conflict does arise, it should be declared in writing to more senior management, who must make sure that the individual is insulated from any decision-making or operation in the area of the conflict of interest.

BP supports the principles set forth in the UN Universal Declaration of Human Rights and will respect the 2000 International Labour Organisation 'Tripartite Declaration of Principles

concerning Multinational Enterprises and Social Policy' and the 2000 OECD 'Guidelines for Multinational Enterprises'

Business Unit Leaders are expected to engage in open dialogue and consultation with local communities and their representatives, non-governmental organisations and government at all levels to ensure that potential issues arising from our operations are identified and the risks addressed. Whether we continue to operate in a country with serious human rights issues will be determined in the light of our ability to fulfil our policy commitments in our own activities and to act as a force for good over the long term.

BP will not employ forced labour or child labour

We will not use child labour in our own operations or in the provision of our goods or services and we will seek to facilitate the transition to alternatives to child employment, such as apprenticeships, training and further education.

Before we make major investments in a new area, we will evaluate the likely impact of our presence and activities

These assessments will consider the likely impact of major developments on local communities and indigenous peoples, local infrastructure and the potential for conflict and its implications for security.

BP will never make political contributions whether in cash or in kind anywhere in the world

BP will continue to engage in policy debate on subjects of legitimate concern to the company, its staff and the communities in which it operates by processes such as lobbying.

BP welcomes its employees' participation in the political process in ways that are appropriate to each country.

Fees for services rendered by third parties, including agents and consultants, must be for legitimate business purposes that are demonstrably commensurate with the service provided.

We will not choose business partners who contravene these commitments

We will not employ agents to carry out actions that conflict with these commitments. In joint operations, we will apply these commitments where we are operators; where we are not, we will seek to influence our partners such that the joint operation adopts similar commitments.

As at June 2003. Reproduced by permission of BP p.l.c.

appendix D

twelve steps for implementing a code of business ethics

1. **Endorsement**
   Make sure that the code is introduced with a statement of corporate values and endorsed by the Chairman and CEO.

2. **Integration**
   Produce a strategy for integrating the code into the running of the business at the time that it is issued.

3. **Circulation**
   Send the code to all employees in a readable and portable form and give it to all employees joining the company.

4. **Personal Response**
   Give all staff the personal opportunity to respond to the content of the code. An employee should know how to react if he or she is faced with a potential breach of the code or is in doubt about a course of action involving an ethical choice.

5. **Affirmation**
   Have a procedure for managers and supervisors regularly to state that they and their staff understand and apply the provisions of the code and provide an opportunity to raise matters not covered by it.

6. **Contracts**
   Consider making adherence to the code obligatory by including reference to it in all contracts of employment and linking it with disciplinary procedures.

7. **Regular Review**

Have a procedure which involves senior management for regular review and updating of the code.

8. **Enforcement**

Employees and others should be aware of the consequences of breaching the code.

9. **Training**

Ask those responsible for company training programmes at all levels to include issues raised by the code in their programmes.

10. **Translation**

See that the code is translated for use in overseas subsidiaries or other places where English is not the principal language.

11. **Distribution**

Make copies of the code available to business partners (joint ventures, suppliers, customers, etc.), and expect their compliance with the principles of your code.

12. **Annual Report**

Reproduce or insert a copy of the code in the Annual Report so that shareholders and a wider public know about the company's position on ethical matters. The Annual Report should also make reference to how the code is being used in the organization.

A revised (2003) version which appeared first in *Applying Codes of Business Ethics*, IBE, London 1995. Reproduced by permission of the Institute of Business Ethics

Glossary

accountability Preparedness of a business or individuals to justify their actions and decisions. In the context of CSR and reputation risk management this means being answerable to those with a legitimate interest in the business i.e. the business's stakeholders. Accountability is seen as comprising transparency, responsiveness and compliance.

assurance Assurance is a positive declaration intended to give confidence and enhance credibility. In a business context it refers to the confidence of one party (all/ part of a business or its stakeholders) in the assertions of another party (part of a business, its management and/or auditors). The provision of assurance goes beyond mere verification that stated facts and figures are accurate; it implies a more qualitative check that controls and actions to manage risk are operating as intended. Assurance can come from an organisation's monitoring and reporting system, self- or peer assessment and internal or external audits, inspections and reviews.

audit An audit examines systems, procedures and ways of working to ensure that the right controls are in place and that they are having the desired effect. An audit is a form of assurance.

compliance Acting in accordance with specified laws, regulation, standards, codes and guidelines (both statutory and voluntary)

consequence (or impact) The outcome of a risk occurring. Outcomes can be positive or negative and can be expressed qualitatively or quantitatively. There may be a range of possible outcomes.

control (internal control)   A policy, procedure, action, performance measure or working practice designed to manage a risk to the business. The aim of the control should be to bring exposure into line with the organisation's risk appetite.

corporate governance   The system by which companies are directed and controlled. It relates to the series of relationships between a company's management, its board, its shareholders and other stakeholders as well as the structures, policies and processes used to set and attain corporate objectives and monitor and report on performance.

corporate social responsibility (CSR)   CSR is the commitment of business to contribute to sustainable economic development, working with employees, their families, the local community and society at large to improve their quality of life (World Business Council for Sustainable Development).

CSR is about a business placing the core value of ethics, integrity, fairness, accountability and transparency at the heart of all its activities. It's about considering the wider impacts of the business on society and the environment and finding ways of minimising negative impacts and maximising positive impacts. It's also about taking into account and responding to the needs and expectations of the diverse stakeholder groups on which the future success of the business depends.

early warning indicator   An indicator, integrated into your business reporting systems, which will give you advance warning that a risk may be materialising. It should aim to sound alarm bells sufficiently early for corrective action to be taken. Early warning indicators differ from embedded monitors as they are designed to anticipate and pre-empt risks that are about to materialise, rather than provide regular information on the changing status of existing risks.

EBITDA   Earnings before interest, tax, depreciation and amortisation: a measure of financial performance commonly used in the USA.

embedded   Seamlessly integrated into the fabric of organisation, its processes and behaviours, thus becoming part of the business's DNA and 'the way we do things round here'.

embedded monitor   A performance or other indicator, integrated into your business reporting systems, that will give you regular information on the status of particular risk. Embedded monitors are part of the risk assurance process. Embedded monitors differ from early warning indicators as they are designed to provide information on the changing status of existing risks, rather than to anticipate and pre-empt risks that are about to materialise.

environmental audit   An environmental audit assesses the effectiveness of business policies and procedures in complying with relevant regulations and managing environmental impacts in a way that minimises negative effects.

ethical audit   An ethical audit is generally regarded as an internal management tool that tests the consistency of the application of values throughout an organisation by examining its systems and the behaviours of its employees.

ethical or socially responsible fund An investment fund which does not rely solely on financial criteria in stock selection, but also uses ethical non-financial criteria.

greenwashing Public relations campaigns or 'spin' that aim to anticipate and deflect criticism of a business by majoring on its 'responsible' credentials, even when this is not backed up by a solid foundation of policies, procedures and ways of working.

impact (or consequence) The outcome of a risk event. Outcomes can be positive or negative and can be expressed qualitatively or quantitatively. There may be a range of possible outcomes.

internal control (control) A policy, procedure, action, performance measure or working practice designed to manage a risk to the business. The aim of the control should be to bring exposure into line with the organisation's risk appetite.

legitimacy The answer to the question 'What gives them the right to do that?'

likelihood A qualitative description of probability or frequency.

materiality A 'material' factor or risk is one that is considered relevant and essential to an understanding of a business's past, current and future performance. Omission of a material factor could result in stakeholders being misled about the value drivers, dynamics and future prospects of a business.

monitor To check, supervise, observe critically, or record the progress of an activity, action or system on a regular basis in order to identify change. (Australia/New Zealand Risk Management Standard AS/NZS 4360: 1999)

NGO A non-governmental organisation is an organisation that is neither a business nor represents a government. NGOs like Greenpeace and Friends of the Earth campaign on social issues such as the environment or human rights. An NGO such as the International Chamber of Commerce can equally represent business.

reputation A collection of perceptions beliefs, both past and present, which reside in the consciousness of an organisation's stakeholders.

reputation risk Reputation risk is any action, event or circumstance that could adversely or beneficially impact an organisation's reputation.

residual risk The remaining risk exposure level after implementation of the agreed risk responses (such as risk treatment, etc.).

responsiveness Willingness to take into account the needs, concerns and expectations of stakeholders in formulating future strategy, developing targets and improving processes to enhance the organisation's future performance.

risk Risk is an event or situation that could adversely or beneficially affect a business's ability to achieve its objectives, maintain a good reputation and meet stakeholder expectations.

risk management The culture, processes and structure that are directed towards the effective management of potential opportunities and threats to an organisation.

SEE Social, environmental and ethical.

social auditing A social audit measures how an organisation's external stakeholders and its employees perceive the organisation, to what extent it is seen to meet its goals and work within its own values statements. Social auditing assesses the social impact and ethical behaviour of a business.

socially responsible or ethical fund An investment fund that does not rely solely on financial criteria in stock selection, but also uses ethical non-financial criteria.

socially responsible investment (SRI) 'Investment that combines investors' financial objectives with their commitment to social concerns, such as social justices, human rights, economic development, peace or a healthy environment' (UK Social Investment Forum). The investment decision-making process takes into account not only financial risk/return parameters, but also the social, ethical and environmental impacts.

stakeholder An organisation's stakeholders are those groups who affect and/or are affected by the organisation and its activities. Some organisations prefer to describe their stakeholders as 'partners'.

stakeholder dialogue A process in which organisations and their stakeholders work together to develop mutually beneficial solutions by striking a balance between the needs and expectations of the different parties. It involves frank and honest discussion of perceptions, issues, concerns, requirements and expectations and can be a vital source of threats and opportunities to reputation.

sustainability/sustainable development Progress that meets the needs of the present without compromising the ability of future generations to meet their needs.

Transparency In the context of business reporting and communications, providing a full, honest and open account which comprehensively covers all material issues and risks.

USP (unique selling proposition) That single attribute of your offering to customers that differentiates you from your competitors.

verification Making sure or demonstrating that something is true, accurate or justified. For example, external independent verification of a business's social or sustainability report can help to bridge the credibility gap and assure stakeholders that a business is, in practice, doing as it says.

Index

Index compiled by Annette Musker